THE RAPE OF THE
CONSTITUTION?

Copyright to the individual contributions:
© Keith Sutherland 2000; © Tony Benn & Andrew Hood 1993
(updates: 2000); © Jonathan Freedland 1998 (updates: 2000);
© Peter Hitchens 2000; © Jonathan Freedland 2000;
© Gillian Peele 2000; © Simon Hughes and Duncan Bracke 2000;
© Nevil Johnson 2000; © Bernard Weatherill 2000;
© Michael Spicer 2000; © Peter Carrington 1999;
© J.R. Lucas 2000; © Andrew Tyrie 2000;
© Michael Rush 2000; © *Sunday Telegraph* 2000;
© Simon Jenkins 2000; © Tam Dalyell 2000;
© Diana Woodhouse 2000; © Roy Jenkins 1999;
© Jeremy Black 2000; © Norman Tebbit 1999; © Peter Shore 2000;
© Peter Oborne 1999 (updates: 2000); © Mick Hume 2000;
© Moshe Berent and Keith Sutherland 2000;
© Anthony O'Hear 2000; © Mike Diboll 2000

Published in the UK by Imprint Academic
PO Box 1, Thorverton EX5 5YX, UK

Published in the USA by Imprint Academic
Philosophy Documentation Center, Bowling Green State
University, Bowling Green, OH 43403-0189, USA

ISBN 0 907845 70 3

British Library Cataloguing in Publication Data
A catalogue record for this book is available from the
British Library

Library of Congress Card Number: 00-101083

Front cover design: AB Graphics, Exeter
Rear cover graphic: Mother ®

Printed in Exeter UK by Short Run Press Ltd.

THE RAPE OF THE CONSTITUTION?

Edited by
Keith Sutherland

Foreword by
Michael Beloff QC

IMPRINT ACADEMIC

Contents

Authors

Tony Benn is Labour MP for Chesterfield.

Moshe Berent teaches in the Department of Political Science at the Open University of Israel.

Jeremy Black is Professor of History at the University of Exeter.

Duncan Brack is a former Director of Policy for the Liberal Democrats and now edits the *Journal of Liberal Democrat History*.

Lord Carrington was Leader of the House of Lords 1963–4, and Leader of the Opposition in the Lords 1964–70 and 1974–9.

Tam Dalyell is Labour MP for Linlithgow.

Mike Diboll is a freelance writer who lectures and researches in history and comparative literature.

Jonathan Freedland is a columnist and leader-writer for *The Guardian*.

Revd. Anthony Freeman is Managing Editor, Imprint Academic.

Peter Hitchens is a columnist with *The Express*.

Simon Hughes is MP for North Southwark and Bermondsey and Liberal Democrat Shadow Home Secretary

Mick Hume is editor, *LM*.

Lord Jenkins was President of the European Commission from 1977 to 1981.

Simon Jenkins is a columnist with *The Times* (Editor 1990–2).

Nevil Johnson is Emeritus Fellow, Nuffield College, Oxford

J.R. Lucas is a Fellow of the British Academy and was formerly a Fellow and Tutor at Merton College, Oxford.

Peter Oborne is political columnist with *The Express*.

Anthony O'Hear is Professor of Philosophy at the University of Bradford.

Gillian Peele is a Fellow and Tutor in Politics at Lady Margaret Hall, Oxford.

Michael Rush is Professor of Politics at the University of Exeter.

Earl Russell is Professor of History at King's College, London.

Lord Shore is Chairman of the Labour Euro-Safeguards Campaign.

Sir Michael Spicer is Conservative MP for West Worcestershire

Keith Sutherland is publisher, *History of Political Thought* and *Polis: The Journal of the Society for Greek Political Thought*.

Lord Tebbit was Chairman of the Conservative Party, 1985–7.

Andrew Tyrie is Conservative MP for Chichester.

Lord Weatherill was Speaker of the House of Commons, 1983–92 and until recently Convenor of the Cross-Bench Peers.

Diana Woodhouse is Professor of Law at Oxford Brookes University.

Dedication and Editor's Note

This book is dedicated to the memory of Max Beloff who died shortly after confirming his own contribution.

The editorial policy was to include scholars, politicians and journalists from all points on the political spectrum who would not normally share the same platform or address the same audience. Whilst most of the essays are new, a small proportion are revised and updated versions of previously published material.

Notwithstanding the diverse provenance of the authors there is a surprising degree of agreement. Although it would be misleading to imply that everyone was 'singing from the same hymn-sheet', the main difference between the *English Hymnal* and *Hymns Ancient & Modern* is the colour of the cover.

Keith Sutherland
Brampford Speke, Devon
February 2000

Michael Beloff

Foreword

My father, Max Beloff, would undoubtedly have regarded the title to this compelling collection of essays as an example of mealy-mouthed meiosis. He never knowingly understated anything. Although it had always been an intellectual fantasy of mine that one day we should collaborate on a book on the British Constitution (a dynamic Diceyan duo *de nos jours*), in fact the only time that we put joint pen to paper was in attacking Lord Mackay's Green Paper on the reform of the legal profession, and, in particular, his proposals for civil service involvement in the profession's regulation. Even then we quarrelled over whether it was appropriate to say (as Max wished) that 'lay' was simply a synonym for 'ignorant'.

My father was of course a political scientist and latterly a legislator of passionate views. I am a lawyer — a construer, not a maker of legislation — whose views are necessarily subordinate to the interests of my clients. It is improper to express them in court, and (in my judgment) unwise to broadcast them too loudly outside it. Our interests overlapped, it may be said, to a greater extent than our ideologies. One of my father's last public pronouncements was to defend the retention of the hereditary peerage; he genuinely wished *défendre l'aristocracie*, and not merely *épater la bourgeiosie*. It fell by coincidence to me, as an advocate, to appear before the Committee of Privileges to argue on behalf of the Conservative Hereditary Peers that the (then) Bill to abolish the hereditary element in the House of Lords from the end of the session was ineffective to attain its end. My submission was that, on its true interpretation, the Bill failed unambiguously to cancel rights to sit which resulted from response to the Monarch's writ of summons to Parliament. The Committee's decision was that, whatever might be or have been the incidents of the medieval writ, the Bill was clearly designed to override them. It was a stark reminder that Parliament can undo, if it wills, the legacy of centuries in the course of a few months.[1]

Yet I would argue that one of the most profound recent changes to the Constitution (I squeamishly abjure notions of rape, or even indecent assault) results not from the designs, benign or brutal, of New Labour or Thatcherite Tory, but from the activities of the third branch of government, the judiciary, which have themselves infringed the sovereignty of Parliament – an impregnable given for those reared in the traditions of Blackstone and Dicey.

True it is that the major change was wrought by the accession of the United Kingdom to the Common Market, its signature of the Treaty of Rome, and the enactment of the European Communities Act of 1972. The critical consequence of those decisions, underplayed at the time, was not so much that it gave the European Court of Justice ultimate authority in matters of community law – although, of course, it did that – as that it gave English judges, for the first time since the seventeenth century, power – whose legitimacy was beyond doubt – to hold that domestic primary legislation was invalid as incompatible with directly effective community law. When Lord Bridge said…

> Under the terms of the Act of 1972 it has always been clear that it was the duty of a United Kingdom court, when delivering final judgment, to override any rule of national law found to be in conflict with any directly enforceable rule of community law[2]

…he spoke of what may have been clear to the eminent Law Lord but must have been obscure to lesser mortals.

I was myself involved in two of the major cases which revealed the dimensions of this new reality. In *Marshall v. Southampton Area Health Authority* (1986 QB 401), I persuaded the European Court of Justice that different retiring ages for

[1]   The Motion of Lord Mayhew of Twisden (TLR 12.11.99; HL Paper 106–1).
[2]   *Factortame No.2*, 1991 1 AC 603, p. 659.

men and women offended against the Community principle of non-discrimination.[3] In *R. v. Secretary of State for the Home Department ex p. The Equal Opportunities Commission* (1995 1 AC 1), I failed to defend for the Government in the House of Lords provisions of domestic law which laid down time limits before rights to redundancy payment or compensation for unfair dismissal could be claimed. The Appellate Committee held that these were indirectly discriminatory against women, contrary to Article 119 of the Treaty of Rome and the Equal Treatment Directive. The Committee went on to describe the Government's attempt to justify them on grounds of employment protection in brutal language as 'not containing anything capable of being regarded as factual evidence demonstrating the correctness of these views' (p. 26). *The Times* editorial suggested that the decision showed that for the first time the United Kingdom might have a constitutional court.

Enjoying the feel of powers conferred adventitiously from without, the judges exploited to the full inherent powers which had atrophied during the long winter of administrative law which spanned the '30s, '40s and '50s. Although the grounds[4] for judicial review[5] did not allow (the sphere of Community law apart) an attack on statute, or even the overturning of an administrative decision on mere merits, the devil lay in the application of those grounds. In *Secretary of State for Defence v. Guardian Newspapers* (1985 AC 339) Lord Diplock repudiated the notion of a 'constitutional right' in the British context as no more than a 'evocative phrase' (at p. 345). By 1999 it had become an enforceable concept, so that in *R v. Secretary of State for the Home Department ex p. Simms* (1999 3 WLR 328), the principle of legality had come to mean, in the words of Lord Hoffmann (p. 349), that 'fundamental rights cannot be overridden by general or ambiguous words'. Without support from a Bill of Rights, without even parliamentary fiat, the judges had decided that the common law elevated cer-

---

[3] And in its sequel, *Marshall No.2* (1994 QB 126) that the cap on compensation for sex discrimination under the domestic Acts was equally unsustainable.

[4] Illegality, irrationality, and procedural impropriety.

[5] As from 1979 the procedure for judicial control of the executive came to be called.

tain rights, which they, the judges, selected, to superior status in the hierarchy of legal norms. Irrationality and procedural impropriety were equally open textured concepts. While paying lip service to the decision maker's primary right to decide what was reasonable and what was fair, the judges were able to imprint their own views as to whether either test was satisfied.

Now from 2 October 2000 AD fresh impetus will be given to judicial creativity and authority by the substantial domestication of the European Convention on Human Rights in the Human Rights Act 1998 ('HRA') which will shift the whole focus of public law from consideration of executive wrong to that of citizens' rights.[6] And the ingenious device entitling judges under section 4 of the HRA to make a declaration of incompatibility of domestic statute with Convention rights, while preserving the forms of parliamentary sovereignty, further undermines its substance. Faced with such a declaration, Parliament will be confronted with a constitutional Hobson's choice of amending the legislation or mounting a rearguard (and, in probability, unsuccessful) defence in the Strasbourg Court.

The Lord Chancellor, before he ascended the Woolsack, spoke with eloquence, if apprehension, of the risks of 'judicial supremacism' which has extended even to speculation by judges in lectures (although not yet in judgments) that in certain circumstances judges might decline to enforce Acts of Parliament simply because they offended (in the judges' view) against fundamental rights and natural law — a position last taken by Sir Edward Coke in the seventeenth century.

There are, of course, arguments in favour of giving judges overriding authority even in a democratic society: the United States of America provides the paradigm example where this has been chosen as an appropriate procedure for a free people. But, it seems to me, such changes should come about by choice

---

[6] Interestingly, in a variety of cases the judges have already decided cases as if the HRA were in force; see from my own case file *Ex p. Amin* (TLR 16.11.99) — is entrapment evidence admissible in criminal cases?; *Stern v. Official Receiver* (Independent Law Report. I6.2.00) — is compelled evidence admissible in civil regulatory proceedings, *e.g.* for director's disqualification?

and after long and anxious debate, not by stealth. The corollary of enlarging judicial power is to invite outside control of the judiciary. When judges become involved in decisions of a political character (even if not fairly characterized as political decisions), politicians will wish to become involved in their selection. The system which gave the USA Brandeis, denied them Bork. Irrespective of the relative merits of those two lawyers, I am unpersuaded that the bargain is a good one, because at some future date, who knows, a Brandeis might be denied status on the grounds of some fashionable political correctness.

These essays suggest that there are two routes to a good constitution as an integrated whole: tradition—in which it is slowly fashioned by the experience of time, and reason—in which it is more swiftly fashioned in the crucible of analysis. It is a matter of concern to all of us that the British Constitution is arguably being altered in a manner which is distinct from either.

Michael J. Beloff QC
President, Trinity College, Oxford

Keith Sutherland

Introduction: Bagehot Revisited

In his collection of essays, *The English Constitution*, Walter Bagehot painted a vivid picture of the gap between real and symbolic power. In his view, 'efficient' power (in 1867) was in the hands of a small secretive parliamentary committee (the Cabinet). By way of contrast the monarchy, the House of Lords and even, at times, the House of Commons contributed to the 'dignified' part of our constitution but was in reality little more than window-dressing.[1] In the introduction to his 1963 edition, Richard Crossman showed how power had moved away from the Cabinet to the Prime Minister and the party managers. Bagehot described Victorian England as a 'disguised republic'.[2]

The orthodox (Whig) view of the Constitution is based on the principle of the separation of powers (executive, legislative and judicial) and the steady progress from power in the hands of one person — the 'executive magistrate' to a more distributed and democratic system, replete with 'checks and balances' on executive power. Bagehot pointed out that this was

---

[1] However, despite his journalistic cynicism, Bagehot acknowledged that the British Constitution was the basis for a sound system of parliamentary government which allowed for effective rule by the majority party and yet embodied a variety of checks and controls on the executive. Parliament is ultimately responsible (although only indirectly), for the appointment (and dissolution) of the Cabinet, as it 'elects' the Prime Minister. When a new House of Commons is returned, or when there is a ministerial crisis, Parliament exercises real sovereign power.

[2] One hundred years later Lord Hailsham thought that our political system had evolved into an 'elective dictatorship'.

largely baloney even in the mid-nineteenth century — the high point of classical parliamentary government:

> The efficient secret of the English Constitution may be described as the close union, the nearly complete fusion, of the executive and legislative powers.

In Bagehot's view this 'fusion' of powers, in conjunction with the aforementioned parliamentary constraints, produced an informal but effective constitutional system. But, owing to its reliance on delicate matters like custom and precedent, he was concerned as to how it would survive the extension of the franchise introduced by Disraeli in 1867. The authors in this book describe how constitutional balances have in fact been progressively eroded during the twentieth century,[3] which poses the question whether this process is best described as serial rape or consensual intercourse. Are the constitutional innovations of the present Government a sufficient exception to the rule of gradual evolution to constitute rape, or does this description entail a 'considerable degree of terminological inexactitude'? (Vernon Bogdanor, private correspondence.)

In the Introduction to his 1963 edition Crossman argued that since Disraeli's extension of the franchise in 1867 there has been a remorseless trend towards the centralization of power in the hands of the Prime Minister. Arguably the PM now has fewer checks on his powers than Charles I ever had.

To flesh out this argument we need to go back to Bagehot's distinction between the 'dignified' and 'efficient' parts of government. Bagehot argued that the formal separation of powers within the two trinities — on the one hand the Executive–Legislative–Judical divide and on the other the Crown–Lords–Commons — was simply a discourse we construct in order to conceal the true location of power. In this, and many other respects, his analysis was remarkably close to his contemporary, Karl Marx. The two men only differed in their views on the philosophy of history.[4] It was quite clear to Bagehot that real power rested in the Cabinet, that one body that has no formal constitutional role at all (J.S. Mill scarcely

---

[3] See especially **Dalyell**; **Johnson**; and **Weatherill**. References in bold throughout are to authors in this book.

[4] Marx operated within the tradition of Hegelian dialectical philosophy, whereas Bagehot had a journalist's disdain for all such flim-flam.

mentions the Cabinet in his competing analysis). The Cabinet was an eighteenth-century innovation, although its distant origin was the informal circle of advisers to the medieval kings. As Parliament progressively annexed the powers of the Crown — making a mockery of the separation of the executive and the legislature — the Cabinet continued to be the focus of effective power. The only change was in who picked its members.

Bagehot was perfectly happy with this arrangement for a number of reasons. First of all, as editor of *The Economist*, he subscribed fully to the view that government should be in the hands of the educated middle classes. It seemed quite natural to him that the country should be run by a 'Board of Directors' along similar lines to the banking or business community. Secondly, at that time party disciplines were very loose, so the power of parliaments to vote in the replacement of cabinets was still very real. Governments were frequently defeated in parliamentary divisions by their fellow party members, and this was seen as part of the normal day-to-day business of parliamentary government. Thirdly, like most conservative Liberals of the time, he believed in 'government by conversation'. As it was almost impossible for a club of some 500 members to have a meaningful conversation he felt this was best left in the hands of the smaller group of the Cabinet.

Twentieth-Century Developments

Bagehot was apprehensive about Disraeli's extension of the franchise in the Second Reform Act of 1867 to include much of the male urban working class, although he realized it would take a generation before the true impact could be assessed. He had no problem in principle with a broader franchise, but argued that to give the vote to people without the education and wisdom to exercise it properly was unwise. Like most of his peers, he was opposed to party politicians making opportunistic concessions to democracy that would, in his view, substitute government by ignorance and brute numbers for government by discussion. In the eighteenth century, the Commons was effectively run from the Lords through the power of patronage. The First Reform Act of 1832 largely put a stop to that but, with a limited franchise, corruption was still widespread. Although Disraeli's Reform Act ended this form of patronage, it just meant that other methods had to be used. The growth in power of the political parties, which used to be little more than clubs for like-minded MPs, is a direct consequence of 1867. Although it was not possible to buy votes directly, all governments since the time have continued to woo the electorate through promises of state benefits to come. Arguably, corruption has just moved on to a larger political arena.

The role of the political party continued to grow until it became a centralized extra-parliamentary machine, constantly seeking to impose its discipline and its doctrine on the MP and the party-worker alike. The net result of this is that the House of Commons ceased to be the 'electoral college' for the Prime Minister and the Cabinet, and ended up as merely a forum of debate between well-disciplined political armies, of late staged more for the benefit of the television cameras than for the advancement of sound government.

Although the first example of the modern mass party was Joseph Chamberlain's Birmingham caucus, the recently created Labour movement, lacking the traditions and resources of the established parties, had to build a disciplined party machine for its own survival (and the Conservatives followed suit). By the middle of the twentieth century, the two great party oligarchies had appropriated most of the sovereign powers that Bagehot ascribed to the House of Commons.

The politics of the last decade of the twentieth century have sharply accentuated this trend — Mr Hague's muscle-flexing towards errant Peers and Shadow Cabinet members is a direct reaction to the perceived 'weakness' of his predecessor. Although the autonomy of the individual MP and his relationship with his constituents used to be important bulwarks of our democracy, this failed to impress the electorate in 1997. Mr Blair was elected for his perceived emphasis on strong leadership and party discipline, whereas Mr Major was rejected for trying to see both sides of an argument.

Crossman argues that the other cause of the drift towards centralization of power has been the two World Wars. In the paradigm case of the separation of powers, as established by the US Constitution, the main focus of activity of the President, and the areas where his powers are relatively unchecked, is in the declaration and prosecution of war, and the defence of the security and trading arrangements of the nation. This again was based on the English experience, where the prosecution of war was the prerogative of the executive (the Crown). But when the executive evolved into a committee of parliament (the Cabinet), this became our Achilles' heel in times of war. Both World Wars led to (temporary) increases in power of the Prime Minister, but, as tends to be the case, executives are loath to abandon their newly-won powers on the cessation of hostilities. The war-time centralization of power was not reduced by Mr Attlee, and decisions which in the 1930s might well have been taken by the whole Cabinet, were transferred to the Cabinet secretariat, committee or the Prime Minister himself.

The other major historical trend since the time of Bagehot is the matching of the reduction in the power of Parliament and the Cabinet by the enormous growth in state bureaucracy, both at local and national level. As Bagehot predicted, the professional civil service has largely taken over the common-sense business decisions that would normally be the prerogative of the inexpert minister in his department, or of collective Cabinet decision. The conflict between Sir Humphrey and Paul Eddington's hapless Minister for Administrative Affairs in *Yes Minister* is an amusing portrayal of the declining role of ministers in the conduct of departmental affairs — even though this trend was partly reversed after 1979. No doubt this has made public administration far more efficient, but there is always a price to pay. Since 1919 the civil service has been unified under the Secretary of the Treasury, and the regulation requiring the consent of the Premier to senior appointments has given a further boost to Prime Ministerial power. This means that loyalty, rather than independence of thought, has become the supreme virtue in both the political party and the civil service.

Arguably even at the time of Bagehot the Prime Minister's powers were, at least in theory, little short of presidential. He could select and dismiss his Cabinet at will, he could announce Cabinet decisions without taking a vote, and had control, through the Chief Whip, over patronage. But in practice things were rather different. Political parties used to have much of the character of aristocratic clubs, containing, in part, people without whom a leader simply could not govern. After 1945 this characteristic has more or less vanished — parties have become bands of standardized professionals who, having chosen a leader, are then obliged to fall in line behind him/her.

As a consequence the power of the Prime Minister has increased steadily, through the centralization of the party and state bureaucracy under his control. However Cabinet ministers are still collectively responsible for decisions that are not of their own making, as Douglas Hogg and Angela Browning discovered at the time of the BSE crisis. As this collective responsibility now extends down to the level of the PPS, it means that an ever-increasing proportion of the parliamentary party is held hostage to the Prime Minister's decisions.

All these developments have led to the situation where the Cabinet has now followed the Commons, the Lords and the Crown from the 'efficient' to the 'dignified' part of the constitution. **Tony Benn** goes further (p. 60):

> Today it would be more accurate to describe the House of Commons as the dignified part of the constitution, which is there to 'excite and preserve the reverence of the population' while the powers of the Crown, controlled by the Prime Minister, are the efficient part 'by which [government], in fact, works and rules'.

Power is now effectively in the hands of the Prime Minister and the permanent civil service. Although the outward display of Cabinet government is still maintained, there are times when it is revealed as a clear fiction — for example the decision to test Britain's first atomic bomb was not even discussed in full Cabinet.

Crossman notes that the centralization of power in the state has been parallelled by a similar process in finance, business and industry. During the 1980s the abolition of exchange controls and the development of global trading systems meant that real power moved to multinational corporations and global capital markets. As the regular daily flows of speculative capital are in excess of the GNP of many small countries there is an understandable sense that our own economy is beyond our national control, as there is often no direct relationship between the value of a currency and underlying economic fundamentals. George Soros has acknowledged that the assault on the pound that bounced us out of the ERM in 1992 was partly motivated by his personal resentment over the treatment he received on his arrival as a pennyless immigrant in Britain. Arguably, attempts by a small country to regulate capital flows would be just as futile as attempting to control the Internet,[5] but politicians of all colours are reluctant to admit their impotence in the face of global capital, so the debate never really seems to get off the ground.

More worrying still is the centralization of ownership and control of the mass media. Unlike the case in the United States, most British TV and radio channels are effectively national;[6] most of the daily papers are published in London and many are owned by the same publishing groups. Rupert Murdoch is widely believed to have been the kingmaker behind the last two election victories — the support of the *Sun* is perhaps the most valuable electoral asset — but it would be naive to think that there was no price attached.

Perhaps on account of all this happening during a period in which there was a steady rise in the standard of living, the general drift towards centralization (on both sides of the Atlantic) has been accepted with a shrug of the shoulders by a generally apathetic electorate. President Clinton's personal self-help mantra ('it's the economy, stupid') won him a second term and also helped him survive impeachment. Similarly the relaxed attitude towards allegations of sleaze in Mr Blair's Government is in sharp contrast to his predecessor's experience. The crucial difference is, of course, the 'feel-good factor' that is largely the product of a stable and buoyant economy.

Although opinion polls still show that most people are opposed to EMU and the abolition of the pound, they also show a majority believing that we are powerless to resist the

---

[5] This is probably the strongest argument in favour of European integration, leading **Roy Jenkins** to argue (in parallel with the UKIP), that Britain needs to be either wholly out or else wholly in. 'In Europe but not run by it' is a nice soundbite but in practice means little, as the EU is clearly much more than a free-trade zone. However **Peter Shore** and **Norman Tebbit** comment on the duplicity of past governments who sold the Common Market to the British people on the assurance that it was precisely that.

[6] Notwithstanding a small amount of regional programming.

inevitable drift towards deeper European integration. If it is the case that decisions will increasingly be made in Brussels, then a lack of interest in the finer points of our constitutional arrangements is understandable.

Crossman was clearly troubled by the developments that he witnessed after the war, but ends on a note of cautious optimism:

> In theory — but also in practice — the British people retains the power not merely to choose between two Prime Ministers, and two parties, but to throw off its deferential attitude and reshape the political system, making the parties instruments of popular control, and even insisting that the House of Commons should once again provide the popular check on the executive. It is my hope and belief that this will happen.

I cannot see how a commentator writing 35 years after Crossman could hold out much hope for such an outcome. As **Peter Oborne** demonstrates, the penetration of the Government Information and Communication Service by Labour Party special advisers has led to much resentment and the prospect of a further undermining of the political independence of the permanent civil service. As for Crossman's hope that we might finally shrug off our deferential heritage, all that has happened is that the new ikons of youth, image and charisma have replaced our traditional deference to birth, status and the great institutions of state.

The 1997 intake of young career MPs, with their lack of experience outside politics or the public sector, pagers to keep them on-message and lists of planted questions for PM's question time can hardly be relied on to 'provide a popular check on the executive'. The great tradition of parliamentary oratory is all but dead, leaving the role of the MP as little more than lobby fodder. The drift towards PR and the closed party list can only enhance the dictatorial powers of the Prime Minister and his party managers. The incorporation of the European Convention on Human Rights (see **Johnson**) and the constant stream of regulations from Brussels have serious implications for the independence of both our judiciary and legislature. The appalling quality of public debate and the blatant partiality of large sections of the media[7] means that the fourth estate now appears to have joined the other three (Crown, Lords and Commons) on the benches of the 'dignified' part of our Constitution.

Perhaps 'media bias' is nothing more than the natural sympathy for a centre-left agenda that one would expect from the humanities and social-science graduates of the 1970s. But another viewpoint is that it reflects the power of government patronage. As we enter the free-for-all era of digital broadcasting the BBC is naturally concerned to preserve its standing (and licence fee), so managers and editors are wary about offending a government with strong links to the Murdoch empire. But more worrying is the tendency of government press officers to exclude hostile media from their unofficial briefings. The present Government has a policy of leaking policy statements first, with parliamentary announcements playing a very secondary role. The attack on Iraq in January 1999 was announced to the press on the steps of 10 Downing Street, rather than to Parliament, and it would appear that the editor of the *Sun* was gifted with this scoop several hours before anyone got round to telling the Leader of the Opposition. There is a genuine fear amongst editors that, if they overstep the mark, the Prime Minister's Press Secretary will make sure that any government-orchestrated scoops will go to their competitors. Given the intense competition amongst the national dailies, any newspaper that consistently misses the important stories will rapidly lose readers. We are now said to live in the 'information age' and the value of government patronage over access to information is enormous. There is a good case for this uniquely modern form of patronage to be subject to the same scrutiny as other forms of government influence. Once again, the public and media focus on more 'dignified' forms of patronage – in particular the honours system – has helped to conceal the modern 'efficient' form (the ownership and distribution of information).

According to Bagehot's analysis, the 'dignified' part of the constitution – the pomp and pageantry that is a reminder of our feudal past – plays an important, but anti-democratic, role. He reached this conclusion largely on account of his own

[7]   Peter Oborne, 'The Silence of the Sheep', *The Spectator*, 15 January 2000.

modification of utilitarian and rationalist psychology. Bagehot's insight was that although *rational* behaviour is motivated largely by self-interest, nevertheless human beings are,
for the most part, creatures of *habit, circumstance and tradition*.
'It is the dull, traditional habit of mankind that guides most
men's actions.'

This being the case, the role of the 'dignified' part of our
constitution is to satisfy our habitual attitudes and traditional
loyalties, and to provide a smokescreen for the 'efficient' part
of government.[8] Bagehot was convinced that most English-
men believed that they were still governed by the Queen. I am
reminded of a plumber friend who went to service a central
heating installation, only to find that the room thermostat was
not connected to the boiler. Nonplussed, he questioned the
householder, who replied that it was 'just for the missus' and
pointed out where the real (hidden) thermostat was located.

The American Experience

Mr Blair is not best known for his love of history. Indeed the
current debate largely ignores the historical dimension, so it
might be helpful to compare and contrast our own Constitution, which is by and large the product of happenstance, with
that of the United States. The latter was the product of design
— specifically the special constitutional assembly that met in
Philadelphia in 1787.

The US Constitution represents a compromise between a
number of different factions, so to understand the guiding
principles of the Founders we are better off examining secondary documents. The debate over the ratification of the
Constitution (by the state assemblies) largely took place in
newspaper columns. Both sides of the argument (the federal-
ists and the anti-federalists) were anxious to prove their solid
republican provenance and assumed appropriate *noms de
plume* like 'Brutus' and 'Publius'. However, despite the deference to classical republican theory and rhetoric, the federalist
argument was firmly grounded in modern political *experience;*

---

[8] It should not escape our notice that much of what passes for the ancient cere-
monies of state was deliberately manufactured at the beginning of the twentieth century by officials at Buckingham Palace, largely in response to the
altered political landscape that followed Disraeli's Reform Act.

in the words of John Dickinson, one of the framers of the Constitution, 'experience must be our only guide; reason may mislead us'.[9]

Although the newly-independent Americans had just emerged from a bitter struggle with their old colonial masters, they nevertheless had enormous regard for the British constitutional model — the American Revolution was 'not against the English constitution, but on behalf of it'. The formal analysis of the division of power between the three estates (the king, the nobility and the commoners) was felt to accurately reflect society at the time — the challenge to the Founders was how to adapt this to an egalitarian, republican model.[10] Similarly the principled separation of executive, legislative and judicial function was an important part of the British Constitution and essential for the preservation of civil liberty.[11] Thus elected members of Congress were prohibited from serving as government ministers, and the President only had the right to return legislation to Congress for reconsideration.

But to James Madison, one of the trio whose arguments appeared in various New York newspapers under the pen-name 'Publius', freedom depended on more than the formal separation of powers. Madison's main concern was the pres-

[9] Iain Hampsher-Monk, *A History of Modern Political Thought* (Blackwell, 1992).

[10] It was also felt that the mixed constitution was an important defence against moral decay and the preservation of civic *virtù*. Scholars still disagree as to whether classical republican ideas like this or the modern notion of the pluralistic balance of power were the prime influences on the thoughts of the Founders. However, notwithstanding this controversy, it is fair to conclude that the Founders were well aware that large-scale republics could not rely on consensus or the inculcation of human goodness by civic or religious means. The only answer was to design a set of political institutions that ensured public virtue, notwithstanding private 'interest'. In this sense the US Constitution was very much a product of the Scottish Enlightenment. See **Berent & Sutherland**.

[11] Of course Bagehot argued nearly 100 years later that this was largely mythology. Although normally referred to as the 'separation of power', it is more accurate to refer to the division of each analytically-distinct power and the distribution of its parts amongst two or more departments. In both the English and the American case there is considerable overlap of powers between the formal estates, both in theory and in practice. Discussions of 'legislative', 'executive' and 'judicial' powers refer more to the abstract analysis (James Madison's 'parchment barriers') than individual units of government. What is important is that power should never be wholly concentrated in one pair of hands or in one group of people. (Hampsher-Monk, *op. cit.*)

ervation of the rights of individuals and minorities (and the protection of private property). The anti-federalists argued for a system of small-scale representative democracy, whereas Madison and his colleagues were concerned about the danger of popular demagogues and their factions (usually the poorest members of society). This led to the call for large, broadly-based electoral areas and all that implied for the emergence of a natural aristocracy of merit. Madison also made much of the necessity for balancing the power of the different departments of government through the exercise of veto: 'Wherever the real power in a Commonwealth lies, there is the danger of oppression.' Although the Founders had just emerged from a war against a single executive and an unrepresentative parliament, they were still aware that the greatest threat to private rights was the unchecked power of the majority: in a republic one must 'not only guard against the oppression of the rulers; but…guard one part of the society against the injustices of the other part'. Authorities like Locke and Montesquieu were cited in support of this—uncontrolled legislatures could be just as tyrannical as absolute monarchs. Madison argued that democracy was only suitable for small cohesive communities, and America effectively ended up with an elective republican aristocracy, albeit one of wealth and reputation, rather than birth. This was because, like Montesquieu, Madison realized that political freedom depended on moderate government—direct or populist democracy would be anything but.[12]

The US Constitution has not been without its critics, but looking back on the arguments of the Founders the clear division of responsibilities has held up reasonably well over the last two centuries. This has been largely because the need for pluralism, checks and balances was explicitly recognized and incorporated into the Constitution at every level.

By contrast, the English Constitution is not so much the result of design (notwithstanding the events of 1688/9) but of the progressive erosion of feudal power. It is unwritten, and is a cocktail of historical events, parliamentary laws and judicial

---

[12] Although the US centre of gravity has moved more recently in the direction of direct democracy, the increased reliance on referenda is almost entirely at the state level rather than at that of the federal government. Of course Madison would also have been unable to foresee the rise of focus-group politics and the influence of the mass media.

decisions. The problem is that the three estates (Crown, Lords and Commons) are now only of interest to the heritage industry and cannot in any meaningful way be said to represent a system of balances or checks on the exercise of power. As we saw in the first section, Bagehot described how the progressive erosion of these feudal estates has ended up with pretty well all of the balancing influences moving over to the 'dignified' part of the constitution. This is an inevitable consequence of the movement from feudalism to modernity but, such is the force of the myth of the separation of power, the erosion has happened without most of us even noticing.

The problem of the American Founders was how to develop a system of government that did not depend on the checks and balances provided *naturally* by the three estates of Old England. The result was the elaborate system of *formal* checks that makes up the US Constitution. As the natural checks and balances of the English system have now all disappeared, a Royal Commission on the Constitution would find itself faced with exactly the same set of problems that the Americans grappled with over 200 years ago. If anything is crying out for the holistic approach of 'joined-up government', it has to be constitutional reform. Yet Labour's approach so far — in particular in the areas of devolution and Lords' reform — has been piecemeal and opportunistic.[13]

It is no doubt the case that the bulkheads separating the executive, the legislature and the judiciary have always leaked. No one could sensibly claim that judicial decisions were ever taken in a political vacuum. But recent decades have seen an increase in the use of the process of judicial review — the rulings of Home Secretaries have frequently been overturned by the judiciary. Added to that, the split decision of the Law Lords in the Pinochet case was largely along ideological lines, as was freely admitted when Lord Hoffman was rebuked for failing to reveal his close links with Amnesty International. The incorporation of the European Convention on Human Rights into British law now requires our judges to make decisions that should rightly be in the hands of elected politicians. There is nothing democratic about the appointment or dismissal of our judges, and they are only accountable

[13] See **Carrington**; **Dalyell**; **Johnson**; and **Peele**.

to themselves (and their peers). It is ironic that the power of one unelected group in our Upper House is growing at the same time that the Government has effectively dismantled the far more modest powers of other members of that chamber.

But the biggest problem is the relationship of the executive to the legislature. British observers of the US polity tend to be put off by the built-in tendency to gridlock. How could anyone design a system that can set off a Democratic President against a Republican Congress? But the system seems to work, more or less, and one of the benign consequences is a built-in moderation — given the powers of Congress to refuse to bankroll the government, and the powers of the executive to veto or return legislation, anything that eventually makes it on to the statute book has to be broadly acceptable.

In practice the British system is entirely different — the ministers of the Crown sit in the Commons and are appointees of the majority parliamentary party. The majority party in Parliament and the executive are effectively one and the same — a clear travesty of the principle of the constitutional separation of powers. Given the power of the party whips, and the impotence of the Upper House, this means that the leader of the majority party has a five-year electoral mandate for dictatorship.

Reform of the House of Lords

If anything, the only part of our constitutional arrangements that was working more or less as intended was the unreformed House of Lords. As the hereditaries (who made up the vast majority of the Lords) did not owe their position to the patronage or support of anyone among the living, they were in an ideal position to exercise the independence of judgment that our informal constitutional arrangements depend on.[14] Although they were in the most part Conservative, the whip did not lie very heavily on them and on occasion they showed

---

[14] As the Earl of Onslow charmingly put it: the Lords work[ed] so well just because the hereditaries 'don't give a bugger'. This wasn't a reference to their Lordships' views on parity in the age of consent for sexual relations. He meant that the hereditaries were free from all pressures to toe the line and were only answerable to their consciences. Coupled with an inbred sense of duty and public service this made for the ideal scrutinizing chamber, in stark contrast to the party-political posturing of the Commons (see **Lucas**).

a surprising degree of independence of judgment. Most of them were acutely aware of their own illegitimacy (democratic, that is), that the hereditary principle was almost impossible to justify to the modern mind-set and that they were only there because no one had been able to come up with a better system. In the past this led to a general acceptance of the Salisbury Convention, whereby legislation for manifesto commitments is let through intact, but the hereditaries — at least before they acceded to the Weatherill amendment — felt that they had an additional role in the protection of the Constitution from attack by the government of the day.

But, however well the House did its job, it was undermined by its own composition, leading **Peter Carrington** to realize as early as the 1950s that reform was necessary. Although the powers of the House were very limited, it was considered that the Lords had no right to challenge the 'will of the people' as manifested in the elected House of Commons. Although a sensible compromise was agreed by all three parties in 1968, this was torpedoed by the 'curious alliance' of Michael Foot and Enoch Powell.

Michael Rush commends the Wakeham Report as focused, skilfully constructed, and politically realistic. By contrast **Conrad Russell** argues that this was a prime opportunity to redress Hailsham's problem of the 'elective dictatorship' at the heart of the British Constitution. Although there is a case for a degree of nomination to preserve the independence of cross-benchers, nevertheless Russell claims that 'election is the only language that the Commons understands'. The unchecked power of the Commons is in danger or corrupting *of* absolutely. We are at a crossroads: constitutional government is in danger of turning into 'something else'.

Interestingly, the Conservative Party Mackay Report also called for an elected second chamber, a view developed here by **Andrew Tyrie.**

Local Government

Local government since the Second World War has been a story of remorseless centralization, according to **Simon Jenkins**. In parallel with the nationalization of hospitals, prisons and welfare provision in the 1940s, the freedom of local councils to raise and spend local taxes has been curbed. Although this began in the '70s under Tony Crosland, Margaret Thatcher launched a wholesale assault on local democracy in the mid-1980s.

The context for all this was the degeneration of local democracy into party cabalism. 'Loony left' councillors imposed huge rate rises, safe in the knowledge that most of their electors were protected by social security, leading to the capping of local rates in 1984.

Lady Thatcher recalled in her memoirs that the Community Charge was intended to revitalize local democracy by sowing a few nettles in the grass. Councils would have to raise the money they needed for the level of services that they chose to provide, and answer for that choice in a local ballot.

Just as the American colonists raised the cry 'no taxation without representation' as they threw King George's tea into Boston Bay, Thatcher attempted to bring home the revolution with the poll tax. But in the process she effectively reversed the slogan to 'no representation without taxation', allowing opponents to claim that the poll tax was an attack on fundamental democratic rights.[15]

Several other factors conspired to frustrate the attempt to revitalize democratic accountability. In order to be acceptable to the poor, the tax had to be set at a low rate,[16] meaning that central government continued to provide the majority of funding. The final nail in the coffin was the Treasury insistence that the tax should continue to be capped.

As is so often the case, the centralization of local government has had unforseen ramifications. Councillors were left

---

[15] It should be noted, in passing, that the very people who took to the streets to protest against the poll tax now seem to have accepted some of the principles that lay behind the tax, but recast in the Newspeak of the 'relationship between rights and responsibilities'. Thatcherism had little time for such 'Third Way' abstractions.

[16] Nevertheless the poll tax was pilloried as a regressive 'tax on the poor', leading to the rallying cry 'can't pay, won't pay'. Arguably the National Lottery is, in practice, an even more regressive form of taxation, as the average weekly spend of £5.37 (by the one-third of households who play the game twice a week) is concentrated among the lower socio-economic bands. It would appear that people have no difficulty stumping up the 'bread' if there is a hint of future circuses but, given the infinitesimally-small chance of winning the jackpot, perhaps after all the Lottery is just a tax on the gullible.

with the responsibility to administer local services but were stripped of the power to set levels of taxation. Electors were quick to spot the power vacuum so interest in local politics hit an all-time low. Most people are unable to name their own council representative and local newspapers pay little attention to Town Hall debates, preferring to fill their pages with 'human interest' stories.

Whereas people used to take their housing and other domestic problems to their local councillor, nowadays MPs' surgeries and postbags are occupied with matters that should really be dealt with at the local level. **Bernard Weatherill** notes that there are currently 40,000 letters coming into the Palace of Westminster every day, causing MPs to stay in their offices devoting their time to matters that don't really concern them. The role of an MP is, in Gladstone's words, to 'hold the Government to account', and if MPs are not in the Chamber this means that the Government could 'get away with murder'. As Weatherill's essay is entitled 'The Law of Unexpected Consequences', he obviously takes a charitable view of the reasons behind this development, but those of a more cynical disposition might conclude that governments would in general prefer *not* to be held to account.

Devolution

One of the first acts of the New Labour Government was to address their manifesto commitment over devolution (Scotland, Wales and the London mayoralty). This is often cited as evidence that Mr Blair's reputation as a 'control freak' is exaggerated. Simon Jenkins gives New Labour great credit for these developments, describing them as 'setting out to reverse the centralist tendency of government since the Second World War' and 'the most radical for over a century'.

However, as **Dalyell**, **Johnson** and **Peele** are quick to point out, the commitment to devolution was mostly a question of 'unfinished business' and scant attention has been paid to the constitutional implications for the United Kingdom as a whole. **Diana Woodhouse** argues the need for a Constitutional Court to deal with disputes over the devolved powers and a radical reappraisal of the role of the Lord Chancellor.

Moreover we are only just beginning to see the effects of devolution on the English. For centuries, as the dominant nation in the Union, the sense of English national identity has been deliberately suppressed — subsumed under the concept of Britishness, now seen by an increasing number of historians as a manufactured construct. The end of empire and the diversion of overseas trade from the Commonwealth to the European Union have all served to damage the notion of Britishness, but the final nail in the coffin has been the establishment of devolved assemblies for Scotland, Wales and Northern Ireland. This has led to an outpouring of books and television and radio programmes all debating the imminent demise of the Union and the resulting identity crisis of the English.[17]

Just as Scottish nationalism achieved a great fillip as a result of the imposition of Thatcher's hated poll tax, a similar sense of injustice is fuelling the emergence of English nationalism. Why should the Scots have their own Parliament and continue to be massively over-represented at Westminster and in the Cabinet? Why is regional aid weighted to favour the Scots over other equally-disadvantaged English regions? This has led William Hague to argue for 'English days' at Westminster when only English MPs are allowed to vote on English issues, but there is a growing minority calling for an English Parliament and the conversion of the United Kingdom into a federal state, partly as a preemptive defence against creeping Euro-federalism.

What is to be Done?

There is a danger that reviewers and readers might regard this book as little more than the rantings of a collection of modern-day Jeremiahs and Cassandras, lamenting the passing of the golden age of 'government by conversation'. So, given some

[17] Vernon Bogdanor, *Devolution in the United Kingdom*; Jonathan Bradbury, *British Regionalism and Devolution*; David Cannadine, *Britain in Decline?*; Linda Colly, *Britons: Forging the Nation, 1707-1837*; Norman Davies, *The Isles*; Simon Heffer, *Nor Shall my Sword*; Peter Hitchens, *The Abolition of Britain*; Andrew Marr, *The Day Britain Died*; Tom Nairn, *After Britain*; Jeremy Paxman, *The English*; John Redwood, *The Death of Britain?*; Michael Wood, *In Search of England*.

measure of agreement on the nature of the problem, we now need to move on and ask the question 'what is to be done?'

One possible course is the path of reaction—a perfectly proper approach unless you happen to be a hardline Whig and claim that history is as irreversible as the thermodynamic 'arrow of time'. Tam Dalyell[18] locates the Indian summer of representative democracy as the early 1960s, so why not just attempt to consciously recreate the conditions that prevailed at the time?

Dalyell pinpoints several factors leading to the end of 'government by conversation'. Some of these are simple and straightforward—for example, before the construction of expensive office buildings most MPs had to make do with a locker. This meant that the main locus of 'government by conversation' was the Smoking Room of the House of Commons. It would be a comparatively simple matter to flog off the offices and kick out the secretaries and 'research assistants'. If this means that MPs are less able to service the burgeoning needs of their constituents then so much the better as, according to **Simon Jenkins** and **Bernard Weatherill**, this is a usurpation of the role of local councillors. If MPs are to spend their time in the Chamber holding the government to account then they can do a much better job if they are not in their offices, waiting for the division bell to ring.

The other urgent reform needed, argues **Peter Hitchens** (in tune with both **Tony Benn** and **Jonathan Freedland**), is the curb of the royal prerogative, handed on from monarch to government after the 1688 revolution. Much of this power could be given to a strengthened and more independent House of Commons in which, most importantly, the power of the party whips had been curbed. Unfortunately the chances of a government choosing to cede these historic powers voluntarily is on a par with a turkey voting for Christmas.[19]

---

[18] Tam Dalyell, 'On the Decline of Intelligent Government', in Ivo Mosley, ed., *Dumbing Down: Culture, Politics and the Mass Media* (Imprint Academic, 2000).

[19] However these things do happen from time to time: the establishment of a full range of departmental select committees by the Thatcher Government in 1979 provided a very real boost to the power of MPs to hold the government to account (see **Johnson**). **Bernard Weatherill** suggests a number of ways in which such reforms could be extended.

Douglas Hurd has argued that in addition to the power of the select committee, departmental question time and meetings of backbench MPs place a

But of course the problem runs deeper than that, and is part of a much broader shift in society. The last few decades have witnessed the rise of the professional politician — young MPs with little or no experience of outside life are becoming the norm. The death of Alan Clark appeared to mark the end of the era of the MP of independent means who cared little for party discipline or public approval, and the Nolan and Neill committees have made it far harder for MPs to combine politics with extra-parliamentary commercial interests. Even if the power of patronage and party whips were curtailed, it is hard to imagine a return to the golden age of the independent-minded private Member. As Burke put it, 'There can be no independence of mind without independence of means.'

Most of the reforms that would be required would be deeply unpopular with MPs, besides which the evidence for elites reforming themselves is patchy. Traditional representative democracy and 'government by conversation' also require a culture of deference based on the notion that the political elite knows best and should be left to get on with its business without the constant intrusion of media scrutiny. **Bernard Weatherill** describes how when he was Conservative Deputy Chief Whip and then Speaker his primary concern was to maintain the dignity of the institution of Parliament. This entailed the House looking after its own disciplinary matters, and errant members were usually advised to retire on grounds of ill-health. According to Weatherill, the independent watchdog culture has been nothing less than disastrous.

The decline in respect for our parliamentary institutions is also the result of an increasingly intrusive press. **Peter Oborne** recounts how the attitude of the 'lobby correspondent' to the government used to be almost as deferential as it was towards royalty. But all that changed in the 1960s when political journalists were first courted by Harold Wilson. However .

---

very real constraint on the power of government ministers. According to Hurd, the fashionable Whig view that the British system of 'fused' government supports a secretive and tyrannical executive is an exaggeration. The way to address the failings of the British parliamentary system is to build on the strengths of our fused system, with a smaller House of Commons and a reduction in the number of career politicians (Douglas Hurd, 'The Whig Illusion', *Prospect*, February 1997.) Unfortunately the tide would seem to be flowing in the opposite direction.

once the media started to flex their own muscles the tail soon began to wag the dog. The growth of the broadcast media, coupled with the televising of Parliament meant the end of government by conversation. Even if **Peter Shore**'s suggestion is taken up that ministers should be compelled by force of law to make announcements first to the House of Commons, we now live in an age of instant communications and this in itself calls for revisions to our model of government.

All this has coincided with a widespread cynicism among the general public towards all the great public institutions — the church, the monarchy, parliament, the professions and authority in general. Is it possible that such a process could be reversed?

Historical precedents are few and far between. In some ways there are parallels between our present times and the cynicism that was endemic at the beginning of the nineteenth century. Historians like Gertrude Himmelfarb[20] have charted the transition from the decadence of the Georgian and Regency period to the revitalization of our great national institutions in the reign of Queen Victoria.

However, as Himmelfarb is quick to point out, the civic revival was largely a reflection of underlying religious trends. Following the rise of Methodism in the eighteenth century, and the ensuing religious revival associated with Evangelicalism and, later on, the Oxford Movement, there was a notable shift in both personal and civic morality, leading the Victorians to take genuine pride in the great institutions of the nation. However there is no reason to think that another such religious revival is likely, notwithstanding the Prime Minister's attempts to emulate Moses at the 1999 Labour Party Conference (see **Diboll**). Although some Conservatives might hanker for an *imposed* return to traditional values in morality, education and civics there are equal opposing forces on the libertarian Right.

Peter Hitchens focuses on the monarchy as the key genuinely popular obstacle to what he calls the 'government's creeping putsch'. And there are historical precedents: Charles I saw himself, rightly or wrongly, as the defender of both the rule of

---

[20] Gertrude Himmelfarb, *Marriage and Morals Among the Victorians* (I.B. Tauris, 1989).

law and government by consent; it took a republican regime to impose a military dictatorship. So strongly was the monarchy perceived as the best insurance for liberty and the rule of law that these powers were formally retained in 1689. More recently the retention of the monarchy in Italy, albeit as something of an empty husk, ultimately led to Mussolini's downfall, since in 1943, after 22 years of fascist rule, a group of disaffected fascists and opposition politicians were able to rally around the King against Mussolini. In an interesting example of the monarch providing a focus for the forces of liberty, it was Victor Emmanuel who personally signed Mussolini's arrest warrant.[21]

The Prince of Wales has shown a robust independence from the government of the day, as evidenced by his snubbing of the Chinese delegation and the 'monstrous blancmange' at Greenwich, his opposition to GM foods and continuing support for country sports. Such a monarch could well become the focus of dissent against an authoritarian government, using nothing other than the very real legal powers retained in 1689.

---

[21] Hitchens also suggests another parallel between *Il Duce* and the current occupant of No. 10 Downing Street. In his view Mr Blair is only the front man, an 'attractive figurehead', selected for his telegenic and thespian powers by the cabal which took over the Labour Party in the 1980s. Whilst this smacks of conspiracy theory it remains the case that this was one of the factors that led to the Party rallying behind Blair rather than Gordon Brown after the death of John Smith, and Mr Blair's ability to adapt his image, views (and accent) to suit his audience is well known.

In his authoritative biography of Mussolini, Denis Mack-Smith remarks that 'Mussolini [should be seen] as an actor or dissimulator, an exhibitionist who changed his role to suit the occasion' (D. Mack-Smith, *Mussolini*, Weidenfeld, 1981, pp. 111–12)

Lada Rafanelli, Mussolini's one-time mistress noticed:

> ...that at some times he seemed to her like a burlesque actor; he appeared to lack a well-defined inner personality — he told her he did not understand his real self...He had the disconcerting habit of changing his mind in the course of a single conversation in order to agree with what she said; other people in later years confirmed that he always tended to agree with the person to whom he had last spoken...and he confessed that he felt much more at home on a public rostrum than in a private conversation. (*ibid.*, p. 21)

Bringing Home the Revolution

What might be the radical-progressive solution to the decline of parliamentary government? As the American Constitution was based on the 'English experience', **Jonathan Freedland** argues that it is time that we repaid the compliment and 'brought home the revolution'. He is quick to acknowledge the problems with American democracy — the legislative grid-lock, the 'bland, blow-dried candidates', the excessive power of lobbyists and pressure groups, the grease of 'pork-barrel' politicians and election campaigns sold to the highest bidder (or to the candidate with the most charisma). On the other hand, one might argue that anything is better than living under an 'elective dictatorship' and continuing to suffer the dramatic swings that have characterized British politics throughout the twentieth century.

To many people American culture — McDonald's and 100-channel TV networks with nothing worth watching — is tacky and vulgar, and the less we have to do with it the better. 'We're becoming just like America' is a standard British lament on a par with 'going to the dogs'. In Freedland's own words, 'America is the land of Bible-quoting fundamentalists, lamé-suited game-show hosts and gun-toting maniacs.' Why on earth would we want to emulate the United States?

The trouble is we already import American culture 'by the crate-load' every day of the week. Cultural 'globalization' is in reality a synonym for American cultural imperialism, and the popularity of Microsoft, Starbucks and McDonald's is only a reflection of consumers' free choice. We have the worst of both worlds — we import American junk culture in wholesale quan-tities but we do not benefit from the political freedoms and sense of control over our own destiny that Americans enjoy.

Freedland acknowledges that his ten-point programme will attract and repel both progressives and conservatives in equal measure. The main problem for the Left is accepting that their 'century-long flirtation with Marxism' was a false seduction. Freedland offers the interesting observation that socialism (in practice, if not in theory) and paternalism ('one-nation' con-servatism) are two sides of the same coin — a permanent elite tending to the needs of a permanent proletariat. Both attitudes have their origin in a quasi-feudal view of society, with a rigidly-stratified class structure. The welfare state handing down benefits to its citizens is just the twentieth-century equivalent of *noblesse oblige.*

By contrast the Americans never had a feudal society to dismantle or a mainstream socialist tradition to flirt with. The US Constitution from the start was based on the principle of equality of opportunity, hence the fact that the slogan 'hand-ups not hand-downs' has been imported to this country from the US. Whilst the Thatcher era marked the effective end of paternalistic 'one-nation' conservatism, the Left has yet fully to come to terms with the abandonment of socialism — as we have seen from the difficulties the Blair Government has experienced over welfare reform.

The other problem for the Left with the American system is that public opinion is consistently more right-wing than most political elites. Time and again opinion polls have shown a majority in favour of the return of the death penalty, the reintroduction of corporal punishment, and the loosening of our ties with (or even withdrawal from) the European Union. Similarly it would appear that public opinion is solidly behind the retention of Clause 28, banning the promotion of homosexuality by local education authorities. All these things are anathema to radicals, and lead to a cautious approach to democracy, American style.

The main problem, though, with progressives is the deeply-entrenched notion that the state should be the main, or possibly the only, source of welfare provision. We have spent a century equating the state with compassion; any retreat from public provision is immediately condemned as a betrayal of government's sacred obligation to protect the weak. In America the voluntary and charitable sectors are considerably stronger, but to British radicals words like 'charity' evoke images of the workhouse.

However, the architects of the welfare state are beginning to have second thoughts. Michael Young, the author of the 1945 Labour manifesto, has recalled that the Labour Party — by disposition more Methodist than Marxist — has a long tradition of voluntary association and self-help. Young suggests a return to the reciprocal ethic in housing, health and education. Local government, says Young, should be — as in America — more truly local, with smaller councils reflecting a sense of communal identity (*Guardian*, 19 March 1997).[22]

An interesting parallel can be drawn between Young's proposals and an early-'90s discussion document prompted by the Adam Smith Instititute in which John Patten urged the replacement of the 'Nanny State' with a network of local quasi-voluntary associations. The suggestion was that much of the responsibility for policing could be handed over to local groups developed out of neighbourhood-watch associations, and that the WRVS would provide a better basis for community care than social services departments.

From the analysis above it would appear that conservatives have more to gain from the adoption of American-style politics. The main difficulty for the Right, however, is the two R-words in the title of Freedland's book.[23]

The conservative abhorrence of revolutionary change goes back at least as far as Burke's *Reflections*, but if you ask most Conservatives what was their proudest post-war achievement it would more than likely be the restructuring of the economy during the 1980s. But there was nothing *remotely* 'conservative' about the economic policy of the period, it was a classic example of free-market liberalism. In Lady Thatcher's view a state that appropriated and redistributed nearly 40% of the national wealth was socialist and needed to be taken apart. Given both her philosophical individualism and the stability of our democratic institutions, the only tool left in her handbag was the 'invisible hand' of the market. Thatcherism was nothing less than the first of Freedland's R-words (revolution) applied to the economy. Although this was painful at the time, it is now accepted by most people that the economy is in vastly better shape than before. Freedland argues that we need to apply the same Thatcherite principles to political life.

Which brings us on to the second R-word — republicanism. The Conservative Party has always been a staunch defender of monarchy and the hereditary principle. But the acceptance by

---

[22] Gordon Brown's 2000 Budget announcement of additional tax breaks for charities and encouragement for 'civic patriotism', 'active citizenship' and nineteenth-century views of individual, family and civic obligations is an encouraging sign of a change in Government policy for the voluntary sector.

[23] Jonathan Freedland, *Bring Home the Revolution: The Case for a British Republic* (Fourth Estate, 1998).

the party of the Weatherill amendment and the effective abolition of the rights of Hereditary Peers marks a true turning
point in the history of the party. There are many who say the
fight should have been taken to the bitter end, or even that the
Queen should have intervened in the defence of our Constitution. No other democracy would accept such a fundamental
constitutional change on the strength of a party mandate that
was supported by just 44% of the electorate, most of whom
knew little and cared less about the reform of the House of
Lords. But that is now history and Conservatives have to re-
adjust to the new political landscape.

The important thing to remember is that all the historic
powers of the Crown have been appropriated by the Prime
Minister.[24] As **Tony Benn** explains in his essay, the Crown is
the source of all political power in Britain and a nostalgic
clinging to the institution of monarchy is the ultimate source
of our 'elective dictatorship'. The monarchy is the main symbol of the fact that power in Britain is top-down, dispensed by
the Crown-in-Parliament (the Prime Minister) to the *hoi polloi*,
in the same manner that the Queen dispenses pennies to her
grateful subjects on Maundy Thursday.

The Conservative Party has a long association with royalism. The Tories tended to support the king, who was the main
bulwark against radicalism. But now that the powers of the
Crown have been appropriated by political parties with very
different agendas, the Conservative preference for strong government is an anachronism. Clement Attlee's nationalization
agenda was on the strength of a 48% mandate. Large as that
may be, it's hard to imagine such a radical programme suc-
ceeding in the US given the built-in gridlock of an innately
conservative political system. Of course the converse is also
true: Margaret Thatcher's programme of privatization would
have been equally gridlocked under the US system. But there
would have been no need for it in the first instance. Gordon
Brown may have removed the causes of 'boom and bust' by
allowing the Bank of England to set interest-rate policy, but

---

[24] Indeed, judging by the millennium-eve shenanigans at Greewich it would
appear that the Queen's presence at major national occasions is now only
grudgingly accepted by her Government. Her Majesty's role that evening
was confined to opening the gate to allow the children through to pull down
the drapes, and holding hands with the Prime Minister.

the rest of the British Constitution is just as vulnerable to the violent political swings that have beset our history throughout the twentieth century.

A Liberal Realignment?

One of the factors that encouraged me to publish this book was an experience at the conference 'Britain in Europe', organized by the Institute for Constitutional Affairs (22 March 1999). I was amazed to see the very same people who rose to give a standing ovation to Norman Tebbit give the same treatment to Tony Benn. Of course you could argue that the debate over the European Union is the exception that proves the rule, but I would like to argue that incidents like this are a sign of a deeper shift in political alignments.

Although the terms 'left' and 'right' go back to the French Revolution, in the twentieth century they have more often been seen as markers on the socialism–capitalism axis. Hence since the end of the Cold War they appear to have lost much of their meaning. After the fall of the Berlin Wall it has been argued that we have reached the 'end of politics' and are all now (supposedly) committed to the principles of liberal democracy, free trade and market capitalism. This has left figures on the old Left with something of an identity crisis, searching around for somewhere to hang their hat.

However there is another continuum of political alignments — the axis of liberty–statism. Many radical thinkers of the old Left have been quick to divest themselves of the socialist fascination with the state and have returned to their historical territory — the defence of liberty, and here they share a common agenda with right-wing libertarians. **Mick Hume**'s editorials in *LM* (a magazine previously known as *Living Marxism*) sit very comfortably alongside leading articles from the *Daily Telegraph*. The Prime Minister's contempt for what he refers to as 'Libertarian Nonsense' led Hume to consider renaming his magazine *LN*.

If there is anything that unites the disparate writers in this book, conservatives and progressives alike, it is a love of freedom and democracy and a mistrust of the aspirations of the state. But surely the governments of the 'Third Way' share the same commitment? After all Tony Blair was elected on the back of the abolition of Clause Four and a rejection of socialist interventionism — at least as far as the economy is concerned.

A cursory examination of New Labour policies show that statism is still the driving force. The slogan 'standards not structures', as applied to our schools, means a dramatic increase in the role of prescribed curricula, inspection and other such Whitehall-led approaches. Although the National Curriculum and OFSTED were both Conservative innovations — introduced in response to concerns over abysmal school standards — Tories felt more at home with the other policy strand — parental choice and the liberation of schools from the tyranny of the LEAs. Many Tories are privately committed to a free-market voucher scheme in education but lack the political will to put this into practice.

The first act of the incoming Labour Government was to end opting-out and the assisted places scheme. The curriculum for the literacy and numeracy hours gives teachers detailed minute-by-minute pedagogical instructions. Chris Woodhead has suggested that OFSTED should now take on the inspection of child-minders in private homes, and the new scheme for teaching citizenship in schools could well blur the line between education and indoctrination.

Similarly Labour's first action in the NHS was to abolish the internal market.[25] Doctors and hospital consultants are to be subjected to a regime of inspection, and healthcare policy is now decided by the National Institute for Clinical Excellence (NICE). Many Labour politicians view the family doctor as an unacceptable relic of a bourgeois tradition, and would prefer to bring GPs under increasing state regulation, under the pretence of ironing out inequalities or clamping down on poor clinical practice (no doubt the public enquiry announced in the wake of the Harold Shipman trial will provide the opportunity). The NHS is in a permanent state of crisis — mortality rates for cancer and heart-disease are five times worse than in the US and there is no evidence that New Labour's top-down approach will do anything other than deepen the problems — indeed the first action of NICE was to refuse to licence the flu

---

[25] Although according to Labour Peer Robert Winston they haven't even got that right.

drug Relenza for use in the NHS, thus precipitating a crisis in emergency care during the 1999–2000 flu 'epidemic'.

Although the Labour Government no longer wishes the state to own and manage industry, **Michael Spicer** claims that this is not really a conversion to the free market. Investment decisions, environmental policy and the fixing of levels of profit are still made by state-appointed regulators. Coupled with the ever-increasing burden of employment legislation emanating from Brussels and Westminster, commercial-sector policy is still run along European Bonapartist lines, coupled with a rhetorical commitment to the American model of free-enterprise. Government ministers have even been known to interfere with the management of football teams.[26]

The burden of taxation and national insurance has increased remorselessly under governments of all persuasion. Any economy in which the state taxes and redistributes nearly 40% of GDP is, arguably, a *de facto* 'socialist' state, irrespective of the ownership of the means of production. Entrepreneurs and managers may still like to consider that they run their own businesses, but in the end it is the state that is making many of the important decisions.

Conservatives and radicals alike need to do some serious thinking as to how they are going to give substance to the rhetorical injunction to 'roll back the frontiers of the State'. In his essay 'On Being Conservative' Michael Oakeshott dismissed the 'essentialist' view of conservatism.[27] Conservatism has nothing to do with a belief in natural law, a providential view of history, an 'organic' theory of human society or the primordial propensity of human beings to sin. Neither is there any necessary connection between conservatism and royalism or Anglicanism. According to Oakeshott conservatives believe, with Hobbes and Hume, that human beings are naturally passionate and proactive creatures who, left to their own devices, will engage freely in all manner of enterprises, according to their varying dispositions. The task of government is that of the umpire in a cricket match, or the very *limited* one of ensur-

---

[26] Glenn Hoddle's fate as England manager was sealed by Mr Blair on the TV chat-show *This Morning with Richard and Judy*, and David Blunkett has demanded the sacking of the manager of Sheffield Wednesday.

[27] Michael Oakeshott, 'On Being Conservative' in *Rationalism in Politics and Other Essays* (Indianapolis: Liberty Fund, 1991).

ing that people don't collide excessively with each other while going about their chosen business. Such a minimalist approach to government works best during times of social stability, thereby ruling out most of the twentieth century.[28]

But what does it mean to be of a conservative disposition at a time when the status quo is that the state already runs so much of our lives? And why should conservatives wish to defend the institutions of a neo-establishment which has moved such a long way to the left of the man on the Clapham omnibus?

At the end of his essay Jonathan Freedland argues that conservatives and liberals should bury the hatchet and concentrate on the next phase of the Thatcher revolution—namely the extension of liberalism from the marketplace to the political arena.[29] The problem with the word 'liberalism' is that it has taken on so much baggage as to have become totally meaningless. Jack Straw recently castigated the 'woolly liberals' who were opposing his jury-trial reforms, yet we have just described 1980s conservatism as 'liberal'.

Liberalism, as Freedland points out, in its original eighteenth-century form was a movement of freedom and liberation against the state. In the nineteenth century this meant a rebellion against monarchical privilege, against the hereditary principle and against restrictions on free trade.

At the close of the nineteenth century the Liberal Party was torn apart over the Home Rule issue and then eclipsed by the rise of socialism (Freedland's 'false seduction'). The mantle of individualism then fell on the Conservatives, who sought to defend freedom by their usual method of bolstering up the traditional institutions against the onslaught of socialism. But this was no more successful than King Canute's earlier efforts, and it required an altogether more powerful medicine. If Thatcherism was liberalism applied to the economy then Con-

---

[28] Oakeshott would have disagreed with the widespread description of the twentieth century as the 'conservative century'. His theory of human psychology, despite its dated prose style, is in keeping with findings at the cutting edge of cognitive science—with reseach on autopoietic and self-organizing cybernetic systems confirming his view that order is a natural emergent property of social systems. By contrast the Third-Way emphasis on external control and regulation is beginning to look rather dated.

[29] I hope that Freedland and his colleagues will appreciate the irony of the claim that the spirit of Thatcher is alive and well in the offices of the *Guardian*.

servatives and Liberals need to reunite and extend the liberal agenda to the sphere of politics.[30] **Simon Hughes** and **Duncan Brack**, however, locate British Liberals within the 'social liberal' tradition and argue that right-wing admirers of the liberal inheritance often fail to recognize this.

Of course Tony Blair has himself sought to put on the mantle of Gladstone and nineteenth-century Liberalism. No doubt he would argue that his Kosovo adventure was in the great Liberal human-rights tradition, as opposed to the Conservative impulse towards the defence of national interests and a more cautious approach to internationalism.[31] And he would go on to argue that the repeal of Clause Four and the acceptance of market capitalism marks the end of the Labour Party experiment with socialism.

However the words 'freedom' and 'liberty' rarely come up in Mr Blair's speeches. Notwithstanding the programme of devolution, Mr Blair has shown a marked reluctance to allow people to choose their own leaders: the imposition of Alun Michael and Frank Dobson on the Welsh and London Labour Parties respectively would indicate that Mr Blair's commitment to genuine self-rule is largely rhetorical. **Gillian Peele** dicusses the difficulty of reconciling new structures with old political attitudes.

Mike Diboll and **Anthony O'Hear** argue that the low priority that the Blairites give to freedom and liberty has potentially sinister overtones. Both authors draw parallels between Mr Blair's oratory and the early speeches of Sir Oswald Mosley (at the time he broke away from Labour to set up the New Party). It is a mistake to see fascism as a right-wing movement as it is more accurately described as an extremism

---

[30] One can only speculate as to why Lady Thatcher never grasped the need to extend her liberalism to our political institutions. Was this a question of the unfinished revolution, or was it a case of an intuitive conservatism with respect to the practices and methods of politics in Britain? However the latter did not prevent her undermining local authorities or other institutions (such as universities) that prevented the realization of her economic and social objectives. The latter point could also be applied to the present administration, except that in this case it is harder to say what the objectives are.

[31] See **Jeremy Black**, who points out that so-called 'ethical' interventionism is often ineffective (as in Kosovo) and usually has unanticipated geopolitical consequences. Cynics also question whether the moral stance taken up is genuine or just an attempt to placate public opinion in a televisual age.

of the centre, with its emphasis on consensus government and a 'common national purpose'. **Berent and Sutherland** point out that the rhetoric of consensus has been associated with centrist totalitarian regimes since the time of Plato, leading to the following exhortation from **Diboll**:

> A battle needs be fought for the conservation of meaningful democracy in British politics. The right and the left should, for the present, put aside their differences, just as the Western democracies once made common cause with the USSR against the Axis during the Second World War. The forces of radicalism on the right and on the left must be deployed against the incremental totalitarianism of the extremists of the authoritarian centre: tomorrow must not belong to the Blairites.

Some readers no doubt will feel that this is all a bit over the top and would agree with Bernard Crick's acerbic comment: 'Incremental totalitarianism indeed. Such partisan exaggeration defames the memory of the dead' (private correspondence). In February 1999 Max Beloff published an article in the *Times*, which presented a 'Third Way–Third Reich' opinion, prompting the *Guardian*'s Hugo Young to attack a 'once great newspaper publishing the thoughts of a once-great thinker'.

Clearly there will be no consensus over such controversial claims. However if this book has a take-home message, it is that our informal, unwritten constitution — so heavily dependent on intangibles like custom and precedent — is potentially vulnerable to usurpation by an unchecked executive with an agenda of their own. It is hard to think of another example of a modern democracy where fundamental constitutional arrangements can be altered on the strength of a simple parliamentary majority, and it is this structural defect that needs to be addressed as a matter of urgency.

Acknowledgements

I am grateful to Jeremy Black, Tam Dalyell, Anthony Freeman, Nevil Johnson and Ivo Mosley for their comments.

Tony Benn

How Democratic is Britain?

What is this metaphor called a Crown, or rather what is monarchy? Is it a thing, or is it a name, or is it a fraud? Is it a 'contrivance of human wisdom' or of human craft to obtain money from a nation under specious pretences? Is it a thing necessary to a nation? Tom Paine, 1791

All the rights and duties of the British people stem from the powers of the Crown. The legal authority of the state is the monarch — thus defendants in court are prosecuted by *the Crown* and not *the people*. This is a surface reflection of a deeper reality; that the executive powers of the state — the powers to sign treaties, make state appointments and go to war — do not derive from a democratic constitution, but are the prerogative powers of the Crown.

The mythology and magic surrounding the Crown and the Royal Family have always been used both to entrench this culture of deference and to veil a whole range of undemocratic powers protected by the concept 'royal prerogatives'. It is a potent combination.

The royal prerogative has its roots in the oath taken by William the Conqueror. When he crowned himself in Westminster Abbey on Christmas Day 1066, he vowed 'before the altar of Peter the Apostle, and in the presence of the clergy and the people, to defend the holy churches of God and their Governors, *to rule over the whole people subject to me*, justly and with Royal Provenance, to enact and preserve rightful laws, and strictly to forbid violence and unjust judgments'.

The prerogatives represent a formidable array of legal powers. The nationalization of the Church of England was effected by royal prerogative, the establishment of the Royal Mail in 1660 by Charles II was by royal prerogative.

The powers have been moderated and modified by the influence of the Commonwealth period (1649–60) and the Glorious Revolution of 1688, when Parliament allegedly invited William and Mary to replace James II, and the prerogatives have been restricted by statute from time to time. Many have been ceded to the control of the government. But whether in the possession of the government or the monarch, they remain immense in scope and supersede many of the powers of the elected Commons.

Certain executive powers are always vested in the head of state, as such powers normally derive either from the written constitution of a country or from statute passed by Parliament.

Not so the British Crown, which can in law dissolve Parliament, ask an individual to form a government, declare war, sign treaties, make ministers, create Peers, appoint archbishops, bishops and judges, grant pardons or issue commissions without consulting Parliament at all. All but the first two powers are actually exercised by and with the advice of the Prime Minister and, in theory, any Prime Minister could be brought down in the Commons if the powers were grossly abused. One important prerogative is the right to go to war without consulting Parliament. The House of Commons has no legal right to be consulted. The Falklands and Gulf Wars were never put to the vote for decision.

Treaty making has acquired enormous importance and again treaties do not have to be confirmed by the Commons. The government in Britain can enter treaties openly or secretly: the NATO treaty being an open one, the agreement to permit US bases in Britain a secret one. This power has acquired a new and greater importance since 1973, when Britain joined what was then the Common Market, because the signature to the Treaty of Accession was given under royal prerogative: and when Prime Minister Edward Heath signed it, the text had not even been published. Likewise, although in the event the Government declined to use the royal prerogative, it could have done so to ratify the Treaty of Maastricht in 1993, and bypass Parliament.

The most useful prerogative of the Prime Minister is the power of patronage exercised by him or her: the appointment and dismissal of ministers; the appointment of Peers, archbishops and bishops; and an extensive system of honours and titles. It takes 43 million electors to elect 651 MPs, but took only 10 Prime Ministers, from Attlee to Major, to make 840 Peers.

When too many powers are vested in the person of the Prime Minister, voters are voting for a multiplicity of interests. Democracy should not be about the appointment and dismissal of, in Hailsham's words, an 'elected dictator' but about accountability throughout the period of a government.

The powers to dissolve and to invite an individual to form a government are formidable in theory and could also be in practice. If the Prime Minister had a majority but the establishment wanted for some reason to get rid of him or her it would be open to the Crown, in the person of the Queen, to dissolve Parliament. That is her personal prerogative. The dismissal of Gough Whitlam, the Australian Prime Minister, by Governor-General Kerr in 1975 was the last example of that power being used, and although the Palace disclaimed any responsibility for the decision itself, it was taken under the devolved prerogatives which came from the Crown.

Circumstances might arise whereby a government had been popularly elected but against it was a lot of international pressure, the polls were beginning to turn, the City was very discontented and the Crown decided to intervene. The Prime Minister could find him or herself removed and could do nothing about it. No British monarch would dare to do such a thing if there was a risk of the person thus dismissed being re-elected in the general election that would follow. Such an act would bring about a crisis in the relations with a freshly-elected government and that could lead to a reaction against the Crown in favour of a republic. But a well-timed dissolution at a moment when a government was unpopular would not be so difficult to engineer. The courts would have to uphold such an act under the powers of the Crown, and any Prime Minister displaced in that way who appealed to the judges (all of whom owe allegiance to the Crown personally) to declare the dissolution illegal would be told that his or her power to head the administration had been removed quite legally.

For the same reason the *personal power of the Crown* to grant or refuse a Prime Minister a dissolution if he or she requests one is also of the greatest significance. In refusing a dissolution the Crown could obstruct a government that wished to take an issue to the people, as Edward Heath did over the coal strike in early 1974. If the Crown had refused that request, Heath would have had to fight out the battle with the miners with the public against him, and this might well have had a profound influence upon the balance of political power in this country.

The obverse of this power of dissolution personal to the sovereign is the power to decide whom to ask to form a government. In the past the Crown did have the deciding word on the choice of Prime Minister. Until 1965 the Conservative Party leader 'emerged' after mysterious consultations and the Crown was advised by various people as to whom it might call. When Bonar Law was retiring on health grounds in 1923, Lord Curzon was expecting to be appointed, but King George V was advised that it was no longer suitable to have the Prime Minister sitting in the Lords, and Baldwin was chosen. In more recent years, in an ironic twist, Lord Home emerged from the Lowlands of Scotland to succeed Macmillan after Rab Butler had been considered and rejected by the charmed circle. Home then had to divest himself of his peerage and be found a Commons seat.

In circumstances of a hung Parliament the question of whom the monarch should invite to form a government becomes enormously important. Suppose after a general election all three main parties had the same number of seats. The monarch could call any one of the three with equal legitimacy but each one would require an alliance with one of the others. A Prime Minister, thus chosen, could begin a period as PM, move into No. 10, make announcements and appoint a Cabinet, so gaining an unfair but all-important advantage before the new Parliament met.

If a Prime Minister of a minority government could not get his or her legislation through Parliament, he or she could apply to the Queen for a dissolution to hold another election.

But the Queen *could* refuse and the Prime Minister would then resign and she would have to summon someone else. The granting or withholding of such power is potentially very great.

The limiting factor in the exercise of the royal prerogative is fear by the monarch or royal advisers of making a mistake. Supposing the Queen had refused Heath a dissolution in February 1974: he would have been in conflict with the monarch. Alternatively, if the Queen had dissolved Parliament against the wishes of a Prime Minister, and the same Prime Minister had won the election, there would be a constitutional crisis. For these reasons the Crown might very well wish to rid itself of this power.

These are by no means imaginary circumstances to contemplate. The only limitation at present upon the effective use of such personal prerogatives would be the extent to which the royal advisers felt it wise to use them, bearing in mind that the survival of the Crown will always be their prime concern.

If a particular monarch became an embarrassment to the British establishment that person would be removed – as James II was and replaced by a stronger, Protestant king. Likewise when Edward VIII visited the Rhondda Valley in 1936, witnessed the terrible unemployment there and said 'Something must be done', that alarmed the establishment, and when he subsequently persisted in his marriage plans to an 'unsuitable' woman, Baldwin threatened him with the resignation of the government. After consultation throughout the empire the British establishment decided that they would rather force the monarch to abdicate than allow him to marry a divorced woman.

Oaths – The Real Constitution

Underpinning the constitutional arrangements of the Crown is a hidden written constitution – the network of ancient tribal oaths of allegiance to the Crown. Everyone with British nationality is a subject of the Crown, bound by a personal obligation of loyalty to the monarch. The betrayal of that duty can, in certain circumstances, constitute the offence of High Treason.

Over and above any general duty as subjects, all those who hold positions of responsibility within the state are required to swear an oath, or make a solemn affirmation, of allegiance to the Queen personally, and to her heirs and successors.

This oath is imposed upon all Members of Parliament and Peers and is a pre-condition of their right to take their seats in Parliament. Gerry Adams and Martin McGuinness, who as Sinn Fein MPs are not willing to swear that oath, cannot take their seats in the House of Commons, even though they have been elected as Republicans and for a political allegiance which was openly canvassed.

Adams and McGuinness's elections were thus effectively cancelled out by the Crown. Had they attempted to take their seats without swearing the oath they would have been guilty of a serious offence and subject to a heavy fine.

One hundred and seventy-five years ago, no Roman Catholic could be admitted to the Commons. The oath of allegiance established by an Act of the Scottish Parliament of 29 August 1681 to secure *'the protestant religion against Papists and Phanaticks'* required the people to *'bear Faith and true Allegiance to the King's Majesty, His Heirs and Lawful Successors'.*

It also states the claim of the established church—nationalized by Henry VIII—to be the sole interpretation of the Word of God. The people must swear, it said in 1681, *'That [they] Allow and sincerely Profess the True Protestant Religion'* and *'believe the same to be founded on and agreeable unto the Written Word of God; And [they] Promise and Swear, That [they] shall Adhere thereto all the dayes of [their] Life-time; And shall endeavour to Educate [their] Children therein.'*

Though the modern oath is worded differently, it seems preposterous to have a single orthodoxy of this kind enforced as a test of loyalty to the Crown. Yet the position is very little changed. The Church of England remains the established state religion. The oath of allegiance still exists, though requiring that those in authority swear to *'be faithful and bear true allegiance to Her Majesty Queen Elizabeth, her heirs and successors, according to law'.*

There remains an implicit oath of religious allegiance since the Queen in her coronation oath swears *'to the utmost of [her] power [to] maintain and preserve inviolably the settlement of the Church of England,...[and to] preserve unto the Bishops and Clergy of England, and to the Churches there committed to their charge, all such rights and privileges, as by law do or shall appertain to them or any of them'.*

So the constitutional obligations of the monarch are to preserve the power and privileges of the established church, one particular religious denomination among many within Britain, while the rights of the people are nowhere mentioned within the oath. In return the bishops are required to make a homage to the Queen recognizing that she is *'the only supreme governor of this realm in spiritual and ecclesiastical things as well as in temporal'*. One particular religious tradition has been cemented into our constitutional arrangements, while democratic rights are absent.

Cabinet ministers are required to take a second oath to the MPs' oath, in their capacity as members of the Privy Council. The Privy Councillors' oath requires no affirmation or consent. It is read out to an incoming Minister and is thereby 'administered', and the administration of an oath is precisely that, like an injection. The wording of the oath, for years an official secret, was drawn up long before universal adult suffrage and Parliamentary democracy. It imposes upon Cabinet Ministers the duty that they will to their *'uttermost bear Faith and Allegiance unto the Queen's Majesty; and will assist and defend all Jurisdictions, Preeminences, and Authorities, granted to her Majesty...And generally in all things [they] will do as a faithful and true Servant ought to do to Her Majesty'.*

The potential legal effect of these oaths is very serious. In certain circumstances these oaths would be enforced by the courts, in the same way that the courts have been used to enforce the duty of life-long confidentiality owed to the Crown, as became apparent during the *Spycatcher* case. According to the Radcliffe Report on ministerial memoirs of 1975, it is the Privy Councillor oath that places retiring Cabinet Ministers 'under an obligation to protect official information entrusted to them' even from the people by whom they were elected and to whom they are accountable, *i.e.* ex-Cabinet Ministers cannot in theory reveal in retrospect discussion or decisions made by elected governments.

While in other modern democracies, the President, as head of state, takes an oath to uphold the constitution, the oaths of allegiance in Britain contain no obligation to serve the interests of the people or to respect democratic rights. The governing principles of the Constitution remain centralizing and hierarchical, dividing those in power from those who elect them.

Indeed, in this country the nature of democracy is hardly discussed at all. We are taught 'government' as an endorsement of the status quo, not in any analytical way, and when school children visit the House of Commons they are shown where the Queen sits for the state opening of Parliament, the route the Speaker's procession takes to the Chamber, where the Mace is deposited, etc., but not any of the commemorations of democratic advance — because there are very few of them.

Insofar as any advance in our democratic arrangements is discussed it is the 'Glorious Revolution' of 1688, which was actually a coup d'état by the Protestant William and Mary of Orange. The period of Cromwell's Commonwealth is commonly referred to by the traditionalists as the Interregnum — the period between two kings. There are no official memorials in the Commons to the Chartists or the suffragettes or any of those who fought for the vote or opened the Commons to Catholics, atheists and Jews.

Prime Ministerial Power and Accountability

We are told that power has moved over time from the throne to the Lords, from the Lords to the Commons and from the Commons to the people. But in practice power has now moved to the Prime Minister who then, exercising the powers of the Crown without explicit consent from Parliament, dominates the whole system.

A Prime Minister with these constitutional powers is in theory accountable to Parliament, whose support any Prime Minister requires to stay in office. But the Prime Minister is in practice able to use the fact that he or she is leader of a normally disciplined majority party, and in addition controls access to a range of governmental posts and state honours with which to provide a cushion of loyal and generally reliable support in Parliament.

The House of Commons is the only elected part of Parliament and democratic principles should require that all prerogative powers be controlled by that House.

At present any Prime Minister must depend upon the support of powerful ministers or interest groups both inside and outside Parliament, but reliance on the consent of the governed is minimal. A modern Prime Minister controls government like a feudal monarch, exercising Crown powers but dependent on key interests to support the regime.

Powers of patronage are one weapon at the disposal of the Prime Minister granted by the Crown. The problem of patronage begins long before any honour or government position has been awarded. The influence of patronage extends far beyond the number of people who actually receive an honour or appointment, to those who expect or desire one. For a very large number of people, their position, promotion or honour depends upon the favour of senior ministers, and civil servants who have the ear of the Prime Minister. They would be less than human if this did not in some way affect their conduct.

Hopes of patronage help to cement the loyalty of those in the parliamentary parties who aspire to office in government and opposition. The threat of dismissal and the ability to reallocate important portfolios ensures that those within government remain loyal to the Prime Minister. Government ministers have to agree to abide by rules of conduct which the Prime Minister issues personally. These rules are laid down in a minute entitled *Questions of Procedure for Ministers* drawn up by the Cabinet Secretariat and issued by each Prime Minister when he or she takes office. These procedural minutes have never been submitted to Cabinet for approval, but contain regulations governing everything from a minister's exposure in the media to the use of official cars.

The most important of these rules is the convention of collective responsibility, originally established when the monarch still presided over Cabinet, in order to strengthen ministers against the Crown. When the franchise was extended, collective responsibility became an instrument for sustaining the Cabinet against Parliament and the electorate. If collective responsibility is to protect individual members of government from being picked off one by one, the government must present a united face, take collective responsibility for actions, and then stand or fall together. If Parliament were to defeat the legislation of one minister, it could be held to be a defeat for the Cabinet as a whole. If the government were then forced to resign it could cause the dissolution of the Commons, ending the life of the Parliament and jeopardizing MPs' seats. The intertwining of the interests of the Cabinet with the interests of the legislature gives the government considerable power—the Commons will only use its ability to defeat the government as a last resort. 'Either the executive legislates and acts, or else it can dissolve.' Either the government and its majority in the Commons stand together or they fall together.

The outcome is that government back-benchers, who will generally want to see their party continue in power rather than risk losing all at a general election, can usually be relied upon to fall into line. Back-bench rebellion against governments has therefore been limited. The 1950s and '60s saw very few outbreaks of cross-party voting against a government due to the strict enforcement of party whips. Dissent has increased since the 1970s partly because it has been shown that a government can stand a number of minor defeats and resignations without falling. But it probably remains the case that on an issue that might be a threat to the government, or which might precipitate a vote of confidence, party discipline will be severe and when it really matters back-benchers will support the government, such as was evidenced in the Conservative Government decision to close large numbers of coal-mines and its back-bench rebels fell into line.

Collective responsibility not only galvanizes back-bench support for government, but disciplines rebels and dissenters within government. 'Difficult' ministers can be blocked or moved to the sidelines by threats of dismissal by the Prime Minister, the removal of responsibility for a specific policy or by letting it be known to the senior civil servants in that department that the minister is out of favour with the Prime Minister. In this situation, civil servants withdraw active cooperation from the minister.

The power to threaten the collective dissolution of Parliament through a Prime Minister's own resignation and a call for an election has in fact never been tested in practice. John Major, was forced to retreat on one motion in Parliament on

Maastricht, and when Wilson threatened in 1969 to resign unless the Parliamentary party accepted the White Paper on trade unions, *In Place of Strife*, he was advised that if he tried to dissolve Parliament the then chairman of the Parliamentary Labour Party would follow him to Buckingham Palace to request that James Callaghan take over. Wilson capitulated and the White Paper was dropped.

However, in certain circumstances the threat of resignation can be effective and votes of confidence within Cabinet can succeed where hours of persuasion have failed. An alternative sanction for a Prime Minister will be to threaten the sack, potentially destroying a ministerial career.

In these ways the Prime Minister is able to make personal decisions, in consultation with a few key colleagues, binding on the whole government so that decisions which are not collectively taken must be collectively supported in Parliament and in the press. In Callaghan's *Questions of Procedure* it had already been established that 'Decisions reached by the Cabinet or Cabinet Committees are binding on all members of the government.'

Wilson had previously required that those members had a duty 'not merely to support the Government but to refrain from making any speech or doing any act which may appear to implicate the Government'.

In spite of the assumption that collective Cabinet responsibility is a convention of the Constitution, it was waived by Wilson in 1975 over the issue of the referendum on European membership. Later Callaghan, in a parliamentary answer, made it clear that collective Cabinet responsibility applied when he said it did.

When it is in force, collective responsibility does not simply bind Cabinet ministers, but applies to all members of the government including Ministers of State, law officers, Under-secretaries of State and the whips, who will be expected to support the decisions of the Cabinet, both in Parliament and elsewhere in public. It will also be expected to apply to MPs who serve as Parliamentary Private Secretaries to ministers. In consequence the Prime Minister can expect up to half of his or her parliamentary majority to be guaranteed by virtue of these MPs being members of government, however junior, and therefore on what has been dubbed 'the pay-roll vote', which increases in keeping with the appointment of more ministers and their Parliamentary Private Secretaries.

A large amount of government business passes through a system of Cabinet committees, staffed by ministers appointed by the Prime Minister. At any one time there are likely to be over 100 ad hoc and standing committees. Through this system difficult ministers can be bypassed and problematic issues can be removed from the agenda of full Cabinet, a system used extensively by Margaret Thatcher. According to the 1992 *Questions of Procedure* they buttress 'the principle of collective responsibility by ensuring that, even though an important question may never reach the Cabinet itself...the final judgment will be sufficiently authoritative to ensure that the Government as a whole can be properly expected to accept responsibility for it'.

In other words decisions made by a Prime Minister and his or her appointees in Cabinet committee have the force of a Cabinet decision, even though the issues may never come to Cabinet or be discussed with interested ministers. The Prime Minister can even keep the minutes of committees secret from Cabinet Ministers not present.

Harold Wilson wrote in 1974:

> The fact that no Minister is in practice able to participate in the decision-taking process over the whole range of Government policy does not alter the position. The obligations of collective responsibility are binding on all members of the Government, in the sense that it is unacceptable for any Minister publicly to dissociate himself [sic] from the policies and actions of the Government of which he is a member. If he feels impelled by reasons of conscience so to dissociate himself, he must resign in order to do so. This applies to all Ministers; it applies especially to members of the Cabinet.

Prime Ministers have a position in Cabinet which is very much more than first among equals, and they can ensure that policy is made in highly personalized and secretive form under their own direction. But in spite of the personal character of many of the decisions, all members of the government will be expected to support the decisions made in committee.

The Civil Service and Accountability

A further element of personal control of government is given to the Prime Minister by his or her position as head of the civil service. The relationship is not one-way. The senior ranks of the civil service have their own particular agenda and the fact that they hold the key to substantial control of the Whitehall machine gives them a great deal of influence over the Prime Minister.

In parallel with each Cabinet committee is an official committee sharing the same title as its ministerial counterpart, but with the suffix (0). The most important of these is the Committee of Permanent Secretaries known informally in Whitehall as Cabinet (0). Taken together, this network of civil service committees forms the permanent government, and plays an important part in coordinating — and shaping — government policy.

The Prime Minister, as head of the civil service, controls a substantial executive machine. His or her control is exercised quite simply: the Prime Minister appoints and confirms permanent secretaries and has some control over their status and operational conduct. The result is that permanent secretaries within each government department are likely to have greater loyalty to No. 10 than to their own minister. Indeed, civil servants have been known to keep Prime Ministers informed of the activities of ministers who act against their implied wishes. In addition the Cabinet Office has its own extensive research facilities and will prepare briefings and papers for use in Cabinet, which support the Prime Minister's position on any matter, including those which are the specific concern of a Cabinet Minister.

But while the Prime Minister as head of the civil service commands great power, senior civil servants tend to view governments as visitors to the royal suite at the Grand Hotel and they themselves comprise the real permanent government, loyal to a sense of national interest embodied in the Crown. Despite attempts by Margaret Thatcher as Prime Minister to break this inherent resistance to radical policies, through a series of fundamental reforms, the power of the permanent secretaries remains strong. Because of the high degree of centralization, civil servants are able to maintain a broad continuity in policy between different governments in line with their own judgment of what is best.

Former head of the Civil Service Department (subsequently Cabinet Secretary) Robert Armstrong spoke frankly when he wrote in 1974 that 'it would have been enormously difficult for any minister to change the framework [of policy], so to that extent we had great power'. Adding 'I don't think we used it maliciously or malignly, I think we chose that framework because we thought it the best one going.'

A similar attitude was held by George Young, deputy head of MI6, in 1979. He says quite openly that:

> The higher reaches of the Civil Service undoubtedly make most of the decisions for Ministers and put them in front of them and say 'Minister do you agree?' The ethos of the higher reaches of the Civil Service is not one of stirring up hornets' nests, particularly if some of your best friends are hornets, but in my experience of dealing with Ministers...they don't hear what you say; you tell them something, it goes in one ear and it's out of the other and they're busy thinking up the next Parliamentary answer to the next Parliamentary question.

The present constitutional arrangements are such that elected governments may not be able to pursue policy on which they are elected and which they believe is in the public interest since they may be obstructed by the guardians of the interests of the Crown. According to Ian Bancroft, a former permanent secretary of the Civil Service Department, 'the Service belongs neither to politicians nor to officials but to the Crown and to the nation'. The Crown becomes a device with which civil servants can defend the 'nation' from what Ferdinand Mount, a former policy adviser to Mrs Thatcher, calls 'the instantaneous, immediate, hot-and-strong breath of public opinion. The civil service is a self-regulating, self-selecting, self-perpetuating, self-disciplining corps which regards loyalty to the Crown in its capacity as the embodiment of the nation as a great deal more than a mere shibboleth.'

The civil service — and experts in general — can at best only reflect *their own perception* of the public good and at worst a prejudicial view of people as unable to decide what is in their own interest. Such perceptions will almost always favour continuity against reform, since the bureaucrat will be part of a hierarchy, and his or her activity will be weighted with one eye on promotion, and so will favour the known preferences of superiors. In this way new ideas, challenging ideas and the ideas of the elected government can be filtered out by the power of the dominant institutional ethos.

In addition, membership of the European Union has greatly increased the dependence of ministers upon civil service expertise. Senior civil servants from all European Union countries meet in a body called the Committee of Permanent Representatives or COREPER. Most decisions reached in the Council of Ministers will have been agreed in advance by COREPER. These pre-negotiations between civil servants are of substantial importance, and can be used by EU civil servants to press a common agenda on the various governments. Civil servants are in a key position where they are trading information on their government's bargaining position and intentions. In negotiation they will aim to reach agreement on an agenda of 'feasible' policy options. Government objectives filter down from Cabinet and ministers but the decisions are taken in a whole network of EU committees, panels and organizations.

This may be the case with any large bureaucratic structure, but the European Union remains a special case because of the policy-making role it gives to 20 appointed Commissioners. Substantial areas of government are under the control of the Commission, which is charged with both the initiation and execution of EU policy. The Council of Ministers in the European Union is a law-making body and the Commission serves as its 'government'. The structure is far from democratic. Yet more and more power is being poured into the EU. Member governments will have to concede to majority voting in the EU on a range of issues and if they fail to do so the EU can use British *courts* to overturn the policies of British governments.

Loyal but Not an Opposition

The most significant of the democratic constraints on Prime Ministerial power is the timing of a general election. But when a large amount of power is vested in one person, and a vote has to be cast across a multiplicity of issues determined over the previous Parliament, the outcome cannot be a continuous democratic accountability for government. In addition, at just the time when the Prime Minister is most vulnerable, party loyalty will be at its strongest.

The opposition is assumed to be the most significant of the controls on government. An effective opposition can embarrass the government and cause it to spend time answering questions away from its chosen agenda, but the effect is limited in important respects, not the least of which is that in recent times the opposition parties have come to share many of the policies of the party in power. That the opposition party represents a Prime Minister and government-in-waiting poses a permanent threat to the security of the present incumbents. But for an opposition's attacks to have any force, its alternative programme must have support and in fact the opposition's desire to be seen as a government-in-waiting can hinder its function as critic of government policy and principle.

The outcome is not effective opposition, but effective consensus — a situation not unlike that existing between the Whigs and the Tories 140 years ago.

All parties now agree on membership of the EU, on the role of NATO, on the maintenance of nuclear weapons and on the primacy of free markets. Her Majesty's loyal Opposition seems almost to have become persuaded that its loyalty supersedes its opposition.

Government by consensus has been helped by the extension of the Select Committee system under reforms implemented in 1979. It was intended that these would give back-benchers an opportunity to prise information from civil servants and ministers. In reality party whips have come to control the appointment of individual MPs to committees and their membership reflects the balance of the parties within the House. The Select Committees have become effectively a network of coalitions, knitting government and opposition back-benchers together through a common desire to reach unanimous conclusions. They are able to extract information from civil servants and ministers on the minutiae of policy, but may not explore alternatives to policies which the government undertakes. The Permanent Secretaries, having initially viewed the committees with some trepidation, have realized that they provide an additional route by which controlled information can be officially disseminated.

This consensus is strengthened by the magic circle of the Privy Council, whose members are supposed to consult together confidentially, without risk of information 'leaking' outside. In the parliamentary context this is an important system which maintains close relations between the government of the day and the opposition leaders. Backbenchers as a whole are excluded from the deliberations.

This club lubricates 'the usual channels' — which are the inter-party talks that go on all the time between the main front benches about the conduct of business in the House — and in a war situation, such as the Falklands in 1982, provides an opportunity for highly confidential briefings to be undertaken to win the Opposition over to the acceptance of the Government line. There is in this system an element of the conspiracy by the governing class against the governed which has serious implications for freedom of information and makes for an unhealthy consensus on some issues. In this sense the Privy Council is an undemocratic feudal club.

This process is reinforced by attempts to co-opt those who propose radical change to the system of consensus government.

Radical politicians are vulnerable to being co-opted — it is very flattering for a shadow minister to be called in and told in confidential Privy Council terms about, say, Northern Ireland affairs. Even in the Labour Party the accountability of the Parliamentary party to the national party has been to some extent undermined by a parallel system of centralized power which is buttressed by patronage.

Such temptations are used in Britain to sustain a status quo which is unfavourable to the interests of the majority of the British people.

Assaults on Democracy

Britain is like a motorbike with four-wheel braking. It is amazing, given the existing constitutional and cultural constraints, that we make any progress at all. There was a flourishing renaissance of appointed public and semi-public posts under recent Conservative governments, to the real detriment of more representative bodies. Health authorities have been restructured to reduce the number of elected representatives and to replace them with appointees, budgets have been given to the Training and Enterprise Councils (TECS), consisting of appointed businessmen and women who now control substantial public funds; Urban Development Corporations have been appointed and given control of massive budgets of upwards of £200m, such as the London Docklands Development Corporation. With wide planning and development powers previously under the control of local elected councils and accountable to their electorates, the UDCs have applied criteria for which they are accountable to no one save the minister.

Britain's problems are intimately connected with the continuance of such aristocractic and technocratic hierarchies. Some industrialists would apparently rather be made Peers, put on quangos and made Governors of the BBC, before finishing on the Arts Council, than try to be successful businessmen or women. Individuals including many Labour leaders, are seduced by ribbons and ermine, and bemused by ritual and privilege. All hierarchies want to preserve rather than change institutions as each person looks upwards to please the person above, rather than downwards to provide what people below need.

The House of Lords, now reformed, can still present a substantial obstacle to a government, particularly one which might attempt what a Conservative MP called 'any stupid or revolutionary law if the Commons were so minded to do such a thing'. Governments must be subject to checks and balances, but these should be democratic, not imposed by appointed and hereditary elites.

Under the 1949 Parliament Act the House of Lords can delay legislation, passed by the House of Commons, for one year, unless the legislation is a Money Bill. Therefore, because there is still an in-built Conservative majority in the Lords, a Labour government theoretically has a life of only four years, while a Conservative government, with a majority in both Houses, has a full five-year term within which to pass legislation. Although the House of Lords will usually favour a Conservative government, its natural preference for the status quo will provide a brake on radical legislation from right or left, as the Lords' defeat of the War Crimes Bill in 1991 illustrated.

But neither the 1911 nor the 1949 Acts have removed a Lords veto on subordinate legislation, *i.e.* legislation made on the authority of powers delegated under statutes passed in the Commons. As the volume of government business increases, substantial legislation is made by ministers and local authorities under delegated powers without debate in Parliament. The Lords retain the right to strike down all legislation of this type, and could put a serious brake on a government whose policies they considered 'stupid and revolutionary'.

Democratic checks and balances were provided at local level in the early years of elected local government. But today local government has been reduced to little more than a tier of administration. When local government is squeezed from the centre, central government is not just restricting political opposition but restricting the system of democratic checks and balances. If the party of government objects to what local government is doing, it should campaign locally to defeat it: local councils should come under no form of control other than by the police station in the event of corruption, and the polling station in the event of unpopularity.

But Conservative governments of the 1980s crushed the challenge that local government posed to their power by constraining and, in the case of the GLC and the other metropolitan boroughs, eliminating local councils. Those councils that remain are forced to operate within severe financial restrictions set by central government.

By law now if local councillors vote for policies for which they have been elected which exceed centrally-imposed spending limits, they can be made personally liable for any overspending judged to have taken place. Councillors may be made bankrupt or disqualified from office. No such punishment was imposed on government ministers after the financial debacle of Black Wednesday when £10 billion of public funds were lost. Nor was there provision to hold ministers or their appointees personally to account for the millions spent on developing Canary Wharf in the Docklands fiasco.

Local government has been reduced so that unwilling councils now have a role similar to that performed by the magistrates and the Lord Lieutenants in the early nineteenth century, offering very little challenge to the power of the executive.

Official Secrecy

Nowhere has lack of accountability to the democratic process been more apparent than in our security services, trusted with substantial powers which leave them free from any effective democratic control. The extraordinary complacency with which the allegations in *Spycatcher* were received was the end result of monotonous propaganda over the years that such incidents were in the interests of the Crown and the defence of national security.

A major part of the work of the security services, traditionally closely connected with the military, has been for domestic purposes. The army has intermittently put down colonial and domestic revolts, as in Northern Ireland, and the security services have been used in the surveillance of domestic activity including that of trade unionists, members of CND and workers of the National Council of Civil Liberties. That there is a role for the security services is itself an issue for the people to decide, but such a service should certainly be democratically accountable for its actions. Parliament does not have to be told what the security services are planning to do in advance, only that people should know, after the event, on what grounds phones have been tapped, on whose authority individuals have been placed under surveillance or had their homes searched, which foreign governments have been undermined, which supported and why.

But instead, ex-members of the security services have explicitly rejected democratic control.

On a Channel 4 programme, *After Dark*, Lord Dacre, himself an ex-employee of MI6, and former Master of Peterhouse College, Cambridge, was asked whether the secret service should be democratically accountable. He replied:

> I would like to see it accountable indirectly by having the ultimate authority outside party politics, and if there were a body which consisted of respectable people, respected by all sides, then it wouldn't be dependent on the government of the day...It wouldn't be subject to a particular party which happened

to be in power and it would be subject to the state, not to the government.

Currently the security services are free to choose their own enemy under loose definitions given at different times. In the 1970s the Labour Home Office Minister, John Harris, defined subversives as 'those who try to undermine the government of the state by violent or other means'. If you argue for constitutional reform you may be a subversive. Earlier, the Home Secretary, Maxwell Fyfe, gave a directive that the security services were free to act at a distance from ministerial control. Individual ministers, even senior members of government, have little access to security material even when it is of direct concern to them. Gerald Gardiner, Labour Lord Chancellor in 1964, one of the most senior Privy Councillors, asked to see his own security file and was denied access. The security services do remain formally accountable to the Prime Minister, but as Peter Wright demonstrated, members will flout that accountability if it conflicts with their own perception of the interests of the nation or state.

There is a complex intertwining of British and American security interests. American influence over British security was accepted during the 1950s and '60s under the royal prerogative of treaty-making as part of a deal to share American nuclear secrets and maintain a British nuclear force, notionally independent but under American control. It was because of this link that, according to some considerable evidence, James Angleton of the CIA was able to instruct MI5 agents to place Harold Wilson, when Prime Minister, under surveillance as a suspected Soviet agent. 'The accusation was totally incredible but given the fact that Angleton was head of the CIA's Counterintelligence Division we had no choice but to take it seriously,' Wright wrote.

Wilson was not the only target of these activities, which extended to Edward Heath, who was apparently considered by some in the security services to be too weak to be trusted with the premiership. All these activities conducted against politicians and others were undertaken by a small group or groups who nonetheless had convinced themselves that their duty was to the Crown. Empowered to act by the royal prerogatives, they were also excluded from accountability by a duty of lifelong confidentiality owed to the Crown.

The whole *Spycatcher* affair, whatever the culpability of the individuals concerned, highlights a constitutional process, a structure of government, which permits state powers to be exercised against elected government and in secret.

Secrecy provides probably the most significant constraint upon effective opposition and accountable government. The new Official Secrets Act, introduced in 1988, eased some controls and allowed the disclosure of mundane matters, but extended other controls over information necessary for proper accountability. In particular the Act extended official secrecy to cover all matters concerning international affairs. The increasing integration of British policy into a European Union framework means that more and more aspects of government policy can be protected by official secrecy, if the Prime Minister so chooses.

The Prime Minister's control of information, in particular that related to the national interest, has led to Parliament being deliberately misled on several occasions. The invasion of Egypt in 1956, for example, was claimed to be in response to an Israeli attack. In reality, it was part of a pact between the Israelis, the French and the British to invade Egypt and topple Nasser. Indeed Peter Wright seems to confirm what others have claimed that 'at the beginning of the Suez crisis, MI6 developed a plan, through the London Station, to assassinate Nasser using nerve gas'.

It was also on the grounds of national security that the prerogative was used to establish the 130 permanent American bases in Britain after the Second World War. Parliament was told that these were for training missions, although it soon became clear that they were fully operational military bases. Similar Crown powers were used to commit substantial public funds to the development of nuclear weapons in the 1940s and, more recently, to the Chevaline and Zircon projects without the knowledge or approval of Parliament.

Whereas Britain has a 30-year rule covering the release of secret information, the vast majority of US government activity is open to public scrutiny. The case of Oliver North and Peter Wright provide a very interesting comparison. Colonel North was brought before Congress for his part in the illegal selling of arms to fund right-wing political activities in Nicaragua. Peter Wright, by contrast, confessed that he took part in the destabilization of an elected government and yet, rather than trying to establish the truth or falsity of his allegations, the Government tried to silence him.

The British state is a leaky ship. Civil servants who have access to sensitive material are in a position to make damaging disclosures to the opposition front bench and can cause substantial embarrassment to the government. The Prime Minister can of course leak anything he or she pleases through lobby briefings of the press, but at the same time can initiate a leak enquiry into any disclosure of information which has not been approved by him or her (such as occurred in the Clive Ponting case, not because he was passing sensitive information to the enemy, but because he had leaked information to the British people which discredited the Government). In fact the new Official Secrets Act has been reformed to plug the gaps by which civil servants could justify leaks as being in the public interest. It has also brought much tighter restrictions to bear upon ex-members of the security services to prevent repetitions of the *Spycatcher* affair.

There is some role for official secrecy, but not to keep the activity of government and the process of decision making under wraps, or to limit the ability of Parliament to enforce effective accountability. Unless the Commons can claim, on behalf of the electorate, a greater knowledge of what is happening, its role will slowly shrink back to that of ex-post-facto and ineffective auditor of decisions already taken, leaving government MPs as lobby fodder, merely rubber-stamping government decisions.

The European Union and Parliamentary Government

A development of potentially extraordinary significance has breathed new life into the authority of the royal prerogatives, adding greatly to their strength and to the government freedom to implement them against the wishes of Parliament. This change came with British membership of the European Union. Membership of the EU has increased the power of *government* and reduced the law-making role of *Parliament*, transferring law making to the executive in a manner which uses the prerogatives on a scale not seen since 1649.

Until 1972 the prerogatives could only be used with binding legal force by the Prime Minister or executive in areas that were consistent with law made in Parliament. The House of Commons could set the boundaries within which Crown powers had their freedom. Britain's entry to the European Union removed control of laws, made under the Crown prerogatives in the EU, from direct control by Parliament.

The European Union is sustained by treaties, and therefore legislation made in the EU has effect in United Kingdom law under the prerogative. The 1972 Act, which is an enabling Act, allows EU law to become binding in United Kingdom courts without any requirement for further parliamentary approval.

Section 2(1) of the Act states that:

> All such rights, powers, liabilities, obligations and restrictions from time to time created or arising by or under the Treaties, and all such remedies and procedures from time to time provided for by or under the Treaties, as in accordance with the Treaties *are without further enactment to be given legal effect* or used in the United Kingdom shall be recognised and available in law, and be enforced, allowed and followed accordingly.

This means that law is able to be made using Crown powers which then have immediate and direct effect in British courts.

As a result there are now two law-making authorities in operation in Britain. Under the present treaty arrangements EU legislation will override any law passed in the House of Commons.

A ruling of the European Court of Justice in 1978 made this point clearly. It instructed any national court to give primacy to the provisions of EU law:

> If necessary *refusing of its own motion to apply any conflicting provision of national legislation, even if adopted subsequently*...it [would not be] necessary for the [national] court to request or even await the prior setting aside of such provisions by legislative or other constitutional means.

In consequence, legislation passed in the House of Commons will only become law if it does not conflict with legislation made in Brussels. Even so it will only remain law as long as the EU does not legislate to supersede it. The constitutional irony of this position is that whereas, before entry to the European Union, Crown powers could only be exercised in the legislative space left by Parliament, the position has to some degree been reversed: Parliament now only has law-making power in the space left for it by Crown prerogatives exercised by British ministers in Brussels. The Crown now sets the boundaries within which the House of Commons has legislative freedom.

The legal implications of this position were demonstrated on 10 March 1989, when the British High Court granted an interim injunction suspending the 1988 Merchant Shipping Act. The Act was referred to the European Court which overturned it on 26 July 1991, on the grounds that it was in breach of European Community law. In his judgment in the High Court Lord Justice Neill made the point clearly: 'One cannot over-emphasize that, where applicable, Community law is part of the law of England.'

Taken together, the Treaties have acquired a quasi-constitutional status in British law, giving courts the power to decide which policies are legitimate on criteria determined under the Crown prerogatives.

British governments are therefore bound by a large volume of legislation in the form of regulations and directives made in Brussels. This has placed very real legal obstructions in the way of any British government's free choice of policy and the right of the electors.

Entrenched in the Treaty of Rome and the Single European Act is a commitment to the free movement of labour and capital. Any policy that would seek to intervene significantly in the operation of free markets in Britain is formally against the treaty commitments and could be enforced as such by the British courts.

The Treaty of Rome explicitly prohibits any support to industry which might distort competition between member states, and the Maastricht treaty imposed a strict budgetary discipline upon member states, forcing the Public Sector Borrowing Requirement to fall and establishing an independent

European Central Bank, so effectively removing constitutional control of monetary policy from the governments of member states inside the Eurozone.

Every British government is obliged to inform the European Commission if it plans to give financial support to industry, and if the Commission decides that the aid is against EU rules it will outlaw it. The 1974 Labour Government was forced to give way on several policies, including regional employment premiums, temporary employment subsidies and government aid to offshore drilling supplies, which were judged contrary to the laws of the then Common Market.

Therefore if short-term market interests dictate that a factory has to close – even in circumstances where it was decided by the government that it would be in the long-term interest of the country to keep it open – the obligations imposed by the treaty might outlaw any government assistance, even if it had been a major policy in that government's manifesto to provide such assistance.

This severely limits the freedom of government and the electors to decide on policies of their own choosing. A similar situation would never be accepted in America: California cannot ban imports of goods from New Mexico or Texas, but it is quite free to subsidize its own industry. Under the American Constitution a socialist government would at least be constitutionally legal and could be elected with the freedom to carry out interventionist policies. But a government with a similar programme in Britain would be ruled to be in breach of our European treaty commitments. The Treaty of Rome has effectively put us in handcuffs, binding us to a constitution drawn up under Crown powers, which, to a significant degree, entrenches free-market capitalism.

Much of the European Union debate has become, quite wrongly, entangled with the idea of sovereignty. Various commentators and critics of Europe lament the inability of Parliament to have sovereign control of its own territory. But no government – or monarch for that matter – has ever enjoyed complete independence or freedom from external circumstance. As is often said, it is peculiar to speak of a reduction in the sovereignty of the British Parliament by closer membership of Europe when, in or out, Britain's economic policy is influenced by interest rates in the Bundesbank and foreign policy by resolutions in the UN and decisions within NATO. Absolute sovereignty, in this sense — especially of Parliament which is a false notion anyway — has never been possessed by anyone. There have always been important external constraints on the freedom of governments to act. It has never been true that government could do what it liked.

But it is a severe limitation of democratic government and the electors when they are to lose control of their own legal order or the laws placed on the statute book and government is not able to choose how to respond to external pressures or events.

Even were the government fully accountable to the British people, the people are clearly not in a position to control the basic rules governing society and their lives if laws made in Brussels can over-rule domestic law made in Parliament.

Against the striking impact which membership of the European Union has on the British system of government, it is argued in Europe's favour that it can provide Britain with far more progressive legislation and rights than will come from domestic government. Cynicism with British government encourages people to look to Brussels to save them from the mess. Many people have lost faith in the British political system to recognize their claims. The incorporation of the EU social chapter by the current Government is yet another expression of the British tendency to look elsewhere in order to solve domestic problems. While the previous Government was able to negotiate an 'opt out' from legislation to limit the working week, claiming this to be a victory for workers' rights, and was able to exclude itself from the social chapter and to campaign for Britain's right to be a low-wage economy, governments of all colours have used EU law to entrench market forces which allow companies to close factories and remove their investments from Britain without any check by British law.

People should be asking why Britain cannot have a social chapter of its own, why we don't have progressive legislation to protect the environment and why governments have so drastically reduced the power of local democracy. The answer to these questions is not to be found in Brussels, and the cost of trying to find it there is immense, in terms of our capacity for democratic self-government.

Conclusion

The position described by Bagehot in 1867 in *The English Constitution* has effectively been reversed. Bagehot described the Monarch as the 'dignified' element of the constitution, providing legitimacy to the disguised 'efficient' exercise of power by Parliament. Today it would be more accurate to describe the House of Commons as the dignified part of the constitution, which is there to 'excite and preserve the reverence of the population' while the powers of the Crown, controlled by the Prime Minister, are the efficient part 'by which [government], in fact, works and rules'.

But the crux of the matter is not that the Prime Minister has unlimited power—the Prime Minister is quite clearly not a dictator—but that the structures which determine what is politically feasible are generally undemocratic. The Prime Minister is able to use the prerogatives, and in particular the powers of patronage, to create a distance between his or her own executive actions and the controlling influence of the Cabinet, and in particular the control of the House of Commons, where the party and MPs, particularly in the case of the Labour Party, can quite properly constrain the Prime Minister's freedom of action. Once isolated from the source of democratic authority the Prime Minister will be open to extra-Parliamentary action from powerful interest groups and elites, not the least of which are the City, big business, the European Union, the civil service, the military, the media and, in the case of a Labour government, the unions, not to mention international pressures from foreign agencies and governments.

The Prime Minister will make compromises in order to retain the support of these groups and remain in power. As a result the semi-elected Parliament is reduced to one of a number of centres of influence which collectively determine the exercise of the prerogatives.

Acknowledgements

This essay was abridged and updated from Tony Benn and Andrew Hood, *Common Sense: A New Constitution for Britain* (London: Hutchinson, 1993).

Jonathan Freedland

Ten Steps
To the Revolution

They're rewriting our Constitution! Never mind that it's unwritten, as far as the traditionalists are concerned, the British Constitution is being transformed out of all recognition. The most gloomy, led by the likes of Peter Hitchens and Frederick Forsyth, are convinced there is a grand masterplan underlying all these changes, stashed away in the New Labour safe. Devolution and reform of the House of Lords are mere elements in a secret, Blairite plot to abolish Britain. The ultimate objective: absorption into a European superstate.

The less lurid, more realistic view is that Britain is changing — but in a typically British, on-the-hoof, spatchcocked way. There is no grand design, just a series of separate moves whose consequences have barely been thought through. Indeed, to reformers this is a lamentable flaw in Labour's programme of change. For Britain does need to govern itself in a new way and that kind of reform requires a clear eye on the big picture. Such a vision need not be out of reach. On the contrary it is there already, waiting to be found in our deepest intellectual heritage. It lies in the ideas which began in the Britain of the seventeenth and eighteenth centuries, but which only flourished in the land our ancestors created across the sea: America. There, in the core beliefs which animated the American revolution of 1776 we might find the outline of a revolution of our own.

1. Popular Sovereignty

The place to start is America's fundamental view of power. Adopting it means turning our current doctrine on its head and declaring that power does not flow from the top down, but from the bottom up. The British people would be placing itself in charge, insisting that government is its servant.

For sovereignty in Britain currently rests not with the people, but with a much trickier concept: the Crown-in-Parliament. It is this notion of parliamentary sovereignty which results in Britain's trademark concentration of power. If, for example, a statute stands in the way of the government, ministers can simply change it, even when the obstacle in question is common law, evolved over centuries. The conservative philosopher Friedrich Hayek understood the danger when he warned, 'The triumphant claim of the British parliament to have become sovereign, and so able to govern subject to no law, may prove to have been the death-knell of both individual freedom and democracy.'

Traditional defenders of the British system dismiss such talk as pure alarmism. Parliament is elected by the people, they insist; its sovereignty can surely amount to nothing more than the indirect expression of the people's will. But it is worth remembering that a parliamentary majority is not the same as a popular one. Tony Blair won only 44% of the votes of the British people in 1997, yet that translated into a 179-seat advantage in the Commons. Clement Attlee nationalized in the 1940s with a 48% mandate; Margaret Thatcher privatized in the 1980s on the strength of 42–44% votes in her election victories.

Even if one concedes that voters at least have the final say on polling day, it remains true that once a Commons majority is in place it can do what it likes — no matter what the people think. Blended with the Crown, it and it alone is sovereign. As Rousseau witheringly wrote more than two centuries ago, 'The English people believes itself to be free; it is gravely mistaken; it is free only during the election of Members of Parliament; as soon as the Members are elected, the people is enslaved; it is nothing.' We seem to understand that truth ourselves. A 1995 MORI poll found 85% of Britons believed ordinary voters had 'little or no power' over public policy. The solution is popular sovereignty.

2. More Democracy

Few would ever object — at least not out loud — to calls for greater democracy. But, under the surface, there runs a thick streak of British ambivalence towards the rule of the people. One can see it in the dire warnings of 'mob rule' which greet any proposal for direct democracy, or in the instant criticism levelled at politicians who consult opinion polls or focus groups. If a TV programmer wants people to watch his station, he is immediately accused of sinking to the lowest common denominator. Some traditional High Tories are bold enough to admit their lukewarm commitment to democracy. Sir Peregrine Worsthorne happily describes himself as a reactionary who still harbours doubts over the wisdom of the Great Reform Act. Even that champion of the classless society, John Major, once let the mask slip while explaining his resistance to a referendum on the Maastricht Treaty. He said the issues involved were 'highly complex' and that the electorate might be swayed by 'irrelevant' distractions when they came to make their decision. Such condescension betrays an almost nineteenth-century view of the fickle, unscrubbed mob.

Not that the Left's record is much better. It was a Labour minister, Douglas Jay, who wrote that, 'In the case of nutrition and health, just as in the case of education, the gentleman in Whitehall really does know better what is good for the people than the people know themselves.' Jay's heirs today are the fair-weather democrats, those well-intentioned liberals happy to rely on undemocratic means when they aid their own cause — whether it be a favourable ruling from an unelected judge or a benignly paternalistic vote in the House of Lords.

The textbook example is Parliament's refusal to restore the death penalty, despite colossal public demand for its return. Few liberals acknowledge that the real victory over capital punishment will come by winning the argument among the public. The model here is Vermont or Massachusetts or any of those ten other liberal American states — places free of the death penalty because that is what people have voted for, again and again. They have abandoned judicial killing

because democracy has spoken; in Britain we are without it
because democracy has not been heard.

Perhaps death row is not the greatest advertisement for a
vigorous democracy, while others might find the power of
pressure groups, the grease of pork-barrel politics and the
dominance of charisma equally unappetising. But these features of American life are hardly legitimate grounds for the
rejection of greater democracy. Just as genuine believers in
freedom of speech follow Voltaire and support the freedom to
express even those ideas they find repulsive, so full-blooded
democrats have to back the system even when it yields outcomes they despise. For British progressives that will mean
returning to first principles: if we truly believe in democracy
then we must construct a system which lets the people decide.
Such a transformation will not make outright victors of either
Left or Right. Democracy applied consistently in Britain
would probably disappoint the Left on capital punishment,
but please them on handguns or fox-hunting. It might upset
the Right by extending self-rule to the English regions, but
delight them by safeguarding the monarchy.

The Americans have a set-up which, for all its flaws, works
by letting the people decide. The principle should hardly need
to be stated: in a democracy, direct elections are the obvious
way to select people for public service. Education authorities,
health trusts, magistrates — they should all be directly elected
by the people they hope to serve.

Allied to this core democratic principle is the question of
accountability. If the voters of North Carolina decide that, say,
Tom Funderburk has done a poor job as Labor Commissioner
they can throw him out next time. By comparison, a Briton
unhappy with the people who oversee hospitals, schools,
training, housing or urban development — to say nothing of
the police and the courts — is powerless. Not only do we have
no idea of quangocrats' qualifications or policies before they
start, we have no way of making them answerable to us once
they are in place. Elections are the straightforward solution.

They offer another advantage too — ensuring the governors
look more like the governed. America's mayors, judges and
sheriffs include women and ethnic minorities because the
people vote for them. Britons often lament the homogeneity of

the nearly all-white, all-male, all-Oxbridge British bench—
elections might produce a more varied complexion.

The election of judges is instructive, if only because it probably marks the limit of people's appetite for democracy. Many
Britons would reject such a move, preferring Solomonic wisdom, rather than desire for re-election, to be the guiding
motive of the judiciary. But here, too, the US precedent can be
of help. The Americans elect only local and state judges. Federal judges and members of the Supreme Court—all those
responsible for interpreting the Constitution—are not elected,
but nominated by the president and ratified by the Senate.

Besides the allocation of public jobs by election, there is
another American democratic device we might want to bor-
row: the referendum. Traditionalists object that representative
government is threatened if direct democracy takes its place
too frequently. The American position is different, holding
that too much public participation is better than too little. It is
the same tension that exists between parliamentary and popular sovereignty. If we are serious about shifting from one to the
other, and letting the people decide, then a change in our attitude towards referendums is in order.

3. A New Republic

If the name of the game is popular sovereignty, then the British
people needs to wrest control from the combined force now in
charge: the Crown-in-Parliament. Some changes to parliament are suggested below. But what of the other half of this
constitutional double act? It is a touchy subject, even among
radicals. It was not so much as mentioned in Labour's manifesto in 1997. And yet the Crown is at the heart of Britain's
problems with sovereignty, democracy and equality.

To the first Americans it was obvious: in a democracy there
could be no place for heredity. It was the people who were sovereign, not one social caste. In the new republic there would be
no royal dynasty and no formal role for an aristocratic elite. In
The Rights of Man Thomas Paine lambasted the British system,
which reserved both the throne and the Upper House for persons selected by bloodline. That was more than two centuries
ago. Yet, until the brink of the third millennium, the very same
system was still standing.

Traditionalists insist that today's monarchy enjoys merely ceremonial and symbolic power, but such a view is either ignorant or disingenuous. Although she arrives at parliament in a gold coach wearing a fairytale crown, the Queen is not just a bauble. Only electoral fluke has prevented the situation in which the monarch would have to exercise real power: a hung parliament. As recently as 1931, the King handpicked a prime minister during a time of political and financial crisis.[1] According to the veteran student of Whitehall, Peter Hennessy, the Queen has had at least five similar moments of decision since 1949, crises triggered by prime ministerial resignations or narrow election results.

Not all royal power is exercised by the monarch. The prime minister can govern like an absolute ruler because he has appropriated the royal prerogative: as Her Majesty's First Minister, he has inherited her powers to rule the United Kingdom. No republic starting from scratch would ever grant such powers to a president. But in Britain they were already there, bundled together and tied with purple string. They were simply passed from one hand to another in the Glorious Revolution. If Britons want to reform the elective dictatorship which concentrates more power in the hands of the British prime minister than almost any comparable executive in the world, they will have to attack the source of that power — the Crown.

Even putting aside both the residual powers the Queen exerts herself and the Crown prerogative bequeathed to Downing Street, monarchy would still matter. Those who dismiss it as purely symbolic make a mistake: symbols count. The trouble with royalty is that it symbolizes two of our ugliest traits. By conferring enormous status and wealth on one family, the monarchy enshrines the worst values of a semi-feudal class society. Worse still, the Crown symbolizes the very essence of our political culture — declaring loud and clear that power in Britain flows from the top down, with the throne at the summit of the pyramid.

---

[1]   In the words of Harold Laski, '[Ramsay] MacDonald was as much the personal choice of George V as Lord Bute was the personal choice of George III.' MacDonald's emergence at the head of the National Government was 'a Palace Revolution'.

The grand American experiment in self-government began with a break from royalty. The US precedent is particularly useful in reassuring those fearful of abolishing the monarchy. Older Britons are often scared by the mere word 'republican-ism' (even when they are not associating it with the IRA). They imagine public beheadings for the beloved royals, the severed heads of Charles or Philip rolling into a basket carefully placed by the guillotine. Such lurid fantasy has held back the cause of the republic nearly as much as the tendency of British reformers to shy away from the question. Though it may seem obvious, republicans need to say out loud that their historical guide will not be the Jacobins of 1789 but the first Americans. They did not execute George III, they simply proclaimed their desire to be free of him. The Windsors would still live, but they would follow the precedent set by King Haakon of Norway, who once remarked that the only thing he was allowed to poke his nose into was his handkerchief.

To the pragmatic royalist argument — that kings and queens boost tourism — the United States also serves as handy rebut-tal. Tourists flock to Washington to admire the trappings of democratic rule just as much as they come to London to gawp at the vestiges of absolutism. There are queues around the White House at all hours, and permanent homage to those shrines of self-rule: the Washington, Lincoln and Jefferson memorials. The French precedent is perhaps even more apt. The Palace of Versailles continues to attract seven million visi-tors annually — more than two centuries after anyone lived there. There is no reason to imagine that Windsor Castle or Buckingham Palace would be any less popular.

Moreover, the US stands as proof that a head of state chosen by the people can still inspire the awe and respect once aroused by monarchy. The Americans love their presidents and worship the presidency, no matter how much tabloid slime is thrown at it. In celebrating the office, if not the man, they celebrate themselves — and their own experiment in self-government. That is why they carve the faces of their greatest leaders in the granite rock of Mount Rushmore — where they can pay homage, as if to ancient gods.

Not that Britain would have to follow the American lead all the way and install a US-style executive president. The scope of the prime minister's powers means he is quite presidential enough as it is. Indeed, it is debatable whether Britain would need to replace the monarchy with a new, separate head of state. The head of government could take on both tasks quite comfortably, as he does in the US or South Africa. If people cannot accept the prime minister as head of state, there are plenty of alternatives. Candidates could be selected by national ballot or a vote of parliament. Simplest of all would be the elevation of the Speaker for the handful of state occasions where Britain needs an independent figurehead.

Letting go of monarchy will not be easy. For older Britons especially it occupies a key place in our national heritage. In a world that is increasingly uniform, we will be losing something distinctly British. But those comforting sentiments of familiarity and nostalgia should be weighed against their cost. Monarchy instils fresh generations of Britons with a feudal history of inequality in which they are mere subjects. By gently putting the whole institution to bed, we shall be declaring that there is only one sovereign in our land: ourselves.

4. Separation of Powers

The doctrine of the separation of powers which so influenced the American Founders was modelled on the British 'triple cord' — the three estates of the Crown, the Lords and the Commons. We have seen since that time a steady decline in the authority of the House of Lords, in parallel with the declining economic power of landed interests. However there is still a need for an effective second chamber, in order both to safeguard our constitutional freedoms and to provide additional scrutiny over legislation — in short, to hold the executive in check. Now that only a rump of the Hereditary Peers remain, there is still the problem of how the reformed second chamber should be constituted. Critics argue that an Upper House filled with party placemen would be a dreadful prospect, leading to proposals for a democratically-elected second chamber — much like the US Senate.

Such a major change could not happen in isolation. A second house with its own electoral legitimacy would pose a serious challenge to the current dominance of the Commons. Equipped with genuine muscle, it would break Britain's age-old concentration of power — which bundles the branches of government into a single, mighty centre – and move closer to the US system, where power is spread around. Traditionalists and democrats alike need to ask which works better – Britain's 'fused' system or the separated powers of America.

Critics of divided government – including many Americans – bemoan the 'gridlock' it can cause: voters elect a President on a set of promises, only to see him stymied by a hostile Congress. It is as if the American law-making beast suffers from a dire and chronic constipation.

This can be irritating when the frustrated law is one you care about. But gridlock has its advantages too. The built-in restraint of a separated powers system can prevent impulsive, ill-thought-out plans – 'panic legislation' – from becoming law. Witness the fate of Bill Clinton's counter-terrorism bill, proposed days after the bombing in Oklahoma City. Determined to be seen as a man of action, the President suggested the FBI be given increased wire-tapping and surveillance powers. Civil libertarians immediately saw the dangers, as did some cooler heads in Congress. An alliance of Democratic and Republican libertarians used their Constitution-given right to be difficult and won a delay, allowing time for the bill's worst excesses quietly to fall away.

Contrast that with Britain's Dangerous Dogs Act of 1991. That bill barrelled through parliament like a toboggan on the Cresta run. The result was an unwieldy and costly law which created as many problems as it solved, and which had to be humanely put down in 1997.

It is not only in cases of emergency that gridlock can come in handy. A spasm of paralysis can be especially useful when a politician's grandest scheme is at stake, Margaret Thatcher's Community Charge being the classic example. The tax was regarded as illegitimate, even by traditional conservatives. Yet there was nothing inside the parliamentary system to block it. The people were driven to extremes, finally resorting to a riot in Trafalgar Square. Even then, it took the toppling of Margaret Thatcher to kill off the policy once and for all.

The poll tax would never have got off the ground in America. Congressmen anxious to save their own skins would have voted against it. If they had not, a few Senate hearings taking evidence on the pilot scheme would have rapidly exposed its flaws. If somehow it had become law, it would have been struck down by the Supreme Court as an unconstitutional restriction on the right to vote — which it surely was.

Bill Clinton knows the process only too well. The jewel of his first administration was to be his proposed overhaul of the US healthcare system. It never even came to a vote in the Senate and it did not deserve to. Its heart was in the right place — seeking to provide basic medical cover for all — but it called for a comically complicated bureaucracy. The separated powers of the US did to healthcare reform what the fused system of Britain could not do to the poll tax — it stopped a bad law in its tracks. Moreover, the US filter mechanism operated even in the absence of conventional gridlock: the healthcare debacle happened in 1993-4 when the Democrats controlled the White House *and* both houses of Congress.

The secret of divided government's success in restraining ideas too extreme, too stupid or both can be expressed in a single word: scrutiny. Defenders of the British system like to trumpet the accountability it offers, obliging the prime minister and his Cabinet to appear before their fellow MPs in the House of Commons. Nothing like Question Time exists in the US, they boast. Below that surface, however, parliament's record as a scrutineer is not good. The serial failure of MPs to weed out flaws in legislation is well known, with the pension reforms of 1986 often cited as an example.

In recent times, Parliament's weakness as a watchdog has been dramatized through its failure to punish or even notice the corrupt and rotten behaviour of government ministers. The sleazy antics of Messrs Hamilton and Aitken were uncovered beyond Westminster, through the endeavours of an inquiring press. In the arms-for-Iraq affair ministers failed to tell the truth to MPs, and got away with it. The Iraqgate investigator, Sir Richard Scott, concluded that executive power had been abused, thereby lending 'substance to the charge that the constitution has become an elective dictatorship'.

In the United States, Congress is always on the prowl, its eyes and ears open. Admittedly, the separation of powers means the president — who has no place in the legislature — is not routinely grilled by Congressmen in the chamber. But, as Bill Clinton learned through painful experience, that hardly puts the White House beyond the scolding reach of Capitol Hill. Besides the 'nuclear option' of impeachment, Congress is armed with its own committees, staffs and budgets—all aimed at holding the executive to account. Congress can summon Cabinet members and lower-level administration officials—including the head of the military, the chairman of the joint chiefs of staff—to appear in televised hearings. Not for them the half-hour Punch-and-Judy of Question Time; the interrogation can last hours, with questions of mind-bending detail. The congressional record on policing sleaze is also impressive, a reputation burnished by Capitol Hill's dogged pursuit of the Watergate scandal.

On any of these measures, then, the US system appears to serve its people better than Britain's: it filters out panicked or extreme legislation and keeps the executive branch properly supervised. It works by separating powers, not concentrating them—the efficient secret of American democracy. The old British claim that divided or 'weak' governments damage the health of their nation looks suspect when one considers the United States: the country continues to dominate the world economy and to enjoy a standard of living that is the envy of the planet. In the US, at least, divided government appears to have done little harm and plenty of good.

If Britain wants to learn that lesson, the first move will be to use Westminster the way it was intended: as a parliament of two chambers. The executive would remain, as at present, in the House of Commons. But legislative functions would be shared with a democratically-elected second chamber. As in the US, the Upper House would represent larger constituencies: while the Senate is made up of states, Britain's might consist of regions. Such a set-up would both avoid duplicating the local responsibilities of the Commons and fit well with any future acts of devolution, by providing regional parliaments with a direct counterpart at Westminster. The key step would be the staggering of elections to the second chamber, with some seats up for grabs during a general election and others fought in 'off years'—when there are no ballots for the Commons. (The Americans contest one-third of Senate seats every two years.) Opposition parties would often win those off-year elections, as they do in most mid-term polls. As a result, the second chamber would frequently have a majority of a different political colour to that of the Commons.

At a stroke Britain would have adopted a system of separated powers, with the second house serving as an automatic check and balance to the executive. That, after all, is the whole point of a two-chamber system—a system we exported to the world, but which we allowed to rot at home. The executive would finally face some genuine scrutiny—not just the gentle squint over the shoulder allowed by the current system. The present Westminster committees are too often poodles of the majority party. In a genuinely bicameral apparatus, committees of a Conservative-controlled second chamber could be vigorous watchdogs, able to hound members of a Labour Government, and vice versa. No longer would we hear the pressure group drumbeat for a 'new independent body' or an 'immediate judicial inquiry' to monitor some aspect of the executive's conduct or work, whether on MPs' ethics or the safety of football grounds. Suddenly those demands could be met within Parliament itself, by a second chamber committed to watching over the executive. It is a clear index of Westminster's decline in the public esteem that serious scrutiny is seen as a task for others—judges or the great and the good—rather than our own elected Parliament.

A second house could also take on the ratification and rejection of appointments to senior public posts, including Cabinet ministers and senior judges—granting a measure of independence to the former and democratic accountability to the latter. In the Commons such hearings would be a mere formality, with the governing party's in-built majority guaranteeing approval for all its choices. But hearings in a potentially hostile, elected second chamber would be meaningful. As the US Senate's televised interrogations have shown, such a procedure also adds a healthy dash of sunlight to public life.

Replacement of the House of Lords will require the removal of an equally decrepit part of our system: the post of Lord Chancellor. Even before Derry Irvine compared himself to Cardinal Wolsey it was clear that this most ancient office was a medieval leftover. For the Lord Chancellor is the embodiment of the 'fused' powers which Britain ought to remedy. He is simultaneously head of the courts, Speaker of the House of Lords and a senior member of the Cabinet. In other words, he occupies commanding positions in the judiciary, legislature and executive—and he is not even elected!

If we made these changes, our political culture would be transformed overnight. In place of an elective dictatorship crushing a powerless opposition would come a new, and ultimately less adversarial, politics. The prime minister would no longer rule with a royal sceptre, but would have to negotiate across party lines, building alliances with opponents. The old pendulum-rhythm of British politics — in which power changed hands and the country changed direction — would be broken, as politicians, often in spite of themselves, were forced to govern in the national interest. Centrists who have long hankered for the European style of coalition-building, consensus politics — complete with horseshoe-shaped chambers — would see their dream come true. The irony is, they do not have to copy Europe to get there: such politics already exists on Capitol Hill, in a system evolved directly from our own. The US example suggests that this style of consultative politics does not rely on proportional representation; the Americans have come close to it with a first-past-the-post system.

The establishment of an elected second house would give democrats everywhere cause to celebrate. Instead of granting all power to whichever party gains a majority once every five years, a two-chamber system with off-year elections would ensure Britain is governed by a set of 'rolling majorities' — representatives elected at different times during different public moods.

5. A Culture of Rights

All this democracy will need a counterweight. For when we speak of 'the people' suddenly taking charge, what we mean is the *majority* of the people. What of the minority? The US Founding Fathers were aware that popular sovereignty could soon collapse into the tyranny of the majority, happily passing laws that suited its purpose but which trampled on others. Their solution was to enshrine John Locke's notion of truly limited government. This held that the will of the majority was not always sovereign, that it could govern only certain aspects of people's lives. Specifically, the majority could not infringe on personal liberties.

To this day the Bill of Rights and its custodians, the Supreme Court, stand up for the reviled minority against the clamour of the rest. In the federal set-up of the United States, the Supreme Court is especially necessary. It is there to ensure that none of the 50 states violates any of the constitutionally-enshrined rights of their citizens. The most dramatic instance came in 1957 when President Eisenhower flew the 82nd Airborne Division into Little Rock, Arkansas. The Supreme Court had ruled that all American schools had to be racially desegregated — even if a majority of Arkansans thought otherwise. It took troops to enforce the Constitution, and to defend the rights of the black minority, but defend them they did. If British citizens are to establish popular sovereignty, they too will want safeguards for the minority. As local and regional self-rule expands, the case becomes especially urgent. A Bill of Rights will ensure basic safeguards across the whole country.

Some will argue that this is a need we satisfied long ago. After all, we wrote the Magna Carta when the rest of mankind was still in loincloths; our 1689 Bill of Rights came a full century before the French drew up theirs. Both stand as landmark documents in the evolution of constitutionalism. But neither work as clear rosters of our rights as individual citizens living in Britain today. The Magna Carta is concerned with the relationship of 25 barons, the king and the church. Its language is all but impenetrable. The 1689 document is not much better, defining the liberties of parliament rather than people, and ending in a genuflection by Westminster before the throne.

Our rights, like our Constitution, are wreathed in a fog of aged common law, custom and precedent. In the sleepy days of consensus maybe that was sufficient. But in recent years we have learned, all too painfully, that rights which are left vague or unstated are not rights at all — they can be snatched back by government in a heartbeat. Witness the Major administration's alteration to the 1689 Bill of Rights, made solely to enable the disgraced Neil Hamilton to proceed with a libel action. The roots of the problem are the monarchical origins of our system. Citizens have rights; subjects have to be content with entitlements, privileges strictly limited by the royal prerogative. Britons fall into the latter category, granted only as much autonomy as the Crown allows — an indulgence which can be taken away on a whim.

An immediate, if partial, solution has been provided by the incorporation into British law of the European Convention on

Human Rights. It not only spells out some basic freedoms, it has the added advantage of placing a seal on the fact that European law is already supreme in British courts. But it is far from perfect. Most of the key rights are subject to so many qualifications, they are hardly guaranteed at all, yet still the European Convention arouses unease in traditionalists. Critics warn that any charter of liberties poses an automatic threat to parliamentary sovereignty. Acts passed in the House of Commons would no longer be supreme, but could be struck down if deemed incompatible with the bill of rights. Westminster would suddenly be subordinate to a higher authority.

All that such criticism reveals is a failure to understand the original, Lockean point of a bill of rights. Its whole purpose is to place certain liberties beyond the reach of the majority represented in parliament. If that challenges parliamentary sovereignty, then we should celebrate, not apologize. Limiting the authority of parliament is not a drawback of a bill of rights. It is the goal. For that reason, the European Convention should occupy the same place in Britain as the Bill of Rights does in America. It should be the restraint of last resort, a champion for the minority against the majority.

Such talk instantly prompts a related anxiety. Does not an entrenched rights charter give enormous authority to the judges who enforce it? Surely such a document takes all the key dilemmas of the age out of politics and into the courts. Life-or-death questions of medical ethics, sexuality and race will no longer be determined by democratically elected politicians but by a closed, job-for-life set of robed wise men, suddenly empowered to interpret a document with greater authority than parliament itself. The US seems to confirm such worries. The thorniest American debates of modern times have been settled by the Supreme Court, including decisions on affirmative action for minorities, the legitimacy of single-sex education and the nature of religious freedom.

Such fears are, unfortunately, out of date. Britain's judges already take pivotal decisions of life and liberty, just like their counterparts in the US. Through the process of judicial review, they already strike down actions taken by government ministers, quangos and local authorities. The difference is that, while American judges are limited by a written constitution, ours have no such restraint. The British judiciary will enjoy fewer unfettered powers *with* a bill of rights than they do now.

Nonetheless, there is something perverse about an un-elected judiciary exercising even that restricted power in a democracy. If a top rank of judges is to act as custodian of Britain's constitutional liberties — formally empowered to slap down the government when it violates the constitution — then it will have to be chosen more democratically. After all, it is not only their technical ability that is relevant; their political and moral views are of legitimate public interest too. The US system offers a solution. Selecting those members of the American judiciary who rule on the Constitution through a blend of presidential nomination and Senate ratification injects just the right dose of democratic accountability into the US Supreme Court, while life-tenure insulates it from the daily gusts of public opinion. Members of a new, British constitutional court could be chosen by a similar procedure, starting with nomination by the prime minister in the Commons followed by ratification in an elected second chamber.

The second fear of a bill of rights is inflexibility. Opponents worry that rights which we assert now will be written in stone, while those we leave out will be ignored for ever. Times and mores change, yet we risk being saddled with a document too brittle to accommodate those changes. The majority of the future will be bound by the majority of the past. The US Constitution appears to be a case in point. On account of the second amendment, for example, serious gun control is impossible because the Constitution has locked America into a 1776 view of arms.

But this is poor logic. If Americans really wanted to be rid of the bullet the Constitution could not stop them. Of course, changing it is hard; that is the whole point. Yet a straightforward process does exist for amending the Constitution and the Bill of Rights. Prohibition is the obvious example. When Americans wanted to ban alcohol, they passed the Eighteenth Amendment in 1919. When they wanted to drink again, fourteen years later, they simply had to pass the Twenty-first Amendment and it was done.

Finally, many Britons fear that establishing a culture of rights will import to Britain an outbreak of that quintessentially American disease: litigiousness. But America's stampede to the courts might owe less to the Bill of Rights than it does to the more mundane fact that going to court in America costs nothing. The 'no-win, no fee' system—universal in the US, but only narrowly in use in Britain—coupled with the no-cost rule, which frees losers of any obligation to pay winners' legal costs, means an American can launch a court case as a gold-digging expedition, confident that if he loses he will not pay a dime. Of course, there is a value to a legal system fully open to everybody, but the US experience suggests the no-cost rule acts as an invitation to litigation. By ensuring that losers still pay, and that the poor remain covered by some form of subsidized insurance against costs, Britain could establish a culture of rights while still avoiding a rash of US-style law fever.

Although Britain has now entrenched the European Convention, the task is still not complete. There are some reinforcements Britain should make to the document, drawing on America's tradition of free speech. One of the reasons why the US is a land of such wide extremes—from the Klan to political correctness, televangelism to Howard Stern—is that all sides are allowed a hearing. Restricted expression keeps everyone within the cosier, narrower banks of the mainstream.

But free speech need not collapse into anarchy, as the US illustrates. For even the First Amendment allows freedom to be tempered with responsibility. As the jurist Oliver Wendell Holmes famously remarked in 1919, 'The most stringent protection of free speech would not protect a man in falsely shouting fire in a theatre and causing a panic...' With that as justification, direct challenges to public order, including explicit threats to kill the president, can and have been outlawed. The law of conspiracy punishes the speech of villains plotting a crime. Child pornography is banned because its production requires the commission of a further criminal act. In other words, the United States' commitment to free speech does not leave it defenceless against evil.

Similarly, looser libel laws do not inevitably foster an irresponsible press, suddenly able to smear individuals with impunity. After all, when it comes to aggressive vigour, few US newspapers can hold a candle to the British tabloids. For America's relaxed rules apply only to coverage of *public* figures: private individuals defamed in the media still have the law on their side.

There are two specific moves for Britain to make. First, we must formally establish our right to free speech. The European Convention's Article Ten is a step in the right direction, but it allows far too many exceptions. Britain should go further, with a more unambiguous statement of its own. Added to it would be a Freedom of Information Act, premised on the belief that since government works for us, we should have the right to know what actions it takes in our name.

Second, we must reform our libel laws so that they are no longer biased in favour of the powerful. That will mean shifting the burden of proof from the defendant to the plaintiff and allowing for a public interest defence.

But for Britain truly to establish a culture of rights will require action outside the law. Indeed, it will mean resorting to law less often. It is striking that when Americans come across something they do not like, they only rarely demand that it be banned — the reflexive response in Britain. Americans prefer the consumer boycott. So when tapes surfaced of senior staff at Texaco trading racist and anti-Semitic jokes, black Americans threatened a boycott of the company's petrol stations. The American preference for the boycott over the ban is typical in a country which opts for citizen action over state intervention. But it is also a sign of a deeply entrenched culture of rights. Instinctively Americans shy away from anything that might compromise the liberty of someone else.

6. A Written Constitution

Once they had declared the sovereignty of the people, and secured the rights of the minority, the early Americans had one last innovation: they wrote it all down. This was more than an administrative gesture. The Founders understood that a written constitution was, in itself, a crucial component of popular sovereignty. The first Americans knew they needed it the same way a person who buys a house needs a set of deeds — as proof of ownership. More deeply, they understood that a written constitution — irrespective of its content — was critical for popular sovereignty simply because it would let the people know how their system worked.

In this area, as in so many others, Thomas Paine was the pioneer. He lamented that the British system was as full of baffling arcana as the rules of a clandestine masonic lodge. Paine believed all the tinsel and paraphernalia of 'tradition' was used by the aristocracy to dazzle the people, to blind them to the truth of democracy. It served to intimidate them into believing that government was a complex, unknowable task best left to an anointed priesthood. A straightforward document, setting out the rules of the game, would let people participate. Paine was hopeful: 'The age of fiction and political superstition, and of craft, and mystery is passing away.'

But Paine was too much the optimist. The trappings of superstition which made government seem unknowable in his time endure to this day. The MORI poll of 1995 found two in three voters knew 'just a little' or 'hardly anything' about the way parliament works. Britons rely instead on the small academy of 'constitutional experts' who get to play witch-doctor as they stare into the black and somehow perceive the secrets within.

In a more mature polity, Paine believed, there would be no need for the fog of ritual. Writing a century later, Walter Bagehot also believed that monarchy and the 'dignified' elements of the constitution could be jettisoned if the electorate was sufficiently advanced to accept a republic undisguised:

> Where there is no honest poverty, where education
> is diffused and political intelligence is common, it is
> easy for the mass of the people to elect a fair legisla-
> ture. The idea is roughly realised in the North Amer-
> ican colonies of England and in the whole free States
> of the Union.

Bagehot's observation holds good even today. In the US, there is no mystery and nowhere for it to begin. Americans know their way around their own system. They learn their Constitution in school and venerate it thereafter. It inspires a near-religious reverence, its authors accorded similar status to the writers of the gospels.

Britain should learn the lesson. The superstitious nonsense of a constitution written in invisible ink, which so incensed Thomas Paine, is still with us, exerting the same effect now as it did then — casting government as the exclusive preserve of a set of initiates. We need to assert that this is *our* country; we have a right to see the rules by which it is organized. They should be laid out on paper, containable in a booklet small enough to fit in a pocket. Schoolchildren would read it and learn about the country they live in—and own.

Traditionalists warn that such a document will sacrifice the flexibility of our current, unwritten arrangements. But who benefits from such flexibility? Is it the people—or the politicians, who can do what they like, without restraint? With a written constitution, any changes have to be debated in the open, rather than undertaken inadvertently, incrementally or, worst of all, by stealth. All three situations have occurred in our own time, from the erosion of ancient rights of the accused in the criminal justice system to the transfer of key powers to the European Union.

Furthermore, the US actually offers a way to maintain flexibility and keep the Constitution as a living, evolving document. We could learn from their system of amendment and revision, perhaps demanding two-thirds majorities in both Houses of Parliament coupled with the approval of three-quarters of the regional assemblies around the country. Such a stiff requirement would certainly be better than our current situation, where a single party with a simple majority in the Commons—and usually less than 50% of the popular vote— can, if so minded, violate even our most basic liberties.

7. Local Power

Putting the people in charge will require one enormous change in our political culture: a vast switch of emphasis from central to local government. Devolution in Scotland, Wales and Northern Ireland and the mayoralty in London represent a good start. The US, with its mini-parliaments in each of the 50 states, is a useful guide to how the distribution of power could go further. Since we do not have a president in London, we will probably avoid installing US-style executive governors in Edinburgh or Truro, but the idea of democratic assemblies for each nation or region in Britain is hard to oppose.

The next step will come in the cities. America has shown that directly elected mayors not only ensure accountability but also eliminate the facelessness that so often bedevils low-profile local councils. An individual held responsible for a town or city — whose re-election and reputation depends on bins being emptied and streetlights that work — will demand the clout to do his job properly. Britain's cities should expect nothing less. We could spread democracy further, electing chief constables and all local officials in control of sizeable budgets. What competition is to economics, elections are to politics: they give people an incentive to work harder.

Like their American counterparts, Britain's new regional and city-wide authorities should have tax-raising powers — even if they barely use them. The American rebels taught the world that there is no taxation without representation, but the reverse is also true: without power of taxation, there is not much representation. If local authorities cannot raise or spend money, they fast become impotent (the precise fate of British councils in recent years).

All this will help — and be helped by — a change in the culture. We should encourage the American habit of local specialization, in which different cities are allowed to dominate different fields. After all this is how we used to be. At the beginning of the twentieth century and the end of the nineteenth, Britain's cities were proud, muscled places, confident enough to build the ornate libraries and grand town halls which still stand today. Economic times have changed. The industries which were once their *raisons d'être* have moved on or vanished altogether. Inevitably, those economic changes have helped rot the British cities, like damp in an old house.

But our political culture has made matters worse. For all its rhetoric about rolling back the frontiers of the state, Thatcherism actually extended the reach of central government, crushing local autonomies wherever it saw them. The task now is to reverse the centralism of our politics, our economy and our national culture. Not everyone will applaud such a shift away from the centre. Critics on the left, for example, might raise the question of equality and fairness. If local authorities go their own way, then poor areas will have less money to spend on rubbish collection and schools just because rich people do not live there. That seems plain unfair, but perhaps that means local diversity and nationwide equality of provision are incompatible goals, that more independent communities will always be more unequal communities. Maybe Britons will simply have to choose between diversity and equality.

It is a serious problem, and one Americans continue to wrestle with. Children in Massachusetts *do* have more money spent on their education than their counterparts in Alabama. But there are some instructive attempts at solving the problem. Local jurisdictions can be drawn so as to include a mix of rich and poor neighbourhoods. Taxes on sales or on businesses can work a similar magic, ensuring commuters and even tourists make a contribution to the upkeep of a community, and federal cash can be used to bring poorer states in line with their better-off neighbours.

Besides, it is not as if the British system—under which Whitehall gives finely calibrated allocations to local authorities—is a model of fairness. Standard Spending Assessments, which originated as measures of local need, soon became excuses for 'capping', with Whitehall barring democratically-elected councils from drawing up their own budgets and setting their own tax rates.

Which leads to the second probable objection to local autonomy. Critics on the right fear the result will be a string of mini-Stalingrads raising taxation across the land. Yet such fears are illusory. For one thing, local authorities in Britain already levy funds from their constituents through the Council Tax—they are just not allowed to keep or distribute the money as they see fit. It is a ludicrous situation, in which they have responsibility, but no power. Local democracy would remedy that situation, by simply allowing local councils to spend the money they already bring in.

The American experience should bring the tax-wary critic further peace of mind. Although a New Yorker may pay three sets of taxes—a city levy to the Big Apple, state tax to Albany and federal tax to Washington, DC—he will still pay less tax overall than his counterpart in Britain. The difference is that his money is spent where it is raised—locally.

The third fear of devolution is emotional. Traditionalists fear that expanded autonomy for Wales, Scotland and the English regions will lead to the break-up of the Union. Once again, they should look to America. People in Texas or Virginia or California enjoy the institutions of self-government in their states, but consider themselves no less American.

Indeed, the federal structure of the United States has actually strengthened national unity by preventing any one region from feeling subordinate to another. Anyone in Scotland during the long years after 1979 would agree that it is that sense of subordination, and *lack* of autonomy, which endangers the integrity of the Union. Americans see no conflict between their state identity and their Americanness, chiefly because the latter evolves out of the former: after all, it is the United *States.* In Britain, where even limited autonomy has been so long denied, local and national allegiance are in conflict. A MORI poll in 1995 found that 34% of Scots and 21% of the Welsh felt more Scottish or Welsh than they did British, while similar numbers did not feel British at all.

The final objection dwells on timing. All this talk of decentralization makes no sense, say the sceptics, when Britain is edging towards ever closer integration with the European Union. Power is moving upwards, to Brussels, not downwards to Bristol or York. But such a view misses something crucial to the European project. Eurocrats speak enthusiastically of a 'Europe of the Regions' and of 'subsidiarity' — the notion that power should be exercised at the lowest level possible. That means whichever decisions are not taken at Brussels will be handed on to Halifax or Huddersfield, not Westminster. The visionaries of Europe see a future in which some power goes to the centre, but much more goes to the communities — much as it does in the federal United States.

8. Civil Society

Taking charge will mean breaking another long-held British habit. We will need to curb the instinct which makes us look to the state, not ourselves, to solve our problems. For popular sovereignty entails not only rights but responsibility: if we are masters of our own society, then it is up to us to make it work. During most of our history we have looked upwards — first to the Crown and then the state — as if to a benign parent, ready to scold us when we have been naughty but also obliged to look after us, 'from the cradle to the grave'. That needs to change. We have to see that habit for what it is — a feudal relic from the time when those at the bottom looked to their masters for succour. Even the cherished welfare state has its roots in the old class system, in which a permanent elite felt obliged to tend to a permanent proletariat. The paternalists and socialists who built it were people of the noblest intentions, but their creation turned too many of us into passive recipients – as grateful for a state handout as subjects on a Maundy Thursday, bowing their heads to receive a purse from a kindly king.

For many Britons this will be a hard step to take. After Oklahoma City, America's traditional hostility to the state is hardly enticing, while our own trust in government has seen us construct a health service and welfare state of which the Americans can only dream. We have spent a century equating the state with compassion, believing that if there is a social need, government should meet it. Any retreat from public provision is immediately condemned as a betrayal of government's sacred obligation to protect the weak. But a move away from central authority need not be a mandate for callousness. Instead it could mean shifting the burden of care off the state and placing more of it on our own shoulders. The goal is a smaller welfare state – embedded in a welfare nation.

In America the state is not the only outlet for good deeds, and taxes not the only means by which people look after one another. Ordinary Americans help in the provision of education and welfare, independent of government. British liberals get squeamish when they hear such talk. Words like 'charity' and 'voluntary endeavour' evoke images of the Dickensian workhouse. But such anxiety is unwarranted. For British radicals have their own, distinguished history of mutual aid, separate from central government. The author of the 1945 Labour manifesto, Michael Young, has recalled that before the party made a fetish of state ownership it pursued a philosophy of self-help, embodied by the Victorian Friendly Societies, the Sick Club, the Slate Club, the Co-operative Society, the trade unions and the building societies. Young suggests a return to the reciprocal ethic in housing, health and education. Britain's 1,500-plus self-help medical groups could be involved in the NHS, while parents become more active in the classroom. Local government, says Young, should be more truly local, with smaller neighbourhood councils nurturing a sense of communal identity.

Such ideas, spearheaded by the people Young calls 'social entrepreneurs', represent a real future for British radicals. Of

course, many tasks will remain the province of central government, as they should. Defence is the most obvious example.
Economic data also show that healthcare is provided more
efficiently by public rather than private means. The state will
sometimes be the obvious lead investor in industrial enterprises requiring risk and vision, two qualities in scarce supply
among our notoriously short-termist financial elites.

But where ordinary citizens can take on tasks traditionally
left to government, they should. A virtual circle could
develop. The more we rely on ourselves, the smaller our need
for the state; the smaller the state, the more we will learn to
work together. The pattern works in reverse, too, as Alexis de
Tocqueville saw all those years ago:

> The more [the governing power] stands in the place
> of associations, the more will individuals, losing the
> notion of combining together, require its assistance:
> these are causes and effects that unceasingly create
> each other.

De Tocqueville noticed a further phenomenon: when citizens
shoulder duties ordinarily performed by the government,
they develop a fuller, richer civil society. British progressives
have recently become more alive to the importance of civic
connectedness, an impulse which has led some of them
towards communitarianism. But communitarians often floun-
der on how best to *achieve* the apple-pie goal of stronger communities, many of them reduced to nostalgic pleading for the
return of the activist central state. The US suggests at least two
ways to replenish the nation's stocks of social capital.

The first centres on the policy moves government and others can make. Dan Coats, a Republican senator from Indiana,
once proposed a package of 18 Bills designed to strengthen
civil society, chiefly by an intelligent combination of tax
breaks and subsidies. Mentors and parents would get help
teaching 'character' to their kids, while neighbourhood
groups and grassroots bodies would qualify for financial aid.
The US tax code would reward donations to charity, in order
to encourage new ways of providing welfare for the needy,
distinct from the top-down provision of the state.

Away from Capitol Hill, local policymakers can have an
impact, too. The American introduction of community col-

leges—small mini-universities serving a town or city and often majoring in supplemental, adult education—has helped cultivate new social ties. Industry can also play a role—many enlightened US corporations have sought to transform their firms into communities, complete with a mission statement—ties of trust binding employees to each other. They should be encouraged to extend that logic, to recognize the worth of connectedness in the wider community—which is, after all, their market. British chief executives might think twice about replacing corner shops or village post offices with vast 'superstores'—for such moves can only rupture precious civic links which are, ultimately, good for business.

The second step is less obvious. Britain's churches, synagogues and mosques should move away from the top-down hierarchies of old—which have always reflected the pyramid structure of the British state—and move towards the looser, grass-roots congregations found in America, which have done so much to boost civic connectedness. For the Church of England this will entail a truly radical move: disestablishment. While Sunday attendance is at rock-bottom in the established, state-backed Church of England, worship is at mass levels in the unestablished, independent churches of America.

It defies all our prejudices and 50 years of received wisdom, but trimming back the state could make Britain more of a society, not less; one that is more caring, not less. It means shaking off the last, feudal vestiges of *noblesse oblige* and serf- like expectation and deference. In their place can develop a new resolve to do things ourselves. We would be declaring that there *is* such a thing as society—and we are it.

9. The Classless Society

If we move away from the old paternalistic welfare state, we will need not just an upsurge in civic endeavour but a whole new approach to equality. Our starting point should be the American Dream and its commitment to social mobility.

Could Britain adopt a similar vision? It may have to. How else could Britain justify its increasing abandonment of the old welfare ethos, except by expanding social mobility? Put simply, it is only legitimate to deprive a man of a handout if you give him a hand-up instead. Either society protects the weak and the poor or it allows them the chance to become better off. There is no other moral choice.

Constructing a British Dream of genuine social mobility is not pure fantasy. On the contrary, this US-style conception of equality fits our instincts. Take a close look at what most Britons actually mean when they speak of an equal society. They do not hanker for sameness or uniformity; few sincerely believe that a road-sweeper should be paid the same as a brain surgeon. We object if the reward seems disproportionate — but we do not object to merit-based pay in principle. In its most obvious form, this is a rejection of the hereditary principle. We may not begrudge Richard Branson his millions, but many of us do have a problem with the Duke of Westminster. The Victorians drew a distinction between the deserving and undeserving poor. We have quietly revived the idea, applying different standards to the deserving and undeserving rich. It is not all about desert, however. We do not resent winners of the national lottery, even though they have hardly 'earned' their fortunes. The key point is the fairness of equal chances.

The challenge for Britain is to construct a society of equal chances, one that sets limits on no one. In policy terms, it will entail a move from handouts to hand-ups. One American aphorism expresses the difference well: Give a man a fish and he'll eat for a day, teach him *how* to fish and he'll eat for life. While British prime ministers from Benjamin Disraeli to James Callaghan fretted about feeding their subjects, the Americans wanted everyone to be able to feed themselves. While we spent more money on welfare, they spent more on education.

Traditionalists of the old Left have always considered the American opportunity-centred approach to be the soft option. But that is scarcely true. Opening up British society to full social mobility would require massive investment in education — the starting line in the running race of life. Next, Britain would have to spend substantial amounts training adults, enabling them to reach their potential. Such a project would, of course, mean removing the head start some in our society enjoy over others. It might also entail a shake-up of the armed forces, the public schools, Oxbridge and all the other citadels of privilege. No more glass ceiling penning in women, no more prejudice holding back black Britons. And the government would have to apply these same principles to itself — no more quangocrats appointed by a friendly word in the ear.

Those still doubtful of such a project's radical credentials should chew on three thoughts. First, the bulk of spending would have to be directed at the least skilled and poorest — those most inhibited from shinning up society's ladder. Second, the emphasis on a hand-up rather than a handout would only apply to those whose problem is a lack of opportunity. That is not everyone. Some people — the chronically sick, the elderly or even lone parents who want to stay home with their children — do not need work, but help. Third, establishing genuine social mobility will require sacrifice from the well-off. The middle classes have tended to do very nicely out of the old welfare state. Despite the best intentions of the paternalists and socialists, the experts agree that welfare spending has frequently served to reinforce the advantages of the middle class.

A British Dream of social mobility will also require an end to dogma. Education is the most important area, and will also be the most controversial. Some are bound to say equal chances means common schooling for all — closing down the public schools and investing enough money in today's 'sink' institutions to make them as good as any in the land. Others might argue for a return to academic selection, allowing children with sufficient ability to go to the best schools they can — regardless of where they live or their parents' income. A case could even be made for the return of the IQ test as the only mechanism which could factor out the advantages of background and good tutoring, so removing the middle class's current advantage to make room for a wholly classless, merit-based system.

10. A New British Identity

If Britain were to take the nine steps outlined above it would automatically take the tenth: it will have constructed a shared project, and with it a nationalism of ideas, not blood. If America is any guide, our national pride would become more inclusive at home, less aggressive abroad and richer in optimism and possibility. The lesson of America is that such a nationalism is of the civic kind, based on a set of ideals. Put simply, when we have a national project, we will have national pride.

Sceptics will wonder how Britain could possibly develop an idealistic nationalism of this kind. After all, ours is not a created society. We live in an ancient land, not a deliberately constructed community. No one would pretend that Britain is brand new. Still, we can use the end of the twentieth century and the beginning of the new millennium as a fresh start, as the moment to embark on a national project. This can have a powerful effect on patriotism. Look at South Africa, where blacks switched from loathing their national institutions to loving them — simply by making their country their own.

The new South Africa understood the importance of symbols for such a collective endeavour. Along with their new Constitution and bill of rights, they designed a new flag and wrote a new anthem (a highly symbolic blend of the old Afrikaner standard and the music of the ANC). Britons could do the same. We could have a national competition for a new flag, one that does not stand for our imperial past but for our democratic future. The same goes for our current anthem, which barely deserves the name. It is less a national anthem than the bleat of subjects, begging to be dominated ('Long to reign over us…'). It is not a celebration of ourselves, but a hymn to an unelected ruler.

The beauty of a nationalism of ideas, rather than blood, is that it allows an equal place to everyone who joins it, whether their family has lived in Britain a thousand years or none. In practice that is less likely to lead to a radical reform of our immigration laws than to a shift in attitude to the 4.5% of our population which is not white.

A Liberal Reunion

It is a full list — ten steps that would alter Britain profoundly. They form a coherent whole in the shape of the United States, which has bound them together in the creed Gramsci called Americanism. Viewed through a British prism this agenda can seem a pretty mixed, if not confusing affair: it is left-wing on some questions — demanding abolition of the monarchy and the House of Lords — but right-wing on others — urging a move from the central state towards the voluntary sector.

There is indeed something for both Left and Right in such a programme. Before the twentieth-century infatuation with the

state and central planning, liberty was always the project of
the Left. Freedom was the rallying cry of the first radicals,
whether they were the heroes of the Peasants' Revolt, the Lev-
ellers, the Roundheads, the Whigs, the nonconformists or the
Chartists. To tame the state, and win greater liberties for the
people, might represent a break with the Left's recent past —
but it would be a reunion with its earliest roots.

For the Right, the conversion to Americanism should be just
as natural. Margaret Thatcher dedicated herself to rolling back
the state from the economy; curbing the power of the state
over ordinary Britons' lives should mark the next logical step.
The reforms on offer here — from directly elected mayors to
abolition of the Crown prerogative — would achieve precisely
that goal, draining power away from the centre.

But the deeper point is that the old labels of Left and Right
are increasingly out of date. Relics of the Cold War era, they
fail to capture the distance by which politics has moved on.
Surveys of young Britons reveal a whole new world view, one
that defies the easy polarities of the past. This next generation
is fiscally conservative but socially liberal, wary of state intervention and high taxes, but open to diversity of race, sexuality
and family life. In short, they want more freedom, economically and personally. The smart money says the politics of the
new century will be dominated by libertarianism.

If that is right, then it will represent for Britain not so much a
new wave as a return to our roots. For what the doctrine of
Americanism may amount to is an idea whose name has
become so distorted as to lose all meaning: liberalism. Applied
to the economy, liberalism translates into a preference for the
market over the state. Applied to society, it means shifting
power closer to the people themselves.

British liberals have only ever gone half-way. In the nineteenth century, the Manchester School took up the economic
liberalism of *laissez-faire*, but left political and social reform to
others, chiefly the Liberals. The Left, meanwhile, abandoned
liberalism altogether, looking instead to socialism. In our own
time, Margaret Thatcher revived economic liberalism but she,
too, had little stomach for the political implications of her
programme. She could not see that once she had opened up
the economy, society would have to open up too. For more

than 100 years economic and social liberalism have been kept apart.

Now might be the time to reunite these twins, separated in their infancy. The triumph of market forces under Margaret Thatcher locked economic liberalism firmly in place. Now it must be joined by political liberalism for the triumph to be complete — and legitimate. To have one without the other is to have the worst of both worlds: none of the paternalistic protections that justify a strong government, and none of the freedoms that legitimate a weak one.

The Americans understood all this long ago. In a turn-of-the-century visit to the United States, H.G. Wells concluded that only one ideology ruled in America, and that it animated both Republicans and Democrats. It was liberalism, as pioneered in Britain:

> The liberalism of the eighteenth century was essentially the rebellion...against the monarchical and aristocratic state, hereditary privilege, against restrictions on bargains. Its spirit was essentially anarchistic — the antithesis of Socialism.

Wells's words still ring true today, as a clarion call to British radicals of every stripe, beyond the timeworn labels of Left and Right. From now on the British political contest will be between progressives and traditionalists, with representatives from both of the old sides, Left and Right, in each camp. Reformers will need to follow the American lead and reunite the two halves of liberalism, to build on the state-taming work already complete in the economy and extend it to politics. That means a rebellion against the top-down 'monarchical and aristocratic state' which still stands. That will be painful for the right. But it also means a rebellion against the top-down methods left over from state socialism. The left needs to see its century-long flirtation with Marxism as a false seduction, in which state-centred Bonapartism was the real suitor. We need to recover our own freedom-loving tradition, one inherited from the liberalism of Locke, the anarchism of Shelley and a thousand dreamers in between. We need to reclaim the ideas that were born in Britain but which only flourished in the United States. They are ours, and we want them back.

Acknowledgements

This essay was abridged and updated from the author's book *Bring Home the Revolution: The Case for a British Republic* (Fourth Estate, 1998).

Peter Hitchens

A Slow-Motion Revolution:

How New Labour rediscovered
its republican roots

The British Left have long suffered from a strange belief
that republics are in some way more free than monarchies,
simply because they are republics. A swift glance at the rest of
the world should cure this delusion. Even now that we have
said farewell to the German Democratic Republic, there are
plenty of countries which manage to repress their citizens
very effectively without the need for a crown or a throne.
Meanwhile, modern Europe contains several constitutional
monarchies which are models of law and freedom. However,
the British Left have failed to notice this glaring truth because
they tend not to notice foreign tyranny when it has any kind of
radical roots or links.

Since the Cold War ended, life has been simpler for them. It
is no longer necessary for socialists to try to defend or excuse
the wretched political slums which have at last been cleared
from central Europe, let alone the ghastly prison camp that
was the USSR. China's adoption of the belief that 'to get rich is
glorious' has removed the People's Republic from the pan-
theon of heroic countries, something which millions of need-
less deaths and the savagery of the Mao period could not do.
Cuba's long and dismal encounter with socialism is no longer
fashionable or appealing, as Fidel Castro's beard grows grey,
thin and weedy and his government stumbles towards a now
inevitable end.

The Maximum Leader's loathing for homosexuals has also
damaged his popularity among those who were quite prepared to forgive his repression of free speech and his vindic-

tive persecution of political foes. There is not much left to idealize except for the new South Africa about which it is still—just—possible to believe that its future may turn out better than its past.

Perhaps this helps to explain the willingness of some of the cleverer radicals, such as Jonathan Freedland, to look once again to the United States as a model for a British or English revolution. For many decades, the USA's identification with international anti-Communism overshadowed its revolution-ary past and its embrace of socialism under FDR. But the elec-tion of Bill Clinton has helped many British liberals to understand that North America is no longer the arsenal of reaction, but actually a fount of their own sort of thinking. Mr Clinton himself has rather more in common with the romantic third-world heroes of the 1960s than he does with any other US President, and his foreign interventions, whether in Ireland or Yugoslavia, have been idealist and hos-tile to conservative ideas of the nation state. His attitudes towards drugs, the military, progress and abortion are those of the 1960s generation. During the Clinton years, the USA has become a multicultural weakling state, its great newspapers and broadcasting networks are almost entirely dominated by the liberal left, and its universities gave birth to the intolerant progressive conformism and censorship which is unwisely laughed at as 'political correctness'.

So it is at first sight surprising that Jonathan Freedland is, so far, almost alone on the left in seeing the United States as a model for Britain's future. Mr Freedland found much to admire when he lived in the USA, but the experience, so unlike the preconceptions of most educated British people, has probably set him apart from his fellow radicals forever. America's paradox is easier to love and to support if you have experienced the profound and moving generosity of Ameri-cans, and savoured the richness and optimism of their con-stantly-maligned culture.

So he may have been upset to find that so few wanted to fol-low where he had led. He may even have been perplexed when he won the support of that radical republican American, Rupert Murdoch, for his views. This is not the sort of company that *Guardian* columnists are expected to keep. It is rather as if a group of Hell's Angels had arrived at a pacifist meeting, offering to act as stewards. Something doesn't seem quite right here, and nor should it. For Mr Murdoch is not quite the sort of libertarian that gentle liberals like. And the USA, for all its radical republican panoply and grandiose language about liberty and equal creation, is actually a strange mixture of monarchy, mob and mandarin rule. Mr Freedland can say what he likes, but I do not believe he would really be able to stomach a system which reintroduced the death penalty to Britain. In fact, his fellow liberals in the USA have done all they can, through shameless manipulation of the appeals procedure, to ensure that a man sentenced to death is still far more likely to die of old age than to be executed. On the still more contentious issue of school integration, both sides in the argument have spent 40 years frustrating each other. The Supreme Court may technically have ended school segregation, something Congress could not then have done, but white America has responded by moving house, so creating an unofficial apartheid as stark and rigid as any that existed in Malan and Verwoerd's South Africa. Liberals can frustrate the wishes of the majority and use the courts to make the majority more enlightened but the majority is also free to frustrate the elite. As someone who loathes racial discrimination, and supports the death penalty, I think these two examples show that the US Constitution is sadly imperfect from a purely democratic point of view.

In some ways the best thing about it is the Presidency, an elected version of an eighteenth-century monarchy. It stands, as Mr Freedland says, as 'proof that a head of state chosen by the people can still inspire the awe and respect once aroused by the monarchy'. It *can* do so, but it very often does not. For every FDR, Abraham Lincoln and Thomas Jefferson there are ten embarrassing Warren Hardings and Jimmy Carters. Those who inspire the greatest enthusiasm are often the most divisive. It must be very hard to be a passionate admirer of both John F. Kennedy and Ronald Reagan, though both certainly inspired the sort of loyalty once given to monarchs, and used their offices much as Hanoverian kings must once have done. The White House's power to appoint, particularly Supreme Court justices and Secretaries of Defence and State, still gives it immense and lasting power over both domestic and foreign policy, and Bill Clinton probably survived in office for so long because his feminist supporters trusted him to appoint pro-abortion judges, even while they despised his private behaviour. It is this combination of focused loyalty, grandeur and real power which has helped to ensure the survival of the USA and brought about its rise to global power. It is hard to see a partisan Prime Minister seeing it as his duty to fight a civil war to preserve the Union, or to bend the Constitution to save an ally from Hitler. It is surely easier for a President, who is supposed to climb above the level of daily politics as soon as he swears his great oath, to do such profoundly illogical and dangerous things in the service of the great national ideals. Both Lincoln and Roosevelt faced grave political difficulties when they decided to follow principle rather than expediency, but I like to believe that some element of ancient kingship, a last whisper of divine right quietly lurking implicitly in the Constitution, saw them through.

This is why I think it rather feeble of Mr Freedland to hang back from the full implications of what he is saying. Have a republic because the USA has a successful republic, he says. But then he swerves away, and advises us to have an entirely different sort of republic:

> The scope of the prime minister's powers means he is quite presidential enough as it is. Indeed it is debatable whether Britain would need to replace the monarchy with a new, separate head of state. The head of government could take on both tasks quite comfortably. (*Bring Home the Revolution*, p. 193)[1]

He goes on to suggest that if people cannot accept a Prime Minister as head of state there are plenty of alternatives. But he does not truly explore them. A President selected by national ballot would be an immensely powerful rival to the Prime Minister and the majority party in Parliament, so unbalancing the Constitution in an alarming and unpredictable way. A candidate selected by Parliament would be a tool of the political class and a creature of the whips. Similar dangers attend the idea, often canvassed, of giving a heightened ceremonial role to the Speaker of the House of Commons. The government already intervenes far too much in the selection of

[1] Quoted on pp. 67–8, this volume.

this supposedly independent figure. If the post took on greater importance, there would be more intervention. Given the current government's habit of arrogating more and more power to Downing Street, it seems highly likely that it would prefer the 'Prime Minister as head of state' model. Mr Freedland also does not dwell on the rather important subject of how to get rid of an unsatisfactory, incompetent, corrupt or otherwise undesirable President. The American system has not really overcome this difficulty yet, because of the huge reluctance of Congress to unseat such a majestic national figure.

If this were an argument for freedom, rather than for greater Prime Ministerial power, then it should concentrate on the royal prerogative, handed on—as Mr Freedland says—from monarch to government after the 1688 revolution. A true libertarian reformer would seek to take much of this power away and give it to a strengthened and more independent House of Commons, in which, most importantly, the power of the government whips had been curbed and the tyranny of the full-time salaried politicians had been broken. But this could easily be achieved without any move towards a republic. In fact, it could probably most easily be achieved by leaving most of the rest of the Constitution alone, especially its independent elements. A cry for liberty hardly squares with support for the crude abolition of Hereditary Peers which—dressed up as democracy—has actually destroyed independence.

Americans, supposedly our model for this revolution, simply would not be prepared to grant Freedland-type powers to a single person without the strange popular anointing process of the Presidential election. And his task of representing the nation yesterday, today and tomorrow simply could not be separated from his party loyalties—unless we went a stage further and became a one-party state as well. Perhaps that is the way in which our politics are now tending, as leading politicians increasingly break with the old adversarial position and the idea is spread that New Labour is now the natural party of government for the coming century.

As it happens, the enormous powers which the current British Prime Minister has chosen to use so aggressively have given him a sort of presidential aura, but it resembles the near-dictatorial French Presidency of Charles de Gaulle far more than the limited, semi-monarchical Presidency of the USA. Mr Blair's republican practice has, in my view, revealed the hard and unpleasant truth that lies behind the republican theory now fashionable among the sniggering classes of the media and political London. To understand the sudden rebirth of this idea it is necessary to look at what has happened to the Labour Party in recent years.

II

Labour has never been an openly republican formation, but nor is it as royalist as it would like us to believe. Anyone who has, as I have, belonged to a local Labour Party will know that its core membership is republican by conviction and instinct, and privately despises the institutions of the monarchy. The subject is so important to them that they have deliberately avoided discussing it in public for almost 80 years, as I shall explain later.

It is sometimes claimed that Labour leaders have got on well with monarchs, and they have certainly found it wise to do so. Until the Second World War, Labour was viewed by many people as being radical and revolutionary, and it was most anxious, especially in the 1920s and 1930s, to show that it had nothing to do with Soviet communism and was prepared to work within the Constitution. However, the relationship has not always been as good as has been alleged. Harold Wilson's claims that he was much caressed at Buckingham Palace have recently been exploded by Cabinet papers of the time. But the real attitude of the party was fully exposed on the one occasion when it debated the monarchy at its London conference on 29 June 1923. It has not been debated since, not because there has been no desire to do so, but because the leadership are well aware of the likely outcome of any debate, and do not feel it electorally wise to reveal their party's republican leanings in public.

The 1923 debate came a few months before elections which were even then expected to put Labour into office for the first time since its foundation. It was a dangerous moment, and the Party spent much of the conference noisily distancing itself from the wilder parts of socialism. Much time was spent rejecting an application for affiliation from the Communist

Party. The platform knew that this subject would attract plenty of press attention, and that they could lose the next election in a matter of hours if they failed to handle it correctly.

Speakers from the floor urged an open republicanism. The platform, knowing perfectly well what was the mood of the delegates and those who had sent them, responded tactically. Some of the leadership were undoubtedly monarchists, but chose not to make protestations of loyalty. Instead they pleaded with the membership to lay this issue to one side while Labour got on with the business of obtaining power. They chose George Lansbury to give their answer. Lansbury sought to silence the republicans by assuring them that he was really on their side:

> I personally am a republican and have always advocated republicanism, but the group of delegates among whom I am sitting are very strongly divided on this issue. Therefore why should we fool about with a question which is of no vital importance and which will be settled whenever the economic conditions are settled...

> When the workers have the social revolution, they can then be quite sure what they will be able to do with the King, President or anybody else. One of these days we will not have a king or a queen, but what is the point of bothering about that just now?

The matter was postponed to a more suitable moment. It seems likely that this suitable moment is now approaching. In many ways, that social revolution was accomplished during and after the Second World War, a period which destroyed the architecture of deference and class distinction on which the monarchy rested, along with the remaining religious sentiment which upheld it as a sort of semi-divine office. It has since depended on a kind of air-cushion of popularity, created during the war, sustained by the early glamour of Elizabeth II, but deflated rapidly since the days of Diana, Princess of Wales.

But there was also to be a revolution in the Labour Party itself, which very nearly died from lack of support and money in the 1980s, but in a startlingly short time revived itself. The party, which in 1923 was overwhelmingly a manual-workers party concerned with trades union rights and state ownership of heavy industry, has accidentally returned to its radical beginnings as the heir of Tom Paine and the Chartists. George Lansbury's monarchist neighbours in the conference hall would have been trades union men, patriotic and monarchist by instinct, concerned with wages and conditions above all else. So were most Labour voters. But thanks to the 1945 social revolution and the series of industrial revolutions which have followed, Labour has once more become a middle-class party, supported by the beneficiaries of high taxation – schoolteachers, NHS workers, local authority staff, academics, BBC journalists – the whole over-educated new elite which has formed the backbone of all the twentieth century's radical and revolutionary (and usually illiberal) movements, and which concentrates its loathing on the old aristocracies, military and clerical elites which it seeks to replace or subdue to its will.

Because, in Britain especially, the old elites are strongly identified with the monarchy, the nation and patriotism, that loathing is often actively anti-patriotic, internationalist and, as discussed above, privately republican. Anthony Holden, who is a member with Mr Freedland of the republican dining club 'Common Sense', wrote recently about the private discourse of the Labour leadership. He says that long-time friends of the Blairs 'recall Tony chortling merrily as Cherie trashed the royals over their pre-Downing Street dinner-table'. There is no reason to believe that this private contempt has diminished. Combined with Labour's growing understanding that the monarchy is a potential obstacle to its plans to expand the executive power of Downing Street, it seems likely to lead to the sidelining and, quite possibly, a removal of the throne in the medium term, with the best opportunity provided by the end of the present Queen's reign. Such a move would also help to satisfy and encourage the revived eighteenth-century radicalism of New Labour, which is actually far more revolutionary on constitutional issues than the grouping which George Lansbury addressed back in 1923.

We have Margaret Thatcher to thank for this. By destroying the great industrial unions and by breaking up the old nationalized heavy industries she broke the hold of the conservative and patriotic working class over the Labour machine. Many observers thought that this meant that Labour could now be trusted with government, after what had seemed to be a period of ultra-Left chaos. While they had been right to distrust the people who tried to take over the movement in the 1980s, they mistook the nature and direction of the counterattack launched by the Blair faction. I call it the Blair faction though Mr Blair himself was almost certainly no more than an attractive figurehead who did not fully understand what was being done in his name or who was guiding the magic carpet which lifted him from obscurity and wafted him to Downing Street.

The group which increasingly took control of Labour during this period has never issued a manifesto, and tended to prefer backstairs methods and manipulation to open conflict with its foes. It has only appeared occasionally in the open, as over the controversy about Labour's symbolic Clause Four, in which a vote-losing and widely-understood principle was replaced by a deliberately cloudy and evasive formula. What did that formula really mean? It is important to note that Margaret Thatcher only dismantled one small part of Britain's state industries, namely the ones which actually made anything.

The National Health Service, the largest single employer in Europe now that the Soviet Army has been severely reduced, actually grew under her control, and grew even more under John Major. So did the numbers of people employed in government agencies, by local government, by the huge number of new 'universities' which the Tories created as part of their policy of appeasing the new class. It was nothing like enough to satisfy the new radical class. This group, by its nature articulate and well-organized, required a far more regulated and highly-taxed society than the Tories could ever deliver. Regulation provided it with jobs, and taxation would pay for it. Yet it knew that they could never get such policies past the British electorate, especially under the existing winner-takes-all system, and they feared that they could never get their policies through the Westminster Parliament as it was constituted until 1997. They may even have been concerned that the other part of the permanent government, the impartial civil service, might be an obstacle too.

The solution was set out for them by Jacques Delors, then President of the European Union, who made a deliberate effort to explain to the British Left that Brussels was not, as they imagined, a wicked conspiracy of world capitalism, but a deeply socialist enterprise. This truth had been understood by a very few Marxists for some time, especially those who grasped the paradox that large-scale multinational business was as hostile to the conservative nation state as they were themselves. Others began to see that the European Courts could be used to impose policies upon the British economy and society in general that they would not dare place before the electorate. It is reasonable to speculate that some British reformers were even more cynical. Is it possible that ministers and would-be ministers felt they could appear to be reluctant victims of outside interference, while privately welcoming the change? If so, this was only one step beyond the 1960s radicals' ruse of using what were officially Private Members' Bills to make revolutionary changes in social policy, by allowing them the government time without which they would have almost no chance of passing into law.

It is reasonable to assume that 'the Project', the almost cabalistic term used by the inner circle of New Labour to describe their guiding purpose, took on a highly European character some years ago. This would certainly explain the astonishing loyalty shown to the European Single Currency by Labour's high command, despite the fact that it is obviously deeply unpopular. This is at least one highly significant example of New Labour refusing to bend to the wind of the opinion polls, something they are normally only too ready to do. There is surely a serious explanation for this, and also for the complete failure of the British media — itself largely in the hands of the new class radicals — to examine the colossal impact of European Union integration, the most significant political change since the end of the Cold War yet barely examined except by such independent spirits as Christopher Booker. The only explanation that makes sense is that the new radicalism believes it can achieve its aims through European, rather than British, institutions and laws. This of course means that *all* British institutions, from the Westminster Parliament to the Crown, are now open to question, scrutiny, reform and replacement if they get in the way of the Project or seem likely to do so. This is another reason for Labour's implicit republicanism—the monarchy is an embodiment of UK sovereignty, and therefore incompatible with the EU sovereignty which the project's supporters prefer.

One other result of Labour's programme for Britain's conversion to socialism via Brussels, Strasbourg and Frankfurt seems to have been the sudden collapse of the party's traditional support (on the British mainland at least) for the Union. The temptation to outflank Scottish and Welsh Nationalism by supporting devolu- tion had always been there, but was sternly resisted by the Labour hierarchy. They presumably recognized that a United Kingdom party which often depended on Welsh and Scottish MPs for its Westminster majorities could not afford to break up its own supporters into national groups. However the adoption of the Project, which if successful will make the Westminster Parliament irrelevant, seems to have removed that constraint.

I would argue that it is hard to make sense of the government's constitutional programme unless it is seen as preparation for the merging of the United Kingdom into the European Union, which will require a different relationship between the nations which make up the UK. Constitutional reform appealed to the Blair faction because they had used similar methods so successfully in their takeover of the Labour Party and had discovered—like Lenin and Stalin before them—that the party machine, properly handled, is a mighty engine for transmitting power downwards. All that is needed is to reverse the current, making the leadership, instead of the membership, the source of all decisions, and enforcing strong centrally-enforced loyalty codes on MPs, party workers and activists. Similar Leninist methods were to prove effective in overcoming civil service caution and neutrality. Political figures were rapidly installed in what had once been career civil service positions. At the same time, the government press service was a perfect means by which Downing Street could place its loyalists at key positions in every ministry. This action allowed the government to use what was supposed to be a neutral body for far more blatantly partisan and political purposes. It was supported by an unprecedented amount of spending on opinion research and government advertising. Not long afterwards plans were announced for new performance measurements in the higher ranks of the civil service, which many saw as a way of promoting those who were sympathetic to the government, and of getting rid of those who were not.

The control of the Commons, which ought to have been the toughest task facing the reformers if British democracy was in good condition, was easy to achieve. This was thanks to the fact that most MPs, and almost all Labour MPs, are now career politicians or public-sector employees with no other source of income or support other than the state and other politically-controlled or tax-funded bodies. Once, MPs would have been able to resist the pressures placed on them to follow a pre-set 'line to take', to wear pagers at all times, to be ordered 'not to bring the Party into disrepute' and to be instructed, in a semi-circular conference hall that 'they had been elected as New Labour and would govern as New Labour', *i.e.* that they owed their existence to the party and its leader, and must be obedient. Very few were secure enough to resist this, and they could quickly be isolated by exclusion from office. Such isolation was not always enough, however, and it was noticeable that several independent spirits were not prepared to remain in the Commons and announced their retirement quite early in the first Blair Parliament.

The House of Lords, however, was harder to crack. Its hereditary members were quite immune to any pressure and, although they had not used their freedom as much as they should have done, these Peers were a potential source of trouble to a truly radical government. They also held on to the vestigial power granted under the Parliament Act of 1911, which allowed them and them alone to permit the extension of the life of a Parliament. Using the entirely specious argument that Hereditary Peers were undemocratic (all Peers are undemocratic), the government took advantage of the dismal level of public discourse to destroy the hereditaries in a matter of months. The Tories, as usual failing to grasp their own principles, were easily divided and headed off by an offer of temporary, conditional reprieve for a few of the old inherited titles. It now seems likely that this is where things will end, though the remaining hereditaries will certainly be abolished if they cause serious trouble and we can expect large numbers of new government Peers to be appointed so as to avoid any repeat of the Home Office's embarrassing defeat in January 2000, on the issue of limiting jury trial.

III

The monarchy, whose powers and influence are shadowy and ill-defined, is a serious potential obstacle to European integration since it embodies a clearly national United Kingdom. It also remains surprisingly popular, and the Prince of Wales himself has recently shown a surprisingly sure touch with his espousal of popular concerns, such as the disquiet about the purpose and nature of GM foods and the Government's apparent indifference to the culture and economy of the countryside. He has shown signs that he might be less willing than his mother to accept any further attacks on the Constitution, but the implication — that he might have to seek alliances with other politicians against the Government — is an alarming one. If such a contest ever came about, both parties would be badly damaged, but a determined Prime Minister would hold all the strongest weapons and would be likely to win. Even so a Prime Minister would prefer not to face such a fight, and if he is wise, will even now be looking for ways to avoid it. The marginalization of the monarchy would be one way of achieving this.

I believe that this is why the throne has come under a shadowy, ill-defined and subtle assault (which I will deal with in a moment) and it is a pity that Jonathan Freedland, who shows every sign of believing in liberty, should have allowed his very different ideas to get mixed up with the government's highly illiberal centralization of power. If Mr Freedland were to argue unequivocally for the replacement of the British monarchy with an American type of Presidency, and a generally American-style Constitution and Bill of Rights, many British conservatives would have difficulty in disagreeing with him. Republicanism, as practised in the USA, has managed to preserve many features of English conservative society and can even be described, without stretching things too far, as a variant of monarchy. English republicanism, as we know, failed in several significant ways, all but destroying Parliament, subjecting the country to more or less military rule, and eventually failing to solve the problem of succession without inheritance. The Restoration of 1660, the Glorious Revolution of 1688, and the bloody outcome of the French Revolution, effectively made its revival impossible. New Labour's covert republicanism seems to be rather more like that of the European continent, centralized, party-based and drawing much of its practice from the unchecked authoritarian monarchies that used to flourish there.

Anyone seriously worried about liberty and the dangers of dictatorship in modern Britain would seek to reform two things—the pitiful weakness of the Commons since MPs became full-time politicians unable to resist party pressure, and the appalling powers of Downing Street under the Royal prerogative. He would also try to disentangle Britain from the influence of the European Union, whose undemocratic institutions have usurped far too much of Parliament's power.

Without these faults, the virtue of the winner-takes-all election system—strong, decisive government which can even so be removed without violence—would be in the ascendant. But strong, decisive government is far less attractive when Parliament is a poodle and the Prime Minister can decree enormous changes and take huge decisions without parliamentary scrutiny.

The only restraints on an unscrupulous Prime Minister are those of custom, tradition and precedent—the very forces which are represented in the Constitution by the throne. The Prime Minister has edged himself into a contest with the throne over its ceremonial role, while at the same time trying to nudge the monarch into a more partisan position. This behaviour, though not apparently co-ordinated, once again has a pattern to it which suggests a decided purpose somewhere in Downing Street

The Queen herself, in a serious lapse of judgment, made a statement praising the highly contentious Belfast agreement reached at Easter 1998. She has also been tempted into other statements, such as 'cigarettes are nasty things', which she should probably not have made, and her speech from the throne in 1999 was widely seen as having been written in an unacceptably political and propagandist style, quite different from its normal spare, skeletal prose.

But most of her worst problems resulted from the death in a car accident of Princess Diana, a death exploited ruthlessly by the government. The Prime Minister's use of the phrase 'The People's Princess' to describe the dead Diana, placed him firmly on the side of the Diana partisans who saw the monarchy as 'stuffy' and 'outdated' and who were very soon besieging Buckingham Palace and demanding some sign of royal remorse — a sign they duly got when the tradition of centuries was broken and the Union Flag flown at half-mast from Buckingham Palace — the people's flag, as it has now become, supplanting the royal standard. This deeply republican, revolutionary moment was followed by a number of other apparently deliberate humiliations: the decommissioning, on specious and incredible grounds of cost, of the Royal Yacht Britannia; the use of the Royal Train by Mrs Blair; the invasion by Mr Blair of the Queen's Golden Wedding celebrations; and of course the Prime Minister's invasion and takeover of the events following Diana's death — meeting her body on its return from France and reading the lesson at her funeral, when he had no technical, constitutional claim to do either (and certainly no personal one either). There were also unconfirmed but persistent reports that the Prime Minister was often failing to attend his regular audiences with the Queen. Constitutions like the British, based upon habit, are most easily changed by *faits accomplis*, and the reversal of precedent, in the hope that the change will not be noticed until it is established.

Another breach of this kind was made after the Kosovo war, when Mr Blair sent a Christmas message to the services saying how well he had been served by 'his' armed forces. Surely there was somebody in his entourage who understood that the Navy, Army and Air Force owe their allegiance to the Crown, for very good reasons? Did they believe it did not matter, or did they wish to alter this arrangement? Taken alone, it could be seen as a mere blunder. Set beside the other actions of this Government, especially the suggestion by the Home Secretary that the police oath of loyalty may be altered, it is significant. These things only become important when people wish to change them. For a long time now, the British monarchy has had a similar role to that of the king on a chessboard, important not as an active attacking piece, but because he occupies a square that others would like to hold. The loyalty of soldiers to the Crown is a picturesque device now, symbolizing their attachment to the interests of the whole nation; but if attempts were made to end it, it would become a grave issue of control.

It is possible to foresee the outlines of a British or perhaps English Republic, very unlike the jolly American demi-paradise urged on us by Mr Freedland. Imagine a country whose foreign and economic policies are in the hands of Brussels, Strasbourg and Frankfurt, whose law is increasingly brought into the jury-free continental system, whose House of Commons has been moved to the hemicycle chamber already provided for some debates, whose parliamentary deputies are elected by some form of proportional representation, proba-bly using the party-controlled single-list system. Its armed forces might be part of a European command, and its police might serve European Union law. Local government might be in the hands of remote regional authorities, again elected by PR and party list. Politically-correct speech codes might be extended to cover 'sexism', 'homophobia' and, most impor-tant of all, 'xenophobia', severely limiting public discourse and criticism of the European Union. If this seems far-fetched, ponder the astonishing changes of the past two years, from the Diana frenzy to the Macpherson report, and their direction.

With this dreary future in prospect, and with the monarchy the only genuinely popular obstacle to the government's creeping putsch, those who truly value freedom and democ-racy may yet find themselves fighting under the ancient ban-ner of Crown and Sceptre, yet for exactly those liberties which Americans sought when they cast these alleged baubles to one side.

Jonathan Freedland

Response to Hitchens

Well, you can take the man out of the hard left, but you can't take the hard left out of the man. Peter Hitchens, veteran of the Trotskyite struggle, may have become one of British conservatism's sharpest and most incisive champions, but he has not lost his Dave Spart touch. Like his former comrades in the International Socialists, Hitchens retains his fondness for conspiracy theory and for an all-encompassing theory of everything.

In this case, it's his belief that New Labour's hotch-potch of constitutional reforms amounts to a cunning plot to destroy Britain — leaving nothing but a desolate Airstrip One ready for occupation by the European superstate. By sweeping away Westminster, the church, the army and finally the Crown, Tony Blair and his masters (for he is but the smiling dupe) aim to remove any last obstacle which might have stood in the way of the invading Eurocrats. These New Labour fifth columnists, charges Hitchens, want to offer Britain up — plucked, feathered and finally carved into regional quarters — to feed the gluttony of the lip-licking Europeans. They may say their plan is all about modernization, but really it is treason — a secret plot to betray Britain to foreign powers.

One does not have to be a defender of New Labour to see the flaw here. On the contrary, it is New Labour's critics who will disagree with Hitchens most passionately. For their precise complaint against Blairism is its lack of an over-arching vision. Many of them would read Hitchens' exposé of a grand design and cry, 'If only!'

The mundane truth of the matter is that there is no plan. If there were, it would surely not have included the serial

cock-ups which brought such amusement to political specta-
tors in Wales and London. As the kerfuffles over Alun
Michael and Ken Livingstone both illustrate, there is no big
idea: just a mess.

Besides, what kind of idea would it be? If one believes
Hitchens, the Blairites are the first political conspirators in history to be plotting their own emasculation. Their first move is
to lose power by giving chunks of it up, in London, Cardiff
and Edinburgh. This has a side effect, which Hitchens notes.
By dividing its own supporters into national groups, a Labour
party which has often relied on Welsh and Scottish MPs jeop-
ardizes its own chances of winning future majorities at Westminster. Yet they go ahead with it all the same.

Why? Because the object of their entire strategy is to hand
power over to Romani Prodi and his friends in Brussels.
According to Hitchens, New Labour represents a new breed of
politician, one bent on depriving himself of a job. As political
plots go this one gets full marks for originality. Perhaps Robert
Ludlum will buy the rights to Hitchens' essay for a future
novel: *The Kamikaze Conspiracy*.

Unfortunately the dodgy reasoning does not end there.
Peter Hitchens casts New Labour as congenitally Europhile —
yet misses the Government's failure ever to make a robust case
for the single currency. Genuine Europhiles would not
recognize Hitchens' description of this government; they
believe it is maddeningly tepid on Europe. The same can be
said for Hitchens' discovery of a republican streak just below
the surface of New Labour. Ministers may indeed offer only
weak endorsement of the royal family in private, but they do
not go much further than George Lansbury's message to the
Labour Conference of 1923 — 'there are more important things
to worry about, comrades'. Indeed they rarely go that far. Few
in the upper reaches of today's Labour party would dare come
out as republicans the way Lansbury did all those years ago.
Once again, the response of conviction republicans as they
read Hitchens' assumptions can only be: if only.

His reading of the United States is more complicated.
Hitchens understands America much better than most on the
Right and writes about it well. The trouble is, he has to bend
and twist what he sees there to make it fit his own world-view.
He sees that a US President can act, in the cases of Lincoln and

Roosevelt, with extraordinary vision and statesmanship. Yet America is a dreaded republic. How does Hitchens wriggle out of this bind? 'I like to believe that some element of ancient kingship, a last whisper of divine right quietly lurking implicitly in the Constitution, saw them through.'

He might well 'like to believe' that, but he would be wrong. What gave Honest Abe and FDR the clout to act was the sovereignty of the American people, as expressed in the Constitution. There is no 'whisper of divine right' in that document. Quite the contrary. It is such a radical text because it directly junks mystical mumbo jumbo about blue blood and replaces it with a new concept: popular sovereignty. The idea could not be clearer, expressed in the text's first three words: We the people. This is where power lies in the US, and what makes the US presidency such a singular office. (Hence the enduring respect the institution enjoys among the American people. Hitchens may cite the Hardings and Carters, but he misses a crucial distinction: no matter how disdained these men were, the office itself remained revered — because the people know it is filled by them and them alone.)

Which brings us to Hitchens' most searching point. Admitting that he too has admiration for the institution of the presidency, he attacks any form of republicanism that lacks America's direct, nationwide election of the head of state. I share his enthusiasm for the clarity such a mandate generates and it is undoubtedly true that an American President draws daily on the unique authority it gives him, making him the only truly national figure in the US system. But he is wrong to believe that it is this single fact, direct election, which makes American republicanism appealing — and equally wrong to imagine that, without it, no positive republicanism is possible.

Other countries have conflated the roles of head of state and head of government, and still allowed that person to be chosen via the indirect route of a parliamentary system. Nelson Mandela became President of South Africa the way Tony Blair became Prime Minister of Britain — as the leader of a victorious political party. Mandela did not enjoy a US-style presidential mandate, since he was technically elected only by the voters in his parliamentary constituency. Did it matter — or did he, and his office, enjoy just the authority and stature Hitchens so admires in the American system?

I'm afraid direct election is not the magic ingredient. Hitchens surely recognizes as much when he cites, as an unattractive model, the French presidency. This post, as he well knows, relies on 'the popular anointing process' of a US-style direct election yet he describes it as 'near-dictatorial'. The conclusion is clear: Hitchens is looking in the wrong place for the factor *x* which makes one republican model appealing — even to him — and another ugly.

The clue is in the word 'limited', which Hitchens himself uses to describe the US presidency. What could make a British Prime Minister wholly acceptable as a head of state on US lines are checks and balances. This, after all, is the efficient secret of the American system, the complex machinery by which each branch of government stands guard over the other. Sure, my suggestion that a British premier could simultaneously serve as head of state does, taken out of context, sound alarming: an already overmighty British PM elevated yet higher, winched up by the sash of head of state. But that is to ignore the rest of the argument, which would embed the Prime Minister in a much less centralized British system — with far less power concentrated in Downing Street. This is the form of republicanism I advocate, not the Aunt Sally version constructed by Peter Hitchens.

There is a larger point here. Genuine British republicanism is not a plot for European takeover; nor is it anti-patriotic. (Hitchens should know better than to suggest that the likes of Tony Benn and his fellow republicans are anything other than full-blooded in their love of country.) On the contrary, by its insistence that the British people should be sovereign over its own destiny, with no master — not even a symbolic one — but itself, republicanism is a staunchly patriotic creed.

This is what patriots like Hitchens have to hit head-on. In their constant incantation of British sovereignty (against the European threat), they need to ponder what that sovereignty consists of — and who it belongs to. Can it continue to be meaningful when it still resides not in us, the British people, but in a blend of politicians and a family none of us choose?

Only when the Right addresses this issue can they make sense of the modest reforms proposed by Hitchens. Ending both the weakness of the House of Commons and the royal prerogative are good ideas — but they are inseparable from the much more radical reform I outlined in my earlier essay. MPs behave like pager-wearing robots not because they are bad people but because our system, which fuses legislative and executive power in a single chamber, requires them to act that way. As Roy Jenkins has admitted, MPs are glorified members of an electoral college which meets each day to reconfirm the prime minister of the day in his job. They must be slavishly loyal, or else the system will collapse. That is why, in Hitchens' words, 'Parliament is a poodle' and a British PM can 'decree enormous change' with next to no scrutiny. Tinkering with the professional complexion of the Westminster class won't change a thing. Only reform of the entire system—establishing a genuine separation of powers by installing a powerful, legitimate elected second chamber to keep tabs on the Commons-based executive— can remedy the situation. As for Hitchens' spirited attack on the royal prerogative—well, he almost sounds like a republican.

The truth is that of course we can be a republic and British at the same time, without dissolving ourselves into some bland Euro-mush. But, and this is the tougher point for Peter and his friends, it goes further than that. The Right needs to ask itself whether Britain can be Britain much longer *without* becoming a republic. If they are calling on Britons to assert their sovereignty against the long arm of Brussels, won't they first have to assert Britons' own sovereignty, distinct from the ancient hand of royalty? If they believe that Britons should be masters of their own fate, able to write their own laws and choose their own rulers — as Hitchens declares every day — then might they not have to follow that logic to its conclusion? Might they not start to see that all this talk of independence and sovereignty can only mean one thing— a republic? Gosh, I can almost feel another Hitchens turn coming on.

Gillian Peele

New Structures;
Old Politics?

The constitutional reforms initiated by the Labour Government elected in 1997 together promise to transform the institutional structure of the United Kingdom. The Scottish Parliament and the Welsh Assembly are the most tangible signs of this transformation but other constitutional reforms are either in being or well under way, including the Human Rights Act of 1998 (incorporating the European Convention on Human Rights), a directly-elected mayor for London, a reformed House of Lords and Freedom of Information legislation. Although reform of the electoral system for Westminster now seems a somewhat distant prospect, the 1999 elections to the Welsh Assembly, to the Scottish Parliament and to the European Parliament were all conducted using electoral systems very different from the traditional first-past-the-post method.[1]

Yet underlying this rush of constitutional reform (and even its supporters have gasped at the speed with which Blair's administration moved to implement some of its constitutional agenda) there remain a number of questions fundamental to any attempt to analyse the long-term significance of the current preoccupation with matters constitutional. Do these institutional innovations taken together amount to anything approaching a new constitutional settlement? What conse-

[1] For the 1999 Scottish Parliament and Welsh Assembly elections a form of Additional Member System was used. For the 1999 European Parliament elections a system of proportional representation using the d'Hondt formula and closed party lists was used.

quences—direct and indirect—may we expect for the British political system as a whole from the reorganization of so many features of British government? And how will the changes alter the pattern of this country's politics?

Towards a New Constitutional Settlement?

Extensive though the reforms introduced by Labour have been, it is difficult to see in them a new constitutional settlement in the sense of a coherent set of measures which can be expected to take root. There are three reasons for this scepticism about the status of the current constitutional initiatives. First, the various changes—devolution, the Human Rights Act, the limited House of Lords reform, freedom of information legislation—have not been 'joined up' in any purposeful way. Of course there have been statements suggesting that one set of reforms (such as reform of the second chamber) should take account of others (the advent of devolution and the prospect of regional assemblies); but the various reform measures have for the most part been approached incrementally and pragmatically. The various pieces of legislation have been separately drafted with different lead departments and they have reflected their different origins.[2] One could construct an underlying constitutional vision from the speeches of some of the protagonists of constitutional reform.[3] Yet it is not at all clear how deeply or broadly that vision is shared within the Government. It is known that there have been divisions in the Cabinet between Lord Irvine and Jack Straw over the Human Rights Act and major disagreements both about the electoral systems to be used for the Scottish and Welsh assemblies and about proportional electoral reform more generally. Robin Cook, who was the key Labour Party negotiator on the pre-election joint committee with the Liberal Democrats on constitutional reform, remains the most significant supporter of electoral reform for Westminster elections within a Cabinet dominated by opponents of change.

[2] Freedom of Information legislation, for example, was widely thought to have become less robust when responsibility for it was transferred to the Home Office from the Cabinet Office.
[3] See for example Lord Irvine's December 1998 lecture to the Constitution Unit 'The Government's Programme of Constitutional Reform'.

Second, far from being a settlement, the present arrangements have much of the character of unfinished business. House of Lords reform has been put on hold for three years and efforts to strengthen the role of the House of Commons through such devices as the use of Westminster Hall for additional debates are experimental in status. The character of the United Kingdom's territorial relationships is far from fixed despite the enormous amount of attention given to the devolution question in recent years. Even without the uncertainties created by the efforts to reestablish an assembly in Northern Ireland as part of the 1998 Good Friday peace initiative, the introduction of devolved institutions for Scotland and Wales was seen by many as the beginning of a process, not a stable settlement. What it is leading to — whether independence, federalism or a more far-reaching form of devolution — is, of course, a matter of dispute between the parties. Nationalists see the process as leading to independence; others such as the Liberal Democrats would prefer a federal solution for the United Kingdom as a whole.

It may also prove difficult to build solid public support for the asymmetrical form of devolution introduced into the United Kingdom. Ironically, by March 1998 a majority in Scotland appeared (by 47% to 40%) to prefer a fully independent Scotland in the long term than to continue with devolution within the United Kingdom.[4] After the establishment of the Scottish Parliament and the Welsh Assembly public opinion in both Scotland and Wales expressed disappointment with the results thus far achieved.[5]

Public opinion is not the only reason for viewing the devolved institutions as not entirely stable. In addition to changes in the character of the devolved institutions which may occur as a result of pressure from Scotland and Wales for more autonomy, it will take time to build the important informal relationships between London and Edinburgh on the one hand and London and Cardiff on the other. It is highly likely

---

[4] MORI/*Mail on Sunday* 26–27 March 1988 (quoted in Simon Atkinson and Roger Mortimore, 'Blair — One Year On' (Paper delivered to the Political Studies Association, Keele 1998).

[5] See Peter Riddell, 'Devolution has disappointed the customers', *The Times*, 23 February 2000.

that different patterns of inter-governmental relationships will emerge in the two cases, reflecting the different needs of the two areas. At the same time, supporters of greater autonomy for Wales, especially Plaid Cymru, are bound to use the Scottish comparison in their arguments for greater powers. Already there appears to be some support for giving the Welsh Assembly a tax-raising power.

The very different powers accorded to the Scottish Parliament (which has power over primary legislation and tax-varying power) and the Welsh Assembly (which has neither) are but one anomaly in the devolution arrangements. Equally, if not more troublesome is the anomaly now popularly known as the 'West Lothian question' as a result of Labour MP Tam Dalyell's persistent highlighting of a paradox inherent in the devolution arrangements.[6] The anomaly which has so troubled Dalyell (and others) is that, after devolution, Scottish MPs are able to vote on a range of domestic issues affecting English constituencies (for example education) while neither English MPs nor Westminster's Scottish MPs are able to vote on such issues in relation to Scotland because they have been transferred to the responsibility of the Scottish Parliament.[7] Labour ministers and others have argued that the British Constitution is full of anomalies and such paradoxes have to be tolerated, or better still, ignored. It is however much harder to overlook anomalies which are the product of recent constitutional design than ones which appear as the product of historical accident. It would thus seem inevitable that sooner or later the problem will have to be addressed whether through a radical reduction in the Scottish and Welsh representation at Westminster or through some device such as an English Grand Committee which would allow English MPs to consider legislation relating solely to England.

The repercussions of devolution on English political consciousness are at this stage difficult to judge. Regional government, which has been put forward as one solution to the need

---

[6] Tam Dalyell's constituency has been redistributed and renamed and he now sits for Linlithgow.
[7] For a full discussion see T. Dalyell, *Devolution: The End of Britain?* (Jonathan Cape, 1978).

for decentralization within England, is an option not a given, adding another uncertainty to the issue of the UK's territorial arrangements. Moreover, local government, although already subject to extensive and expensive reorganization in the period since 1972, seems set for another bout of experiment, especially if directly-elected mayors catch on. So, far from a stable settlement of the problems of what has been an unusually centralized state, what we have at this stage is a recipe for an almost kaleidoscopic pattern at the sub-central level.

Third, a settlement assumes a degree of consensus at the elite and popular level. It is extremely doubtful whether any such consensus exists. It is true, of course, that the Labour Party was returned to power in 1997 with an overwhelming majority (179) of parliamentary seats, though the crushing majority of seats was won on the basis of a much less impressive share of the vote (43.2%). The scale of the Labour victory in seats won has caused many commentators to speak of 1997 as a critical election which signalled a new pattern of politics in the United Kingdom. From a policy perspective, Labour's plans to modernize the Constitution were clearly signalled in its manifesto of 1997, its earlier policy documents and its unusual and public cooperation with the Liberal Democrats on constitutional reform. For adherents of traditional constitutional practice these factors should be sufficient to give Blair a mandate for any and all of the changes he has initiated.[8] It is difficult under existing constitutional arrangements to deny that the Government has the *right* to introduce far-reaching constitutional reforms. Certainly the Government is in a much stronger position than the Callaghan Government was when it attempted unsuccessfully to introduce devolution in the late 1970s.

If, however, the question is posed slightly differently and put in terms of how much underlying support for comprehensive constitutional reform exists, a rather more mixed picture emerges. Constitutional reform is a topic with low public salience and, as opinion pollsters recognize, it is rarely men-

---

[8] They might even be evidence of a sufficient degree of consent to acquit Labour of any charge of 'rape' of the Constitution since adult voters in 1997 may be presumed to have known what they were doing when they opted for a Labour government.

tioned unprompted when voters are asked to rank the most important issues facing the country.[9] In the case of devolution (and the creation of a Greater London Assembly with a directly-elected mayor) voters were required to endorse the new schemes directly through referenda. Apart from increasing the familiarity with referenda in Britain, these exercises in direct democracy allow us to test the depth of the support for constitutional innovation. In Scotland the support for a Scottish Parliament, on a turnout of 60.4%, was overwhelming (74.3% to 25.7%), but the degree of support fell off somewhat when voters answered the question of whether such a parliament should have tax-raising powers. Then 63.5% approved as against 36.5% who did not want such a parliament to be able to vary tax levels. In Wales, however, enthusiasm was much less marked. On a turnout of 50.1%, the Welsh opted for an Assembly by a tiny margin — 50.3% to 49.7%. In London the innovation of a new Assembly and directly-elected mayor were approved overwhelmingly (by 72% to 28%) but the vote was tarnished by the extremely low turnout of 34%. Thus although the referenda were positive in all three cases, only in Scotland could the results really be seen as a solid endorsement of the change and the low turnouts in London especially posed a serious question-mark over the legitimacy of the new institutions.

There is also uncertainty about the attitudes towards constitutional reform of the major actors in the system — the political parties. Until the 1990s Labour displayed little interest in the topic of constitutional reform, perhaps because of the Left's long-standing suspicion of the judiciary and the Party's preference for using executive power to introduce radical social and economic reform. Constitutional reform is very much a programme adopted by 'New' as opposed to 'Old' Labour and indeed in many ways Blair's constitutional reform ideas were the most, if not the only, radical part of his 1997 agenda. It was also a key part of the broad Labour project, highlighted after coming into office, to reach beyond the Labour Party and to include Liberal Democrats in a progressive majority. It remains to be seen how far the cooperation with the Liberal Democrats can survive the retirement of Paddy Ashdown

[9] See for example the comments of Atkinson and Mortimore, *op cit.*

(who as leader was personally committed to much closer links with Labour) and the sidelining of the Liberal Democrats' key goal of electoral reform for Westminster. Electoral reform for Westminster elections, while to some extent a generational issue, deeply divides the Labour Party and while the government appeared to be moving in a reforming direction by establishing the Jenkins Commission, a referendum on the issue looks unlikely while Labour has a secure working majority.[10] There may however be further changes to the electoral methods used for other elections, including a switch to a proportional system for local elections.

The Conservatives for their part have often toyed with constitutional reform while out of office — as in the period 1974-9 — but have lost interest in it when returned to power and concern about the perils of elective dictatorship faded. The Thatcher years left the Conservative Party a distinctive and unconstructive legacy on constitutional reform. By comparison with the emphasis on rational analysis and radicalism which marked economic argument and substantive policy debates, constitutional questions, such as the Scottish issue, were either neglected or responded to in terms of a dogmatic defence of the status quo. The Thatcher years also saw a greater centralization of power in the executive alongside (or, as some critics would say, because of) the greater freedom allowed to market forces.[11] Civil liberties groups (and prominent members of the judiciary) as well as journalists and academics increasingly pointed to the limited ability of the British system to defend the individual in a conflict with the state.

Now the Conservative Party finds itself in the awkward position of having to work out a policy on the constitutional reforms initiated by Blair. At the moment it appears at best to accept these measures as a *fait accompli* and there is still a tendency to treat them as the product of the unrepresentative chattering classes. Although it is unlikely that the Conservatives on return to office would repeal such measures as the Human Rights Act or devolution (especially if a second

[10] *The Report of the Independent Commission on Voting* (the Jenkins Report) Cm. 4090, 1998.
[11] See, for example, Andrew Gamble, *The Free Economy and the Strong State: The Politics of Thatcherism* (Macmillan, 2nd. edn., 1994).

Labour term allows them to 'bed down') the Conservatives' ambiguous attitude towards them raises questions about how they would work under a different political regime. A Conservative government could alter the detail of the reforms, and we might in any case expect a different party at Westminster to bring a different set of values and style to the internal relationships with the component parts of the United Kingdom.

The Implications for the United Kingdom

The constitutional reforms themselves, together with other innovations brought about by the Blair Government, have profound consequences for the United Kingdom as a whole, although much of the debate about the individual reforms, especially devolution, has tended to neglect these more general systemic points. Some of the implications for the management of the political system are already apparent. The conduct of inter-governmental relations at Cabinet Office level is bound to absorb more central government time. And if the crisis over funding for Wales is a precedent for the future the Exchequer is likely to be drawn into the internal crises of the Assembly.

On a different level it is apparent also that the already distinct pattern of party politics in the sub-units of the political system will become more separate with the creation of the Scottish Parliament and Welsh Assembly. There has been an erosion of two-party dominance in the United Kingdom since the early 1970s; but in Scotland and Wales the pattern of party competition offers a choice of four parties: Labour, Conservative, Liberal Democrats, and the SNP in Scotland and Plaid Cymru in Wales. The creation of important new political arenas for party competition in Scotland and Wales is likely to have repercussions for the major parties at Westminster if voters develop new loyalties as a result of voting for nationalist parties in the context of the Scottish Parliament and Welsh Assembly elections. The results of the Scottish Parliament election — in which Labour failed to secure an overall majority and had to enter a coalition with the Liberal Democrats — were interesting in two respects. First they pointed to the relatively small room for manouevre within the Scottish sub-system given that a coalition with the Scottish National Party was deemed out of the question because of the SNP goal of complete independence within the European Union. Secondly the results underlined how quickly Labour in Scotland might be forced to distance itself from Labour in London in order to satisfy the local need for a coalition. The deal was done by Labour reluctantly accepting the Liberal Democrat policy to abolish university tuition fees, regardless of the many anomalies which such a move would produce in relation to students across the United Kingdom. For the most part, though, the Scottish institutions were established smoothly and, despite some wrangles over such issues as the pay and privileges of members, the Scottish Parliament has developed a strong committee system and displayed its determination to develop a different approach to the legislative process from Westminster's.

The Welsh results, by contrast, were deeply discomforting for Labour and highlighted the potential for administrative and political turmoil in relation to the administration of the country. The perception that Blair had forced Alun Michael (as opposed to Rhodri Morgan) on the Welsh Labour Party after its previous leader Ron Davies was forced to resign in 1998, boosted support for Plaid Cymru. In the 1999 Assembly elections Labour was, as in Scotland, unable to secure an overall majority, taking only 28 of the 60 seats and losing once-solid Labour seats such as Islwyn and Rhondda. Labour, rather than forming a coalition, decided to operate as a minority government, a decision which made it vulnerable to political assaults from the opposition parties, especially Plaid Cymru. In February 2000 the anticipated loss of a confidence vote in the Assembly forced Alun Michael to resign in a move which was widely interpreted as a huge political embarrassment for Tony Blair. Michael's successor, Rhodri Morgan, was seen as the popular choice for Wales because he was more overtly independent of Blair.

Clearly the advent of multi-partyism in Scotland and Wales may be expected to threaten Labour's long-term ability to dominate Westminster elections. If in addition the Conservatives successfully sharpen their identity as the party of England, Labour's electoral position could be seriously undermined. Thus far the Conservative Party has not revived in the polls, but its increasingly Euro-sceptic stance, together with the lack of a strong base in either Scotland or Wales, makes the strengthening of its English identity a very possible scenario. In these circumstances it would, of course, be vital for Labour to hold on to the votes of middle England and to tilt its appeal even further from its traditional heartlands. Political calculations apart, the experience of both Welsh and Scottish devolution thus far show that the administration is going to become far less predictable than in the past and that regional variations in the shaping and delivery of policies will become more marked.

A More Powerful Judiciary

One indirect consequence of the spate of constitutional reform is an acceleration of the already growing political importance of the judiciary within the British system of government. The role of the British judiciary has been quietly changing for some time, although the constitutional reforms of the Blair government — notably devolution and the incorporation of the ECHR — will mark a qualitative shift in the relationship between courts and the political system. It is worth pausing to note why judges and courts have acquired more prominence in recent years. One factor has undoubtedly been the growth and elaboration of administrative law and the remedy of judicial review. The growth of administrative law is a remarkable product of the creativity and ingenuity of the judges themselves. Since the 1960s judges have broadened the scope of judicial review, turning it into a potentially powerful weapon to check the executive, although some authorities have cast doubt on the extent to which judicial review is as useful a curb on the abuse of power as is sometimes claimed.[12] Nevertheless the growth in the number of challenges to the decisions of public bodies (itself a reflection of the growing reach of the state) has necessarily brought the judiciary into political controversy, especially when the actions of ministers have been challenged. Under the Conservative governments of 1979–97 ministers found themselves subject to judicial scrutiny as well

[12] See for example, L. Bridges, G. Meszaros and M. Sunkin, *Judicial Review in Perspective* (London, 1995) where it is pointed out that despite a small number of high-profile cases, judicial review has been more significant as a weapon against *local* than central government.

as no little judicial criticism as a result of government sentenc-
ing policies and efforts to reform the delivery of legal services.
Conservative ministers found they liked judicial activism no
more than their Labour predecessors had done.

The UK's membership of the European Union has also
brought a role for the courts and the judiciary rather different
from the traditional one of subservience to Parliament. The
European Union is a legally-defined order in which British
domestic law is subordinate to European law and the British
courts have had to adapt to this fact of life. The most spectacular example of this was perhaps the *Factortame* case of 1990 in
which British judges had effectively to prevent the application
of an act of Parliament (the Merchant Shipping Act of 1988)
because it impeded the exercise of rights under European
law.[13]

Labour's constitution reforms will have a further impact on
the judiciary. The incorporation of the ECHR into domestic
law is bound to create a much more prominent role for judges
who will have to adjudicate disputes about the compatibility
of British legislation, past and future, with the ECHR.
Although the Human Rights Act does not allow judges to
strike down laws in the manner of the US Supreme Court, the
right to declare laws incompatible with the ECHR means that
not merely will judges have a new and politically-sensitive
caseload; their expression of views on human rights issues
outside the court will also acquire a new legitimacy, making
them much more influential actors on the public stage if they
choose to exercise the power.

In addition to the Human Rights Act the judiciary will necessarily find itself required to intervene in a range of other
constitutional issues. Devolution will inevitably create a vast
number of jurisdictional conflicts similar to those found in the
federal courts of the United States and Germany. Special procedures, both formal and informal, have been devised to handle disputes about legislative competence. The extensive role
given to the Judicial Committee of the Privy Council (JCPC) in
the resolution of 'devolution issues' means that what may be
highly contentious disputes between the Scottish Executive/
Parliament and London will be decided in a court, and it will

---

[13] *R v Secretary of State for Transport ex parte Factortame (No. 2)* [1989]AC 603.

be the JCPC which will have to decide devolution issues referred to it from ordinary court proceedings. This constitutional jurisdiction of the JCPC is not, of course, new; but what *is* new is its exercise over such a range *within* the United Kingdom.

The new and expanding role for the judiciary presented by constitutional reform inevitably raises questions about the adequacy of existing legal structures to discharge these new functions as well as about the appropriateness of the judiciary to handle politically sensitive issues. The use of the JCPC has seemed to many observers a short-term solution pending the creation of a proper constitutional court which could hear both devolution issues and important human rights cases. The issue of the representativeness and capacity of the judiciary to fulfil a wider political role remains a significant one, though under both Lord Mackay and Lord Irvine some limited changes have been introduced to make the process of appointment to the judiciary more transparent.[14]

Adapting to Change

The series of constitutional reforms introduced by Labour will bring new institutions and procedures to the machinery of British government. Whether they will change the behaviour and values of British politicians is another matter entirely. It is difficult to change the traditional assumptions and values of politicians so deeply socialized into a political system which has emphasized adversarial politics, partisan identity and loyalty, and parliamentary sovereignty. The politicians charged with operating the newly-devolved institutions of Scotland and Wales have talked about the 'new politics' — meaning a more cooperative, cross-party style of politics — which aims to be inclusive rather than confrontational. But party has continued to be a major factor in the calculations of politicians both in the devolved areas and in London, as the bitter debates surrounding the survival of Alan Michael's administration in Wales showed.

---

[14] See also Sir Leonard Peach's review for the Lord Chancellor: 'Independent Scrutiny of the Appointments Processes of Judges and Queen's Counsel', December 1999.

On a slightly different level, the architects of the major constitutional reforms have often proved coy about how far they really wanted to change existing constitutional practices. Jack Straw, in the context of debates about the Human Rights Act, has talked about promoting a 'rights culture' in the United Kingdom and other politicians, including the Lord Chancellor, have acknowledged the extent to which these reforms are indeed intended to change Britain's constitutional habits. On the other hand, the same politicians have frequently spoken as though the reforms could co-exist quite happily with traditional attitudes and practices. Thus Lord Irvine commented in the House of Lords on the way in which the Human Rights Bill had elegantly squared the circle of reconciling the protection of human rights with the notion of parliamentary sovereignty. 'The logic of the design of the Bill', he said, is that it 'maximizes the protection of human rights without trespassing on parliamentary sovereignty.' It is difficult, however, to see how a new and more balanced constitutional order can be created without trespassing on a parliamentary sovereignty that has effectively come to mean executive dominance of the legislature.

The difficulty of reconciling new structures with old political attitudes has already been seen in relation to Labour's efforts to control both the candidate selection processes for Scotland and for Wales and in the selection of the Welsh Labour leader. In both the process of selecting the Welsh Labour leader and in the selection of its candidate for mayor of London, New Labour appeared to be using the old time-honoured machine methods of electoral control using the unions to help influence the result. (In the London mayoral race the Prime Minister's candidate, Frank Dobson, defeated Ken Livingstone only as a result of the support of two unions which had not balloted their members.) The devolution of power and decentralization of decision making thus make uneasy bedfellows with the tendency within New Labour (which affects the core executive as well as the Party) to centralize and control power more effectively.

For the Conservatives the problem of adapting to constitutional change reflects the varied analyses of the Party's political prospects. There is a tension in the Conservative Party between those who wish to attack the Labour reforms root and branch and those who wish to promote a process of reasoned and constructive thinking about constitutional arrangements. While the Conservatives in opposition are inevitably acutely and painfully aware of the advantages which the executive has in the British system, the memory of being in government is perhaps still too strong to prompt a radical rethinking of how best to check the executive through parliamentary or other means. The myth of parliamentary sovereignty dies hard even for an opposition, and within the Conservative Party devotion to the cause of parliamentary sovereignty has acquired a new lease of life in the rhetoric of the Euro-sceptics who wish to resist European Union expansion at the expense of national policy control. Only the Liberal Democrats have consistently recognized the extent to which constitutional reform entails a major alteration of our traditional assumptions and practices.

Conclusions

The constitutional reforms which are currently being implemented have generated a host of questions about the operation of our country's government. Uncertainty by itself is not necessarily bad and in many respects the reforms offer an opportunity to develop a new style of politics. But there is at present a mismatch between the logic of the reforms and the attitudes of the politicians who will have to operate the new institutional arrangements. Some of that mismatch is the result of the highly partisan character of our traditional political system; but some of it stems from the fact that these important reforms have been generated as a product of governmental fiat rather than cross-party agreement and public consensus. We need not weep for the loss of the traditional constitution; we should be concerned about the extent to which sustained and rational reform is difficult to achieve in this country.

Simon Hughes and
Duncan Brack

Power, Politics and Modern Liberalism

The new century is bringing with it potentially far-reaching shifts in the focal points of political debate. Devolution for Scotland, Wales and Northern Ireland, the establishment of regional development agencies, a new government for London, debates over freedom of information, the incorporation of the European Convention on Human Rights into UK law, the enlargement of the European Union — all are ensuring that the reform of Britain's constitutional framework is featuring more highly on the political agenda than it has for perhaps ninety years.

Many of these reforms are long overdue, a response, although in many ways incomplete, to deep-seated changes in the way in which British citizens view their state and its powers. Yet they are being introduced by a party which has never, historically, shown a particular interest in them, which clearly does not possess a coherent approach to their implementation and implications, and which in many cases is motivated primarily by short-term political considerations. With a few exceptions, there is little fundamental sign, in either Labour or Conservative Parties, of any real process of rethinking the structure of relationships between citizens, public officials and elected politicians through which society is governed. Liberals, however — by which we mean those who derive their political beliefs from the philosophy of Liberalism, whether members of the Liberal Democrats, or of their Liberal Party and SDP predecessors, or of other parties, or of none—have consistently argued for a different way of dispersing and controlling governmental power in Britain. This follows from the primacy that Liberalism itself has always given to the distribution and use of power in society.

Liberal proposals for constitutional reform have often been criticized as irrelevant to the 'real needs' of the country. This has, of course, never been true, but the way in which the government is going about its reforms is rendering it even more obviously untrue than before. The new agenda therefore offers great opportunities for modern Liberals, if they have the courage and ability to grasp them, to bring their thinking and proposals centre stage. This chapter provides a critique of the current reform process and sets out a different vision—a Liberal vision—of why it should and how it could be done.

The Liberal Critique

> We want no more gods and emperors, no more saviours of any kind. Democracy, freedom and happiness are the only goals of modernization.
>
> *Wei Jing Sheng*[1]

Many of the other chapters in this book explore the defects of the present government's reform agenda. From a Liberal viewpoint, the fault running through many of the changes is that governmental power remains insufficiently dispersed and is subject to inadequate democratic control. Furthermore, since the reforms have been introduced in a piecemeal and incoherent manner, they are generating further needs and demands that have not yet been addressed or even thought about.

In Westminster, central government seems stronger than ever: it is supported by a huge majority in the Commons, yet it displays an obsession with control of its back-benchers that

[1]   Chinese dissident, Tiananmen Square (attributed).

would seem excessive in a party with no majority at all. New Labour's rapid abandonment of its earlier and greater commitment to freedom of information, depressingly familiar to students of government, reveals its antipathy to substantially open and participatory politics. Its failure to democratize the House of Lords, and the real possibility that it may proceed no further than a largely or even wholly appointed chamber, reveals its propensity to give in to the temptation to accumulate power.

Devolution for Scotland, Wales and London — limited and unsatisfactory, but at least better than the *status quo ante* — is in place or under way; but it is clear that the current Labour leadership distrusts this dispersal of power from the centre, and will go to some lengths to limit and control it. Fortunately, it seems impossible to put this particular genie back in the bottle. Indeed, as recent opinion polls show, despite the uncertain beginnings of the Scottish Parliament and Welsh Assembly, they seem only to have whetted the appetite of the Scottish and Welsh people for further devolution — genuine home rule, with full legislative authority and the unconstrained power to vary tax levels. Even the brief first experience of the recent Stormont Government has proved popular in Northern Ireland. The Scottish Parliament's abolition of university tuition fees for Scottish students has shown how the current system is bound to throw up anomalies, with implications for the UK as a whole, which cannot easily be resolved. All these developments, coupled with the over-representation of Scottish and Welsh MPs at Westminster, the 'Barnett formula' for distributing public spending amongst the nations of Britain, and the establishment of appointed regional development agencies, have generated interest in elected regional assemblies in England, and possibly an English parliament (a topic of particular relevance to the Conservative Party, which historically has tended to win a majority of English seats). This, together with the fact that regional groupings of local authorities are already coming together to coordinate funding approaches to the EU, in turn raises the issue of the balance of national, regional and local taxation and the relations of different parts of the UK to the EU's decision-making and representative structures. These are all entirely predictable consequences of Scottish and

Welsh devolution, to which Labour appears to have no thought-out answers at all.

At the local level, the government has relaxed some of the most unjustifiable restraints of its Conservative predecessors, but has again shown a desire to construct structures of power—elected mayors and cabinet, rather than committee-style administrations—which concentrate power into fewer hands rather than disperse it more widely.

The UK is one of the few countries in the world which possess neither a written constitution nor some kind of supreme court. Yet the implications of the long-overdue incorporation of the European Convention on Human Rights into UK law, due to enter into force on 2 October 2000, will raise precisely that question. British, not European, courts will be holding the British government and parliament to account, potentially finding UK legislation to be in breach of the Convention. The consequences of these actions and subsequent constitutional changes remaining uncodified will be a recipe for confusion and conflict—but once again ministers have no answers, and the option of creating a written constitution, though it is highly logical, does not seem to have occurred to them. Similarly, a recent European court ruling on part-time judges in Scotland will help to uphold the independence of the judiciary, but will also have important implications for many other aspects of the UK legal system—including whether the Law Lords should remain members of the second chamber, and how the wholly archaic position of the Lord Chancellor, simultaneously head of the legal system, speaker of the House of Lords and key member of the cabinet, can be justified. The (Liberal) argument for a separate ministry of justice is a logical outcome of these developments, but again not one which Labour appears to be willing to consider.

The utter incoherence of Labour's constitutional agenda is revealed most clearly in its attitude to electoral reform. A manifesto commitment to a referendum on proportional representation—one of the most effective ways to disperse power in Britain's distorted electoral system—has been put off, and many believe it may have been abandoned entirely. Worse still, the lack of any principle or vision and the desire to exercise strong control from the centre has left the UK with no less than five different electoral systems[2] for different structures of government, most of which possess the characteristic that they give more power to the party selection apparatus than they do to the elector. No wonder turnout is falling drastically—yet ministers have blamed 'voter fatigue' from the greater number of elected bodies. (Our ancestors did not appear to suffer from the symptom, even when they cast their votes far more frequently—in Sunderland in the 1870s, for example, a population of 112,000 elected a total of 362 representatives to twenty different assemblies, with various functions and responsibilities.[3]) If citizens believe that their vote makes a difference—in the election because it can affect the choice of candidate, and afterwards because the body to which they are electing exercises real power—than the strains of walking to the polling booth once or twice a year may not be too difficult to overcome.

It should be clear that Labour is implementing a set of potentially far-reaching reforms without any coherent plan of where they may end up. This is not surprising given the party's history, which reveals a general lack of interest in reforming a system that has from time to time given it largely unfettered power, modified only in the 1980s and '90s as the Conservatives' seemingly unstoppable series of election victories pushed it towards support for Scottish and Welsh devolution, and for a referendum on proportional representation. It is possible, however, to adopt a different approach: to address these questions, and to draw up proposals for reform, with a set of underlying principles dealing with the distribution and use of power. These are offered by the philosophy of Liberalism.

---

[2] First past the post for Westminster; first past the post for local government (except in Northern Ireland, which uses the single transferable vote (STV) system of PR); additional member systems for Scotland, Wales and the Greater London Assembly; STV for the Northern Ireland Assembly; a closed regional list system for the European Parliament (except in Northern Ireland, where STV is used); and a limited alternative vote system (two preferences only) for the London mayor.

[3] Eugenio F. Biagini, *Liberty, Retrenchment and Reform: Popular Liberalism in the Age of Gladstone* (Cambridge, 1992)—cited in Conrad Russell, *An Intelligent Person's Guide to Liberalism* (Duckworth, 1999), p. 45.

The Liberal Vision

> It has been said that Socialism is about equality. If
> you ask for an equivalent short-hand description of
> Liberalism I should say that it is about freedom and
> participation.   *Jo Grimond* [4]

All political philosophies begin with a view of human nature.
Liberals start from the belief that individuals are essentially
rational beings — that, in most circumstances, they exercise
their freedoms wisely and responsibly, and do not seek to
impose on others what they would dislike themselves. This is
not to say that individuals will *always* behave in this way: the
appeal of essentially irrational forces such as religious dogma,
xenophobic nationalism or class war can be very powerful.
But these forces can be countered — through, for example, education, a widening of personal horizons, a removal of depend-
ency, and guarantees of personal security and of freedom from
fear. Difficult tasks yes, but not in principle *insuperable* ones.

This is an optimistic view; Liberals believe in the essential
goodness and what, in a more religious age, would be termed
the improvability of humankind. This is in sharp contrast, it
should be noted, to the basic ingrained pessimism of Conservatives about human nature, and about what individuals will
do to others given the chance. From the French Terror of 1793
onwards, Tories have appealed to those in the electorate fearful of what the future might bring for themselves, their fami-
lies or their country — and have been electorally most
successful when such troubles were at their height. It is more
difficult to identify a clear Labour view (as in so many areas)
on this question. Some of the organizations which joined
together to form the Labour Party in 1900 shared the Liberal
belief in rational, decent and improvable human beings — the
Independent Labour Party, and probably the Fabians, though
a key difference from Liberals lay in the Fabian belief that individuals could best be 'improved' from above, whether they
desired it or not (as Douglas Jay put it in 1939, 'in the case of
nutrition and health, just as in the case of education, the gentleman in Whitehall really does know better what is good for

---

[4]   Jo Grimond, *The Liberal Challenge* (1963).

people than the people know themselves'[5]). The picture was clouded, however, by the influence of the trade union movement, for which the main point of establishing the Labour Party was to enlarge their struggle to protect and extend the interests of the employed working classes. This lent the party a chauvinistic, insular and anti-pluralist set of attitudes that are still visible today.

To develop the argument, given that human beings are essentially rational individuals, Liberals also believe that the extension of new freedoms will itself have an enlightening impact, helping to guarantee that they will be exercised with responsibility and maturity. A good way, for example, to prevent growth in support for Scottish independence from the UK is to introduce home rule for Scotland. When the Scottish people are able to exercise control over the activities of government which are most effectively directed from Edinburgh (as opposed to London, or Brussels, or perhaps Geneva or New York), then the attractions of independence diminish; it is not clear what gains, in terms of good governance, economic prosperity or personal freedom, would derive from it. Conversely, the best way to generate the desire for independence is to deny the Scottish nation any degree of home rule at all.

What, then, are the Liberal principles that flow from this view of human behaviour? Above all else, Liberals believe that, as rational beings, individuals are capable of judging their own self-interest. Indeed, they are the *only* ones able to so judge; no-one else, whether civil servants, priests or politicians, can take that decision for them as effectively. The good society, the one Liberals want to create, is therefore one in which each individual has the maximum freedom to pursue their own ends. The aim of every policy, every act of government, must be to create the conditions within which individuals can best pursue these ends, realize their talents and forge their own destinies.

Throughout history, Liberals have therefore aimed to remove constraints which denied individuals this liberty, whether imposed by state, public opinion, religion or custom. The objects of these struggles have of course varied across

---

[5]   Douglas Jay, *The Socialist Case* (1939).

time, from the Whig opposition to Stuart absolutism and Tory repression, to the Victorian Liberals' gradual extension of the franchise, removal of religious discrimination against non-Anglicans,[6] the opening of the civil service to competitive examination and the abolition of stamp duties on newspapers (to list a few among many) — all achievements which removed barriers to the free expression of thought, opinion and action, and therefore enlarged the liberty of individuals. The 'New Liberalism' of the early twentieth century extended the concept of liberty by recognizing that unemployment, poverty and ill-health were also serious constraints on individuals' capacities to lead their own lives, and were therefore worthy objects of state action to ameliorate. The last Liberal governments introduced old age pensions, health and unemployment insurance, labour exchanges, school meals and progressive taxation; they laid the foundations of the welfare state which Attlee was to build on after 1945.[7] Even after the Liberal Party was eclipsed electorally by Labour, the intellectual inheritance of Liberalism remained alive, and was visible in the economic genius of Keynes, who showed how governments could promote growth and employment without intervening excessively in the operations of the economy, and in the administrative talents of Beveridge, who planned the system of social security which led to a new assault on the financial constraints on freedom after the Second World War.

Power: Dispersal, Control and Diversity

The loudest cheer I have ever had from a party audience was for saying: 'if we were in power we would be just as bad as the others: we would need control

---

[6] A process which is still incomplete — e.g. the prohibition on the heir to the throne marrying a Catholic.

[7] This was a major revolution in Liberal thinking, locating the British Liberals firmly in the 'social liberal' (as opposed to classical liberal) wing of liberalism world-wide, where they still remain. Politicians, from Margaret Thatcher to Tony Blair, who have commented admiringly on the Liberal inheritance (usually to justify some removal of state responsibility) have not often appeared to recognize this.

just as much'. I am proud of my party for that
cheer.   *Conrad Russell*[8]

A Liberal society is accordingly one in which each individual
has the freedom to determine and pursue their own ends as
best they can. Liberals are not, however, either libertarians or
anarchists—they do not accept the fatuous equation of minimum government with maximum freedom. Government is
needed for many reasons: to regulate the market, to ensure
that it works freely and fairly and that it operates within
parameters desired by society (for example to ensure that
prices and decisions reflect environmental costs and benefits);
to provide public services which private enterprise or small
groups of individuals cannot supply, or cannot supply as
effectively; to establish the framework of law within which
one person's freedoms do not detract from another's; and to
provide the social framework (education, income support,
health care) within which all individuals, whatever their personal inheritance and abilities, can develop their talents to the
full.

The key question therefore becomes: how should the exercise of these governmental powers best be controlled? As
Conrad Russell has put it, 'We know that a civilised community needs power, and is not safe without it. Power, like sex,
should be subject to two restrictions. First, it is unlawful if it
does not rest on consent. Second, it is often more enjoyable
and more rewarding if it is set in the context of a relationship.'[9]
Power comes from the people, who confer it on government,
which uses it to enlarge, not restrict, individual liberty.

This has a number of implications. First, that political
power should be dispersed as widely as possible, given that it
is in general easier for citizens to control a tier of government
that is nearer to them, geographically and psychologically;
and, of course, a lower tier is also likely to be more aware of
and responsive to local circumstances and needs. (In the final
analysis, as Tip O'Neill, speaker of the US House of Representatives, said: 'all politics is local'.) It is not surprising, there-

[8] Earl Russell, in Duncan Brack (ed.), *Why I am a Liberal Democrat* (Liberal
     Democrat Publications, 1996), p. 117.
[9] Russell, *An Intelligent Person's Guide to Liberalism*, p. 22.

fore, that in the nineteenth century Liberals were instrumental in creating democratic structures of local government and consistently argued thereafter for enhancing their powers; whereas since 1979, Conservative and Labour governments, whatever the rhetoric, have tended to do the opposite. Similarly with home rule for Scotland, Wales and the regions of England; a long-standing Liberal cause which Conservatives have always opposed, and where Labour have been late and only partial converts.

This is not to say, of course, that all power can or should be exercised locally. There are some powers that can only be exercised, or can be exercised more effectively, at state or higher levels. For as long as the UK is the relevant state, the maintenance of defence, the control of macroeconomic policy and the redistribution of resources from rich to poor communities clearly should be directed from a UK level (though there are arguments for passing up some aspects of these powers to the EU). Other activities, such as the regulation of the international economy or the protection of the global environment, cannot be managed effectively by individual countries, and international cooperation and supranational institutions are required. It is impossible to be definitive about the appropriate level at which any particular function should be best exercised, and in practice many of them require cooperation between different tiers of government; it is the function of the political system to resolve these tensions and to strike the appropriate balance between local accountability and policy effectiveness — and the Liberal instinct is always to push power downwards.

A second implication of the belief that power rests on consent and on active relationships is that control through the ballot box, though necessary, is not sufficient. To quote Conrad Russell again, 'It is not enough to claim that we have an ascending theory of power if it comes up from the people once every five years, and then comes down again in a five-year uncontrollable avalanche from Downing Street'.[10] The power of the executive (at all levels of government) must be capable of being checked between elections — through a structure of

[10] *Ibid.*, p. 27.

law which protects the individual citizen against arbitrary actions of the executive and itself is immune to political interference, and through an active legislative body fully able to amend inadequate legislation and to hold the executive to account. There are other forms of participatory relationship—referendums, citizens' initiatives, consultative exercises—worth experimenting with and using where appropriate, particularly at a local level.

A third implication of the basic principle is that the more diverse and pluralist the society, the more tolerant and liberal—and more open to individual freedom—it is likely to be. We have so far talked primarily about the powers of government, but there are many other kinds of power: that exercised by businesses, particularly by large or, even more, by transnational enterprises; that exercised by the local community; and that exercised by society at large, or by parts of it such as the media. All these can, in some circumstances, act to constrain the individual in the exercise of their freedoms.[11] It is difficult for government to do much directly to create a culture of tolerance and diversity, though there certainly are many creations of politicians that will help: a strong framework of laws that is applied without regard to race, sex, sexual orientation, disability or age; effective and autonomous structures of local and regional government; a common welfare system, including social security, housing and education policies which do not discriminate against individuals because of their membership of a particular group (such as single parents); and government structures which encourage a role for local community initiatives and voluntary groups. There are other things that politicians can *avoid* doing: they can avoid attempting to impose their own moral values on the nation at large, and, especially, they can avoid holding up one particular lifestyle as an object of admiration (Liberal politicians would not, in the way that Tony Blair frequently does, talk about *the* fam-

---

[11] John Stuart Mill, greatest of the Victorian Liberal philosophers, devoted the vast bulk of his best-known work, *On Liberty,* to the threats to liberty from public opinion and social custom; only a few pages dealt with the activities of the state. One hundred and fifty years later, in a world where government is far larger and more far-reaching than in Mill's day, this is still a point worth bearing in mind.

ily — there are many different kinds, incorporating all sorts of formal and informal relationships and networks of relatives, and a tolerant and pluralist society would recognize the value of all); and they can recognize that prohibitions on personal behaviour which may (or may not) have been appropriate to an earlier age but are now widely ignored, because most individuals believe they cannot be justified, should be removed.[12]

The final implication of the Liberal belief that the good society is one in which each individual has the freedom to determine and pursue their own ends as best they can, and that this is mainly achieved through building a framework in which power is dispersed and controlled, is that the concept of equality is central. In fact this has already been referred to when we discussed the promotion of a culture of tolerance and diversity. Such a society cannot exist where individuals are treated differently by the law and by government institutions because of their nature. 'Equality before the law' was one of the great rallying cries of Liberalism from the earliest days of the Whigs; 'equal justice', 'non-discrimination' and 'concern for the underdog' are equally valid ways of expressing it.

The dispersal of governmental power, its effective control, pluralism and the building of a diverse and tolerant society, the principle of equality before the law — these concepts are not normally treated as part of a unified whole. But for Liberals they are, because they are all necessary building blocks in the construction of a society in which individuals can be free.

The Liberal Agenda

[Liberals] are unique in devising a political system which links the concept of fairness to an ideology which says not that: 'Jack is as good as his master',

---

[12] This statement could have referred to a number of issues over the years, but the best example now is the use of cannabis, where Tony Blair and Jack Straw, in the teeth of advice from virtually all the professionals working in the field, and of the evidence of other countries, insist on maintaining a theoretical ban which at best is a waste of police time, and at worst actively encourages users to experiment with hard drugs, because the suppliers (being illegal) are the same.

but rather: 'Jack should be his own master'.

Richard Kemp[13]

We do not have the space here to trace this thread through all major areas of political concern, except to note that, for Liberals, everything else is essentially secondary to the question of power and how it may be controlled. We do, however, need to address some of the major areas of state action.

Economic analysis is not, for Liberals (unlike followers of most other political persuasions), a prime determinant of policy; it is important principally in that it affects the distribution of power in society and can thereby enlarge or diminish the life-chances of individuals. In general, Liberals have tended to support the operation of the free market, mainly because this has appeared to be the system which has the greatest potential to deliver the greatest benefits to the greatest number with the smallest need for government interference. But many Victorian Liberals saw the free market, and in particular free trade, as desirable because it provided a means of protecting the poor against the rich, who possessed the power (then, and to a certain extent now) to fix prices, rig the market and restrict choice. Liberals oppose concentrations of economic power as much as they do concentrations of political power, and for the same reasons. But equally, where the market fails to deliver desirable ends — public services, environmental sustainability, a basic income — Liberals have no hang-ups about government intervention to subsidize these services or directly provide them, and to alter the parameters within which the market works.

Another key area is international policy, and again the principle of the control of power applies just as well. Historically, Liberals have supported the underdogs, nations struggling to be free of empires, minorities oppressed by majorities — though without automatically assuming that independence, which often bears overtones of exclusivist nationalism, is necessarily the best option; various forms of federalism are valid alternatives. Equally, they have argued for the creation of a strong framework of international law, wherein every coun-

---

[13] Cllr Richard Kemp, of Liverpool, in Brack, *Why I am a Liberal Democrat*, p. 84.

try, no matter how small and weak, may enjoy the same rights to equal treatment — say, in a border dispute, or an argument about trade discrimination — as its larger and more powerful neighbours. The creation of effective international and supranational institutions — the European Union, the United Nations and its agencies — is a natural development of this belief and explains why Liberals have always argued the pro-European and pro-internationalist case throughout the twentieth century. The collapse of the Soviet bloc and the end of superpower rivalry, the growing understanding that more and more issues — the control of transnational enterprises, the protection of the environment, the regulation of money markets — can only be tackled effectively at an international level, gives a wider acceptance and greater opportunity for this approach than at any time before, though whether effective structures and policies can be put into place at a global level quickly enough to meet the major international challenges is an unresolved question.

People may argue that there is an apparent inconsistency here, in that we appear to be making the case for the decentralization of power downwards, to bring institutions closer to the citizens whose lives they affect, but also its centralization upwards, so that global problems may be more effectively managed. But this inconsistency is only an artefact, created by the current world of nation-states, shaped by a notion of national sovereignty that developed in the seventeenth century and is long since out of date. The key point, as we argued above, is that power should be located at the lowest level consistent with its effective exercise — and in some matters, recognizing how far the process of globalization has proceeded, this must mean a move upwards (for example, in negotiating over trade policy to the EU). An important point to add, however, is that international institutions, however remote they may seem from the ordinary citizen, must still possess some route of democratic accountability and control. In the EU this means a stronger European Parliament and a more open and accountable Council of Ministers. At a global level it could mean, as a first step, political or parliamentary assemblies of bodies such as the World Trade Organisation or the IMF, and perhaps a democratic counterpart to the government-appointed United Nations General Assembly. Slow and no doubt inadequate steps — but a beginning.

A third key area is environmental policy, which we have touched on above. Again the Liberal approach can be traced back to the concern with the distribution of power, but this time with its distribution *between* generations. It relates to the idea of the exercise of power as a trust, passed to the government by the consent of the people, exercised in their name and for their benefit, and on behalf not just of the current population but of future generations too. Viewed in this way, the need for a strong environmental policy becomes apparent. A society may be able to maintain a high standard of living while ignoring its impact on the environment for a while — but it cannot do so indefinitely, and in most countries in the year 2000 it cannot do so at all any more.

These Liberal alternatives are described in full in the manifestos of the Liberal Democrats, and also in the writings and speeches of Liberals in other parties — we claim no monopoly of wisdom, and some aspects of Liberal thinking pervade, to a greater or lesser degree, many parties. Indeed, it has become commonplace to claim that 'liberal democracy' has become the accepted orthodoxy of all parties in Western politics, that the triumph of free-market capitalism and free elections shows that there is no place for a distinctively Liberal party, whatever that may be. We hope we have shown in this chapter that that assertion, resting on a lack of understanding of the basic tenets of Liberalism, is nonsense; that the enduring Liberal concern with the distribution, use and abuse of power is just as relevant today as it ever was, and that Liberals are the only ones arguing the case.

In fact, we would go further and argue that it may well be *more* relevant. Social values surveys have frequently shown that the motivations, prejudices and behaviour of the individuals who make up British society are changing, in slow but fundamental ways. As society as a whole increases its levels of income and wealth, motivations other than subsistence and consumption are becoming more important — personal growth and self-expression, individual freedom and responsibility, an awareness of the interdependence of individuals and communities. Other indications in recent opinion surveys—increasing concern for the environment, the higher acceptance of gay and lesbian lifestyles and of a racially diverse community, and the growing resentment of New Labour authoritarianism and control-freakery—reveal different aspects of the same thing: a belief in a more tolerant and relaxed society, a greater appreciation of a broader 'quality of life' as opposed to a narrower focus on levels of personal wealth and consumption.

The ways in which political power is used and controlled is crucial to the lifestyles of this new society. This is where the Liberal agenda has much to offer, in its focus on the distribution and control of power, and in its belief in a system within which individuals can best pursue their ends, realize their talents and forge their own destinies. This is the best chance for decades for the rebirth of Liberal Britain.

Nevil Johnson

Parliament Pensioned Off?

Parliamentary government has been the most important political invention of the English. It is, of course, true that representative institutions of various sorts did emerge fairly widely in late medieval Europe, but it was only in England that there was a more or less continuous line of development from the feudal estates to a parliament with supreme authority over legislation and over the formation and survival of governments. It is not surprising, therefore, that Parliament, and more specifically the House of Commons, has been the institution which first in England and Wales and then in Britain as a whole came to embody the theory and practice of constitutional government. What the Constitution has been for the United States of America, Parliament has been in Britain: it has stood for self-government and the successful assertion of fundamental political rights against the claims of that even older institution, the Crown. It has been the foundation stone of liberty and the rule of law, and it is to Parliament and those who fought for it that this country chiefly owes its tradition of limited government by consent.

Yet despite the ease with which the glories of Parliament and its historical achievements can be evoked, its decline has been a familiar and repeated theme of commentary on the British Constitution for much of the twentieth century. By the 1930s it was almost commonplace to deplore the weakening of Parliament in the face of the encroachments of an overweening executive—the 'new despotism' as it was called by a highly critical judge.[1] Though victory in the Second World

---

[1]   Gordon (Lord) Hewart, *The New Despotism* (Ernest Benn, London 1929).

War seemed to demonstrate the inherent vitality and authority of British parliamentary institutions, a belief symbolized by the reconstruction of the Chamber of the House of Commons just as it had been before bombs fell on it during the war, it was not long before books began to appear with titles which suggested that Parliament was after all in serious decline, losing its ability to check governments and no longer able to keep up with the relentless expansion of the powers and responsibilities of the executive.[2]

But this pessimistic assessment of Parliament's prospects led neither to a rejection of parliamentary government nor to efforts to redesign the institution of Parliament altogether. Instead there opened in the mid 1960s a period stretching right down to the present time during which countless proposals for the 'reform of Parliament' were propounded, argued about and in some degree acted upon.[3] Of these reforms perhaps the most notable was the establishment of a full range of departmental select committees by Margaret Thatcher's Government soon after she took office in 1979.

Yet despite decades of intense preoccupation with reform of both the Commons and more recently of the Lords, few would assert with confidence that the decline of Parliament has been halted, still less that it has been reversed. We are left with a situation in which it is clear that Parliament is and has for a long time been unable to perform effectively and regularly those functions of control which have since the closing decades of the nineteenth century been held to be at the heart of its constitutional role. Parliamentary debate no longer shapes public opinion and in fact has little impact on what the Government decides to do; Parliament's influence over the terms of legislation is marginal and over public expenditure negligible; despite a wide range of select committees the functions of scrutiny are performed patchily and members of the executive can often evade accountability for their actions. Thus Parlia-

[2] Titles of this sort included *Can Parliament Survive?* (Hollis, 1949) and *The Passing of Parliament* (Keeton 1952). However the fashion for such gloomy prognoses soon passed away.
[3] Bernard Crick, *The Reform of Parliament* (Weidenfeld, 1964), provided something like an initial manifesto for the parliamentary reform movement. The Study of Parliament Group, founded in 1964, was also to be influential in developing a reformist concern with the strengthening of Parliament.

ment appears to be constantly falling behind in a race it cannot win. Nothing that has so far happened in the present wave of far-reaching constitutional change suggests that the prospects for Parliament, and especially the House of Commons, are going to improve.

For a long time now parliamentary reform has been presented by many of its protagonists as a matter of restoring or re-establishing what is often called 'balance' or 'a better balance' between the executive and legislative powers, *i.e.* between the Government and Parliament. What the weights on the scales should be, where the balance should be struck, and how this better balance might actually be brought about are matters generally left in some obscurity. It is easy to see why. To talk of balance — or better still of checks and balances — sounds impressive and indeed echoes an account of the Constitution that stretches back to the eighteenth century and even earlier. Yet despite its distinguished ancestry 'balance' between executive and legislative eludes contemporary reformers. The reason for this is in fact quite obvious: the direction and degree of constitutional reform have in modern times been determined by the executive, and this has applied just as much to parliamentary reform as to any other segment of constitutional development or change. That the executive is driving the process of reform at the present time is surely beyond dispute; and the reform programme accords but a modest place to parliamentary reform. Nor does it pay any serious attention to the question of 'balance', still less of checks and balances, either in the Constitution as a whole or between Parliament and Government in particular.

In numerous speeches and statements it has been asserted that the reforms now being put in place are motivated by a commitment to the modernization and democratization of British political institutions and practices.[4] The first of these terms can be made to mean virtually anything and is, one suspects, nothing more than a fashionable slogan. The second has to be taken rather more seriously, though it is hard to find

---

[4] Typical of the modernization jargon was the title of the White Paper on reform of the House of Lords: *Modernising Parliament: Reforming the House of Lords,* Cm 4183, 1999. Similarly there was *Modernising Government,* Cm 4310, 1999, a publication on the theme of administrative improvement.

agreement on what it means. But at least it suggests that after the reforms have been carried through there will be wider opportunities for the exercise of democratic rights by citizens and their representatives and that political institutions – or some of them at least – will have become more accountable to those they serve and more accessible to the public. In principle at least an outcome of this kind would not be incompatible with the retention by Parliament, and especially by the House of Commons, of a central place in our constitutional system, and with measures which might help to strengthen it in relation to the Government. But the programme of constitutional change so far enacted as well as those schemes still in the making do not in fact seem to offer grounds for believing that Parliament will emerge in much better health as a result. The strengthening of national parliamentary institutions in ways which might restore to them a capacity to impose checks on the executive is certainly not prominent on the reform agenda. Some of the measures put through – notably on human rights – have little to do with democratization or the democratic accountability of Governments; others, principally those devolving powers away from Westminster, may in some senses be said to establish new democratic rights, but they do so at the expense of elected representatives in the national Parliament, and who is to say with confidence that that will strengthen British democracy?

II

The main argument to be put forward in this essay is that the current reforms are more likely to weaken Parliament still further than to strengthen it. To back up this contention we will look in rather more detail at some of the implications for Parliament of some of the reforms undertaken and projected. We will begin with the Human Rights Act 1998, a piece of legislation that will take effect during the year 2000.[5] In essence what this measure does is to lay on the British courts a duty to interpret British law as far as possible in such a way as to render it compatible with the human rights set out in the European

---

[5] With the setting up of the Scottish Parliament the human rights legislation has already come into effect in Scotland.

Convention of Human Rights, a code formulated and adopted as long ago as 1950. If by the application of this new principle of interpretation it turns out that sometimes a court cannot plausibly establish compatibility between a Convention right and a statutory provision or executive act claimed to be in breach of the right, then it will be open to it to make a declaration of incompatibility. After that it is then in theory at least up to Parliament to decide what to do to bring British law into line with the Convention, though in practice this means that it will be for the Government to determine what to do and how to proceed. Indeed, the legislation provides a 'fast track' procedure for just this purpose.

The procedures for implementing the new human rights standards sound somewhat complicated, and certainly the manner in which Convention rights are to be brought to bear on British law is oblique. The courts are not to be empowered to strike down statutory provisions, but instead will have to assess issues of compatibility and incompatibility. Ostensibly one reason for this crab-like approach to the enforcement of Convention rights lies in respect for Parliament: it is necessary, so it has been affirmed, to preserve the principle of parliamentary sovereignty which would be breached irreparably, so it is held, if the courts were entitled to nullify existing enactments. It is possible to argue for a long time about the pros and cons of this matter, and in political terms the case for parliamentary supremacy may be far stronger than many of the supporters of greater authority for judges will allow. But this is not the aspect of human rights legislation which will be pursued here. Instead, I want to consider what are the likely implications for Parliament of the legislation, given the terms on which it has been designed and enacted. Will it strengthen Parliament, and especially the House of Commons, or weaken it? Will it make much difference to the legislative process and to Parliament's opportunities to influence legislation? Is Parliament likely to come to terms easily or comfortably with the much more legalistic culture implicit in the judicial arbitration of rights claims at a constitutional law level?

None of us can predict the future, and in any event the impact of human rights legislation will be influenced by factors outside British control, such as the further development of the European Union, the nature and status of rights within the EU, and the extent to which Europe as a whole remains committed to a standard liberal rights culture.[6] But at the very least it seems clear that Parliament's discretion will be restricted, and probably in two ways. First, at the stage when legislation is being prepared (usually by a Government department) it will be necessary to avoid any provisions or formulations which might be thought likely to fall foul of the Human Rights Act. Indeed, Ministers putting forward legislation will be required to make a statement vouching for its compatibility with Convention rights. Thus, before Parliament even begins to exercise the discretion in law-making that in principle it still possesses, something like self-censorship on its behalf will have taken place. Second, the amending rights of Parliament are bound to be restricted, at any rate in practice even if not in theory. Were amendments or additions to a Bill to be proposed which the Government's legal advisers thought might be challenged as breaching the Convention rights, then very likely the Government would have no alternative but to oppose them, no matter what might be the political demand for them.

The overall impact of such conditions on the passage of bills might not be great, but they do point to a further narrowing of the scope for parliamentary intervention when legislative proposals are being considered. It might also be found that private members will face an extra hurdle when trying to secure support for measures they would like to bring forward. What will be inescapable is the need to pay more attention to strictly legal questions and to the possibility of conflicting interpretations of whatever provisions are being put forward. All this must in some degree at least be at the expense of a focus on either the practical policy arguments for a particular measure or the political case for it. But it is precisely these features of the legislative function that have generally claimed most attention in the British parliamentary tradition. It has been up to Members of Parliament to say where the shoe

---

[6] There is talk inside the European Union of the drafting and passage in 2000 of a European Charter of Rights. In principle at least this could become justiciable before the European Court of Justice. Such a development would have serious implications both for national charters of rights and for the European Convention of Human Rights. Indeed, one wonders what the European citizen would do with so many rights.

pinches and what should be done about it. Under the new dispensation there may often be no scope for performing this role. Certainly there can be little doubt that unless the attitudes and experience of most legislators change considerably in the future, it will be difficult to secure from them a constructive contribution to the consideration of rights issues.

There remains too the risk of serious conflict occurring between the legislature and executive on the one hand and the judiciary on the other. If we were to imagine the Court of Appeal declaring that parts of a recently enacted statute could not be construed as compatible with the Convention and thus putting on Parliament and Government the onus for changing it or perhaps repealing it altogether, it is then possible to envisage a sharp conflict between an indignant Parliament and an uncomfortable judiciary. Of course, it can be argued that such possibilities are 'academic' and unlikely to arise. But this optimistic view assumes greater agreement on the modern liberal rights culture than may in fact be present in society. Human rights are very fine when there is little disagreement about what they mean and as a result a general willingness to accept judicial arbitration. But if sharp disagreement arises, for example about an issue like abortion or the balancing of freedom of expression against the provision of some protection against the diffusion of pornography, then the tolerance of judicial determination of such matters may well wear thin. The question will be raised whether judges who are both appointed and politically unaccountable are entitled to determine what many people will continue to regard as political issues which ought to be settled by legislator politicians.

III

The perspectives for the exercise of parliamentary discretion under a regime in which human rights have directive force across the board may not be hopeful, though some kind of adaptation may turn out to be possible. In relation to devolution the impact on Parliament is much more immediate and direct. The purpose of devolutionary schemes is to remove powers from the government in London and from Parliament and to transfer them to devolved assemblies and their executive arms. This has been done in the case of Scotland and

Wales and, most recently, Northern Ireland. The schemes differ in significant ways, but they nevertheless all have one feature in common: they reduce the range of matters that can be raised, debated and voted on in the Westminster Parliament. In the case of the Scottish Parliament there is a delegation of substantial law-making powers over all the functions formerly discharged by the Secretary of State for Scotland and his officials in Edinburgh. Thus the bulk of domestic affairs in Scotland become subject to rule-making in the Scottish Parliament and are to be administered by officials serving the members of the Scottish Executive. A limited tax-raising power has been granted to the Scottish Parliament, but it remains uncertain so far whether and when this power will be used.

In the case of Northern Ireland legislative powers are also being devolved along with the responsibility for the administration of the services concerned, but the range of devolution in Northern Ireland is less wide than it is for Scotland. In particular policing and security are to remain under the authority of the Secretary of State for Northern Ireland, at any rate for the time being. In addition the Northern Ireland Assembly would appear to be totally hobbled by virtue of being tied to an all-party executive which in effect can act only under a near unanimity rule.[7]

As far as Wales goes, the good fairy of devolution has been less generous in the powers handed down. The Welsh Assembly receives no rights to pass primary legislation, which means that it and its executive will be confined to the administration of the domestic affairs devolved to them. The Assembly will, however, be entitled to pass subordinate legislation —in effect statutory instruments—within the framework of the primary powers inherited by it or granted to it in the future by Parliament in London.

This is a very simplified summary of complex legislative provisions. Their implications for Westminster are what concern us here. In the first place, it is clear that all Members of Parliament, regardless of the part of the country they represent, will be generally excluded at Westminster from any

---

[7] The Northern Ireland Assembly and Executive were suspended on 11 February 2000. Despite this setback the British and Irish Governments hope for an early resumption of devolved government in the province.

direct involvement with the future government of three important parts of the United Kingdom. The only exceptions to this appear to be legislation affecting England which is intended to apply in Wales and, presumably, issues relating to the allocation of finance to these parts of the United Kingdom. A further exception will be legislation (primary or secondary) on any reserved matters, *i.e.* functions for which London remains responsible. For many Members of Parliament the most serious aspect of this reduction of their powers will arise not so much from the removal of their legislative responsibilities as from the disappearance of the right to ask questions, to raise matters under a variety of procedures on the floor of the Commons, or to approach ministers directly with matters of concern to them and their constituents. In other words, most of their bread and butter casework is taken away from them.

A second effect of devolution concerns specifically the Members of Parliament representing the devolved nations or provinces. For the most part they cease to have any worthwhile tasks to perform at Westminster. To a large extent they become debarred from raising the grievances of their constituents with United Kingdom ministers, if they sit only at Westminster they have no direct rights of access to the devolved administrations and assemblies, and yet they are expected to turn up in order to cast their votes for measures addressed for the most part to England only. To say the least, this is not a dignified role for representatives in the national Parliament, nor is it likely to command respect. Moreover, the serious reduction in the role of Members of Parliament from the devolved parts of the country is bound to create an imbalance inside the House of Commons. On the one hand there will be Members still responsible in principle at least for public policy and spending in England, a country of over 49 million people, on the other Members who have rights in little more than residual functions for the rest of the United Kingdom. What is more, this imbalance will be accompanied by another one of a rather curious sort. Under the devolution legislation there is no provision for incompatibility of mandates. Members of all the devolved assemblies and members of all the executive bodies set up continue to be entitled to stand for election and to sit as Members of the Westminster Parliament.[8] At the present time there is still a noticeable incidence of dual mandates of this kind: there are, for example, 22 Members of Parliament who also sit in the Scottish Parliament or Welsh Assembly. Perhaps over time this practice will decline, if only for practical reasons. Nevertheless it suggests a cheapening of the Westminster mandate if it can become something like a permission to put in an occasional appearance for people whose main responsibilities lie elsewhere.

A third implication of devolution for Westminster concerns broader political effects, especially on political parties and the organization of political life. How these matters evolve will depend very much on how parties and individuals behave and respond to new circumstances and challenges. But past experience in Northern Ireland as well as the experience of many other countries which have devolution in one form or another do suggest certain likely tendencies. The most obvious of these is simply that political life and parties in those parts of the country with devolution will tend to develop in increasing separation from what goes on in England and in the 'national' parties. Provided this does not lead to serious conflict on policy issues between parties in the devolved areas and the national parties, no great harm might be done by this tendency to separate development. However, it is likely to have one consequence which could ultimately constitute a grave threat to the unity of the United Kingdom. This is simply the likelihood that gradually the UK national parties themselves will attract fewer and fewer members from the devolved areas who aspire to reach high office in national politics or are even of the calibre to hold down national office.

This possibility stands in stark contrast to the current position of the Labour party, whose Scottish members make up about a third of the members of the present Cabinet. As the prestige and interest of service at Westminster declines in the wake of devolution for those in the devolved areas seeking a political career, so there is likely to be a return to something

---

[8] There is legislative provision for the abatement of salaries payable to members of a devolved assembly if they also sit at Westminster or in the European Parliament, for example in the case of the Scottish Parliament in Section 82, Scotland Act 1998.

near to 'all-English' UK Governments, a condition almost reached by the Conservative party by 1992 and which did great damage to that party's overall electoral prospects. Devolution may well encourage a similar trend in all parties regarding themselves as national in scope, and this in turn is bound to weaken the political glue that holds the United Kingdom together.

It is worth making one further remark on devolution. This time round powers have been devolved basically on the principle that everything is devolved except what is reserved to Parliament at Westminster. On the face of it this has the advantage of being a generous principle as far as the devolved institutions go and much simpler than any method of enumerating the devolved powers.[9] But there is a grave inconvenience attaching to it and this is the absence of any balancing principle which defines the obligations of the devolved nations to respect the unity of the realm as a whole. As things stand Scotland in particular could in many spheres go its own way. An example of this is the demand in the new Scottish Parliament for the abolition of the requirement introduced nationally under which students at university become liable to pay tuition fees of £1,000 per year. Since higher education is a function devolved to the Scottish Parliament it would appear on the face of it that it is within its powers to legislate in some way in order to rescind in Scotland and for Scottish students this tuition fee liability. But, of course, it is not as simple as that. What in legal terms is a Scottish student and how does he or she differ from an English or a Welsh student studying at Edinburgh University? How would the Scottish Parliament make good the financial loss to universities in Scotland and would it do so entirely out of revenues raised in Scotland and under its own powers? Above all, how can a measure of this kind intended to benefit Scottish students (however defined) be squared with obligations to respect European Convention rights to fair treatment as well as non-discrimination rights under both British statutes and European Union legislation?

---

[9] In the Scotland Act 1978 the powers devolved to the Assembly in Scotland were listed in detail in Schedule 10, whilst in the Wales Act 1978 there was in Schedule 2 an even more complex division of powers delegated and those not delegated.

Here we do have to face up to the fact that within a single state and political society like the United Kingdom devolution cannot simply imply the right of the devolved institutions to use their powers just as they like. Surely they need to recognize wider obligations to respect the interests of all British citizens, to maintain fairness and equal treatment insofar as this is practicable, and to act with some consideration for the interlocking duties of all governmental institutions and public authorities in the system. Unfortunately the devolution legislation is virtually silent on these matters and seems to provide hardly any basis for the development of the kind of understandings that are essential to cooperation within a devolved system[10] or of a jurisprudence defining mutual obligations.

IV

Parliament has so far figured only modestly in the reform process, and then chiefly through the promise of measures of modernization which tend to reduce rather than enhance its effectiveness. The measure which has so far excited most political attention has been the removal of most of the hereditary members from the House of Lords at the end of 1999. A modest number remain (92 in all) as part of what is said to be a purely 'transitional' arrangement pending such decisions as the Government might at some stage take on the recommendations of the Royal Commission on the Reform of the House of Lords. However, regardless of what might (or might not) happen in relation to the composition of the second chamber, it is unlikely that there will be any early change in its powers or, what is perhaps more important, in the manner in which it exercises them. In other words, there are no grounds for believing that this leg of parliamentary reform will be designed so as to make a significant contribution to strengthening the capacity of Parliament as a whole to check or control

---

[10] Some recognition of the need to develop methods of cooperation appeared in the establishment of a Joint Ministerial Committee involving members of the UK Government and of the administrations in Edinburgh and Cardiff. According to press reports this was initially to work through three sub-committees concerned with particular policy sectors (*Daily Telegraph*, 2 December 1999).

the actions or proposals of the executive and thus to reduce the present imbalance.

What then of the Commons? There has been much talk of modernization and of making the Commons more 'user-friendly' both to its Members and to those who come into contact with it and have business to do there. A Modernization Committee was set up in 1997 and has issued several reports; the Committee on Standards and Members' Interests has been strengthened and is supported by an active and perhaps somewhat intimidating Commissioner to whom, in a manner of speaking, Members now report. But the overall effect of these developments on the authority and effectiveness of the Commons vis-à-vis the Government has been modest indeed.

In part, this is because the procedural changes so far recommended and implemented in the sphere of 'modernization' have been limited and unoriginal. Ideally what the Government would prefer to see (and it would not be the first government to have such hopes) is a smoothly-running, fully timetabled and preferably faster legislative process. This would make life much easier and might even allow the Commons to operate on the basis of much shorter working weeks such as are familiar in many continental European Parliaments. But despite the presence of a very large Government majority it has remained so far impossible to achieve such streamlining of legislative procedures, whilst many Members of Parliament retain an obstinate desire to hang about the place rather than to go off to some harmless pursuit in their constituencies. Not even the working hours have been substantially rationalized, though attendance on Friday mornings is nominal and even on Monday is often rather thin.

It is striking that the reform process makes such halting progress at the very heart of our institutional system. There remains, therefore, an alarming gulf between the claims made on behalf of Parliament, and especially on behalf of the Commons, and the reality of the powers that it regularly exercises. Nor can it be argued nowadays that Parliament has that educative role of which Bagehot wrote well over a century ago or that through its proceedings it shapes public opinion in the manner in which it appeared to do even as recently as 40 years ago. In all this it has been supplanted by the electronic media and a populist press. So insofar as a genuine reform agenda is conceivable, it could only be one for reinvigorating Parliament and for enabling it to recover some influence over public policy and the actions of the Government.

But here we run into many difficulties, two of which in particular must be underlined. The first is that obviously governments, no matter what their members might have said in opposition, rarely have a genuine interest in strengthening Parliament. To do so would simply be to make life more difficult for them. So it is very hard to envisage the executive devising or adopting a serious programme of parliamentary reform, except to the extent that it might involve procedural changes making the conduct of specific types of business more efficient or predictable from the executive point of view. The second point is that during the past 35 years or so innumerable schemes for parliamentary reform have been discussed, proposed and in some degree put into effect. As a result it is now very difficult to discern what might be explored or tried out, at any rate so long as parliamentarians remain within the parameters of traditional procedural assumptions. But to leave some of these assumptions behind would be to begin to redefine the role of Parliament and more particularly of the House of Commons. That is not the kind of venture on which many contemporary constitutional reformers have embarked.

This last remark can be illustrated by one example. The House of Commons knows two kinds of committees (apart from that of the whole House): standing committees and select committees. The former handle legislation after second reading and proceed by debating the bill clause by clause, including such amendments as are put forward and accepted for debate and a vote. Basically select committees take evidence and report. The crucial thing about a standing committee is that a minister is in charge, that he or she wishes and intends to make progress, and that the procedure is essentially adversarial as on the floor of the House. This is not a method that makes it likely that committee members—who are as a rule neither specialized nor permanent—can make much impact on the bill. The truth is, therefore, that standing committees in general contribute little to the final form of the bills which pass through them.

In principle alternative procedures could be devised, all of which would be likely to make standing committees rather more like select committees, to substitute what might be called focused discussion for debate, and to take control of the proceedings out of the hands of the ministers sponsoring the legislation. It is, of course, immediately apparent that despite experiments with special select committees to supplement the work of the standing committees no radical reforms of this kind are imminent. This is because they would threaten the ability of the executive to use its majority whenever it chooses in order to gets its way.

Since this is so it is not surprising that the present Government sticks to very modest changes in the House of Commons, preferring to let it drift along more or less as it is. But, of course, neither the House of Commons nor Parliament as a whole are static. They are bound to be strongly affected by the changes going on within the British system of government, not to speak of the powers which are steadily leeching away to the European Union. The changes discussed here—chiefly in the sphere of human rights and devolution—undoubtedly tend to limit Parliament and to diminish the claims to legislative supremacy made on its behalf. Provided the judicial interpretation of European Convention rights becomes established —and it is not certain that this will happen quickly—Parliament will have to acknowledge that there are substantive limits to what it can enact. It will have to adapt to acceptance of an open-ended code of values which may on occasion be found to be in sharp conflict with what many of its Members regard as politically desirable and practically necessary. However, if the courts find against particular statutes, then in practice Parliament will have to knuckle under and pass the necessary amendments to bring them into line with judicial rulings.

Devolution has larger and more immediate consequences. It withdraws devolved functions from the remit of Parliament and at any rate in practical terms takes away its capacity to use powers which have been retained only in a formal constitutional sense. As a consequence Parliament—or more specifically the House of Commons—has surrendered much of its responsibility for the non-English parts of the United Kingdom. At the same time England is left in something like a constitutional limbo. The Westminster Parliament may de facto often be acting as an English Parliament, but few want to say so openly for fear of undermining its claim still to be the

'Union Parliament' to which a 'Union Government' remains accountable. The consequences of devolution for parties and those who pursue a career in politics in them will, however, come through more slowly and only after many in the present generation of active and successful politicians operating at the national level have stepped down. The ultimate irony of devolution may, however, be a return to exclusively English Governments.

The difficulties of parliamentary reform have already been alluded to. One factor has, however, not been mentioned and it has great relevance to the question whether the legislature could ever be strengthened in relation to the executive. This is the survival of parliamentarians in the sense of Members of Parliament who retain some independence of judgment and understand how to use the resources of parliamentary procedure to pursue their varied concerns. If the Commons has over many years become weaker, then this is to a significant extent a consequence of the declining spirit of independence of its members and their surrender to the demands of party discipline. They have become professional politicians in a very straightforward sense, with most of them wholly dependent on the income derived from holding a seat and gaining office. What is more, recent measures introduced before the Blair Government came into office to enforce the public declaration of interests on Members and to subject them to a regime of external supervision of such interests have reinforced the belief that Members can no longer be trusted to police themselves, and that anyway the fewer external interests they have the better.

The latest step is to legislate on party funding in line with many of the recommendations of the Neill Committee.[11] Essentially these measures will have the effect of making it harder for parties to secure private funding. Yet what is always overlooked in the pursuit of such policies is that an austere regime of this sort can only accelerate the professionalization of politics and all the accompanying negative consequences for the health of parliamentary institutions. In such

---

[11] Fifth Report of the Committee on Standards in Public Life (Chairman Lord Neill): *The Funding of Political Parties in the United Kingdom*, Cm 4057-I, HMSO 1998.

conditions it becomes ever more difficult to regard the parliamentarian in the more traditional mould as anything other than an anachronism, a species on the verge of extinction.

Here is a problem to which the modernization movement in the Commons has devoted virtually no attention, and for understandable reasons. For to revive the ideal of a parliamentarian with independent judgment would pose a threat to the very politicians who have done best in the professional stakes. This may, at any rate subconsciously, be one of the reasons why a significant number of politicians and party managers have sympathy for two further measures often advocated as 'reforms'. One of these is a shift to electoral provisions based on the principle of proportional representation. Its main effect would be to increase the security of tenure of those elected and, as a rule, the ability of party managers to steer the selection of candidates and their subsequent career prospects. The other is the introduction and extension of public funding for political parties. Such a step would also make life far easier for party managers, as well as putting the seal of approval on what would then tend to become publicly funded oligarchies. So much then for the dream of democratization!

Parliament has been the instrument by which important constitutional changes requiring legislation have been made during the past two years or so. These measures have decisively altered the context within which Parliament has to operate and imposed upon it many new constraints and limitations. But Parliament itself, apart from the issue of the composition of the House of Lords, has not been central to the wider reform project. Indeed, the House of Commons has had the status of a residual element in the mosaic of reforms. By now it can hardly be doubted that Parliament has been left behind by much that has been done. It has lost powers and is subject to the enervating impact of the thorough-going professionalization of political life.

But in addition to the impact of the institutional changes discussed here there has also been the effect of purely political developments which it has not been possible to consider in this essay. Most important of these has been the presence of a Government with an overwhelming party majority. This has created a situation which makes it all the more difficult for Parliament as a whole to make a reality of its traditional functions—critical debate, scrutiny and control. At the same time the Opposition has been so severely weakened that one of the basic features of parliamentary politics, that is to say, the dialectic of the competition for public opinion between the Government and the alternative Government, seems to be called into question. In such circumstances it is hardly surprising that the appearances of Ministers before what was once regarded as 'the grand inquest of the nation' have shown signs of becoming ever more perfunctory. Increasingly the House of Commons begins to look like a chamber on the verge of being pensioned off to enjoy a quiet life.

Bernard Weatherill

The Law of Unexpected Consequences

Bernard Weatherill invited **Anthony Freeman** *to meet in the House of Lords to discuss informally the role of the Westminster Parliament and its relations with other bodies. He began by reflecting on the inter-relatedness of the elements that make up Parliament.*

In my modest contributions here, I often draw attention to 'the law of unexpected consequences'. Parliament is a whole – both the Lower House and the Upper House – and you can't really make changes in one part without having an effect on another. A very good example of this is the Jopling reforms in the Commons. Michael Jopling was the Chief Whip when I was the Speaker, and as a senior member of the House he was asked by the Commons to see if he could rationalize their hours, which he did. They now sit on Wednesday mornings and no debate goes on after ten o'clock at night. On Thursdays they rise about seven and they don't very often sit on Fridays and it has made it very much easier for them. But it has added vastly to the hours worked in this part of the building. In one of the debates on the reform of the House of Lords it was said that in a recent session of parliament the Lords sent down 4,000 amendments! Well it is our job to amend Bills and polish them up and make them better, but the reason we send down so many is that they have not been properly scrutinized in the Commons. They have not been dealt with.

So you cannot make changes in one part of this building without affecting another. We are currently concerned with the reform of the Lords – and I accept that you have got to start somewhere — but it should not stop here. Thereafter the Royal Commission must turn itself to the Commons because, given that we have devolution in Scotland and Wales and in Northern Ireland, there's no reason why we shouldn't face squarely the West Lothian Question.[1] The Scots are already over-represented in terms of the constituencies. The Boundary Commission, which is a non-party group, carves up the constituencies and makes them broadly equal at around about 80–90,000 voters. But in Scotland some of them are as little as half that number because the areas are much greater. So they are over-represented in Westminster at the moment and, given that they now have their own parliament, their numbers should be reduced. I think there is a very good case for cutting down the size of the House of Commons by at least a third by adjusting the boundaries to about 100,000 electors.

I don't imagine that would be very popular with the Members. How can one MP adequately handle the concerns of 100,000 constituents?

The way things are organized now it is already impossible for MPs to cope with the constituency workload. But that is because they are being asked to do things which are no business of theirs. It really is essential to return to local authorities the powers that have been taken from them by successive governments.[2] Then, not only will MPs be released to do their proper job, local councillors will have the value and dignity of their office restored to them.

At the moment something like 85 per cent of all local government money comes from Westminster — we have rate capping and all those sorts of things — so you could hardly call it 'local'. One of the reasons why in days past we had to get rid of the Greater London Council was that it had no powers left, and decent people won't serve on local government bodies unless there is some power attached to them and something for them to do. So we didn't get very good people and in the end we abolished it. I don't say the same thing has happened in local government in general, because I think there are some

[1]　See Tam Dalyell, page 259, this volume [ed.].
[2]　See Simon Jenkins, page 246, this volume [ed.].

very good people there. But it would be even better if they were responsible for raising their own money. My view is that in a democracy local councils should by and large be responsible for raising their own money — not entirely, because there are regional differences and wealthier areas sometimes need to help out the less well off — but local authorities should raise the bulk of their own resources. Then if the local electorate doesn't like it, they won't re-elect them. That way you will get very much better people sitting on these councils.

Then we have got to stop Members of Parliament touting for business. When I entered parliament in 1964 I succeeded Admiral Hughes-Hallett, who got in at a by-election in the 1950s. He told me about going to see Churchill, who actually said to him, 'Well, Admiral, I hope you're not going to demean yourself by canvassing or anything like that'. To which Duncan Sandys, a Cabinet Minister in that administration, said, 'Well, Prime Minister, times have changed and I do think the Admiral will have to canvas a little', to which Churchill replied 'Well, I hope at least you never set up in the medical business'. By that he meant, 'I hope you won't have a 'surgery' '. Today we all have constituency surgeries and in effect we lay ourselves open to taking on board what are largely local authority questions. I would say that in my former constituency at least two-thirds of the problems were really matters for the local authority and not for me. That should stop.

When I became the Speaker the attendance at my surgeries were vastly increased. People would come to see me just for a chat or would get me to sign things for their grandchildren — a whole range of things — and I was frightfully busy. I said to a man one day, who wanted a council house, 'I don't think I am going to be able to help you'. He said, 'What do you mean, you might not be able to help me?' I said, 'Look, I have a lot of people to see. Could I just explain that if it were called *parliamentary* housing, then I would be able to help you, but actually it's called *council* housing. That really means it is a matter for the local council. If you go into the next-door room with this lady who is a councillor she will be delighted to help you.' He looked at me and poked me in the chest and said, 'Look 'ere, mate, you're paid to do it!' As I was so busy I took it all down and so did she — she sat with me — and she then wrote to me and I wrote to him. It's ridiculous. It's a terrible waste of time.

So what do you think that Members of Parliament ought to be doing?

They should be holding the Government to account, and this relates directly to the previous question. When I was Speaker I got very very few letters about bad behaviour – it's an absolute myth that behaviour in the Commons is bad, in fact it's historically better that its ever been – but I got a lot of letters about the empty Chamber. I used to have to explain that most MPs were present, but they were in their offices answering letters. Here is a very significant statistic: I checked with the postmaster for a debate we had recently who told me that 40,000 letters come into the Palace of Westminster every day. Members are too often beavering away, basically on matters that don't really concern them and should not be coming to them, so they are not in the Chamber and in the process Governments can get away with murder – or could get away with murder!

So what should the Members be doing? The role of an MP is to hold the Government to account. You can't do that if you're not there! Last week the Commons had two days off because it was the schools' half term. What was wrong about that was that the Government went on without anybody questioning them. They don't take time off. I quote Mr Gladstone, speaking to his own supporters: 'It is not your job to run the country; it is your duty to hold to account those who do.' That is the proper role of an MP...

...and that entails being in the Chamber, listening to the debates and asking awkward questions...

Exactly. Returning to local authorities the power to get on with their own business would free 'at a stroke' the Members of Parliament to be in the Chamber to carry out their duty to hold the Government to account. The type of person that is coming into the Commons these days is a professional politician and I think they should be treated as professional politicians. By that I mean that they should be paid rather more than they are, then they should not be tempted to have outside consultancies.

*Reference to 'outside connections' will raise in many peoples' minds
the whole question of undue influence and 'sleaze'. Do you regard
that as a serious problem?*

In my day there was very little sleaze and it was always dealt
with by the House. In my view Nolan was a mistake and quite
unnecessary, though I understand why it was done.

It's always been thus. I was the Deputy Chief Whip for six
years — I was a whip for twelve years and I guess that's a
record — and I remember doing an investigation into the whipping system. The Chief Whip was still called the Patronage
Secretary and until the middle of the last century he received
£10,000 a year from Secret Service funds for which he was not
accountable. It was straight bribery. In the Speaker's house
there were wonderful letters that had been preserved from
Members of Parliament, who would write such things as, 'I
would like the Customs at Harwich'. Speakers had the gift of
the Customs at Harwich!

Arthur Onslow was the greatest of all the Speakers and he
received a handout from the government and of course was a
government man. He was Speaker for 33 years but after his
first ten years he gave up all patronage and became totally
independent and impartial. It was said that at the end of the 33
years, so great was his prestige and the cleanliness of his political life that it raised the whole prestige of parliament. One
man. So corruption has always been there and we've always
dealt with it ourselves.

I remember when I was Speaker one Member had let the
side down. He had taken money for asking a question so I sent
for him and I asked if it was true. He said, 'No' and I said,
'Well, we'd better have a look at this', and then he admitted it
was true. I told him to go and see his doctor and have it confirmed that his health had deteriorated to the extent that he
could no longer remain in Parliament. Then he was to apply
immediately for the Chiltern Hundreds. He asked why he
should do that, and I told him: in that way his own honour
would not be impugned, his family would not be affected, but
also — of far greater importance — the great institution of
parliament would not be brought into disrepute.

Whips of all sides co-operated, through 'the usual channels'. A government with a majority has the right to get

through its business, but that must be balanced by an equal right of the Opposition to criticize. This is arranged 'through the usual channels' and it's a highly sophisticated system. There is no other parliament where weekly business is discussed in such a way and arrangements decided by the usual channels — 'Will it be convenient to have this bill on Monday?' 'Well, our people won't be quite ready for it, could we have it next week?' There is no other parliament in the world where once a week the government offers a day of its business to the opposition parties, which may be used to debate a motion critical of the government. And I know of no other country in which the opposition parties are paid in order to make their opposition more effective. It is highly sophisticated and it works extremely well. So I think the institution of parliament is more important than any of the individual people here. The role of parliament is to act as a searchlight, to expose exactly what is going on. If you had a Speaker who was not completely impartial it could be bent one way or another. It would be very difficult to find out. But Speakers don't. They give up party politics for life and underpinning the independence of the chair is the certain knowledge that the Speaker of the day will never get another political job. You get a modest pension and get sent to the Lords. What is more that peerage doesn't come from Number Ten. According to Tony Benn, I am the only legitimate Peer here: beacause my peerage arises from a motion on the order paper of the House of Commons, requesting her Majesty to grant it as a mark of 'her royal favour and approbation'. So it's a House of Commons' Peerage. That also underpins one's independence. So the Chamber of the House of Commons is a searchlight that exposes for the public exactly what is going on. In my speeches these days I regularly say, 'Look, be critical as you like of those who are in the parliamentary arena, but don't ever be cynical of the institution which exposes to you what is happening'.

If there were less MPs you could afford to pay each one more. But it would take more than higher pay to encourage high-calibre people into parliament. They would need to exercise their talents and gain job satisfaction.

I would make the chairmanship of select committees highly prestigious. The average Member of Parliament knows that he will not be called by the Speaker more than four times a year in a debate. Half the problem—on the occasions when there is bad behaviour in the Commons—is the temptation to signal to constituents, 'I am here but the Speaker has not called me.' There is a feeling that service on committees reduced even further the chances of being called. People used to come to me and say in relation to a debate, 'Mr Speaker, Sir, do you think I could be called before five o'clock', and I would say, 'Well, Anthony, the front benches will hardly be over by five o'clock and I can't guarantee... '. 'Well my select committee meets, you see, at five o'clock'. And I would say, 'Well I think you had better go to your select committee'. During my time I organized a change in procedure which allowed me to call members between six and eight, or seven and nine, if they had not been in the Chamber for the opening speeches of the debate, to make a 10 minute speech. This allowed Members who had been at select committees to come in and make a contribution. But they hadn't listened to the debate—therefore it wasn't really a contribution to the debate. They were just making statements in order to get something on the record, without having heard the arguments. The obvious temptation is to go to a select committee, which is televised, and ask a question of a minister and get on the record in that way. I think the select committees do excellent work, and furthermore there's not much party politics in their deliberations.

Chairmanship of select committees is already prestigious and I would make it even more so. I would treat the chairmen like junior ministers; pay them—put them on the same salary as a parliamentary secretary—and give them a car to take them home afterwards, because they are having to do a lot of home work. Ensure that people want to come on to a select committee and they would become more expert at it too. If they did this they would specialize in certain subjects and therebt they would become better investigators into what's gone wrong. In my time Departmental Select Committees started in what were called the St John Stevas Reforms. Well done to Mrs Thatcher for setting them up, because very few Prime Ministers positively set out to make life more difficult for themselves, but she did. These departmental select com-

mittees monitor a government department. When they started
I used to go upstairs to listen to them and I found the wit-
nesses — especially the civil servants — got away with murder
because the members were not expert in asking the right prob-
ing questions. But gradually they became much more expert
and now they are very expert indeed. To take a good example,
I think David Howell, who was Secretary of State for Energy,
was far more influential and respected — infinitely more — as
the Chairman of the Select Committee on Foreign Affairs than
he was as a minister.

I would like to see matters arranged so that for major events
the committees would always break and return to the Chamber. The Chamber should be the forum of the nation again,
because that's televised and it does go out on the media. The
Parliamentary Channel has now been taken over by the BBC
and with digital TV there will be a dedicated channel for
anyone to watch parliamentary proceedings all day long if
they wish.

*This emphasis on holding the Government to account raises the
question of the large number of MPs on the Government side holding
some form of ministerial post and therefore effectively silenced.*

That is a very important point. As I say, most of the MPs now
are professionals. Many have been research assistants to ministers and for most of them it's a career. If I may give you a very
important quotation from Edmund Burke: 'There can be no
independence of mind without independence of means.' As
professional politicians few have now got independent
means, although my proposed upgrading of the role of the
committees and their chairmen ought to make MPs less
dependent on the favours of their party leaders. Reducing the
numbers of junior ministers and parliamentary secretaries — which has gone up enormously since the 'ministerial
inflation' begun by Harold Wilson — would be another step in
the right direction.

But you have to ask yourself whether these 'professional
politicians' are the right people to run a big department.
Should we not, in an overall reform of our parliamentary system to take us into the twenty-first century, consider giving
the Prime Minister a wider choice of people for his adminis-

tration? Fortunately Tony Blair has got some very bright people, whereas John Major was left with a very poor hand — his predecessor had sacked most with talent and they were not prepared to come back — and I am afraid that it did show. I think the Prime Minister should have a much wider choice, as does an American President.

It's a convention here that ministers can't come up to the Lords to answer questions or make statements, but that could easily be arranged. I think the Prime Minister could draw in ministers from the real world outside and put them in the Lords — as Blair has done it. I think the calibre of ministers up here is rather better than down there, partly because these ministers are older and have had more experience...

...also, if they haven't got constituency mailbags to worry about, they can get on with the job...

Well that's one of the advantages of the House of Lords. Here we speak for ourselves and on our honour. Now [at the time of writing] we don't know what the Royal Commission is going to recommend but the Government has said repeatedly that in future no political party will have a majority in the House of Lords, *i.e.* that the balance of influence will be left with the cross-benches. The cross-benchers will be appointed, not by Number Ten, but by a totally independent Commission. I know there are members on the Tory benches who are suspicious of the Government's intentions, but I am taking them absolutely at face value and I wholly support them. I think its essential to remove these appointments from the realm of 'cronyism'.

But why have a second chamber at all if the scrutiny in the first chamber is being done as it should?

The role of the second chamber is still important, because it can question, and ask the Commons to think again. That is why we have the Parliament Act, which is very rarely operated — until I did it with war crimes it hadn't been operated for thirty years I suppose — but now it has become fairly regular. It is a very delicate instrument and the Lords should remember that, but it does give the Government and the Commons an opportunity to think again and that's the real value of it. Furthermore because Members of the Lords have not got a constituency, they don't have to play to the gallery. If they become elected members they will tend to do so and it will be much more political than it has been in the past.

Lord Crook, who is a cross-bench Peer and formerly Chief Justice in New Zealand, made a telling speech in the House of Lords (Reform) Bill. In New Zealand they went down this road and their Senate became a reflection of the Lower House — a place where 'old boys' could end their lives — and according to him the New Zealanders thought that it was a waste of money and the Senate was irrelevant. So they did away with it. Lord Crook said that since this occurred there had been a case where a Bill was introduced on Wednesday and it became law on Friday. The dangers of a single chamber are colossal because a government with a big majority (we've already got an elected dictatorship anyway) could be a total dictatorship. So that is the real reason for a second chamber, to ask the Lower House to think again, and also of course to participate by amending and improving legislation. The other important function of the second chamber is to have general debates on subjects unlikely to be raised in the Commons — to quote a recent example 'the role of the family in society'.

I can give you an example of the changing atmosphere in the Upper House. Just before Christmas, one of the old Labour Peers — a Life Peer who's been here for ever — said to me:

> 'Ere, Bernard, do you know that last night I went for
> a drink in the bar, one of them new Peers came up to
> me and started talking politics!

I am [at the time of writing] the Convenor of the cross-benchers in the Lords. Robert Cranbourne gave me a drink just before the 1997 election, and he said that something had been intriguing them. He said, 'Do the cross-benchers issue a whip?' I said, 'No', and he said, 'Well we can't understand why we are always being defeated. Since you came in as Convenor we seem to have been defeated far more often. You haven't been telling them what to do have you?' 'Well', I said, 'that would be very reprehensible, wouldn't it? We are all totally independent. But if you want to know why you have been defeated, it's to do with your policies.' He said, 'What do you mean?' So I explained: if anyone comes to me and says, 'Look, have we got a line on this or that?' I say they had better go into the Chamber and listen to the argument. 'Gosh', he said, 'you don't do that do you?' The result is that people here listen to the argument. I would never have got my amendment to the Firearms Bill in 1997 if there had been a strong whip as there is in the Commons. Nowadays you're not allowed to disobey the whip in the House of Commons. You'd not get reselected — in effect chucked out. In my day we did our best to keep people in line, but we couldn't do much about it. My ultimate threat as a Whip was to say, 'What you have done is very serious: you do that again and I'll have you put on a parliamentary delegation to...!' But we couldn't do much about it; we couldn't withdraw their licence.

If you have beefed up councils for local government, as you want, and you have regional assemblies in Wales and Scotland – and possibly English ones as well – and you have Westminster, and you have something in Europe, either the present system or something akin to it...

...then we are in danger of being over-governed!

There is certainly a danger of the buck stopping nowhere – would you concede that?

Well, we have not got a written constitution so we can do what we like. Here it is possible to introduce a bill and get it through in one day — I have seen it done, but it would be an emergency measure. I would say that in the new House of Lords that the regions should be represented, probably by election and probably by proportional representation. And also the European Parliament. When I was the Deputy Chief Whip I persuaded members of the House of Commons to have a dual mandate, because it enabled them to come back to the Chamber of the House of Commons and tell us what was happening in Europe. You don't get that now. We are completely cut off from the European Parliament. In those days it was not called a Parliament it was called an Assembly, and it still is an assembly, not a parliament as we know it. They sit by political groupings, not by countries, and although people got very fussed about the 'closed list' I don't think it is a bad idea. We do not want it in this country, but in Europe there's quite a good case for it. I went down to Croydon, when these debates were going on, and I said to old friends there, 'Who's our MEP?' They hadn't got a clue. It was bad luck on James Moorehouse — whose constituency was about 200,000 — because he was quite assiduous, but nobody knew him. So I think there is quite a good case, since they do sit by parties, that you should elect Conservatives to sit with Conservatives. I think the conduct of the Lords was quite wrong — and I said so several times — to thwart the will of the Commons on this. Of course it was called cronyism and we know why the Labour Party did it — to get rid of people they didn't like — but that was not the point.

Does that mean that you think that the senior position of Westminster vis-à-vis both Europe and local government is actually secure? Because a lot of people do get fussed about this.

No. With regard to Europe I do get fussed about it. This is another very important role of both Houses of Parliament. The directives pour out of Brussels, often untranslated — I cannot begin to tell you the number of times people in the Commons came up with 'Point of order, Mr Speaker. Why are we debating this directive at this time of night when it was all agreed and decided three weeks ago in Brussels and we cannot influence it.' The answer is that the Honourable Member was quite right, but that the Government had put this down for discussion and we must proceed with it — even though it had already been decided.

We have in the House of Lords European committees that are absolutely superb, they are infinitely better than anything they have in the Commons. We have a designated Deputy Speaker, the Deputy Lord Chairman of Committees, specifically for Europe and we have a whole range of committees looking into European directives and bringing them to our attention — not least the one of fraud, on which I once served.

Is that done at a point where something can still be done about the directives?

We have debates on them and we can put pressure on the Government, but the danger of all of this is that it is by qualified majority voting now. Our freedoms were signed away by Mrs Thatcher in the Single European Act, which allowed for majority voting. A Labour MP came to me and said, 'Mr Speaker, you have simply got to stop this. The Government is putting this through under a guillotine [two-day debate] they simply don't know what they are doing, they are signing away our freedoms—you have got to stop it, Sir'. I said, 'Well, I totally agree with you, but it's in order for them to do it and although it is highly dangerous I cannot stop it. However I will arrange for you to go and see Margaret Thatcher'. I did that, and he went up to No. 10 and she said, 'I know all about it, but I've got such a good repayment of our dues—I can't possibly put that in jeopardy. So it has got to go through. Besides, I am absolutely sure I will never allow any of these things to happen'. Well in the event she was no longer in No. 10. It was an Act of Parliament. The Maastricht treaty merely dotted the 'i's and crossed the 't's. It had all been signed away in the Single European Act. It was a classic example of the guillotine being used with inadequate discussion. She suddenly realized, especially after she lost, what she had done, and in the Maastricht debate here railed against it all. I didn't like to get up and say, 'Well it's your fault'. Tebbit was man enough to say it was their fault.

Europe is a very difficult problem and I suspect that economically we may have to join the single currency. I am very concerned about the political implications of it, but I am prejudiced because I don't relish the fact that the Speaker of the United Kingdom, with 800 years of history, is going to be about as relevant as the former chairman of the Greater London Council. I asked my constituency in Croydon back in 1978 if they wanted to join the European Economic Community. I never did ask them whether they wanted to join the European Union and no one has ever put that question. The term European Union was introduced by the Commission in Europe, not by us. It was a unilateral decision that 'We are going to call ourselves the European Union'. No one has ever asked the

British public whether they wanted to join the European Union and I suspect they would say 'No' at the moment. The reason I say that is this: is it wise, at a moment when we see, for instance, what is happening in Yugoslavia, with people speaking different languages and different ethnic groups feeling they are not getting a fair deal. Are my people in Croydon going to be happy paying for French pensions that are not properly funded? I see in this all the seeds of dissension in days to come.

So what should be the role of the public in all this? Lobbying and so forth?

That is very important, but it must be done in the right way at the right time — for instance, in relation to the City of London. I used to say to my friends in the City — and I used to describe myself as a businessman in politics (I came from trade as a tailor) — the first thing you have got to do if you are a businessman is to read the manifesto. When Ken Livingstone was reigning supreme in County Hall I spoke to a group of actuaries who were being pretty critical of Ken Livingstone. I remember saying to them he had every right to do it because it was in his manifesto. They asked, 'Who ever reads the manifesto?' and I said, 'You jolly well should'. You must read the manifesto: that tells you what the government is going to do. And of course there's a bit at the end that says, 'other measures will be brought before you . . .', but I don't know of a Government that hasn't carried out its manifesto *in toto* if it runs a full Parliament. They do — it's their prospectus. So read it, pick out the Bills that are likely to affect you and start lobbying — before they are printed. Once it has been printed it's quite difficult to change it because that has to be done by amendment. Bring pressure to bear early. There is *nothing* wrong with lobbying *at all*, and everything right with it. That's why 'the Central Lobby' in the Palace of Westminster has that name.

Then listen to the Queen's Speech because that will tell you in that session exactly what is going to happen. Then, when the Bill comes up affecting your business, put your television on. Alert your parliamentary people — particularly if there is an amendment down that affects your firm — and listen to what they are saying. Then bring your pressures to bear on your MPs.

There is a good example in the Firearms (Amendment) Bill. After Dunblane the Conservative Government had brought in a bill saying that all handguns had to be handed in and that anybody who had anything to do with young people would have to be vetted against a police record to make sure they were 'safe'. The cost would be between eight and twelve pounds— say ten pounds—a head. I went to see Michael Howard [then Home Secretary] and said, 'Are you in favour of volunteering?' 'Of course we are', he said. 'Well, you are going to slit its throat by this', I said. 'Volunteers will not pay ten pounds a head. The Scouts tell me it's going to cost them £750,000.' He replied that his information was different and that the volunteers would pay. I came back here and went to my cross-bench meeting upstairs and fortunately there was a bishop present. He asked whether Sunday School teachers would be affected by this, and we looked into it and of course they were. 'Well', I said to him, 'do you think Sunday School teachers will pay ten pounds a head for the privilege of looking after children? They'd be up in arms over it!'

I then put down an amendment to this Bill. Here in the House of Lords and the Government put a whip against me. I made an impassioned plea, supported by the Labour Party and the Liberals, and thanks to the defections of the Tories I succeeded. I won!

Sadly I have subsequently heard that the present Labour Government, although it supported me in opposition, was going to bring it back again. I rang up Jack Straw's secretary and she said that he was so busy he wouldn't be able to see me for some weeks. I said, 'Just remind Mr Straw that I am a former Speaker of the House of Commons, that there are thousands of Scouts, Guides, Cubs and Brownies in this country, and thousands of people who go to Sunday School, and just remind him that this amounts to a lot of votes. I think he may wish to see me before we get too far down this rather dangerous road.' She said, 'I will ring you back…' And, of course, he did see me, accompanied by the chief executive of the Scouts and a bishop.

So there is nothing wrong with lobbying, everything right with it, but its important to get in early before it's enshrined in legislation, when the government may not accept an amendment. That's quite a good example of what I think the partnership between MPs, the House of Lords and the general public ought to be about.

Michael Spicer

Socialism on the Sly:

The new parallel government of the regulators

The Prime Minister rightly sees his successful campaign to abolish Clause Four of the Labour Party constitution as the turning point in the fortunes of his party. The scrapping of Clause Four enabled Mr Blair to campaign in the 1997 General Election at the head of a party that appeared to have turned its back on its socialist heritage and now accepted all the benefits of the market economy.

However, just as his pledge not to increase income tax has been bypassed by a welter of indirect 'stealth taxes', his commitment to the market has been undermined by a dramatic increase in the power of regulatory bodies. Why should the state bother to own and manage businesses when it can control what they do more effectively through an army of regulators? The Financial Services and Markets Bill and the Utilities Bill, both currently passing through Parliament are prime examples of this new form of government: rule by regulator.[1]

Very few people appreciate yet the full implication of what is going on. Costing the taxpayer hundreds of millions of pounds, regulatory bodies are being set up to control all the 'commanding heights' of the economy — telecommunications, the postal services, water, electricity, gas, rail and, above all, financial services. The heads of these regulatory bodies will have enormous new powers over the industries they control.

---

[1] Michael Spicer, 'Coming next: the new state planners', *Daily Telegraph*, 25 January 2000.

In the name of consumer protection the Financial Services Authority (FSA) will be able largely to determine a list of 'financial crimes', to judge whether these have been committed and to lay down the penalties when it finds an organization 'guilty'. The penalties can include imprisonment. The FSA will have the powers to determine the precise nature of the business of any company or institution in the City of London. The other regulatory bodies will be given similar powers through price controls and other measures to determine business decisions in the industries they cover.

In the same way that Gordon Brown's 'stealth taxes' have mostly targeted businesses, the new self-financing regulatory agencies (Sefras) charge a levy on those that they regulate. In some cases — the most notorious being the charges imposed by the meat hygiene agency on small craft slaughterhouses — the costs can be such as to bankrupt whole sectors of the industry. The largest Sefra is the Environment Agency (employing 10,300 officials), set up largely to implement EC directives. Of the £623 million it plans to spend in 2000, £450 million will be recovered in charges and levies on businesses.[2]

The genesis of this regulatory form of government lay in the desire of the last administration to prevent previously nationalized industries from operating as monopolies. As such it was a necessary interim measure to smooth the transition from state monopoly to a genuine free market. The medium-term aim was to increase competition and, as this came about, to diminish the powers of the regulator.[3]

As I was the Minister who piloted the 1989 Electricity Act through Committee, I would like to compare it with the Utilities Bill of the current administration. The 1989 Act is highly representative of the previous Conservative Government's whole approach to the utilities and their regulation. The changes to that legislation included in the current Bill are

[2] Christopher Booker, *Sunday Telegraph*, 23 January 2000.
[3] Similarly the capping of local taxation was intended only as an interim measure to combat the huge rate rises levied by some councils, safe in the knowledge that most of their electors were protected by social security. Conservative policy was to replace the cap in the longer term with a revitalized system of local democracy, but that proved harder to implement in practice than in theory.

equally representative of the Labour Government's approach to those matters.

The general idea behind the 1989 Act was to privatize electricity in such a way as to maximize competition over time and, as that increased competition occurred, so to diminish those powers of the regulator. Over time regulation would give way to competition as the best means of protecting the consumer. Several features of privatization helped to meet that objective. The structure militated against the vertically-integrated franchise — the American model. We were against that model, because we did not want vertically- integrated local monopolies. We began with a brave move — we broke up the Central Electricity Generating Board into about five separate players.

However, most important was the fact that we built into the measure a dynamic towards near-perfect competition in an industry to which competitive pressures were extremely difficult to apply. We did that in such a way that not only were there new entrants to generating but the distribution and supply companies were subject to competitive pressures. By 1998, those companies were selling in and out of each others' markets and were entirely free from restrictions on competition, as had been planned at the outset.

The regulator was chosen, not only for his personality but as someone who had competition at the front of his mind. Professor Stephen Littlechild was the nearest thing to a competition expert who could be found at that time. He has now been replaced by someone who, whatever his merits — and Callum McCarthy has great merits — is really a high-flying civil servant. He is interested in politics and in the ways of Whitehall, but he has no experience of the marketplace, nor any particular interest in it.

Another part of the process of setting up a competitive industry was the establishment of a transparent pricing system. The pool may have had its faults but it was a transparent system which the Government now intends to scrap and replace with a system in which bilateral agreements are to be struck behind closed doors. Nobody knows how the contracts will be assured and there is no way of guaranteeing security of supply.

Let us consider a plausible example in which a contract with a large supplier of coal-based electricity receives the Government's blessing. It is more than likely that such a contract already exists. That electricity could be extremely expensive but it fits in with the Government's intention to continue to protect the coal industry. Who knows how that contract came about? Who knows what factors lay behind it? Who knows whether there are political objectives behind it? Nobody knows because a new system of secret pricing is emerging. The truth is that the Labour Government does not like the market-based system that we provided; they like intervening and interfering, particularly to protect certain sectors of the industry with which they have connections.

The effect of the competitive pressure that was built into the 1989 Act has been dramatic. In 1991, two companies — National Power and PowerGen — betweeen them held 74% of the generating market. By 1998 National Power's share was down to 13% from 46% — it is set to fall to 8% in 2000 — and PowerGen's share is currently at 14%, down from 28% in 1991. The two biggest players now have only 22% of the highly competitive generating market between them. Today 30 generators use the pool, as opposed to the five or so who used it regularly at the time that it was set up.

The electricity market has been transformed into a highly competitive market, so why is there a need for a new Bill? The answer is that competition is no longer the Government's primary objective in their regulatory approach to the utilities. The scene is set by the proposed new section 3A (l) in clause 12:

> The principal objective of the Secretary of State and the Authority in carrying out their respective functions under this Part is to protect the interests of consumers in relation to the supply of electricity, wherever appropriate by promoting effective competition.

'Wherever appropriate' is the qualification attached. In the name of 'competition' and by using consumers as a 'human shield', the Government will create a whole new set of regulatory objectives. Clause 12 of the Bill introduces the concept of income distribution, a concept that has nothing to do with competition or electricity. It is questionable whether giving people access to electricity on special terms is the best way to help the disabled and those of pensionable age or on low incomes.

In effect the Bill will create the need for a whole new almoning system in parallel with the social security system. It is wasteful and untransparent to help people in need by regulation and through industry. It raises the question why one set of electricity consumers will have to pay more to subsidize other sections of the community. Would it not be much better to do that through the taxation system or through a more transparent use of benefits?

If the requirement is to subsidize rural communities, that should be done through direct Government subventions in a way that does not distort the market. When the previous Government privatized the bus industry, we made a clear distinction between economic costings and social subventions, which were made through financial means, and proper pricing, which should reflect costs and the marketplace. That is a manifestly sensible way to support the people whom one wants to support but without distorting the market system.

Of course the way in which social benefits and payments are made is a matter for the Government of the day to determine, in line with their manifesto commitments. However, in the electricity industry one set of consumers, some of whom may be poor or deprived but not specifically listed in the Bill, should not subsidize another. That is socialism by the back door, rather than through the ballot box.

Using the example of electricity I have described how since 1989 competition has increased enormously, but under this government this has been accompanied by vastly *increased* powers for the regulator. Competition has ceased to be the limited objective of regulation. Regulators are no longer the guardians of market forces so much as unelected commissars, who apply a widening range of policies which invariably are themselves anti-competitive.

Thus the rail regulator concerns himself with an 'integrated' transport strategy and the FSA is working on rules to develop 'social banking' — the compulsory extension of banking to the two million people who hitherto have not wanted to have bank accounts. The same principle is to be applied by Oftel to telephones—there is to be universal coverage whatever the economic implications. The Post Office regulator has been set the task of determining the level of privatization in postal services and of ensuring, in the words of the minister Alan Johnson, that they meet 'crucial social obligations'. The water regulator has set himself the objective of lowering the dividends paid to investors in water by forcing companies to cut water rates, whatever the effect on investment in water pipes and sewerage. The electricity regulator is setting electricity and gas companies the task of addressing what he calls 'fuel poverty'.

All those regulators are being given social and political objectives, which are antithetical to competition. We are witnessing a parallel system of government emerging. I shall use the idiom 'joined up' because, in their consultation paper *A Fair Deal for Consumers*, the Government suggest having a cabinet of regulators who would work out together each industry's capacity to achieve the various political objectives, which have no bearing on competition. The political imperatives will be provided by the Government and the regulator will implement them with all-pervasive powers of intervention.

None of this has much to do with economics, let alone with competition; most of it is about income redistribution and social policy. If socialism means central intervention and control of the main sectors of industry, then this is certainly socialism without the necessity for public ownership—socialism on the sly—nationalization by the back door.[4] I hope that one of the first objectives of a future Conservative Government will be to dismantle all the regulatory apparatus, except for that

[4]   Although New Labour appears to be committed to private ownership and competition in industry and commerce, it is quite clear from their policy announcements in other areas that this commitment is only skin deep. Although it was a Conservative administration that introduced the National Curriculum and Ofsted to raise standards in schools, most Conservatives recognized that it was the freeing of schools from LEA control and the empowering of parents to vote with their feet that would drive up standards in the longer term. However, as soon as New Labour gained power, the slogan 'standards not structures' was put into practice by ending the system of opting out and introducing far more proscriptive management of the classroom from Whitehall than the previous administration would have dared to contemplate. Ofsted have now suggested that their regulatory powers should be increased to include the inspection of childminders in their own homes.

which focuses on competition because competition is the true friend of the consumer.

The personalities who now head up this parallel form of government reflect the new ethos. I described earlier how in the electricity and gas industry the academic expert on competition Stephen Littlechild has given place to the former Civil Service high flyer Callum McCarthy. He has already made it clear that he intends to stamp his authority on the industries he controls and, in particular, to 'get the generators', whom he sees as the fat cats of the industry. In financial services, the genial but astute professional banker Sir Andrew Large has made way for the ex-CBI proactive corporatist figure of Howard Davies. Other industries, such as water and telecommunications, are controlled by former civil servants.

The regulators are well-versed in the ways of Whitehall. What they do not always have is experience of risk-taking, which lies at the heart of a dynamic capitalist system. They are therefore, in this sense, the antithesis of capitalists. They may not have much idea either of what a customer looks like, although the legislation which gives them their vast powers is littered with the word 'consumer'. The problem is that this legislation makes little distinction between the needs of consumer protection and the requirements of consumer choice. The two are opposites. Ensuring choice is about making the market work; protection is about distorting and intervening in such a way as ultimately to bring the market to a standstill. The new economic supremos, with their roots in the political rather than the industrial process, equipped with enormous new powers and extensive staffs, are formally accountable to no one. At least with the old-fashioned and honest socialism still championed by Tony Benn and Ken Livingstone (and rejected by New Labour), managers of state-run industries are ultimately accountable to the electorate.

The whole process is secretive, anti-competitive, suppressive of enterprise, out of line with British experience, and deeply disturbing for the future of the country. Its implications go well beyond those of the severe burdens it places on the economy[5] — even though this could in the longer term re-

[5] Closely parallelling the growth in Sefras and other regulatory bodies has been the explosion of 'task forces', numbering over 300 at the last count.

introduce the same stagnation that resulted from the previous wave of state intervention. Government by unelected regulators threatens the very essence of our democracy.[6] A future Conservative government must commit itself to abolishing it all except for that which genuinely relates to the achievement of greater competition – which is the true safeguard of the consumer.

Democratically-elected governments have the right to implement the social policies that were mandated by their election victory. But those social policies should be stated explicitly in the election manifesto and then implemented through social legislation. Any political party is free to campaign on a redistributive socialist agenda; what is not acceptable is to use the vehicle of commercial-sector legislation to smuggle in social redistribution by the back door, all the time camouflaged by a rhetoric of competitition and consumer protection. This constitutes an abuse of the democratic system.

Many of these unelected quangos are staffed by government appointees from business. In the case of Michael Grade's First Leisure, Robert Ayling's British Airways, Lord Haskins' Northern Foods, Denys Henderson's Rank, and Graham Hawker's Hyder, appointment to a government task force has coincided with a disastrous slump in their own company's share price. This has given rise to the fear that 'pathological corporatism' could undermine Britain's economic performance. 'Some companies can become so fixated with a government scheme that they become distracted from thinking about their market.' (Tony Barker, Iain Byrne and Anjuli Veall, *Ruling by Task Force*, Politico's Publishing, 2000). It is also the case that 'the inevitable consequence of the quangos' remit, their approach and above all their personnel is that they will recommend further regulation, further intrusion of the state into the private sphere and further use of 'resources' to solve problems.' (Martin McElwee, *The Great and the Good*, London: Centre for Policy Studies, 2000.)

[6]   In his article in this book Lord Weatherill has described the disastrous consequences of the abandonment of self-regulation in the Palace of Westminster. In his view the preservation of the dignity of the institution of parliament used to be the prime concern of every Member. However, this rapidly disappeared with the introduction of the Nolan watchdog culture.

In some respects this is a moral argument: the principle of personal responsibility and self-regulation is derived from the Christian notion of *conscientia* – the silent monitor on our every action – and the feudal notions of honour and faith. Once it is assumed that formerly trusted professionals are not capable of regulating themselves this soon becomes a self-fulfilling prophecy.

Peter Carrington

The Lords are A-Leaping

I remember many years ago, when I was at school, I was asked to write an essay on Pope's famous quotation:

> *Let fools for forms of government contest*
> *What ere is best administered is best.*

To be truthful I don't remember to what conclusion I then came. But one thing is certain, that the human race spends a very great deal of time discussing constitutions and most of them, at any rate at first glance, seem pretty unsatisfactory and largely unworkable.

The French, who change their constitution fairly regularly, have given themselves one which on the face of it shouldn't work. To provide for the possibility or even likelihood of a president and a prime minister of different political parties, who have spent much time opposing each other's policy, and expect them to work side by side in perfect harmony, does not seem to be a recipe for success. But somehow they do manage to make it work. In much the same way, the American Constitution with all its checks and balances, the executive divorced from the legislature, seems set for stalemate and disaster. But again, somehow or other they do make it work.

As for our own, unwritten constitution, we too get by without too much difficulty. *We* do, but do others to whom we have bequeathed it? We have, I think, given independence to some 57 or so former colonies since the end of the Second World War. On each occasion we have handed them a written version of the Westminster Constitution, and on each occasion we have told them how lucky they are to have this paragon of a constitution.

I think you will find that in all cases but one, and that perhaps the least likely, they have fairly rapidly devised a constitution for themselves. India, with its enormous population,
size and diversity, is the one exception. Even in Australia,
which has broadly speaking retained our system, there is provision for referendums on almost any subject you can think of.
I remember when I lived there that there was a referendum in
the State of Victoria to decide whether or not the closing time
for pubs, which at that time was 6 o'clock and which led to
what was engagingly known as the 5 o'clock swill, should be
extended to 10.30. This was resoundingly defeated by the
women of the state, who preferred to have their husbands
home the worse for wear at 6 o'clock, rather than even worser
for wear at 10.30.

What is true of constitutions is even more true of second
chambers. I think one could say without much fear of contra-
diction that the only second chamber that is both credible and
powerful is that of the United States. In many ways the Senate
is more important and prestigious than the House of Representatives. But that is certainly not the case in France or Can-
ada or Australia or, indeed, in New Zealand which manages to
get by with a unicameral constitution.

It is important to remember that *we* did not devise a constitution, it grew from need and circumstance and as these
changed so did our unwritten Constitution. Centuries ago the
king, in order to govern, needed the support of the powerful,
the mighty and the landed. From that need Parliament was
born and later the division between Lords and Commons. For
centuries the House of Lords was equal in power to the House
of Commons and it was only much later on, in the late nineteenth century, that the Commons became the dominant and
all-powerful house. It is interesting to note that from the time
of the first prime minister, Sir Robert Walpole, and the emergence of cabinet government in 1721, until 1900, of the 49
Prime Ministers, 33 were Peers. Since then none, though there
was in the 1920s talk of Lord Curzon as Prime Minister, a prop-
osition rejected largely because he was in the Lords.

The influence of the House of Lords was gradually eroded
in the nineteenth century as the enfranchisement of the electorate took place. Universal suffrage (1867) totally changed
the relationship between the two Houses — as well, of course,

as the abolition of rotten boroughs, though the influence of the territorial magnates in their own areas continued. To take a very small example, my great grandfather became Member for the borough of Wycombe, having decisively defeated Disraeli. Loyal though I am to my great-grandfather, who was a splendid man, I cannot honestly say that politically he was quite in the same class as Dizzy.

Not only did the power and influence of the House of Lords change, so also did its composition. You will perhaps be surprised to learn that of the enormous figure of 932 Barons and Baronesses — and I expect that figure is now long out of date — only 80 were created before 1800 and only 180 before 1900.

There has been a great change in the composition of the House. If I may quote my own family, my forebear, the First Baron Carrington, was a banker and George III did not feel that was the type of person who should be in the Upper House, nor indeed did the members of the Upper House itself who, when he was introduced, got up and walked out because he was 'in trade'. I think it is true to say that some people nowadays think bankers quite respectable.

And so the change has continued, with some fairly disgraceful interludes, such as the sale of peerages in the Lloyd-George era. But the crucial factor in the decline of the House of Lords came in the early 1900s when the House rejected the Lloyd-George Budget. The result of this was the Parliament Act of 1911, very reluctantly passed by the House, mainly because of the threat by the Liberal Government to create enough Peers to swamp the Opposition. The Act curtailed the powers of the House of Lords. Henceforth, legislation could only be *delayed*, not vetoed, for two years. The Act deprived the House of the right to challenge the Government on financial matters and left them with only one absolute veto — that of preventing the Government of the day from prolonging its life.

It is interesting too to note that in the preamble to the Parliament Act were these words 'The Reform of the House of Lords brooks no delay'. Whether you would call 88 years no delay is a matter of opinion!

The main cause of this delay was that no two people, even in the same party, were ever in agreement about what should be done, how the House should be composed and what its powers should be. Things have not changed much.

On the whole it didn't really matter until 1945. There were in those years no clashes to speak of between the two Houses. In 1945 the situation became much more complicated and here I must present such credentials as I have for tackling this subject.

I took my seat in the House of Lords in 1945, when I was still in the Army and, for the last 54 years, give or take those periods in which I was occupied abroad, I have been an active member. I was, in the Home Government, Leader of the House and subsequently, in the Wilson and Callaghan Governments, Leader of the Opposition for some ten years; not something I would wish to repeat! Even if you disagree with me, what I say is from the inside. The House of Lords, and in particular the Conservative Party, was faced with a very difficult problem after the landslide victory of the Labour Party.

In the days of Whigs and Tories and Liberals and Conservatives the problem didn't arise to anything like the same extent. But in 1945 we had a situation, in which there was a great political gulf between the two parties. The government was committed to socialism – the nationalization of all means of production, distribution and exchange (though I may say it didn't really turn out quite like that). That philosophy was anathema to Conservatives; but the electorate, for better or worse, had willed it, and there was an enormous majority in the House of Commons.

The House of Lords, as we know, had the power to delay this controversial legislation for two years and its composition was overwhelmingly Conservative. In 1945, The Lords was not at all as it is now. There were only a handful of Labour Peers. We sat in The King's Robing Room, a small and intimate room, since the House of Commons chamber had been destroyed and the Commons sat in the Lords. It was a very different place from the Commons, as to some extent it still is. The House itself keeps order. There is no Speaker.

There is no procedure for curtailing an interminable or irrelevant speech, other than to move a motion that the Noble Lord be no longer heard, a motion which can be debated at length and probably takes longer than patiently listening to the original speech. It was also very polite. I remember the outrage when one Peer called another 'an oleaginous hypocrite', a remark made that much worse by its obvious accuracy! The attendance was very sparse. There were a large number of very distinguished members of the House. Not just Hereditary Peers, but those like Lords Beaverbrook and Woolton, whose reputation rested on their wartime record.

There were some of the greatest experts in the country on almost every conceivable subject, for hereditary peerages were given to distinguished men of medicine, letters, industry and so on, who did not consider it necessary to attend regularly unless they felt they had a real contribution to make. For example, I remember that the present Duke of Bedford's father was the greatest living expert on the diseases of parrots. Not a subject which frequently appeared on the Order Paper, but there were many others whose expertise was of greater practical use. In the changed circumstance of 1945, however, that really wasn't what was needed.

Lord Salisbury, who was the Leader of the Opposition, and the wise and sensible Leader of the House, Lord Addison, had to devise a means whereby the legislation of a government elected by an overwhelming majority could be enacted and not frustrated by the non-elected House, despite the strongly-held objections of the large majority of its members. If a solution was not found, the future of the House would be in doubt and in a climate not at all favourable to the Conservatives or the Lords.

So came about what are now known as the Salisbury Rules. This in effect was a convention by which the Opposition did not challenge the Second Reading, that is the principle, of any Bill which had been foreshadowed in the manifesto of the government party. In other words, if the Labour Party had said that, if elected, they were going to nationalize steel, then the House of Lords could not reject the principle, though they could seek to amend it, but without frustrating the objective.

In the 1945 Parliament this worked well and though the House of Lords made a number of important amendments which were accepted by the Members to the nationalization bills, some of which were accepted by the Government, there was no constitutional conflict. This was a makeshift solution, but it has worked for over 50 years.

In reality it is manifestly absurd. Nobody supposes for one moment that the electorate has read the party manifestos or that if they have then they agree to every item in the long and unreadable documents that political parties produce. But it was a practical and successful way of overcoming the unfairness of one party having a permanent majority in one of the Houses of Parliament.

Nevertheless, in spite of the Salisbury doctrine, the Government in 1949 introduced a new Parliament Act, which curtailed the powers of the Lords to a one-year delay from the Second Reading of a Bill in the House of Commons. This, in effect, is only a delay of some nine months or less, after the Bill has been through all its stages in both Houses of Parliament.

These remain the powers of the existing House. These are not, as you will readily agree, very draconian powers but it soon became clear that in successive governments the Commons took issue, not because of the powers themselves but because it was considered that the composition of the House of Lords was such that it had no right to challenge the elected members of the House of Commons, or as it was and is termed 'the will of the people'. In particular, in the '60s and the '70s, whenever an amendment was sent back to the House of Commons, the issue of the matter, the substance, was never discussed either in the Commons or in the press, only whether or not the un-elected House of Lords had a right even to ask the Commons to think again, let alone defy them for a year.

Quite early on in the 1950s I came to the conclusion that it was necessary to do something about the composition of the House, if it was to fulfil its function. The membership was almost wholly hereditary and there was an inbuilt Conservative majority. This meant that however well the House did its job — and it did do it well — it was undermined by its own composition. No government until 1968 was prepared to tackle this, not least, as I have said, because no common ground could be found either amongst political parties or indeed within them. But there were certain changes made. Peeresses and Ladies created Hereditary Peers were allowed to take their seats in the House. This was accepted with acclaim and agreed by a large majority, though I remember a most eloquent speech in which the then Lord Glasgow, a splendid old sea dog, protested that the lavatories were neither suitable nor numerous enough to accommodate this alarming innovation.

Mr Macmillan's administration introduced the concept of Life Peers. The idea behind this was firstly to introduce new blood with relevant experience and secondly to create a form of peerage which did not involve the succession of the sons of those chosen.

There is no doubt that this had a galvanizing effect upon the House. Those chosen were both distinguished in their own field, both men and women, and greatly enhanced the reputation of the House. Subsequently, successive prime ministers created large numbers of Life Peers. Sir Edward Heath pointed out, in February 1999, that Harold Wilson had made 226 Peers, Lady Thatcher 216, John Major 171 and, in a fairly short time, the present prime minister 105. His total, he said, was a modest 48. My own view is that Conservative Prime Ministers made a great mistake in creating as many, if not more Life Peers than Labour and if anything, made the imbalance between the two parties worse.

It will be seen from this that the idea of selecting those persons most suitable to enhance the prestige of the House has become a little extravagant. Indeed the idea that you can divorce a Working Peer from an ordinary Life Peer as is now the fashion is, in itself, absurd.

To take but one example, Lord Simpson, the Chairman of GEC, was created a Working Labour Peer, that is to say, somebody who attends the House and takes part in its proceedings and obeys the whip. All I can say is that I very much hope he doesn't, I do not think that would be greatly to the advantage of the company of which he is chief executive. He would be wasting his and his shareholders' time.

Life Peers were originally created to take an active part in the House and there are now far too many. I remember not so long ago being asked to take part in a debate on foreign affairs. I asked how many speakers there were and was told 58. There is no way in which you can have a sensible debate on one afternoon in which 58 people take part. One of the lessons is that a future House must be greatly reduced in numbers.

In 1968, the Wilson Government decided that there should be an effort to reform the Second Chamber. It took the very proper course of forming an inter-party committee to devise a scheme to be put before both Houses of Parliament and which it hoped would lead to agreed proposals.

This is in contrast to the actions of the present Government. In an unwritten constitution as delicately balanced as ours, it is not right that a political party with a temporary majority—however large, still temporary, since all majorities in the end are temporary—should unilaterally change the constitution without, at any rate in the first instance, seeking the co-operation and agreement of the other parties.

The 1968 Committee, of which Lord Jellicoe and I were members under the Chairmanship of Dick Crossman, produced an agreed scheme, accepted by all three parties. This was an amalgam of Hereditary Peers and Life Peers in a House much reduced in size and with the crossbenchers holding the balance between the political parties. This was generally considered to be a fairly sensible compromise between evolution and revolution and when introduced into the House of Lords was passed by an overwhelming majority.

The same could not be said of the House of Commons. The Bill was finally withdrawn after weeks of discussion due to a curious alliance between Enoch Powell and Michael Foot. Enoch Powell, the great traditionalist, appeared almost to believe in the divine right of Hereditary Peers and consequently was against any proposal which diluted the hereditary system, whereas Michael Foot didn't believe in a second chamber at all. They conducted a masterly parliamentary battle in which they eventually emerged triumphant.

I think, on reflection, that though the new House might have been considered a more credible body, it would not, after a few years, be held to be much more legitimate than its predecessor.

And there the matter rested. Mrs Thatcher understandably took the view that the trouble and fuss and time which would be needed to reopen the problem was simply not worth while and there were far more important things for her government to do. That, of course, brings us to the present day.

First of all, as I have said, I do not believe that the government, however big its majority, should unilaterally decide to change the constitution without some attempt at agreement with the other parties. In addition, it seems to have given no thought to the future. Other than getting rid of Hereditary Peers, it appeared to be content with a nominated House, though it subsequently decided—provided the House behaved itself—to accept a temporary composition much along the 1968 lines.

To those of us of a more cynical disposition, all this seemed designed more to appeal to those in the Labour Party who had been carried along on the wave of New Labour, with perhaps not as much enthusiasm as the leadership would have wished. Nobody, after all, would much mind if the right of Hereditary Peers to sit in the House of Lords disappeared and it would be very welcome to those Old Labourites who had to swallow some of the ideas of New Labour and that would be that.

No doubt this was true but, from a purely party-political point of view, it was hardly necessary. The present House of Lords suits them admirably – should it oppose any policies of the Labour Government its composition can be derided and its objections ignored. In the year of the Wilson and Callaghan administration the Government may have been annoyed but barely inconvenienced and never frustrated.

A new House with more legitimacy may prove a good deal less amenable. In any event, it soon became clear that the abolition of the right of Hereditary Peers to sit in the House of Lords was, by itself, not enough. A second stage was necessary and after much delay a Royal Commission was appointed to devise a new Second Chamber, with a very tight timetable. They have wrestled with the same intractable problems which have been rehearsed so many times in the last 80 years. What powers and duties should the House have and how should it be composed to best carry them out?

The revision of legislation is a most important function, done extremely well in the current House. There have been in the last two decades so many Bills rushed through the House of Commons that they arrive in the second chamber ill-drafted and, in some cases, barely discussed. The revision of this legislation means intensive long and hard work, often pretty detailed and dull. A House composed of the great and good or of those busy in their own professions or businesses would have neither the time nor the inclination for these essential chores.

Secondly, the House should have sufficient power of delay to enable public opinion through the media to encourage the Government to have second thoughts and act accordingly.

There is one more power which I would give it. The House of Commons is all powerful and can by a single vote change our Constitution. If they so wish they can curtail our rights and liberties. I think the latter is unlikely in the present circumstances, but the former is not so unthinkable.

I would give the second chamber the power, not to veto any such proposals, but to order a referendum on constitutional issues. I have to say I would not care to draft such a proposal, but there are clever lawyers who could. It would be a formidable power and yet one which did not challenge directly the authority of the Commons.

As to the composition, a purely nominated chamber which, I suspect, is favoured by the present Government, has almost all the disadvantages of the hereditary system. The nominations would be broadly speaking at the behest of the party leaders; they would have to be if there was going to be some kind of balance between the two parties. In effect they would be placemen, put there to vote for their parties and lacking the independence of the Hereditaries and the existing Life Peers in what would necessarily be a more party-political House.

Nor do I think a nominated House would be considered legitimate, whoever appoints its members. 'Who are these placemen elected by no-one to challenge the will of the House elected by the people?' I can hear the refrain now — that is if the placemen ever did challenge the government. Perhaps that situation is precisely what Mr Blair seeks.

The other alternative is election. It would certainly ensure legitimacy. But that in itself creates a problem vis-à-vis the House of Commons. The Commons are most unlikely to accept an assembly which might be regarded as a rival in prestige and authority — even if its powers were not much greater than I have outlined.

But unless the new elected House had worthwhile teeth, who on earth would be prepared to stand for election? There would be a real danger of it becoming a kind of Aldermanic rest home.

These are not very attractive alternatives. A House of placemen, no more credible and certainly less distinguished than the present House. Or an elected House with insufficient power to challenge the House of Commons — with a membership, to say the least of it, of an uncertain quality.

These are the issues over which we have all been mulling over these last 88 years. The most likely eventual outcome, I suppose, is a mixture of nomination and election, with a sprinkling of religious leaders, possibly representatives of the Welsh Assembly and the Scottish Parliament and—God help us—such other regional assemblies as the Government is going to inflict upon us; and, I suspect, with less power than it has at the present time. I do not believe it will be a more successful, more credible or more efficient second chamber than it is at the present time.

What would I suggest? I have not changed my mind since a speech I made in 1977, though I recognize that what I say is most unlikely to be accepted. I would have an elected House, elected at a different time from the Commons, taking into account the Scottish Parliament and other regional assemblies and I would give it the powers I have outlined. Or would I? I remember Lord Hailsham telling me that once you removed a brick from the wall of the Constitution, the whole wall was likely to collapse.

A Scottish Parliament, a Welsh Assembly, regional assemblies. A Prime Minister of Scotland, a Welsh leader, first Minister of England and a cobbled-together second chamber. And above all, it seems, with a House of Commons increasingly ignored and media spin doctors in control. I pray that Lord Hailsham is wrong.

Acknowledgements

An earlier version of this paper was given as part of 'The Last Word' lunchtime lecture series in February 1999 at the Royal Geographical Society.

J.R. Lucas

Constitution and Democracy

When the Royal Commission on the House of Lords held a public meeting in Exeter in May 1999, it appeared that the predominant view of the participants was 'If it ain't broke, don't fix it'. One factor, no doubt, was the difficulty in thinking up a satisfactory alternative to the House of Lords as it now is, but another was a deep sense that what is important is not so much institutions as the spirit in which decisions are actually made. Constitutionalism is a way of doing things rather than a set of rules.

Such a sentiment enshrines a truth, though not the whole truth. Our polity has long been a constitutional polity, and though it has evolved over time, a certain spirit of reasonableness and respect for other people's rights and opinions has been a continuing feature that has served us well. It is easy to pick on this as the key factor that has made us the people we are, and has made our history a success story of which we can be proud. Other countries have fallen prey to doctrinaire political ideals that have led them astray, while we have been preserved from excess by our fundamental common sense.

But this, too, is a doctrinaire doctrine, which can distort our thinking and lead us astray as badly as other countries are by their more articulate views. When changes are necessary, it gives us little guidance as to what changes are best, and it encourages us to define ourselves by contrast with other countries. For many years it was liberty, not democracy, that was our watchword, as we thanked God that we were not under a despotism, even if sometimes benevolent, as our European neighbours were. It was only as we girded ourselves to resist Hitler that we drew the contrast between the Axis powers and the democratic countries of Britain, France, Czechoslovakia and the United States. Democracies, as we understood them, were non-Nazi, non-totalitarian, subject to the rule of law, protective of civil liberties. Periodic elections, whereby the government could be thrown out, were an important feature, but not the all-defining one—Hitler had been democratically elected. During the Cold War the West was uncomfortably aware that communist regimes might be voted into power democratically, and that periodic elections were held in communist countries. There was little public debate about what democracy was, and whether it was a good thing. 'Democratic' became a term of appraisal, with little descriptive content. So that now, when the House of Lords is condemned for being undemocratic, we feel that it is a bad thing that it should be undemocratic, but have little idea of what being democratic would really require.

It helps to move away from nouns and towards adverbs. No real democracies do exist, could exist: even ancient Athens excluded metics, slaves and women. But some decisions can be characterized as being more or less democratically taken, in contrast to others that are taken by lot, by a single authoritative individual, or by an effective group of individuals. But even among the more or less democratically taken decisions, there is, once unanimity fails, room for dispute over the rules for translating diverse individual choices into a definite collective decision. Sometimes a simple majority is deemed to constitute a valid decision on a Yes/No question, sometimes a two-thirds, or even a three-quarters, majority is required. Where there is more than one option, as with elections, many different systems have been proposed, each with its merits and defects. If the House of Commons is elected democratically by separate constituencies on the first-past-the-post principle, then the House of Lords might be replaced by a Senate elected democratically on some other principle—by county councils or by some form of proportional representation.

Bicameralism has its merits. Both chambers are democratically elected, and it has worked reasonably well in the USA. But it engenders conflict between the two chambers, each claiming democratic legitimacy, neither being disposed to give way. Constitutional deadlock is endemic in the United States, often resolved only by the use of presidential patronage to bribe Congressmen to vote for government measures. We should look to other means to arrive at a definite decision when the two chambers do not agree. We might have a double dissolution, as in Australia. More in accordance with the spirit of the present age would be a referendum. If the Lords and the Commons could not reach agreement on the final form of a Bill, there would be a referendum to choose between the two versions. People would be faced with a simple choice between supporting the government that had the confidence of the elected House of Commons and accepting the second thoughts of the Upper House, also elected, though on some different principle. Both Houses would be under pressure to be reasonable, since the more reasonable version would have the better chance of winning. The inadequacies of any particular electoral system would be in part compensated for by there being another chamber whose members were chosen by a system, also inadequate but not inadequate in the same way. It would be possible to meet some demands for a more federal constitution by having the Upper House elected by the regions on some equal footing, like the Senate of the United States. It is conceivable that the United Kingdom may evolve into a federation—if the Scottish nationalists are successful, and are followed by the Welsh and Irish nationalists, there may be a role for the House of Lords as a 'Council of the British Isles' (and there might be an argument for keeping the Scottish Representative Peers against that sort of possibility).

A bicameral constitution could be made to work. But there are grave disadvantages. However much might be said at the outset about the pre-eminence of the House of Commons, the balance of power would shift away from it. Whatever the method for electing its members—first-past-the-post or some variant of the recommendations of the Jenkins Committee or something altogether different—it would be open to objection; no system of election can be perfect, and in the rough-and-tumble of politics there would be occasions when many people, disappointed at the outcome in the Commons would feel that the Lords represented the nation's interests better. We should gradually move towards parity of disesteem, and increasingly resort to the referendum in order to resolve disagreements between the two Houses, each confident of its own electoral legitimacy.

A fully bicameral constitution is not a serious option. It would require a radical alteration of the Constitution, with a complete change in the relations between the government and parliament. It is ruled out by the terms of reference of the Royal Commission and by the political fact that the House of Commons would never agree to a cuckoo possessed of equal electoral legitimacy being inserted into the parliamentary nest. It follows that complaints that the existing House of Lords is undemocratic and demands that it should be replaced by a democratic body are misconceived. There may be justifiable complaints about the existing House of Lords and we may want to improve it, but these must be argued for from an understanding of what constitutionalism requires. Vague uses of the word 'democratic' are out of place, and no substitute for serious thought.

As the Constitution has developed in the last two centuries, the House of Commons has been the chief *locus* of political power. Recently it has become more like the electoral college in the USA, but an electoral college in permanent session with power of recall. There has been growing dissatisfaction with the way the House of Commons works, but governments have been unenthusiastic about reforms intended to increase the power of the Commons to call the government to account. Power now resides in Downing Street and Whitehall as much as in the House of Commons, but formally it is still the House of Commons that has the final say, and the function of the House of Lords is to be construed primarily in relation to the House of Commons. Most of the time it acts as a **Second Chamber**, revising (or occasionally initiating) legislation; on occasion it may act as an **Upper House**, with power to prevent the House of Commons legislating itself into permanent existence; in addition it often is a **National Forum of Debate** in which issues of public concern are articulated and aired, more authoritatively than in the media, less constrained than in the House of Commons.

The need for a Second Chamber arises from the pressures on the House of Commons, both of time and of party discipline, which mean that many measures are inadequately scrutinized

and not criticized trenchantly enough. The different atmosphere in the House of Lords and its different membership
constitute an independent check on what has been approved
by the House of Commons before it is enacted into law.

It is an essential feature of any constitutional regime that
there should be some check on the dominant organ of government. The Upper House is there to protect the country from a
dictatorial and over-whipped House of Commons. In spite of
events in Australia under Mr Whitlam's premiership, this
need has been insufficiently recognised. It is felt that if the
Lower House is democratic, an Upper House that thwarts its
decisions must be undemocratic, and therefore bad. But the
'therefore' is not cogent. A decision may be taken democratically, and still be wrong. The classical case was in Athens, after
the battle of Arginusae. The Athenians had won the battle, but
many ships had been lost with much loss of life. This was
blamed on the admirals, who failed to make sufficient effort to
pick up the shipwrecked sailors. A motion was proposed in
the Assembly that they should be executed forthwith. It so
happened that Socrates was in the chair that day and he
refused to put the question to the vote, as it was contrary to the
law of Athens to condemn anyone without proper trial. There
was a great uproar with many shouting that it was a terrible
thing that anyone should not let the *demos* do what it wanted.
But Socrates was right. What the *demos* wanted to do was
wrong.

A democratically-elected House of Commons could be
wrong too. We like to think that we are too civilized, too gen-
tlemanly, to need any formal restrictions, that our unwritten
Constitution would prevent any party with a majority in the
House of Commons passing a law that was outrageously
wrong. But constitutions come into play when things are
going wrong, and we need to think through such cases and
consider what remedies we should have in such a situation. At
present the remedy is the next general election. However bad
the government, whatever draconian measures are whipped
through the House of Commons, and after a year's delay
passed into law without the consent of the Lords, there has to
be an election within five years of the previous one. The one
measure that cannot be passed into law by the House of Commons alone, without the consent of the House of Lords, is one

prolonging its own existence. It is a crucial safeguard. In the seventeenth century the Long Parliament lasted far too long. In our own century the 1935 Parliament was, quite rightly, prolonged on account of the exigencies of war, and after 1945 there were voices, citing this as a precedent, arguing that the new Parliament should simply pass an enabling act to allow the Government to get on with creating a new society without need for further elections until the job was done. It is to be hoped that such voices would never prevail in any future House of Commons, but it is not to be counted on. In framing constitutional law we need to think about worst possible cases and take steps, while we have the opportunity, to secure ourselves against them.

The present Parliament Act provides protection against the House of Commons, but needs to be strengthened. Bills certified by the Speaker as money bills do not need the consent of the Lords at all. As was pointed out by Dicey, the definition of a money bill should not be left to the sole decision of the Speaker; now that taxation takes a very large proportion of the GNP, the consequences of money bills have wide social implications which call for a second scrutiny. More important is that the restriction on bills prolonging the life of Parliament needs to be more securely entrenched. The Nationalists were able to set up *apartheid* in South Africa by altering the provisions, themselves not entrenched, which determined the validity of entrenched statutes, such as that protecting the franchise of the Cape Coloureds. Any new Parliament Act must give the Upper House a veto, which cannot be overridden after some suitable delay, not only on bills to prolong the life of Parliament but essentially also on bills to amend the Parliament Act itself. Only so can we ensure that an elected House of Commons will not be able to legislate away its obligation in due course to face the electorate.

We might go further. As we have seen in communist countries, bare elections are by themselves no guarantee of real choice. They need to be buttressed by many other provisions securing free speech, effective communication, unintimidated electors, provisions we take for granted as part of our constitutional rights, but ones that could be whittled away by a dictatorial regime. We might seek to establish a distinction between constitutional and ordinary measures, with the House of

Lords being able to delay the latter for only one year, but the former until after the next general election. But it would be a difficult distinction to draw, and difficult to determine how disputed cases were to be decided. If the decision were vested in the House of Lords itself, some sort of Cranborne Convention might operate, but it might be unduly extended over the years, or alternatively whittled away until even the essential restriction on prolonging the life of Parliament was in danger.

Many people recognize the need for some constitutional watch-dog, but would not assign it to the House of Lords. They would follow the example of the United States and establish a Supreme Court to protect the people from Parliament. But there are great disadvantages. We do not want, and ought not to want, to hand ourselves over to the lawyers. In the United States the Supreme Court decides how far its powers extend, and over the centuries has gradually extended them. We should not want to create a Supreme Court that was able and willing to be a judge in its own cause. Moreover, often the issue is not a narrow legal one but a wider political one: the Americans could not put off their elections in 1942 as we did in 1940. Generally the adversarial atmosphere of a judicial court is not the right body for resolving constitutional clashes in an eirenical way. A constitutional watchdog needs to contain people well versed in politics, and people who have had experience of holding high office. Such people may well be recruited for a Second Chamber, but not for a court of law.

Only occasionally does the House of Lords have to act as an Upper House frustrating the will of the House of Commons on high constitutional principle. The very fact that it possesses the power is enough to dissuade politicians from trying dodgy tricks. For most of its time the House of Lords acts as a Second Chamber, revising legislation which the House of Commons did not have the opportunity to think through adequately. If the functions of Upper House and Second Chamber are not separated, we face a dilemma: either the Upper House is strong enough to thwart a House of Commons determined to subvert the constitution, and then it will become too strong and constitutional deadlock will become endemic; or it is weak enough not to obstruct the government of the day on party-political grounds, and then it will be too weak to protect us when we need to be protected. Similarly, if a Second Cham-

ber has power enough to make the House of Commons have
second thoughts, it will sometimes obstruct the Government's
parliamentary programme: if, on the other hand, it does not
possess effective power, it will soon become a cipher — as the
Canadian Upper House is said to be — and competent persons
will not want to waste time being members of it. The main reason why previous proposals for reforming the House of Lords
have come to nothing is the difficulty of devising a system that
will not be impaled on a horn of this dilemma.

The House of Lords sometimes initiates wide-ranging
debates. Parliament was originally a talking shop, a National
Forum of Debate, but the possession of power inhibits free
and frank discussion. Debates in the House of Commons tend
to be dominated by party considerations, and many things are
left unsaid for fear of offending the whips or damaging
chances of re-election or promotion. The Lords, being free of
these pressures, are better able to speak their minds, which
makes for better debating. It is desirable that this should continue. Although the media also provide a forum for debate
they tend to do so on a somewhat superficial level. The Lords
are better informed and go into matters much more thoroughly than most discussions in the media, and have the constitutional clout to ensure that what they say is heard by the
Government. No special powers are needed, since in most
cases the motion is by leave withdrawn, and no vote is taken.
So far as this function is concerned, voting rights are less
important than speaking rights. At present only the Bishop of
Sodor and Man has the latter but not the former, but there
could be others.

The different functions and different powers of the House of
Lords impose different desiderata for its composition. The
Second Chamber works only because there are a good many
regular attenders, who are either former members of the
House of Commons or leaders in some walk of national life,
and have considerable expertise which they can bring to bear
on details of government legislation and policy. It has been
suggested that the new House should have full-time members
who are paid. This makes some sense for a Second Chamber,
but not for an Upper House or a National Forum of Debate.
The function of a Second Chamber is to revise. It is a task that
former civil servants and former members of the House of

Commons can do well. They know the ropes and can understand the intricacies of drafting that mystify most of us. It is desirable that the Second Chamber should contain a core of such people, mostly London-based and able to devote a considerable amount of time to the work of the House. But they should not be the only ones. Bishops can contribute on social and spiritual issues, Law Lords on legal ones. Many other professionals could contribute something, but only occasionally. The present House of Lords contains leaders in various walks of national life who are not regular attenders: they are too busy with their dioceses, universities, medical practices, to come to the House much, except when there is business they can make a special contribution to. Although full-time attendance on the part of some retired politicians is a reasonable demand, it would be inexpedient to make it a general requirement. Many professionals do not have much to offer outside their own sphere. At the very least it would be a waste to have bishops, vice-chancellors and doctors spending many hours listening to debates about agriculture and fisheries. Not only would it be a waste, but it would be counter-selective and counter-productive. It would be counter-selective because leaders in various walks of life would be unable to combine full-time attendance in the House of Lords with their other duties, and unwilling to abandon their profession for Second-Chamber politics. Good doctors might be prepared to devote some time to helping to make the country's medical policies better, but would rather cure patients than listen to an under minister for agriculture read a departmental brief on fish quotas to a somnolent chamber. It would also be counter-productive: it would increase the temptation for those who had nothing to say to say it nonetheless. Absenteeism spares us superfluous speechifying. Debates in the Lords are said to be good: few speak well of proceedings in the Senate of the United States of America. Contrary to much contemporary rhetoric, apathy is an important political virtue. An Upper House needs to contain many members who are generally content to let the House of Commons get on with the business of politics, and will only stir themselves to intervene if it seems that some important constitutional principle is at stake. A largely absentee membership provides a natural way of distinguishing routine business from business of exceptional constitutional importance.

It has been suggested that the Law Lords be extruded, because their impartiality in administering the law might be compromised if they had taken part in framing it. It is an unreal fear: any Law Lord who had been unduly partisan as a legislator on a law he subsequently was called on to interpret could disqualify himself. It would rarely happen, and would be a minor awkwardness compared with not having judicial expertise at hand when debating what the law should be. The presence of the bishops raises the question of there being representatives of other religious traditions besides the established Church. Many who are not Roman Catholics would have welcomed the presence of Cardinal Hume. There is an obvious case for having the Moderator of the Church of Scotland. But we should recognize spiritual difficulties in accepting a Spiritual Peerage. Although Judaism was an established religion, and Isaiah felt at ease in the centres of power, the main thrust of Christianity has been anti-establishment, and the dissenting churches may well be wary of being officially embraced by the establishment. The present practice of conferring Life Peerages *ad hominem* may be preferable. Lord Soper and the Chief Rabbi have been able to contribute without compromising the independence of their co-religionists. Similar considerations may militate against other *ex officio* Peerages. It would be desirable to have leading trade-unionists and industrialists in the House of Lords, but that would involve legislative definition of the qualifying offices, which is something the TUC and CBI might not like. Where it can be done, it should, in order to reduce the burden of selecting *ad hominem* Peerages. It might help restore the morale of teachers if some — say, the heads of Manchester Grammar School and Holland Park Comprehensive School — were *ex officio* intellectual Peers of the realm.

There could be *some* elected members — perhaps the university burgesses who used to sit in the House of Commons, together with representatives elected by other professions and trade unions, if they were not represented *ex officio* by their leaders. But there are many areas of national life that do not form natural constituencies, and it is important that the Upper House should not be composed predominantly of persons elected from among those who put themselves forward for election, but should contain many whose judgment would be widely respected in the country if they deemed some government measure so objectionable that they voted it down. Most Lords, therefore, will need to have Life Peerages conferred on them individually by the Crown. It has been suggested that the core members of the Second Chamber should be nominated by their party leaders without the Prime Minister having a veto over the nominations put forward on behalf of other parties. That would work moderately well, though it would be better if their nominations were scrutinized by an all-party committee, chaired by the Speaker, which could ask awkward questions if dubious manufacturers of raincoats were being put forward. A different procedure is required for the selection of non-politicians, 'the great and the good', who are desirable members of the Second Chamber and essential ones of the Upper House. They need to be very great, so that if they challenge the House of Commons they will be supported by public opinion, and moderately good, so that they will not be tempted to usurp its functions or threaten its primacy. Such people will tend to be old — fame comes only slowly — not necessarily based in London, and with many other calls on their time. It follows that there should be no age limit or need for re-appointment, no expectation of regular attendance, and no pay (except for reimbursing expenses). Even in respect of its function as a Second Chamber, it would be a mistake to make membership of a reformed House of Lords a full-time occupation, but it would be much worse as regards its standing as an Upper House. It would exclude the very people best qualified to adjudicate between the politicians and the people. Isaiah Berlin is often cited as a great and good man of our time whose judgment was widely respected: but he would never have accepted membership of a body that required him to be always in London, and not writing, thinking or talking to friends.

Assessments of greatness and goodness are always difficult. A Life Peerage should be, as it is in popular estimation, a great honour. If the Upper House is to have the prestige to enable it to stand out against the House of Commons, its members need to be those most highly thought of in the country at large; and such people are least likely to have ambitions to become politicians. As far as I can see, the present honours system works reasonably well. If the present system is thought not to be open enough, there could be a committee including some Privy Councillors, some Peers, and some other public office-holders, to make recommendations to the Queen. The Prime Minister might have some sort of veto. The system for making Crown appointments in the Church of England offers a modern example of how the Prime Minister's role as the Queen's chief adviser may be combined with a procedure for garnering from diverse sources opinions about individuals' suitability for appointment.

At least two methods for nominating people for Life Peerages are required, one overtly political, the other perhaps connected with the honours system generally but in any case distinct from political nominations to the Second Chamber. Further methods are required if the House of Lords is to continue to be a National Forum of Debate. The presence of retired party politicians and of cross-bench Peers drawn from the great and the good is a strength, but they share a common defect: even if they are not nominated by the Prime Minister, they are, characteristically, very successful people. They are not representatively ordinary, and it is desirable that ordinariness be represented in national discussions of what public policy ought to be. It has been pointed out, mostly by Conservatives but also by Earl Russell from the Liberal Democrat benches, that the Hereditary Peers are free from the limitation of being remarkably successful people themselves. The Home Secretary has countered by saying that they are limited in another way—they are mostly land-owning Old Etonians (though not, for instance, Lord Calverly, a retired policeman). That is true, and needs rectifying, though not at the cost of throwing out the ordinary baby in order to guarantee an absence of Old Etonian bathwater. We need to have ordinary voices heard near the seats of power. We cannot have them all, and if they are representative in one way, they will not be representative in some other way. Nevertheless, it is good to be able to hear in national debates the voices not only of professional politicians and the great and the good, but of some non-politicians who are not at all great and not outstandingly good. In ancient Athens the *Boule* was selected by lot from the different tribes, and some element of sortition might help the

House to be a sort of citizens' jury: F.A. Hayek had a compli-cated scheme of choosing representatives for each cohort, so as to retain a youthful presence. In a slightly tongue-in-cheek letter to the *Independent* last year, I suggested giving seats in the House of Lords to winners of the jackpot in the lottery. Since very few debates end with a vote, little would be lost in treating the Ordinaries, as we might call them, like the Bishop of Sodor and Man. Some protection might be needed against the development of filibustering as in the Senate of the United States — perhaps Ordinaries could speak only with the permis-sion of the House, which would be granted as a matter of course except to those who had on previous occasions out-talked their welcome.

If a reformed House of Lords is to contain ordinary people, it would be sensible to allow those Hereditary Peers who wanted to continue as Ordinaries. The prejudice against the hereditary principle as such is difficult to understand at the present time. We know now what we have always believed, that genetics is important. The descendants of those enobled for outstanding public service yesteryear, are likely on aver-age to manifest a greater than average devotion to public ser-vice now, though with each generation regressing further to the norm. Family pride and education are also likely to foster an ethos of *noblesse oblige*. Current attacks on the hereditary principle are misconceived — or rather, outdated: they would have made sense at the end of the eighteenth century, but not at the end of the twentieth, when we are at last beginning to understand how heredity works. Rather than spurning it and trying to make the House of Lords entirely meritocratic, we should be making use of it, and adapting it to present needs. We do need to meet the Home Secretary's point, and have non-hereditary, non-meritocratic, non-politician Peers; but the retention of Hereditary Peers would have three merits. It would make the reform of the House of Lords an evolution rather than a radical break, and hence make it much more consensual — very important where any change to the Constitution is involved. It would also give real recognition to the service actually rendered by individuals who have inher-ited peerages — there have been many tributes recently, even from those who think change is called for, and this measure would make those tributes not a matter of lip service only, but real appreciation of work well done.

To summarize: in formulating plans for reforming the House of Lords we need to distinguish three different functions that it performs, which require it to have different powers and suggest different criteria for membership. If the new House of Lords is not to threaten the primacy of the House of Commons, it cannot be democratic. It is very important that it should be able to protect us against abuse of power by the House of Commons, and therefore must have effectively entrenched power to prevent the House of Commons legislating away the need for elections. In order to have this power but not be tempted to use it improperly, it needs to have members drawn widely from the leaders of different aspects of national life, many of whom would not be politicians and would not be frequent attenders. In the National Forum of Debate it is desirable that there should be heard some voices from those who are neither politicians nor outstandingly successful.

Andrew Tyrie

Reforming The Lords: The Democratic Case

Lords reform, despite outward appearances, is a relatively straightforward subject. The crucial decisions turn on the answers to four questions:

- Does the United Kingdom need a second chamber and what functions should it perform?

- What powers does it need to perform those functions?

- What composition most appropriately enables it to exercise those powers?

- If composition is to be by election, can conflict between two elected chambers be avoided?

1. Does the United Kingdom need a second chamber and what functions should it perform?

I believe that the country needs an effective second chamber, both for reasons of constitutional principle and because of the growing strength of the executive in the Commons.

The constitutional arguments for second chambers are well known. Diffusion of power is better than its concentration. Freedom is better protected when it is not entirely dependent on one institution, as it is to the extent that the sovereignty of parliament is coming to mean the sovereignty of the Commons. No doctrine of the separation of powers buttresses freedom in Britain – we remain uncomfortably dependent upon the exercise of self-restraint by the executive.

The practice of modern British government also supports the case for a second chamber. The executive has become steadily more powerful over the last few decades. The professionalization of Commons' politics, the growth of the payroll vote, the increase in the power of the party whips and its corollary, the decline of the independent backbencher, all these have considerably strengthened the position of the executive. In addition the executive now has almost complete control of standing orders, leaving it virtually supreme in the Commons.

Only the most superficial scrutiny of government activity now takes place on many issues and the executive is frequently able to avoid it altogether. It is widely accepted that legislation often reaches the statute book in a poor state. Even the 'bread and butter' task of explaining policy and announcing changes to policy are now frequently made not in the Commons, but directly to the media.

From the above it is clear that a second chamber is needed both to improve scrutiny of the executive and to act as a constitutional longstop. In performing the scrutiny function the second chamber can and should remain ultimately advisory. It can assist the Commons in calling the executive to account and can encourage government by explanation. It can also assist the process of consultation, often the best guarantee of soundly based legislation. Its purpose should not be to stymie executive action but to bring greater transparency and in the process promote a wider understanding, and therefore acceptance, of government decisions. A second and more than merely advisory function is that of constitutional watchdog. The near supremacy of the executive in the Commons suggests the need for some constitutional check on the arbitrary exercise of its power.

There is, of course, a unicameralist response. Some argue that it is possible to imagine a reformed House of Commons performing these roles, without the need for a second chamber, or with a second chamber consigned to little more than a dignified constitutional role. Although theoretically plausible, there is no sign that the executive would permit such reform of the Commons—such evidence as there is points in the opposite direction, that is, to a further accretion of executive power, reinforced by greater control of backbenchers by parties at Westminster.

2. What powers does it need to perform those functions?

The existing powers of the Lords are in most respects adequate to enable it to perform both the scrutiny and the constitutional longstop functions mentioned above. The power of amendment, combined with the power to delay a bill by at least a year, can oblige the executive to think again and provide an opportunity for further public debate. In addition to the power of delay, the Lords retains an absolute veto over bills to delay a general election beyond the statutory limit of five years—an essential minimum constitutional check on executive authority.

These existing powers were not arbitrarily arrived at. They are the product of the compromise worked out after the Lords crisis in 1911 and provide for the ultimate supremacy of the House of Commons over legislation, with the one constitutional proviso cited above.

Nonetheless, there is a case for strengthening the powers of the second chamber. The scrutiny powers could be bolstered by providing a delaying power over statutory instruments, rather than the absolute veto still theoretically allowed by the Parliament Act. The second chamber's constitutional role could also be enhanced by increasing the delaying power to, say, two years, or even the lifetime of a parliament over some constitutional issues.

There is no case whatever for any further significant erosion of existing powers, which would weaken the second chamber to the point where it would not be able to perform its scrutiny and constitutional longstop functions. In particular, any further reduction in the power of delay would leave the second chamber virtually toothless—it is the ability to force the executive to reintroduce a bill in a subsequent session which makes the power of delay valuable to a second chamber. Most of the proposals about powers set out in the government's White Paper would have the effect of further weakening the second chamber, and are therefore pernicious.[1]

---

[1] See particularly the proposals in the White Paper *Modernising Parliament and Reforming the House of Lords*, January 1999, Chapter 7, paras 23–27.

3. What composition most appropriately enables it to exercise those powers?

In my view, in the twenty-first century only a chamber backed by the legitimacy of the ballot box can hope to perform a meaningful constitutional role. A largely, rather than fully, elected House could probably also do so—it could offer a number of other compensating advantages as well. Nonetheless, the democratic case is very strong—the principle, that the electorate should decide upon whom to bestow the authority to legislate over them, seems almost unanswerable.

A crucial question is whether an appointed House could also perform a constitutional role, such as the one outlined above, as well as or better than a largely or fully democratic House. I think it unlikely. An appointed House could not be expected to challenge a democratic House of Commons. An appointed House would carry less legitimacy even than the chamber prior to stage one reform in 1999—at least the pre-existing arrangements had that grain of legitimacy that came from continuity. It is more likely that, however devised, an appointed House would come to be seen as an adjunct to executive or 'establishment' patronage.

Likewise, I very much doubt whether appointees from other democratic institutions, such as local councils or the regional assemblies, could carry sufficient legitimacy, even if elected by those institutions. It is true that within a federation an indirectly elected second chamber can play a valuable constitutional role in representing its constituent parts, but in the absence of elected regional government such a federal approach would be inappropriate for Britain. A House composed of an assortment of representatives from the newly elected regional assemblies, where they existed, and local councils for the rest of UK, where they did not exist, would offer no constitutional coherence. Their right to challenge the will of the executive as expressed in a majority of the House of Commons would carry scarcely more weight than that of an appointed House.

None of these assertions can, of course, be conclusively proved but there is a good deal of evidence to support them. The composition of the pre-1999 House of Lords derived from appointments by Prime Ministers and Monarchs, past and present. The majority of its work was done by Life Peers, eminent, and many of them capable of influencing public opinion on their own account. Yet the pre-1999 House of Lords found itself extremely unwilling to exercise even the limited legal powers it possessed. In that sense we have been perilously close to unicameralism for a long time. In fact we have had the worst of all worlds: the appearance of a bicameral check on the executive, without its substance.

Nor has the exercise of patronage, particularly over the last few years, made the task of advocating appointed Houses any easier — the recent packing of the Lords with government supporters is without precedent in modern history.[2] An independent appointments commission, if carefully structured, might succeed in restraining this exercise of executive patronage but that would not be enough to imbue an appointed chamber with moral authority. This is the biggest single flaw in the Wakeham proposals. The crucial judgment is whether, in a democratic age, the electorate would regard as legitimate the exercise of parliamentary authority by a self-perpetuating oligarchy of the great and the good. I doubt it.

Opponents of democracy often rehearse the canard that two elected Houses would merely duplicate one another and that the second chamber would become susceptible to the encroachment of the whips/executive, as has the Commons. This is a relatively straightforward problem to address: different electoral systems and particularly different electoral terms, if long and non-renewable, would greatly reduce the power of the whips (and hence the executive) in the second chamber.

4. Can conflict between the two elected chambers be avoided?

This would be a serious objection if conflict led to constitutional 'gridlock'. Could the two elected chambers find themselves so gridlocked?

---

[2]   The average number of life peers created per annum by Tony Blair in 1998 was 67 whereas John Major created on average 25 per annum and Margaret Thatcher 18. Source: House of Lords Library note LLN 98/005 *Peerage creation 1958-1998.*

The Mackay Report dismisses this issue as 'a sterile debate'.[3] I would not go quite that far, but I believe that safeguards can be found to the danger. For such a crisis to be avoided it is crucial that the relationship between the two chambers should remain tightly regulated by law, as laid down in the Parliament Acts. The Acts greatly circumscribe the ability of a second chamber to bring about gridlock. It is difficult to imagine a crisis in which the Commons would allow itself to be bamboozled into releasing the second chamber from the constraints laid down in those Acts — the inability to block money bills and the limitation of the power of delay.

Gridlock can therefore be avoided, but any scheme which obliges the Commons to think again would generate some friction. Those who argue that any tension between the two Houses would be unacceptable are making a unicameralist case — the tension and dialogue between the two chambers would form part of the constitutional safeguard which bicameralists seek.

A more subtle concern, particularly of some Commons' colleagues, is that the authority of the Commons could be compromised by another elected House. It is certainly possible that an elected second chamber might come to command a powerful moral authority over a particular issue but it is at least arguable that, were such mobilization of popular opinion to take place, it should be seen as a demonstration of political maturity rather than a threat to the Commons.

In a deeper sense I believe that the objection misunderstands the source of the primacy of the first chamber. The popular acceptance of the role of the Commons in providing strong and stable government is very deeply entrenched. It is perhaps the greatest strength of the British system and it would remain. The ultimate subordination of the Lords to the Commons, on any of the current proposals, including my own, would therefore be buttressed not only by the rule of law in the Parliament Acts but also by the consent of the electorate.

---

[3] See *The Report of the Constitutional Commission on Options for a New Second Chamber*, April 1999, p. 13.

5. Other issues

The foregoing leaves many important issues unanswered. I have dealt with a number of these more fully in Chapter 3 of my paper *Reforming the Lords: a Conservative Approach.*[4] In summary these are:

- The role of Ministers: there is a strong case for excluding Ministers from sitting in the second chamber altogether.

- The scope for the development of joint scrutiny committees: such committees could encourage the resuscitation of scrutiny by the Commons, for example by reviving the flagging standing committee system.

- The system of election: a form of proportional representation commends itself and would entrench the first-past-the-post system and hence 'judgment day' — on which the electorate can judge and dismiss a government — for Commons elections.

- The merit of avoiding extra election days: there is a strong case for holding elections at the same time as the Commons but putting only a proportion (a third or a half) of the membership up for election each time.

- The role of the Law Lords, the bishops, and possibly other groups of particular expertise: the risk of tension between elected and appointed elements in a second chamber could be assuaged by means of a system of 'co-option' of the experts by those elected.

- Size and remuneration: a chamber of about 300 would probably suffice. Cost is the only major argument against a somewhat larger chamber. Remuneration should probably reflect a less than full-time role.

- The relationship between the second chamber and the regional assemblies: without the experience of seeing these chambers in operation for several years it would be premature to try to design a Second House to take a definitive account of them.

---

[4] Conservative Policy Forum, June 1998.

6. Stage 1 and the Wakeham Report

The government's decision to reform the second chamber in two stages has reduced Britain to a condition of near unicameralism. The 'stage one' House which the government has now created is unlikely to be able to command public respect. Without respect the House will be unable to play a meaningful constitutional role.

Outwardly, the composition of the interim House does not appear very different from what it replaces: the majority of the regular attenders from among the Hereditary Peerage have survived. However, the composition of the new interim House leaves it shorn of legitimacy — in fact it is little short of pantomime.

Under the terms of the Blair/Cranborne deal 92 Hereditary Peers will remain in perpetuity.[5] The terms of the deal, now enacted, enable the hereditaries to replenish their 'charmed circle' of 92 by dividing into electoral colleges to elect replacements for those who die — a self-perpetuating oligarchy. The Conservative college contains 42 electors, rather more than the ultimate pocket borough, Old Sarum. As for the Liberals and the Labour party, their colleges contain four peers each: those who survive a death will therefore be able to vote-in a new legislator over tea for three. An institution containing a rump constituted on such an absurd basis cannot hope to command much moral authority.

The interim chamber's other chief distinguishing feature is the greatly increased power of patronage now in the hands of the Prime Minister. He has already appointed nearly as many Life Peers in under three years as Margaret Thatcher managed in just under eleven. He has appointed a higher proportion from his own side than any Prime Minister since the introduction of Life Peerages in 1958. He controls one House and he is now appointing the other. In the absence of further reform he will continue to do so.

---

[5] The terms of the deal, negotiated over a period of several months and sealed in a meeting between Tony Blair and Lord Cranborne, were eventually made public in December 1998. See House of Commons Research Paper 98/105, p. 60.

Both the farce of Hereditary Peers electing one another to a legislature in perpetuity and the massive increase in Prime Ministerial patronage since 1997 will severely erode the credibility of the interim House in the eyes of a wider public and will therefore limit the scope of the chamber legitimately to challenge the executive.

It is true that the removal of nearly half the regularly attending Hereditaries (which is all that stage one reform really achieved) and the introduction of so many new Life Peers has created uncertainty and instability in the interim House. As a result it is more difficult than before to forecast Lords' decisions. Nonetheless, if the interim House acts rationally it will stop short of a major challenge to the executive in the Commons.

In the absence of such a challenge the country is likely to be stuck with the interim House indefinitely. This is because many of the remaining Peers and the Government have an unhealthy interest in seeing it endure. The last thing most Hereditary Peers should want to do is to rock the very lifeboat into which they have just clambered to the point where they might be tipped out. Life Peers will also understandably see further reform, particularly any whiff of democracy, as a threat. Both have an interest in doing whatever is required to make the interim House look permanent. As the sponsor of the Blair/Cranborne amendment, Lord Weatherill, said: 'I'm saying to my friends I believe if this works, as I hope it will work, it's within the bounds of possibility that the Royal Commission may say this has been working well—let's leave it alone. That would preserve continuity...Surely a consummation devoutly to be wished!'

The interim House is therefore likely to maximize the appearance of activity and usefulness, including the adoption of occasional populist causes, while at the same time avoiding serious challenges to the executive in both Houses. Regrettably this is probably what the government wants: the appearance of bicameralism but the reality of almost untrammelled executive supremacy in both Houses. An occasional defeat in the Lords, easily reversed in the Commons, is a small price to pay for that.

For these reasons the Government's justification for two stages of reform – that the Hereditary Peers were a massive obstacle to any reform at all and therefore had to be removed before stage two could be implemented – is bogus. The opposite was the case: the Hereditary Peers, for all their lack of legitimacy, were an (albeit fragile) bulwark against executive supremacy in both Houses.

Lord Wakeham and his Commission could have forced the Prime Minister to loosen his grip on the interim House. He missed the chance. He should have recommended the one thing that can make bicameralism work: democracy. Only democratic legitimacy could give the second chamber a meaningful role in the twenty-first century. I doubt if the public will respect the voice of any other chamber. It was the one recommendation which the Prime Minister would not relish being seen to defeat. Not only would he have had to deploy undemocratic arguments – he would have had to eat his own words.[6]

However Lord Wakeham was reluctant to propose anything that the Prime Minister would veto and so he recommended a largely quango House of appointed Peers, with a residual elected element of only 20% or so. A House constructed on such lines would carry scarcely any more legitimacy than the interim chamber. Worse still, by failing to articulate a clear argument for giving the second chamber a popular mandate Lord Wakeham has left the initiative for further reform firmly in the hands of the executive.

Whether or not Lord Wakeham's proposals are implemented the British parliament is likely to slip further towards *de facto* unicameralism. With stage one reform, far from modernizing Parliament, Labour have entrenched a status-driven second chamber shorn of moral authority – a constitutional shell.

Powerful vested interests now obstruct the route to a more democratic second chamber. The Government will remain deeply wary of any parliamentary impediments to its disposal of power. As they see it, they will not want to create a rod for their own back. Many Commoners will fear that a revived and

---

[6] For example, at the Labour Party Conference in 1995 Tony Blair talked of 'an end to the Hereditary Peers sitting in the House of Lords as the first step to a proper directly-elected second chamber.

largely elected second chamber might erode their monopoly of democratic authority. And then, as already mentioned, there is the existing peerage. Many of the hereditaries, who have survived the stage one cull, will hope that the Blair/Cranborne/Weatherill amendment could become a permanent arrangement, thereby securing the retention of an hereditary element in perpetuity. As for Life Peers, most will fear democracy every bit as much as the Hereditaries. Democracy would mean extinction for them too.

The feature common to all these powerful vested interests is that they are opposed to any further major change, most especially democratic change. It was partly the strength of the democratic case that forced the government to create a Royal Commission in the first place. By articulating that same case, the strength of which far exceeds that of the arguments so far advanced by the various vested interests, the Royal Commission could have played a historic part in framing the British Constitution. They missed the opportunity. That task now falls to the opposition parties and particularly to the Conservatives.

7. Conservatives and the democratic case

How should Conservatives respond to Lords reform? Since 1997 Labour have forced the country on a constitutional journey. If they themselves — as they freely confess — have not identified the end point it is the duty of others, and particularly Conservatives, to make the intellectual effort. In doing so Conservatives must balance their traditional suspicions of abstract constructs with the need to ensure that change accords with Conservative principles. Conservatives should not embark on this task with heady illusions of building a better world.

Conservatives do not turn their minds easily to constitutional theories. Devising neat constitutional arrangements from first principles is alien to them. For the Conservative, political institutions are organic, deriving and learnt from custom and tradition. Most Conservatives agree with Burke: 'politics ought to be adjusted not to human reasoning but to human nature'.

However, it is the very imperfectibility of any constitutional arrangement, based as it is on human nature, which leads Conservatives to certain approaches to constitutional issues: a desire to see limited government and a belief in the need for vigilance in defence of personal freedom against the incursions of the state. Conservatives favour arrangements which provide checks on unlimited authority and which can offer some redress to the inevitable weaknesses of any democratic arrangement. These ideas lie behind the Conservative preference for bicameralism.

It is hardly surprising, therefore, that the Conservatives, more than any other, have been the party of constructive House of Lords' reform.[7] Since the position of the Lords became an issue in British politics, Conservatives have been active in devising schemes to reform its composition and render it a more effective institution. Liberals and particularly Labour have for the most part sought to reduce its powers and effectiveness, or to abolish it.

Since 1918 the majority of leading Conservatives who have examined Lords reform have concluded that some form of democratic solution will eventually have to be found for the second chamber. The list of Conservative contributors to the debate is long and illustrious: Churchill, Curzon, Carrington, Home and Mackay, to name but a few. Conservative support for an elected second chamber, most recently and eloquently expounded in the Mackay Report, has deep roots.

Yet the Conservative Party still stops short of pledging support for democratic reform. Some hanker for the old chamber, now irredeemably lost. Others, understandably but I believe mistakenly, fear the challenge which a more legitimate second chamber could pose to the Commons.

However, a growing number of Conservatives are not only appalled by the gerrymandering of the Constitution which the creation of the interim House represents, they are increasingly aware that only a clear commitment to involve the electorate

---

[7] See *Reforming the Lords: A Conservative Approach, op. cit.*

in its composition can save the second chamber.[8]

Parliament as a whole, and not just a second chamber, has been under attack these past three years. In its defence Conservatives should now be bold. Since Disraeli, Conservatives have never been afraid of radicalism in pursuit of their principles, particularly on constitutional issues. On Lords' reform Conservatives now need to take another leaf out of Disraeli's book. They should embrace democracy for the second chamber (appropriately safeguarded by constitutional checks) and thereby stimulate a wider public debate about the future of Parliament. In doing so Conservatives will be moving with the tide of popular opinion.[9]

The more public debate the better. It will not look unreasonable to argue that in the twenty-first century the electorate should have a say in choosing those entrusted with the power to frame their laws. By making the case, Conservatives can not only ward off the dangers of the interim quango; they can bolster parliamentary democracy.

Acknowledgements

Parts of this article were based on the author's submission to the Wakeham Commission and articles in *The Times* (23 March 1998 and 26 March 1999).

---

[8] In March 1999 almost half of the Conservative backbenches signed Early Day Motion No. 464 in favour of an elected second chamber, since when parliamentary support in the party has probably grown. The motion attracted support from all sides of the House and was signed by 144 MPs.

[9] Opinion polls have consistently shown support from about three quarters of the electorate for an elected second chamber. In the most recent poll, by ICM in September 1999, 84% supported an elected chamber, while only 11% opted for an appointed chamber.

Michael Rush

The Wakeham Report[1]

The Labour Party's 1983 election manifesto promised that the next Labour government would abolish the House of Lords. However, by 1992 that pledge had been replaced by a commitment to an elected second chamber, probably based on regional representation and elected by PR. This was to be achieved by a two-stage process: the removal of the Hereditary Peers and then the creation of a reformed second chamber. The 1997 election manifesto retained the commitment to remove the Hereditary Peers as a first and separate stage of reform, but there was no specific commitment to create a wholly- or partly-elected second chamber. In its place was a general pledge 'to make the House of Lords more democratic and representative', but four clear commitments were made:

- 'The system of appointment of life peers…will be reviewed.'

- 'Our objective will be to ensure that over time, party appointees as life peers more accurately reflect the proportion of votes cast at the previous general election.'

- 'We are committed to maintaining an independent crossbench presence of life peers.'

- 'No one political party should seek a majority in the [second chamber].'

---

[1] Royal Commission on the Reform of the House of Lords, *A House for the Future*, Cm. 4534, January 2000.

The second stage of reform was to be the task of a joint parliamentary committee 'to undertake a wide-ranging review of possible further change and then to bring forward proposals for reform'. There was no mention of a Royal Commission, but in the Queen's Speech in November 1998 the Government announced legislation to remove Hereditary Peers from the House of Lords with a Royal Commission to make recommendations on the second stage of reform. The Government argued that this would allow for a more wide-ranging consultation, encourage public involvement, and allow the matter to be considered while the first stage was being dealt with by Parliament.

The House of Lords Reform Act (1999) removed the right of Hereditary Peers to sit and vote in the House of Lords, but provision was made for a residuary group of 90 Hereditary Peers to be elected proportionately by the three major parties and the Crossbench Peers.[2] In January 1999 the Government published a white paper, *Modernising Parliament: Reforming the House of Lords*,[3] and the Royal Commission was appointed in February 1999. It was asked to report by 31 December 1999. In its white paper the Government said that once the Commission had reported a joint committee of the two Houses of Parliament would be set up to consider 'the parliamentary aspects' of the Commission's recommendations.

Although the white paper did not come down unequivocally in favour of a particular model, it was clear that the Government did not favour a wholly-elected chamber (Chap. 8, paras. 29 and 32). Crucially, but not surprisingly, the Government made it clear that, whatever form of second chamber emerged, the primacy of the House of Commons must remain (Chap. 7, para. 6). On the functions of a reformed second chamber the white paper followed a conventional line that, like the existing House of Lords, it should have significant legislative, scrutiny and deliberative roles (Chap. 7, paras. 12–20) and there were strong hints that it could play a useful role in regional and broader religious representation (Chap. 8, paras. 24–5). As far as the judicial functions of the House of Lords

---

[2] In addition, ten former Leaders of the House of Lords and Peers of first creation accepted Life Peerages.

[3] Cm. 4183, January 1999.

were concerned, it was noted that these could be hived off, but acknowledged that the Law Lords played a useful part in the non-judicial work of the House (Chap. 7, paras. 19–20). The manifesto pledges to prevent any one party from having a majority in a reformed second chamber and to maintain a significant crossbench element were repeated in the white paper (Chap. 2, para. 19). There was also a clear pledge to set up an independent Appointments Commission, but its role would be confined to the nomination of crossbench members; party nominations would remain in the hands of the Prime Minister, although they would be subject to vetting by the Appointments Commission (Chap. 6, paras. 9–14). Finally, the Government saw no need for a significant change in the powers of the second chamber, although some detailed aspects could be usefully examined (Chap. 7, paras. 23–7)

1. The Royal Commission at Work[4]

The Royal Commission began work in March 1999 and embarked on an extensive consultation exercise. A consultation paper was published and 6,000 copies were sent to over 4,500 individuals and organizations. Responses could be made not only through conventional means but also via a website and e-mail. This exercise elicited 1,734 written submissions from a wide range of individuals and organizations, with no less than 76.9% from members of the public, as distinct from Peers (7.3%), various organizations (5.7%), academics and other experts (5.2%), MPs and political parties (2.5%) and religious bodies (2.4%). Yet further public access to the Commission was facilitated by 21 evidence-taking public sessions held in London and seven regional locations, which were attended by 1,026 people. These sessions took oral evidence from various individuals and then invited comments from members of the audience. Those attending were also invited to complete a questionnaire on the functions and composition of a reformed second chamber.

The Commission also commissioned 12 papers on various aspects of its work, including the judicial functions, methods

[4] For details see Wakeham Report, Chap. 1, paras. 1.6–1.15 and Appendices A and B.

of election, religious representation, human rights aspects and overseas experience.[5] In addition, the Commission consulted a number of prominent individuals, including four former Prime Ministers, the Speaker of the House of Commons, the chair of the Commons' Procedure Committee, the Presiding Officers of the Scottish Parliament, the National Assembly for Wales and the Northern Ireland Assembly, two senior Law Lords and religious representatives.

The Commission's report was published in January 2000, but, in addition to publication in the conventional form of a printed command paper, a 28-page summary was also produced and both it and the report were accompanied by a CD-ROM which included the commissioned papers and most of the oral and written evidence the Commission had received.

2. The Commission's Recommendations

The Commission's report comprises 222 pages and contains 132 recommendations. It is some measure of its thoroughness that the report and the accompanying evidence, both oral and written, amounts to over 600Mb on the CD-ROM. That thoroughness is much more clearly shown, however, by a detailed examination of the recommendations, which rest on the basic premise that *functions should determine composition*. The Commission therefore argued that, in terms of its overall role, the reformed second chamber 'should have the capacity to offer counsel from [a] range of sources. It should be broadly representative of society...work with the House of Commons to provide an effective check on the government...[and]...give the United Kingdom's constituent nations and regions...a formally constituted voice in the Westminster Parliament' (para. 3.30). It then went on to consider particular functions — legislative, scrutinizing, protecting the Constitution and judicial — in separate chapters, before turning to composition.

---

[5]   For a list see *ibid.*, p. 216.

The Legislative Function (Chaps. 4 & 7)

Primary Legislation

The Commission did not envisage significant changes to the second chamber's legislative function. In general it argued that the House of Commons 'should have the final say in respect of all major policy issues', but 'the second chamber should have sufficient power...to require the government and the House of Commons to reconsider proposed legislation and take account of any cogent objections to it' (para. 4.7). It therefore followed that the second chamber should retain its delaying or suspensory power over Bills passed by the Commons (para. 4.12) and the existing situation whereby Bills introduced first in the Lords are not subject to the Parliament Acts (e.g. the Criminal Justice (Mode of Trial Bill) should *not* be changed (paras. 4–19). Similarly, the Salisbury convention — that the second chamber would not oppose the second reading of bills foreshadowed in the governing party's election manifesto — should be retained and the second chamber 'should be cautious about challenging the clearly-expressed views of the House of Commons on any public policy issue'. The latter would require the development of a new convention (para. 4.24). Where disquiet persists, informal conciliation procedures could be supplemented by a formal joint committee (para. 4.29).

The Commission makes a number of other detailed proposals concerning primary legislation, *e.g.* the second chamber should continue to play the principal role in dealing with consolidation Bills (para. 4.49), explore means of expediting Bills proposed by the Law Commission (para. 4.51), and deal with more private Bills than at present (para. 4.52).

Secondary Legislation

On secondary legislation the Commission argued that there 'is a strong case for enhanced parliamentary scrutiny of secondary legislation' and that the 'second chamber should make a strong contribution in this area' (para. 7.6). It proposed the systematic sifting of all SIs (Statutory Instruments), either by a joint committee or by the existing Delegated Powers and Deregulation Committee, and that neither House should consider any SI until it has been reported (paras. 7.23, 26 & 28).

The period for the consideration of SIs subject to negative procedure should be extended from 40 to 60 days (para. 7.28).
However, the Commission recommended *against* the second
chamber being able to amend SIs (para. 7.29) and *in favour* of
the removal of the Lords' present absolute veto on SIs (SIs are
not subject to the Parliament Acts). A vote to oppose an affirmative resolution or annul a negative one on an SI could be
overridden by the Commons after three months. In each case
the minister responsible would publish a memorandum
explaining the reasons for the regulation and give the second
chamber an opportunity to reconsider its position (para. 7.37).

The Scrutiny Function (Chap. 8)

Ministers in the Second Chamber

There have been suggestions that no ministers should be
members of a reformed second chamber, but the Commission
took the view that this would reduce the opportunities for
scrutiny and that ministers should continue to be drawn from
the second chamber (para. 8.6). However, it further recommended that mechanisms should be developed to enable *MPs
who are ministers* to make statements and answer Questions in
the second chamber (para. 8.7), rather similar to the practice in
the French National Assembly.

European Union Business

The Commission recognized that the House of Lords already
does important work in the scrutiny of European Union business and made a number of recommendations to extend and
strengthen that role. In particular it suggested that there
should be a specified time for Questions for oral answer on the
EU (paras. 8.16, 20, 23 & 24) and that the second chamber
should consider steps to improve links with MEPs and
develop contacts with the European Parliament and the parliaments of other member states (paras. 8.21 & 26). However, it
recommended against UK MEPs being ex-officio members of
the second chamber (para. 8.20).

Other Aspects of Scrutiny

The Commission also recognized the important part Lords' committees play in scrutinizing the executive and similarly made recommendations for strengthening that role. In general it recommended that the second chamber 'should continue to provide a distinctive forum for national debate' (para. 8.27). This was one of the four second chamber functions identified by the Bryce Commission 80 years before in an earlier attempt to reform the House of Lords and acknowledged by the Government in its white paper.[6] In particular, however, it recommended that scrutiny by specialized committees 'should continue to be an important function' of the second chamber (para. 8.29) and suggested a further role — 'the establishment of a select committee to scrutinize international treaties' (para. 8.42), but rejected a special role for the second chamber in the making of public appointments (para. 8.36) (cf. US Senate).

Protecting the Constitution (Chap. 5)

The Commission argued that 'one of the most important functions of the reformed second chamber should be to act as a "constitutional long-stop", ensuring that changes are not made to the constitution without full and open debate and an awareness of the consequences' (para. 5.4). However, it rejected special and additional powers for the second chamber to protect the Constitution, either generally (para. 5.7) or over particular areas of constitutional or human rights issues or legislation (paras. 5.11 & 12), but did make a number of specific recommendations:

- The Parliament Acts should be amended to prevent their being amended *without* the consent of the second chamber, as happened with the Parliament Act, 1949 (para. 5.15). This would, of course, prevent the House of Commons from removing the provision in the Parliament Act, 1911 stipulating that the life of a Parliament could not be extended without the consent of the second chamber (para. 5.16).

---

[6] See *Report of the Conference on the Reform of the Second Chamber* (the Bryce Commission), Cd. 9038, 1918 and *Modernising Parliament*, Cm. 4183, January 1999, Chap. 7, para. 14.

- The second chamber should establish a select committee on constitutional matters (para. 5.22).

- The second chamber should establish a select committee on human rights issues (para. 5.31), although this could be a sub-committee of the constitutional committee.

Giving a Voice to the Nations and Regions of the UK (Chap. 6)

In general the Commission's view was that '[the] second chamber should be so constituted that it could play a valuable role in relation to the nations and regions of the United Kingdom whatever pattern of devolution and decentralization may emerge in the future' (para. 6.5). In order to achieve this '[a]t least a proportion of the members of the second chamber should provide a direct voice for the various nations and regions of the United Kingdom' (para. 6.8), but 'the second chamber should not become a "federal legislature", supporting a "federal government"' (para. 6.10), nor should it become 'a forum for inter-governmental liaison' (para. 6.12), which should be 'carried on outside parliamentary institutions' (para. 6.12). This direct regional voice should be secured by direct election and Members of devolved assemblies should *not* be 'automatically entitled to sit in or nominate others to join the second chamber' (para. 6.18). Proposals for the direct representation of overseas territories, in the manner of the French Parliament, were rejected (para. 6.30).

However, the Commission did not take the view that the second chamber should not in any way be concerned with devolution; on the contrary, it suggested that a select committee might be established to examine 'the issues raised by devolution'. This could be a sub-committee of the constitutional committee (para. 6.25). In addition, although it did not think the second chamber should meet outside London, its committees, especially the devolution committee, could (para. 6.27).

The Judicial Functions (Chap. 9)

The Commission was firmly of the view that the second chamber should continue to exercise its judicial functions through the Law Lords (para. 9.5) and that the Law Lords should continue to be members of the second chamber (para. 9.7), on the grounds that they made a valuable contribution to its other functions. However, the Law Lords 'should publish a statement of the principles which they intend to observe when participating in debates in the second chamber and when considering their eligibility to sit on related cases' (para. 9.10).

Composition (Chaps. 11, 12, 13 & 15)

The Principles of Composition (Recommendation 70)
In considering composition the Commission initially examined the merits of nomination and election and the optimal size of the reformed second chamber, before coming to conclusions about more detailed aspects. It rejected a wholly- or largely-elected second chamber, indirect election from the devolved assemblies, from among MEPs or by an electoral college, random selection and co-option (para. 11.36). It also rejected a wholly-appointed second chamber, opting for a mixed composition, with the majority of members being appointed and a minority — representing the nations and regions of the UK — elected. Three models for the election of regional members were suggested (paras. 12.26–42) (for details see below).

An 'Appointments Commission, independent of the Prime Minister, the government and the political parties, should be responsible for *all* appointments to the second chamber' (author's italics). The present system of nomination by the Prime Minister would therefore cease. The overall size of the second chamber should be determined by the Appointments Commission (para. 13.28), but the Royal Commission envisaged a second chamber 'in the region of 550 members' (para. 13.27). It also adopted a number of 'principles of composition' which should guide the work of the Appointments Commission:

- 'The political balance in the reformed second chamber should match that of the country as expressed in votes cast at the most recent general election.' (para. 11.36)

- '...at least 20 per cent of the members...[should *not* be]... affiliated to one of the major parties'.

- The Appointments Commission 'should be required to ensure that members...are broadly representative of British society on a range of stated dimensions...[and]... should possess a variety of expertise and experience and various specific qualities appropriate to the role and functions of the reformed second chamber'.

- There should be a statutory duty to ensure that 'a minimum of 30 per cent of *new* members of the second chamber...[are]...women and a minimum of 30 per cent men, with the aim of making steady progress towards gender balance in the chamber as a whole over time'.

- The Appointments Commission 'should be required to use its best endeavours to ensure a level of representation for members of minority ethnic groups which is at least proportionate to their presence in the population as a whole'.

- The Appointments Commission 'should also play a role in ensuring appropriate representation for religious faiths'.[7]

The Appointments Commission (Chap. 13)
The Appointments Commission should consist of eight individuals, three nominated by the Conservative, Labour and Liberal Democratic Parties respectively, one by the Convenor of Crossbench Peers, and four independents selected in accordance with the principles laid down by the Committee on Standards in Public Life. Commissioners would hold office for a maximum of ten years (paras. 13.3 & 14–19) and 'a number..., though not a majority, should be members of the second chamber. None should be an MP' (para. 13.16). One of the independent members would chair the Commission (para. 13.14).

The Commission would submit an annual report to Parliament providing details of the appointments made and the steps taken to ensure that the composition of the second chamber reflects the characteristics laid down in the Royal Commis-

---

[7] This is covered by Chap. 15, in which the Commission recommends that 26 places should be reserved for Christian faiths (21 in England (16 Church of England), and 5 for Wales, Scotland and Northern Ireland). A further 5 members 'should be broadly representative of non-Christian faith communities' (para. 15.17).

sion's report regarding party, gender, ethnic and religious representation (para. 13.23). The Commission should be pro-active in seeking to meet those characteristics (paras. 13.30, 36, 37 & 39).

Term of Appointment or Election (Chap. 12)
Wakeham recommended that appointed and elected members should serve a fixed term of 15 years, with staggered elections for elected members (para. 12.15), subject to a maximum of two terms (para. 12.18). Members of the second chamber would not be eligible for election to the House of Commons until ten years after their term of membership ends, whether they have served a full term or not (para. 12.21).

Three models — one of 65 members, one of 87 and one of 195 — were proposed. The Commission could not agree on one model, but 'Model B had the support of a substantial majority':

- Model A: 65 members elected at the first general election after the legislation setting up the reformed second chamber has been passed, with one third being elected for one parliamentary term and one third for two parliamentary terms. Thereafter elections would be on a staggered basis, coinciding with general elections, with one third of the seats in each region being filled. Because elections would coincide with general elections, terms of office in the second chamber would vary from the 15-year norm. The voting system would be closed list PR (*i.e.* seats would be distributed in proportion to each party's vote in each region) (paras. 12.26–32).

- Model B: 87 members elected at the same time as MEPs, using Euro-constituencies, on a staggered basis by PR, and using either a 'partially-open' list system (majority view) allowing voters to choose different parties for second chamber members and MEPs or a closed list system (minority view) as in Model A (paras. 12.33–8).

- Model C: 195 members elected at the same time as MEPs, on a staggered basis, using the 'partially-open' system as in Model B. One-third (65) of the regional members would be elected at the first Euro-election after the setting up of the reformed second chamber and a further third at the following two Euro-elections (12.39–42).

Transitional Arrangements (Chap. 14)
The Royal Commission decided against a 'big bang' approach to establishing the reformed second chamber. Transitional arrangements for the regional elected members were included in each of the three proposed models. The Appointments Commission would make appointments twice a year and the Royal Commission estimated that there would be 20 to 30 vacancies each year. Existing Life Peers would be deemed to have been appointed to the reformed second chamber for life (para. 14.12). Life Peers appointed between the publication of the Royal Commission's report and its implementation would be deemed to have been appointed for 15 years from the date of the peerage (para. 14.14). Existing Life Peers, including Law Lords, would be able to retire from the second chamber and 'should be encouraged to reach an informal understanding with the Appointments Commission about how long they intend to serve' (paras. 14.16 & 17).

Pay, Services and Facilities (Chaps. 10 & 17)

Full-time versus Part-time Membership
The Commission did not favour a full-time membership. It took the view that the second chamber 'should contain a substantial proportion of people who are not professional politicians...[and that]...part-time membership...should continue to be facilitated and even encouraged (para. 10.18).[8] It therefore recommended not a salary but payment based on attendance. The total payment possible should be less than the basic salary of an MP (paras. 17.9–11). However, members who chaired 'significant committees' should be paid a salary (para. 17.12). The Senior Salaries Review Body (SSRB) 'should consider the issue of severance payments and pension arrangements for members of the reformed second chamber' (para. 17.13).

---

[8] This echoed the view expressed by the Nolan Committee on MPs. See Committee on Standards in Public Life, *First Report*, 1995, Cm. 2850-I, paras. 2.19–20.

Services and Facilities

Additional office accommodation and secretarial resources should be provided to enable committees and individual members to work more effectively (para. 17.15). The SSRB should review the travel and subsistence allowances 'with a view to ensuring that regular attendance is economically viable for [members] who live outside London' (para. 17.17).

3. Implementation

Both before and since its publication, the Wakeham Report has been the subject of much speculation — often involving back-burners, long grass and dusty shelves! It has also been the subject of strong criticism by those who favour a wholly-elected second chamber,[9] notably the Liberal Democrats and Charter 88. But, whatever the merits of such a chamber, it is the least likely outcome. The Government has committed itself to further change in its white paper, but that is no guarantee that there will be a second stage of reform and Wakeham could easily suffer the apparent fate of the Jenkins Report on electoral reform.[10] On the other hand, the Wakeham report is a skilfully-constructed set of proposals: it has responded clearly to the signals in the Government's white paper; none of its major recommendations are politically unrealistic; and it has, for the most part, avoided making recommendations which distract from its main thrust. The *most* obvious example of this is the refusal to propose a name for the reformed second chamber or an appropriate title for its members, preferring that these be 'left to evolve' (Chap. 18, para. 11). It is therefore unfortunate that the Commission could not agree on an electoral model, since it has allowed some in the media to suggest that the Commission was fatally divided, and this may yet prove a distraction. Three possible outcomes may be suggested:

- The Government essentially accepts all the Commission's report, opting for whichever of the three models for elected members it prefers.

---

[9] See Russell; and Tyrie, this volume [ed.].
[10] Cm. 4090, October 1998.

- The Government adopts a significantly *selective response* to the report, accepting some major recommendations, rejecting others. This might, for example, include opting for a wholly-nominated house and rejecting the proposal for an elected element. It might also include rejecting or substantially modifying the proposal for an Appointments Commission.

- The whole question of further reform is delayed indefinitely, openly or not, leaving the 'transitional' house to become the 'permanent' house, repeating the experience of 1911.

There also remains one fascinating unknown: what will be the attitude of the 'transitional' House of Lords to any legislation for further reform that is brought before Parliament. On this, one thing seems certain: the reaction of the transitional House will not be passive. Already it has shown itself willing to assert itself at least as readily as its predecessor by, for example, rejecting the regulations for the London mayoral election, the first such rejection of an SI since the 'old' House of Lords rejected an SI renewing sanctions against Rhodesia in 1968. In 1907 Lloyd George denounced the House of Lords as Mr Balfour's 'poodle'; the transitional House clearly intends to be no one's poodle.

Conrad Russell

Wakeham Report:
A short commentary

There are two trends in parliamentary history that have been operating almost uninterrupted at least since 1688. The question posed by the Wakeham Report is whether these trends will continue to the point where parliamentary government changes into something else, or whether the pendulum has now reached the limit of its swing and they will go into reverse.

The first of these trends is the growing predominance of the Commons within Parliament. The theory of parliamentary sovereignty as formulated under Edward I and Henry VIII was a system of checks and balances. King, Lords and Commons, like the Trinity to which they were sometimes compared, were three in one and one in three. As the ritual of the State Opening, largely developed under Henry VIII, reminds us, the Commons were the least important of the three. The requirement to gain the consent of all three before the sovereign power to pass legislation could be invoked was a very real restriction. Today, as the Wakeham Report brusquely reminds us, 'whatever the theory, parliamentary sovereignty in the United Kingdom ultimately resides, in practice, in the House of Commons'.

Yet at the same time as the Commons has gained authority over the other members of the parliamentary Trinity, it has progressively lost its independence in relation to the ministers of the Crown. The growth of party, the growth of government patronage, and the transfer of government patronage from the Crown to ministers in the Commons have all contributed to this. As a result, the power of ministers with a large majority over the Commons has developed, in Lord Hailsham's famous phrase, into an elective dictatorship. The consequence, as Tony Blair discovered during the coalition that ran the Kosovo war, is that he has more unfettered power than any other leader in the Western world.

To the question of whether the reform of the Lords should be used to put this trend into reverse, the Wakeham Commission has returned a resounding 'no'. In their words, 'our view is that the country's new constitutional arrangements should provide for a second chamber which does not pose a threat to the House of Commons' pre-eminence'. In other words, the Prime Minister should be free to do whatever he likes.

It does not matter whether this power is going to Blair, Hague or Kennedy: whoever gets it, it is bad for him. If it were offered to me I would hope to respond in the spirit of a colleague who once interrupted a discussion of mortgages with the words: 'If I were a banker, I wouldn't lend me that much money.' Arbitrary power leads to intellectual sloth and to unworkable legislation. Every constitution that can pretend to the name must have some check on its highest power.

There are three main ways this can be done. The first is by a written constitution. The second is by proportional representation, which forces a government to negotiate for its majority in the legislature. The third is by an effective second chamber with the power and the legitimacy to impose significant inconvenience on a government that will not consider compromise. This is the only one of the three that is on the agenda at present. What is at stake in the reform of the second chamber, then, is whether we are to have a constitutional government or an elective dictatorship. Many countries have all three of the above-mentioned checks on executive power. To have none is unacceptable.

This is the yardstick by which the Wakeham Report must be judged, and by that yardstick it falls very far short. This judgment will be unacceptable to the Commons, but they, like any other power, must be prepared to answer John Stuart Mill's question: 'When has there been a dominion which has not appeared natural to them that possessed it?'

No one proposes to end the supremacy of the Commons. What is needed is not to take it away but to ensure that it is not unchallenged. MPs must be subjected to a need to compromise so that they do not always get 100% of their own way, but occasionally have to settle for 90%. It is a modest ambition and a procedure for achieving it has been well set out in the Parliament Acts. Those Acts face a minister whose Bill is in trouble in the Lords with a choice between having an amended Bill at once, or the whole in a year's time. That choice concentrates ministerial minds and forces them to decide on priorities. The Parliament Acts were not designed to destroy the supremacy of the Commons.

Ministers have refused to negotiate and have claimed an unfettered right to get their own way 'because I say so'. Reform of the Lords must give it the legitimacy necessary to mount an effective challenge to that point of view. It is not encouraging that on the same day as the launch of the Wakeham Report the Government responded to the overwhelming Lords' defeat of the Bill to restrict trial by jury by saying that they will do exactly what they tried to do before. Do they really want a second chamber?

This is why any discussion on the composition of the second chamber must be subordinate to decisions on powers. It is no good having a second chamber that can merely ask the Commons to think again, and must always knuckle under if they do not. In this context the Wakeham Report's discussion of powers, and particularly of delegated legislation, is deeply disappointing.

The Commission's views on composition are the consequence of their views on powers. The case for election is not just a case for avoiding 'Tony's cronies'. It is that election is the only language the Commons understands. Until ministers in the Lords can no longer get up and intone: 'Now is the time for us to give way to the elected chamber', the second chamber cannot provide effective checks and balances. There is a strong case for nomination to preserve the existence of cross-benchers who prevent the second chamber from being a purely party-political House. There should be election for all or almost all the rest. Even the Wakeham Report option which suggested the largest number of elected members (195), is far short of adequacy. It is even more worrying that the majority option proposes election by closed list, as for the European Parliament. A second chamber needs people of distinction who should be personally elected. To have them chosen by party lists brings back nomination by the back door.

If the Commons rejects these arguments and goes for absolute power, it will find that it leads to the proverbial consequence: it will corrupt absolutely. In the end it is they who will suffer, and the fiction that they represent the people will in the end become a case of the Emperor's New Clothes. Their legitimacy will be in danger too. We are at a crossroads. Is it too late to take the right turning?

Acknowledgements

This commentary was originally published in the *Sunday Telegraph*, 23 January 2000.

Simon Jenkins

Local Government

The reforms now being introduced to the local government of London and other English authorities are the most radical for over a century. Coupled with devolution to Scotland and Wales, they set out to reverse the centralist tendency in British government since the Second World War. In the case of Scotland and Wales, devolution is regional and partial, with wide areas of discretion, most crucially over taxation, remaining to the government in London. In the case of London, there is no freedom to raise taxes, only charges. Even switches between expenditure headings, for instance on police or transport, is controlled centrally. Labour election promises to devolve the new National Business Rate or the use of capital balances have not been fully honoured. Standardization of local services, through Audit Commission and other performance targets, has continued apace. The hand of the Treasury still lies heavy on political reform.

Yet the changes have unleashed new and unpredictable forces. Decentralized democracy in Britain, long shackled, has seen its chains loosened and has begun to move free. Although the new powers devolved to the Scottish Parliament are scarcely more extensive than those enjoyed by the old Scottish Office, the mere existence of an elected parliament sitting in Edinburgh, to which the executive arm is directly accountable, has transformed local politics. In Wales the assembly is little more than a debating chamber. Yet as in Scotland the fact of its existence and the requirement for executive accountability has offered local representatives the opportunity to challenge regional policies and galvanize officialdom. The domestic affairs of a substantial portion of the United

Kingdom have been repatriated. Democracy is now whipping devolution onwards, rather than centralism whipping democracy backwards.

In London, the mere prospect of the Greater London Authority Act has proved seismic. The act itself is so hedged about with 'Henry VIII' clauses restricting the scope of the new authority as to leave the mayor and assembly on paper as little more than statutory agents of Whitehall. They will have less power than their predecessors, the London County Council or the Greater London Council, and less than London's constituent boroughs. That has not seemed to matter. The prospect of direct election has opened public debate on every aspect of the government of the capital. Since the same option is to be on offer to every local council in England, London's experience could well form the template for the rest of the country. If so, Britain will see the most radical upheaval in its democratic institutions since the introduction of the universal franchise.

The extraordinary assault on local democracy in Britain in the 15 years after 1984 was not unprecedented. The progressive usurpation of local autonomy had continued since the growth of the welfare state and the 'nationalization' of hospitals, prisons and public assistance in the 1940s. By 1975, Labour's Tony Crosland was already warning local councils that 'the party is over', hinting that their freedom to raise and spend local taxes would soon be curbed. But it was the degeneration of local democracy into party cabalism in the 1970s and 1980s that offered Lady Thatcher the opportunity to cap rates, curb spending and institute the most homogeneous pattern of local services in any Western democracy. Her fixation with controlling all she surveyed was not new, only more explicit.

The story of the introduction and abandonment of the poll tax between 1988 and 1992 needs no repetition. History holds that it was a once-off aberration, which contributed to Lady Thatcher's fall and was briskly corrected by John Major's in-coming cabinet. I believe this analysis to be false.[1] Certainly one of Lady Thatcher's environment secretaries, Patrick Jenkin, baldly stated that 'there can be no room in our unitary

---

[1]   See Simon Jenkins, *Accountable to None* (Penguin, 1995).

state for unilateral declarations of independence by individual local authorities relying on claims of a local mandate'.[2] But in its early form the poll tax was a real attempt to rectify the democratic deficit in local government which had widened since the capping of local rates in 1984. Capping had stripped local democracy of any accountability for the huge rate rises levied by some councils, safe in the knowledge that most of their electors did not pay rates because they were too poor. Attempts on the part of Michael Heseltine and Norman Fowler to correct this lacuna by expanding the rate base were considered insufficiently radical.

The new tax was intended to sow nettles among the grass roots of local democracy. Councils would have to raise the money they needed for the level of services they chose to provide, and answer for that choice in a local ballot. In her memoirs, Lady Thatcher looked back on the reform through typically rose-tinted spectacles. Claiming that it was just starting to work when she was ousted, she said that its abandonment would mean that 'more and more powers will pass to central government, that upwards pressures on public spending and taxation would increase accordingly'. She was right, but upward pressure had begun with the poll tax, not after it.

For the poll tax to have democratic 'bite' it had, above all, to be uncapped. It had to offend against Mr Jenkin's principle of a unitary state. Councils had to be able to vary service levels, pay for it and account for that variance to their electorates. Yet the poll tax was inherently rigid and too regressive in impact to survive. To be tolerable to the poor it had to be fixed low; it thus delivered insufficient revenue and had to be augmented by central grants. It was hard to collect, since people are more mobile than properties, and it evolved into a miserable 'graduated residents' charge'. But nothing so undermined the case for the innovation as the victory conceded by Lady Thatcher to the Treasury in the course of its passage. Like the outgoing rates, the new tax was to be capped by central government. This wrecked the essence of the reform, which was to make a new fiscal regime locally accountable and thus give local voters the necessary 'bite'. If central government was to cap the

[2] In America or Germany such an assertion of constitutional centralism would have had Mr Jenkin up before a constitutional court.

poll tax as it had capped the rates, why should local electors bother to hold their councils to account? It was a government tax, and so it was regarded.

The poll tax was the most complete 'constitutional rape' of devolved democracy. Councillors could be as irresponsible as they liked 'up to the cap' and were protected from being irresponsible above it. All local expenditure gradually converged on the norm. Almost by accident the government also abolished the discretion on local councils to levy business rates. The chief reason was that businesses had no vote and were being squeezed by left-wing councils more concerned for money than employment. Yet the business rate was not abolished but 'nationalized', its level remitted to Whitehall (where businesses were equally disenfranchised). In 1988 roughly £13 billion of annual cash flow was brought under the control of the Treasury. I calculated that this was the biggest single act of 'nationalization' in postwar British history — and by the Tories. Nobody complained.

By the early 1990s Lady Thatcher had gone and the Major Government had abolished the tax, reinstating the rates in the form of a banded property tax. The poll tax fiasco was estimated to have cost £1.5 billion to set up and dismantle. This was dwarfed by the rebates, safety nets, transitional reliefs and subsidies required by politicians to ease both introduction and abolition. David Butler and his co-authors[3] put the additional cost of the tax at some £20 billion, all borne by central taxpayers. This shift from local to central taxation added 2–3 pence on income tax, and gave local ratepayers a massive tax holiday. They did not notice it and gave no thanks to central government. But by the time of the 1992 Local Government Finance Act the popular view was that the saga was over and could be forgotten.

The 1992 Act restored property taxes but did not restore the status quo. In the early months of 1991 the cabinet even debated a paper suggesting the winding up of elected local councils altogether. Not only had the poll tax been capped, but the new council tax was capped also. The habit had stuck. Local democracy survived, just, but only as a prelude to a

---

[3] David Butler, Andrew Adonis and Tony Travers, *Failure in British Government* (Oxford University Press, 1994).

decade of remorseless centralization. Between 1985 and 1997 upwards of 100 new laws sought, in some way or another, to limit and regiment local councils. At the start of the process, some 60% of local spending was covered by discretionary local taxes. By the end, local taxes covered under 20% and local treasurers reckoned that less than 5% of their spending was in any sense discretionary. Local democracy had won a battle against Whitehall over the poll tax, but it had lost the war. In future, new initiatives in policing, education, roads or public health would depend on special targeted central grants, for which ministers would take the credit.

The Labour opposition fought rate-capping and other measures of Tory centralization, and constantly promised to rescind them. As soon as Tony Blair came to office in 1997, however, the sirens of central control soon won him round. Capping continued, as did the no less *dirigiste* Standard Spending Assessments. Ministers were daily in and out of schools, claiming credit for a service whose quality, two decades earlier, was the responsibility of councillors. Police numbers became a Home Office responsibility. So did such minor investments as school computers, street security cameras and literacy training courses. Local government continued to get an appalling press. The media covered every children's home scandal, every council expenses scam, every planning corruption allegation as it drove a nail in the coffin of local democracy.

By the end of the 1990s the culture of centralization appeared to have reached its limit. Schools were receiving over 200 detailed forms a year from Whitehall. Police forces were estimated to spend 20% of their time on centrally-generated bureaucracy. The calculation of the needs and resources component of central grants took government statisticians into the wilder realms of differential calculus. Performance indicators prepared by the local Audit Commission ran to page upon page of quantification. Some were instructive, such as the number of bin clearances per house, or the number of library books per head. Others were ludicrous, like clear-up rates on recorded crime, with its built-in disincentive to list crimes unlikely to be solved. Others were murderous, like response times to 999 calls, which sent police car accident rates soaring. 'What is measurable became valuable and what is unmeasurable valueless', was the maxim of the day.

With stark exceptions, notably in London's poorest boroughs, most English councils did respond to the new ideas current in public administration in the 1980s and '90s. Competitive tendering was generally a success, transforming direct labour forces, refuse collection and street cleaning. The local management of schools released institutions from much local bureaucracy (before it was replaced by central bureaucracy). The disposal and privatization of housing management greatly improved most council estates. It seemed to pass notice that the two least efficient public services, hospitals and prisons, were those that had been nationalized under Whitehall the longest. The Metropolitan Police, one of the less cost-effective forces in England, was the only one run directly by central government. From my own observation, public land is usually more efficiently used when held locally than when it is owned by central government, notably the defence ministry estates. Despite their offence against democracy, capping and audit did focus attention on cost-effectiveness and waste.

Yet it was small wonder that by the mid-1990s participation rates in British local democracy had collapsed. At the time Denmark was recording local turnouts at 80%, Germany 72%, France 68% and Spain 64%. Britain was down to 40%, or nearer 30% in the big cities. Even for the most trivial complaints electors were turning to their MP rather than to their local councillor. Local government remained popular: surveys conducted for the 1995 Commission on Local Democracy showed it was persistently more trusted than national or European government. But as a vehicle for local accountability it was ineffective. A gulf had opened between the 'local administration of local services', as Whitehall put it, and political responsibility for the level of such services. When roads were pot-holed, people blamed the government. When libraries were closed, it was because of government cuts. When teachers needed new equipment, it came in a budget package from government. The media understandably concentrated on central government and accordingly ignored local. In the 1990s the BBC did not even have a television news programme for London, the capital being regarded as part of 'the

South-East'. With the abolition of London government in 1985 went the abolition of London's political identity. Without media support interest in local politics naturally atrophied.

While the new Labour government seized centralization with enthusiasm, it did carry in its manifesto a number of devolutionary pledges which it could not ignore. These included assemblies for Scotland and Wales, an elected mayor for London and a democratic revitalization of local councils. Unlike pledges on local finance, which Gordon Brown's Treasury disregarded, these innovations were specific and constitutional. They needed white papers and statutes. While the Scottish and Welsh reforms were regional, even nationalist, in character, the reforms to English local government were truly local.

They were not without their conflicts. The resistance to any delegation of serious political power to a new London mayoralty was intense within Whitehall. The new government of London was to be original both in structure and in mandate, and to the Treasury 'original' meant largely ceremonial. It was not to insert a new layer of government, rather to place a new tier of accountability over the functions of Whitehall's existing Government Office for London. The authority was meant to make existing functions more democratic, not find new things to do.

The case for a directly-elected mayor had been set out in detail in the report of the independent Commission for Local Democracy in 1995. Its chief purpose was, ironically, similar to that initially underlying Lady Thatcher's poll tax. It was 'to make local politics more accountable' by raising the profile of local politicians, increasing participation rates and bringing decisions more directly before the public gaze. Evidence from abroad was that direct election achieved this. Germany, Italy, France, Spain and all Scandinavian countries enjoyed more decentralized local government than Britain. Local participation rates were higher. Mayoral systems, for instance in France and Germany, led to impressive political name recognition: 90% of French electors could name their local mayor. Such direct association of service levels with elected officials was the best guarantee against centralization and the surest way of marrying local identity to local service. The same principle underlay the proposal for some division of powers between a mayor and a council or assembly. The secrecy of British local government and the tradition of party cabal had done much to induce helplessness and therefore apathy among electors.

A mayor for London was taken up by Tony Blair personally. It was foisted on a largely unenthusiastic Labour party, opposed by the Tories and appeared in the new Labour manifesto. London politics was instantly electrified. Despite derision at the quality of candidates – the first-round election was bound to yield a harvest of 'parliamentary retreads' – the campaign galvanized London as a political theatre. The primaries saw both parties plunged into chaos. The prospect of Ken Livingstone returning to head London's government brought, inside a week, the Prime Minister, Chancellor of the Exchequer and Foreign Secretary to the hustings in opposition. This was participation inconceivable in local government before. On a number of days in late 1999 the London mayoralty was claiming as much media attention as Westminster politics. This was beyond the wildest dreams of the advocates of the reform.

Nor was it true, as critics claimed, that direct election 'focuses exclusively on candidate personality'. It certainly subverted the smooth working of party cabals. The two early strong runners, Lord Archer and Mr Livingstone, were unlikely to find favour in the back rooms of the Westminster parties. But they were undeniably popular – populists in the American and Continental mayoral traditions. An American friend of mine was mesmerized by the London poll: 'An Oscar-winning actress, a best-selling author, a newt-fancier and a serial adulterer!' he said. 'All we get is a policeman or clapped-out district attorney.'

More to the point, the debate over candidature brought to the surface government issues that had long remained dormant. Personality as much as party is the means by which democratic government is made accountable. Most prominent was the fate of London's public transport, which Whitehall had hoped it could privatize in advance of the mayor taking office. This it failed to do, and had to amend the legislation to retain the Tube and privatize its infrastructure, before allowing the mayor to take charge of its operation. The mayoral candidates united in opposing this. Whatever the actions of central government towards such functions of government in the capital the views of Londoners, however expressed, would clearly be significant. A central Parliament in the pocket of the executive of the day could never hope to equal the independent voice of a London mayor and assembly. London public opinion would in future hold the mayor and assembly to account, however impotent they might be in statute. Whitehall could no longer tell London how to run its Tube.

Similar controversy surrounded parking and other congestion charges in the capital, the one area in which the mayor would be permitted to raise revenue. It was open season for debate. The same applied to the use of the river, the regulation of bus services, police accountability, homelessness and street cleanliness. From the start of the campaign the mayoralty was unlocking cupboards that central government had kept shut for a decade and a half. In addition, mayoral candidates were proposing changes in education and health care that were nothing to do with the mayoral remit. They were proposing taxes specifically outside their sphere of competence.[4] It was soon obvious that whatever statutory powers were conferred on the new government of London, the fact of direct election was raising public expectation of the post generally. Whatever the relevant statute said, the entire government of the capital was on the political agenda. I cannot think of a more vivid illustration of a democratic innovation galvanizing public debate.

London's experience had an impact on local government elsewhere in England. It excited electorates and dismayed sitting council politicians. Already in 1999 a number of cities were pondering whether to jump the London gun and hold earlier mayoral elections — there was talk of this in Glasgow, Birmingham and two London boroughs. The local government minister, Hilary Armstrong, introduced her long-awaited local government reform bill in 1999, with the intention of allowing local cities, counties and districts to choose their own path to constitutional change. Under the bill, each council must put a series of options to their electorates in a referendum. These included a directly-elected mayor, a mayor chosen by the majority party, and a more conventional system

[4] The mayor of New York has six taxes with which to play.

of council cabinet with leader. The existing council structure, composed of cumbersome executive committees, had to be streamlined. Some formal separation of powers should be opened between the executive and the wider council charged with overseeing it. Early signs were that electors strongly favoured direct election of mayors.

The Armstrong reforms were designed to bring much of the decision-taking in local government out of the party cabal, or at least concentrate it on elected leaders, and expose the natural conflicts of domestic politics to public gaze. Councils should be led by full-time executives and held to account by councillors less constrained in time and loyalty by committee membership. The reforms were intended to reduce the scope for corruption and delay, and increase the access for community groups and other informal institutions. Elections for some seats would be held annually, and referendums allowed for changes to local budgets. Above all, the Armstrong bill offered diversity, accepting that different systems may be appropriate for different areas and types of authority. In America, every conceivable model of mayoralty can be found on display somewhere.

The chief shortcoming of this constitutional revolution was its failure to reverse the most specific aspect of financial centralization since 1984. The Institute of Fiscal Studies, in its comment on the 1998 white paper, went straight to the point. 'Local accountability depends both on the existence of a clear and transparent link between local spending decisions and council tax bills, and on councils being genuinely accountable to local people.' As long as rate capping, even in its residual form, remained in place and as long as central government saw itself as responsible for local service 'initiatives', this accountability would be diluted. Compared with recent decentralization in most other European countries, notably Italy and Scandinavia, Britain's changes were paltry. The best that can be said is that they were changes in the right direction.

Yet London's experience suggests that there may be a world of difference between what a statute says and what happens on the ground. I suspect that of all the changes, direct election will prove the most traumatic to the existing constitution of local government. It introduces a new concept into British democracy, that of the primary election, a single name on the city-wide ballot paper and a single transferable vote. Not only will this make it easier for new blood to enter local, and possibly national, politics; more important the election process will be more dynamic than any yet seen, witness the furore that has surrounded the candidacy for the London office. This in turn will expose personal and policy differences far more fiercely than under any party-based system. In other words, the expectations that electors will come to have of their democratic leaders will exceed the statutory remit of their mandate rather than underrate it as at present.

The proof of the new system can only be in the outcome. Democracy is tested, as de Tocqueville said, primarily by how far its participants are satisfied with it. The most localist systems, practised in the cantons of Switzerland, the 'free towns' of Scandinavia and small-town America, are so entrenched that it would be unthinkable to change them. Every survey of attitudes to democracy ever conducted shows people wanting more of it, not less. It is Britain that has least, and Britain that has changed its local government most often in the past quarter century. Satisfaction with democracy is ultimately measured by rates of participation. The test of the new British system will be how many more people it induces to vote. Of that, the year 2000 will be the proof.

Tam Dalyell

Devolution:
The End of Britain[1]

In politics it is much more difficult—in terms of relations with one's party colleagues and friends—to be right than wrong; and, of all political stances, perhaps the least pretty is 'We told you so!' But we did.

It is just not possible to have a subordinate parliament in part, though only part, of a unitary state which, above all, one wishes to keep united. There is not the proverbial cat in hell's chance of the situation remaining stable. Of course, as we predicted, the Parliament in Edinburgh will want more, and more, and more—and so it has proved, within months, not even years.

It is in the very nature of politicians to fight for the institution in which they themselves serve. The very setting-up of the Holyrood Parliament, however disappointing it may have been to many of its champions, and a host of people (including myself!) who wished it well, has meant that we are on a motorway without exit to the end of Britain.

Although I am no fan of the Prime Minister on foreign policy, I think Tony Blair perceived at an early stage, shortly after he became leader of the Labour Party, the difficulties and abysses of devolution. When I went to see him at his request on this topic, in 1995, he rang his hands and said, 'Well, what do you expect me to do about it, now?' And, the truth was that

---

[1] No apology do I offer for giving the selfsame title to this essay as I gave to my book, published in 1978 by Jonathan Cape.

I suppose I could expect an incoming leader to do little else than go along with the policy.

To make sense of the situation we had arrived in by the mid-1990s it is necessary to delve into delicate and personal histories. And in few constitutional matters can the influence and legacy of the deceased have played a more prominent role. At the time of the first attempts at devolution, in the mid-1970s, the Wilson–Callaghan governments were sinking deeper and deeper into the mire of devolutionary legislation. It was the Irish crisis of the last century all over again. Ministers floundered. The Prime Minister, James Callaghan, knew he had to do something to help the minister nominally in charge, Michael Foot (for all his attributes, no man for legislative detail). In desperation he plucked John Smith, an able lawyer and adroit politician, out of the Department of Energy, where he was dealing with vital issues of North Sea oil, and appointed him as number two in the Cabinet Office – in order to act as Callaghan's attorney in the Commons, and deal with the awkward squad of Enoch Powell, George Cunningham, Neil Kinnock (from time to time) and Tam Dalyell. John Smith got the promised reward for completing the job – and was duly appointed to the Cabinet as Secretary of State for Trade and Industry.

Now it may be true that in a West Highland way John Smith favoured a parliament in Edinburgh. All I can say is that up to the time that Callaghan appointed him to this challenging ministerial post I did not detect much sign that a Scottish parliament was one of John Smith's particular causes, or that it was at the top of his list of priorities. What is certain beyond peradventure is that from the day devolution was defeated in the referendum in March 1979 until the terrible morning when he died, John Smith did not give his considerable mind to thinking through the mechanisms of devolution, or how it would actually work.

But the damage was done. Cleverly, the proponents of devolution, led by the messianic Donald Dewar, who has acquired a deep-rooted antagonism to London, latched on to what was little more than a slogan of John Smith – that devolution was 'unfinished business'. Smith's unfinished business became the catalyst of the drive to put a Scottish Parliament and Welsh Assembly at the top of the agenda of the incoming Labour

Government. It became a flagship policy, and Prime Ministers cannot afford to see their flagship policies fail. Yet all this is hardly a justification for wounding the British Constitution and setting Scots on a road on which, I assert, most of the population had never intended to travel in the first place.

At this point I must digress. In the period 1976–9 there were 47 days of debate on the floor of the House of Commons on devolution legislation. All sorts of difficulties emerged. As Enoch Powell colourfully but accurately put it, 'all sorts of creepy, crawly things emerge from under stones, during parliamentary scrutiny'. The proposals were hammered out on the anvil of parliamentary debate—and found wanting. How could it be that the Member of Parliament for West Lothian could vote on matters affecting West Bromwich but not West Lothian? For how long could the Member of Parliament representing Blackburn, West Lothian, vote on education affecting Blackburn, Lancashire, but not the very same matters in Blackburn, West Lothian? How long could the Member of Parliament representing Linlithgow, in Scotland, vote on local government in Liverpool, but not Linlithgow?[2] Twenty-two years have gone by, and answer has there come, none.[3]

By contrast with the scrutiny in the late 1970s, the Scotland and Wales Bills of 1997–8 were unexamined. A Parliamentary guillotine was imposed. Debate was limited. Ministers were profoundly uninterested in difficulties. When replies came from the front bench—and frequently there was no attempt whatsoever at a reply—they were glib and facile.

Francis Pym was right. Government majorities of over 50 are unhealthy. A significant number of MPs who might have taken an interest in the proceedings simply opted out, on the understandable grounds that, faced with a majority of 179, there was little or nothing they could do about the situation, so

---

[2] This question was repeated by me so often that Enoch Powell, with heavy irony, said: 'We have finally grasped what the Honourable Member for West Lothian is getting at, let us call it the West Lothian Question.' I owe Powell this soubriquet, and when I went to see him in Ecclestone Square shortly before he died, he whispered movingly to me, 'I have bequeathed you the West Lothian Question', and so he had.

[3] Nor, indeed did Mr Gladstone find an answer to the dilemma of the 'Ins and the Outs' so pungently described in Morley's life of the great statesman.

why get their political noses dirty and ruin any chance of preferment, all in a lost cause?

The cause was also lost for another reason. After 1979 most of us thought that devolution had been put to bed. We had not foreseen Mrs Thatcher. In the 1980s, those of us in the Labour Party who might have reasonably been expected to continue to oppose devolution failed to make our voices heard.

Actually, I blame myself. But there were lots of other matters on which to campaign — industrial destruction and the Falklands War — and anything such as anti-devolution, which seemed to tally with Mrs Thatcher's view, was taboo.

The pass had been sold. So it is against this deeply unsatisfactory background that Holyrood has come into being. Have the Jeremiahs been justified?

The truth is that judgment cannot be made for some years. I suppose it is possible that somehow we will muddle along. Rape can be coped with in different ways. But the omens are not good. Personally, I absolve Holyrood from its first and damaging contretemps — the fuss about the salaries to be paid to MSPs. Housekeeping is inevitably troublesome and financial problems have to be sorted out.

But since then Holyrood has been besieged by other troubles, of a more serious nature. It is the circumstances of the referendum — the pre-legislative referendum — held on 11 September 1997, which encapsulate the root of their woes. Expectations were blown up: teachers would get significantly better salaries; waiting lists in hospitals would be dramatically cut; any ill — real or imagined — would be remedied. The Scottish media, the leading architects of the whole devolution structure, the impetus behind the schemes in the first place, trumpeted all the goodies that would flow from 'our own parliament'.

Now, all too clearly, such desirable objectives have not been met. Within months the Scottish Executive was on the brink of becoming involved in the first teachers' industrial action for years. There is a flaming row between the Health Minister and the Cardinal Archbishop of Glasgow. The idea, put out in the referendum that this was somehow to be a new type of parliament, characterized by consensus, adult behaviour and tranquillity, is gravely shown up for what it always was — a pipe-dream.

The fact is that the 1997 referendum was a fraud. It was utterly, utterly wrong to use a referendum to give the imprimatur of approval on a set of propositions yet to be defined. The rhetoric had far more to do with the film *Braveheart*, in which the Australian actor Mel Gibson starred as an unlikely William Wallace, than the future constitutional arrangements of the United Kingdom.

Furthermore, there was a particular set of circumstances, which may seem ephemeral but which certainly affected the size of the majority. Three long years before, the American Travel Association had decided for the second time in their history to have their annual meeting outside the continental United States. Some years ago they had gone to Lisbon, so this time they alighted on Glasgow, Scotland.

They chose 9 September as the date of their keynote speech. Guest of Honour? Margaret Hilda Thatcher. Since the campaign, such as it was—distorted by the death of Diana, Princess of Wales, and truncated in length—was for hundreds of thousands of voters about 'Do you want Scotland protected from Mrs Thatcher's poll tax?', it is easily imaginable that her presence at that very moment in Glasgow was manna from heaven for the 'Yes' campaign.

And how the press, the BBC and STV played on it! It was superbly exploited—an example of how the media fought their corner. My friend Noel Dolan, now press officer of the Scottish National Party, arranged a televised debate in Glenrothes on the Monday night before polling.

On the 'Yes' side, was the Faustian combination of Donald Dewar, Alex Salmond and Jim Wallace. On the 'No' side were Michael Ancram, Donald Findlay—the highly controversial Vice-Chairman of Glasgow Rangers Football Club, and not everyone's cup of tea—and myself. Not a minute had gone by before Alex Salmond leaned sweetly across the table and said disarmingly to Michael Ancram: 'Hey, Michael, aren't you the very minister who piloted Mrs Thatcher's poll tax through the House of Commons?'

And of course he was. My point is less hubris than the assertion that it is hardly a basis to make possible the break up of the British state; and break-up is what is on the cards.

Let us take a straw in the wind—tuition fees. How, in a system paid for out of the United Kingdom Treasury, will it be possible to have students in Edinburgh University having fees waived until they are earning over £25,000 per year (a horrendous scheme to administer!) — and students at Exeter University paying tuition fees? Worse still, how long can a system last when students at Edinburgh University, domiciled in Scotland, do not have to pay fees, while those doing exactly the same courses, domiciled in England, have to pay? This situation is the tip of an iceberg. There will be an endless procession of disagreements, and I predict then governments in London will get tired of the Scots and resignedly say: 'Just get on with it, but do not expect us to pay.' I think this would be a tragedy as there are so many family and other connections between Scotland and England.

As Holyrood asserts its right to set levels of spending in areas which gobble up public expenditure, such as student fees, and as the Chancellor of the Exchequer tries to keep the lid on with his so-called 'co-ordinating meetings', the English are becoming impatient. What happens when Gordon Brown, a Scot, leaves the Exchequer and a non-Scot succeeds him, I would not be too confident.

The North of England MPs are becoming uneasy — after all they might be told by their electorate that it is high time the wealth of regions is sorted out. Per capita the figures are London £14,411, South-East £13,549, East of England £11,739, South West £11,213, East Midlands £11,002, Scotland £10,975, West Midlands, £10,669, North West £10,481, Yorkshire and Humberside £10,244, North East £9,473, Wales £9,442, and Northern Ireland £9,235.

Even in the South, the issue is beginning to reverberate. Candidates for the Mayoralty of London are beginning to act like the SNP in the 1970s with their cry 'Give us back Scotland's Oil'.

I am gloomy and doom-laden about the future of the Union.

Diana Woodhouse

The Judicial Committee of the Privy Council

its new constitutional role

Constitutional change in the United Kingdom has never been characterized by coherent programmes of reform. Adjustments have tended to be piecemeal and the Labour Government's package of constitutional measures has continued this tradition. Thus while the individual reforms are of considerable importance, there has been little thinking about their long-term effect and how they relate to each other. Nowhere is the lack of coherence more evident than with devolution, where there has been little attempt to consider it in the context of other reforms, such as the reform of the House of Lords, or to reflect on the implications for England, the regions or, indeed, the United Kingdom as a whole. There has also been a failure to address coherently the location of judicial constitutional authority or to consider whether any changes are necessary to ensure that the courts are suited to their new constitutional role. It is this issue that this essay will discuss.

The legislation which gives effect to devolution measures in Scotland, Wales and Northern Ireland provides for matters of *vires*, or powers, to be determined by the Judicial Committee of the Privy Council, and, by so doing, gives it considerable influence in the sphere of territorial and inter-government relations. Why the Judicial Committee was given this role is not clear. As Lord Wilberforce said during the debate on the Scotland Bill, 'We have heard no reasoned explanations as to why that body was chosen.'[1] Justifications that the Committee, through its position as the final appeal court for the Commonwealth, has expertise and experience in dealing with constitutional issues, are unconvincing, as its Commonwealth jurisdiction has shrunk dramatically and disputes about *vires* have been infrequent. Similarly, suggestions that the Privy Council was the obvious location, because it had previously had that role under the Northern Ireland Act, fail to acknowledge that it was only called upon to give judgment on one occasion. All that might be said is that if a new court is not to be created it is perhaps psychologically better that the Privy Council is given that role, rather than the Appellate Committee of the House of Lords which more readily suggests English domination of the judicial process.

However, in practice the same judges sit in both courts. Moreover, the new role of the Privy Council relates closely to that given to the House of Lords by the Human Rights Act, not least because under devolution legislation it is outside the competence of the new legislatures to pass legislation which is incompatible with any of the rights protected by the European Convention on Human Rights. Thus the Judicial Committee of the Privy Council cannot be viewed in isolation from its sister court and the division of constitutional jurisdiction between them, such that the Privy Council is concerned with matters of *vires* and the House of Lords with upholding Convention rights, through the Human Rights Act, lacks both logic and constitutional coherence.

In fact, the position of either court assuming a role, which requires the determination of disputes about power and competence, raises the question of whether it can acquire the constitutional authority necessary for its acceptance across the territories of the United Kingdom. Such authority depends on a number of factors. These include its *modus operandi*, its independence and impartiality, and its decisions and the philosophy or jurisprudence which underpin them. All of these challenge the Privy Council (and the House of Lords), whose way of operating and institutional position may, in the context of constitutional disputes, be inappropriate and whose ability to develop a constitutional jurisprudence has yet to be tested.

---

[1]   House of Lords Debate, 28 October 1998, col. 1965.

The Operation of the Privy Council

The Privy Council is an amorphous body which, in theory, comprises some 50 or so members, including past and current law lords, Lord Chancellors and Court of Appeal judges. Neither it, nor the House of Lords, sits as a full court. Instead they sit as panels or benches, the composition of which is left to an informal process. Formal procedures are absent. Moreover, no rules on the composition of panels are prescribed by devolution legislation. There is, for instance, no requirement for a panel of the Privy Council to be balanced, with judicial members from all UK jurisdictions sitting, nor is there any stipulation for the country or countries involved in a *vires* dispute to be judicially represented. It is therefore theoretically possible for an entirely English panel to be convened to determine, say, the validity of legislation passed by the Scottish Parliament, with inevitable political consequences should Scotland be found to have acted outside its competence. It might be assumed that such a situation would not be allowed to arise. Indeed, the Lord Chancellor, Lord Irvine, has stated that he expects a convention to develop, whereby 'there would always be at least one Scottish judge — and in practice perhaps more — sitting on the Judicial Committee for Scottish devolution cases.'[2] But it has been known for conventions to be breached or ignored. They do not amount to a legal requirement.

Responsibility for the composition of benches or panels, both in the Privy Council and the House of Lords, lies with the Lord Chancellor, who, of course, has executive as well as judicial responsibilities. At the beginning of the twentieth century holders of the office were not averse to packing panels to secure the decisions they wanted. In more recent times Lord Chancellors have distanced themselves from the process, delegating the responsibility to the senior Law Lord. Yet this delegation is, once more, only by convention and in cases which are politically and constitutionally sensitive the suspicion might arise, or the accusation might be made, that the Lord Chancellor has sought to influence the selection. Given that there is no legal provision to prevent this, we are reliant on the

---

[2] *Ibid.*, col. 1984.

integrity of the Lord Chancellor and the will of the senior Law Lord to resist such an attempt. This leaves what Lord Lester has called 'a potentially embarrassing tension within the rather opaque system of choosing a court'.[3] This is particularly so should the Lord Chancellor seek to sit himself, as he is entitled to do, against the wishes of the senior Law Lord.

In practice the selection of a panel is in the hands of the listing clerk, an official whose choices may be quite limited, for while the Privy Council appears to have a large membership, Court of Appeal judges seldom sit. Panels are therefore more or less confined to the Law Lords and Lord Chancellors. As a consequence the work of the Privy Council has to be coordinated with the needs of the House of Lords. This inevitably limits the number of judges available and it may be limited further by the engagement of some Law Lords in other judicial or quasi-judicial duties, such as the chairing of inquiries. In addition, according to Lord Cooke, 'administrative convenience and even quite minor issues of expense may have some influence on the composition of the committee'.[4] Expertise is also a factor in the determination of a panel. In the context of *vires* this will be lacking initially, but should the practice whereby Scottish Law Lords are whenever possible assigned to sit on Scottish civil appeals be extended to *vires* cases, as Lord Irvine has suggested, this, together with the other factors, may make a panel almost self-selecting.

Whatever the composition of the panel, where human rights and *vires* cases are concerned, its members will be scrutinized in an attempt to determine the likely outcome. These cases will therefore bring judges to the centre of the political arena and, for a foretaste of the treatment they can expect to receive, they need look no further than the *Pinochet* litigation in 1999.[5] After the House of Lords had vacated its first decision, on the basis that the panel, which heard the case, had been improperly constituted (Lord Hoffman's connection with Amnesty International presenting a real danger of bias), the ideological leanings and personal attributes of the judges

---

[3] *Ibid.*, col. 1970.
[4] *Ibid.*, col. 1967.
[5] See: D. Woodhouse (ed.), *The Pinochet Case; A Legal and Constitutional Analysis* (2000, Hart Publishing, Oxford).

listed to rehear the appeal were subjected to considerable media scrutiny. Lord Browne-Wilkinson, for instance, was described by *The Times* as 'humane, liberal and charming', Lord Hutton as 'the most right-leaning of the panel' and Lord Hope as 'quiet with a meticulous style and middle-of-the-road politics'. In the context of cases concerning *vires* there will, no doubt, be discussion as to whether the members of the panel are traditionalist, for whom Diceyan notions of parliamentary sovereignty hold sway, or whether they are open to other constitutional principles and to influences from Europe and elsewhere.

Moreover, because there is choice, even if limited, as to the composition of the court, there will be speculation as to why particular judges were selected and what the decision might have been had different judges sat. It therefore seems that the use of the Privy Council (and the House of Lords) in constitutional cases is flawed. It provides the opportunity for those who dislike a decision to create the suspicion that pressure was brought to bear by, or through, the Lord Chancellor for political purposes and to encourage speculation that if different judges had been on the panel a different decision might have been reached. There is therefore a danger that, in the words of Lord Lester, the Privy Council 'will become a political football, kicked hard by politicians for their partisan ends.'[6] Indeed it would seem inevitable, given the opaqueness of the selection of panels and the fact that, unlike most constitutional courts, there is selection rather than the court sitting as a whole. The result will be an undermining of the court's authority.

The court's authority may also be undermined by its reliance on the arguments put forward by counsel. The *Pinochet* appeals showed how difficult it is for the public, and indeed many lawyers, to understand that a court presented with different arguments can reach a conclusion which diverges from its previous decision, even though the facts remain the same. *Pinochet* may have been exceptional, but in the context of disputes over *vires* differences between panels may act to undermine the authority of the court and be used against it in the political arena. The Privy Council would therefore be well

[6]   House of Lords Debates, 28 October 1998, col. 1970.

advised to look to the practice of the US Supreme Court, where the judges employ law clerks to conduct research on their behalf and *amicus* briefs,[7] filed by parties interested in the case, are used to ensure that no argument that might be relevant is ignored.[8]

All this would seem to suggest that in its new role the Privy Council should always sit as a full court. For this to be the case its membership would need to be confined to an appropriate number, perhaps seven or nine. Alternatively it could designate a panel of judges to hear all *vires* cases. This panel could employ law clerks and make use of *amicus* briefs to aid the development of a coherent jurisprudence. Such reforms are also relevant to the House of Lords when it hears human-rights cases. Indeed, it would seem appropriate for the same judges to hear both *vires* and human-rights cases, as this would enable them to develop an inter-related jurisprudence. Logically this suggests the establishment of a constitutional court, which is what many critics of the devolution reforms believe to be missing.

Judicial Independence

If the way in which the Privy Council operates is important for its authority, the need for it to be seen as independent from executive and legislative bodies is even more so. However, perceptions as to its (and the House of Lords') independence may be coloured, first, by the way in which senior judges are appointed, second, by the Lord Chancellor's role, and, third, by the position of the Law Lords in the legislature.

The Law Lords are appointed by the Crown, which means, in practice, that their positions are in the gift of the prime minister and the Lord Chancellor, who advises him or her. The procedure by which this advice is given is confidential and Lord Chancellors have refused to give details. It is, however, evident that some prime ministers have expected to be more

[7] In the American context *amicus* briefs are pleadings from groups and individuals who are not parties to a case but have an interest in it. They can be partisan or neutral.

[8] For a fuller consideration of *amicus* briefs see, D. Robertson, 'The House of Lords as a Political and Constitutional Court', in Woodhouse (ed.), *The Pinochet Case*.

involved in appointments than others. Mrs Thatcher, for instance, liked to discuss appointments and exercise her right to choose. Lord Hailsham, when Lord Chancellor, therefore developed a strategy of not giving her too many names to consider. Lord Mackay, on the other hand, advised her and subsequently John Major, fully on the field from which the choice could be made and it seems his preferred candidate was not always accepted, although he told the Home Affairs Select Committee inquiry into Judicial Appointments in 1996 that he supported 'wholeheartedly' all the appointments that were made.

The appointment of senior judges is therefore in the hands of two politicians. Lord Chancellors would, of course, argue that they act non-politically in the advice that they give on these appointments and there is certainly no evidence of the old party-political 'spoils' system that prevailed until the early part of the twentieth century. Indeed, a glance at the appointments made under Lord Mackay's Chancellorship shows no correlation between political allegiance and advancement, some of those appointed having little in common ideologically with the government. Yet despite this the involvement of Lord Chancellors in appointing judges does little to foster notions of judicial independence, particularly when, as at present, the incumbent has a high political profile. The part played by the prime minister is even more questionable and as the courts become embroiled in the politically sensitive issues of *vires* and human rights it would seem unacceptable for appointment to lie within the gift of the Lord Chancellor and prime minister alone.

It is not necessarily wrong for politics to play a part in judicial selection, particularly as the judges move towards a more overt political role. After all, the Privy Council and House of Lords do not make decisions in a vacuum but in accordance with the ideology and mindset of the judges concerned. It may therefore be appropriate for the politics of these judges to be a matter for consideration when they are appointed. However, if this were to become the case, it would be essential for the system to contain adequate checks to ensure the safeguarding of judicial immunity from government pressure. The appointing process would therefore need to be separated from the executive, such that senior judges would no longer rely on the patronage of the Lord Chancellor and the prime minister. This separation would, in any event, seem essential, given the constitutional role now assumed by the judges.

Calls for a judicial appointments commission to make the appointment of judges more transparent and independent therefore have added vibrancy. The establishment of a judicial commission was favoured by Labour when in opposition. It has since been 'put on hold' by Lord Irvine, who is of the belief that the current system of appointment does not need reform. Many would disagree. A commission could operate in a number of ways, most likely making recommendations to the Lord Chancellor or his equivalent, and perhaps also involving a committee of Parliament in appointments. This involvement could simply take the form of questioning judges appointed as Law Lords to determine the principles under which they operate and their views on relevant matters. A similar procedure is already operated successfully by the Treasury Select Committee, which interviews members of the Monetary Committee of the Bank of England. More controversially, parliamentary involvement could equate with the confirmation hearings held by the US Senate, which has the power to veto Supreme Court judges nominated by the President.

Devolution presents some problems for the involvement of Parliament in judicial appointments, there being a danger that the process will be seen as dominated by England, even if the parliamentary committee contained representatives from all the countries of the United Kingdom. An alternative might be for the legislatures of the devolved territories to have a role in appointing judges to the Privy Council. However this could be divisive and, in the context of Northern Ireland, highly contentious. A better solution might therefore be for the appointing function to be confined to a judicial commission, whose members are drawn from a wide range of interests, including the political parties.

The need for change in the way in which the Law Lords are appointed also raises questions about the position of the Lord Chancellor, both as head of the judiciary and as judge. The Lord Chancellor is not only theoretically responsible for selecting panels of the Judicial Committee of the Privy Council and the Appellate Committee of the House of Lords, he is also head of the judiciary. In this capacity he represents the interests of judges and protects them from executive pressure, acting simultaneously as a hinge and a buffer. Such a position is clearly contrary to any doctrine of separation of powers. While it may have been acceptable when the courts had no constitutional role and Lord Chancellors were mainly concerned with their judicial duties, the involvement of the courts in the new constitutional settlement and the increased executive responsibilities of recent Lord Chancellors makes it unsustainable. The role should now pass to the Lord Chief Justice.

Similarly, the Lord Chancellor's role as judge and, when he chooses to sit, as president of the Appellate Committee of the House of Lords and Judicial Committee of the Privy Council is no longer appropriate. Concern about his judicial role was apparent prior to the passing of devolution legislation and the Human Rights Act and related mainly to the expansion and changed nature of his executive role. During Lord Mackay's period in office this change in the executive role was evident in the lead taken by him in controversial policy initiatives aimed at making the legal system more efficient and reducing, or at least capping, public expenditure. These policies, notably related to the reform of the legal profession, the civil court system and legal aid, brought the Lord Chancellor into conflict with the judges and the legal profession.

Lord Irvine has shown no signs of loosening the grip of the executive on the administration of justice. Moreover, he has assumed a much higher political profile and a larger role in government decision making. Indeed, his closeness to the prime minister and his role in Cabinet committees makes him the most politically influential Lord Chancellor this century and has resulted in his role as judge being seriously questioned. Concerns about his political role have been shrugged off by Lord Irvine, who has argued that it makes little sense to 'attack the Office at the moment that the Office has come into its own and can be of greatest use to the government.'[9] However, such a statement suggests a lack of understanding of the concern, which is about the balance between political and judicial roles. It is the fact that the Office is of 'greatest use to

---

[9] BBC Radio 4, 9 April 1998: interview with Marcel Berlins.

the government' that makes it unacceptable for the Lord Chancellor to sit as judge.

It has long been recognized that Lord Chancellors should not sit on cases in which there is a party political element or in which the government has a direct interest. Cases where there is an indirect interest have proved more problematic. Lord Mackay was criticized for presiding over the House of Lords in *Pepper and Hart* (1993), not just because it was an Inland Revenue case but also because an important aspect of the case was whether judges should be allowed to refer to *Hansard*, the parliamentary record, when the intention of a statute was unclear. This was an issue in which the government had an interest, as it related to the responsibility of ministers when presenting bills to Parliament, and the hearing of the case by the Lord Chancellor, who is also a member of the Cabinet, did little to engender confidence in judicial independence, particularly when he dissented from the decision of the majority that reference to *Hansard* was admissable.

Lord Irvine has similarly been criticized for his decision to sit, firstly, in a judicial review case and, secondly, in a case (*DPP v. Jones* (1999)) which was concerned with the right to peaceful assembly on the public highway. It therefore involved the rights of the individual against an organ of the state of which the Lord Chancellor is a member. He gave the leading judgment and, in fact, found for the individual, but he might not have done so and, regardless of the outcome, his hearing of the case raised the issue of conflict of interests.

The decisions of Lords Mackay and Irvine to sit in these cases were sufficient in themselves to raise questions about the Lord Chancellor's role as judge. These have become even more pertinent with the passing of devolution legislation and the Human Rights Act, and for a Lord Chancellor to sit in either *vires* or human-rights cases would be detrimental to perceptions of judicial independence. Yet Lord Irvine has refused to provide an assurance that he will not sit in such cases, stating only: 'I will exercise my discretion not to sit where I consider it would be inappropriate or improper to do so.'[10] This is an insufficient safeguard and his comment that there are no cases that can be labelled 'constitutional', which

[10] House of Lords Debates, 20 October 1998, WA 138.

should be 'no-go areas' for a Lord Chancellor,[11] is misconceived. Of course there must be no-go areas for a judge who is
also a Cabinet minister. These include cases brought under
devolution legislation and the Human Rights Act.

The position of the Lord Chancellor as judge may, in any
case, by contrary to Article 6 of the European Convention on
Human Rights, which provides the right to a fair hearing
before an independent and impartial tribunal. The European
Court of Human Rights in *Bryan v. UK* (1995) has stated that
independence is to be determined with regard to the manner
of the appointment of a tribunal's members and their terms of
office, the existence of guarantees against outside pressures
and whether the body appears to be independent. The Lord
Chancellor's position would seem suspect on all three
grounds. First, he is appointed by the prime minister and,
unlike other senior judges, has no security of tenure; he can be
dismissed at will. Second, the only guarantee against outside
pressures is the integrity of the Lord Chancellor himself.
Third, the position of the Lord Chancellor as a government
minister, particularly a high profile one, undermines any
appearance of independence.

These points were reiterated by the Court in *McGonnell*
(2000). The case, which related to a planning issue, was concerned with whether the Royal Court of Guernsey is an independent and impartial tribunal for the purposes of Article 6. It
is presided over by the Bailiff, who spends most of his time
discharging judicial functions, but also has executive and legislative responsibilities. The Court considered that 'any direct
involvement in the passage of legislation, or of executive
rules, was likely to cast doubt on the judicial impartiality of a
person subsequently called on to determine a dispute over...
the wording of the legislation or rule at issue.' In this instance
the Bailiff had presided over the passing of the planning legislation, which was now 'at issue', and this 'was capable of casting doubts over his impartiality'. The Court therefore held
unanimously that Article 6 of the European Convention on
Human Rights had been violated. There are obvious differences between the position of the Bailiff and that of the Lord
Chancellor, but the Lord Chancellor's position would, never-

[11] House of Lords Debates, 17 Februaury 1999, col. 736.

theless, seem vulnerable, particularly as his executive functions are more substantial than those of the Bailiff.

However, whether the Lord Chancellor should sit in the Privy Council or the House of Lords, when they hear *vires* and human-rights cases, should not depend on a decision from Strasbourg. It would be wrong, judicially and politically, for a government minister so to do and Lord Irvine should make it clear that he sees himself debarred. Indeed, given the constitutional status that is now accorded the Privy Council and the House of Lords, it would seem unacceptable for the Lord Chancellor to sit as judge at all, for to do so may undermine the independence of these courts. Appearances matter and a government minister sitting as judge in any case does not enhance the appearance of judicial independence.

The need for the Privy Council and the House of Lords to be seen as independent raises questions not only about the position of the Lord Chancellor but also about that of the Law Lords. They are appointed to the House of Lords to hear and determine appeals but, as Life Peers, they are also entitled to sit and vote in the legislative chamber and speak in debates. By convention they do not speak on matters which are politically contentious. However, during the 1980s and '90s there were a number of instances when this convention was breached, putting the Law Lords in the front line of political controversy and drawing attention to the fact that they not only act as judges and technical advisers on legislation, but also as legislators. A number of Law Lords spoke in opposition to criminal justice measures, the reform of the legal profession, civil justice reform and proposed changes to the legal aid system. They expressed the view that these matters were concerned with the administration of justice and it was therefore acceptable for them to take part in debates. The problem is that as governments have sought to control public spending, issues around the administration of justice have become increasingly political.

The mix of legislative and judicial functions may also be contrary to the European Convention on Human Rights, although the case is obviously not as strong as that against the Lord Chancellor. However, whether or not it breaches the Convention, it would seem inappropriate for those who are hearing *vires* cases to sit in the dominant parliament. The cases will be concerned with political power and the judges need to be seen as independent from those engaged in the power struggle. Regardless of Lord Wakeham's recommendations, the judges should remove themselves from the Upper Chamber, setting up a Supreme Court in place of the Appellate Committee of the House. Ideally such institutional change should be carried a stage further with the establishment of a special Constitutional Court which merges the function of the Privy Council, under devolution legislation, with the appellate function of the House of Lords, in relation to the Human Rights Act and judicial review. The establishment of a Constitutional Court would not only enhance judicial independence, it would provide those judges who sit in it with constitutional authority and thus help to generate the public confidence necessary where *vires* decisions are concerned.

Jurisprudential Developments

The role of the Privy Council, through devolution legislation, will no doubt vary across the devolved territories, which are likely to follow different paths in their development. However, the jurisprudence it develops in relation to *vires* will be influential across the whole of the United Kingdom and, providing there is sufficient public confidence in its decisions, could act as a unifying factor. For this to be the case, the Privy Council will need to relate its decisions to human rights jurisprudence, as it is developed by the House of Lords, and move away from the traditional and stultifying concept of parliamentary sovereignty. It must recognize a constitutional authority grounded not in the supremacy of the Westminster Parliament but in concepts with which the people from all UK regions or territories can identify, such as human rights, shared identities and constitutionalism. But it will have to move carefully, so as not to alienate the Westminster Parliament and precipitate inter-governmental conflict—no easy task.

Conclusion

The legislation which established the Scottish Parliament and the Welsh and Northern Ireland Assemblies provides a key role for the Judicial Committee of the Privy Council. However, there seems to have been little rationale for choosing the Privy Council and little thought as to whether, given the way in which it currently operates, it is suited for a constitutional role or whether it will be able to gain the constitutional authority and public confidence required of a court in this position. Its ability to retain public confidence will depend ultimately on its decisions and its jurisprudence. In the context of devolution this will need to be underwritten by principles with which the devolved territories, as well as England, can identify. These will take time to develop.

But public confidence does not depend on judicial decisions alone and there are a number of reforms which could, and should, be undertaken. The first requirement is for a constitutional court. Lord Irvine has accepted that when the constitutional reforms 'bed down' thought might need to be given to the establishment of such a specialist court. It is to be regretted that the Government did not give this matter thought as part of its reform package, rather than waiting until the current arrangements are found wanting and the Privy Council (and House of Lords) are found to be unsuited for a constitutional role. In the meantime changes could be made to the way in which the Privy Council operates in the devolution context, so that, when considering *vires* issues, it sits as a court and makes extensive use of *amicus* briefs. The second requirement is for the system by which the Law Lords are appointed to be reformed and a judicial commission established. The location of constitutional authority in the Privy Council and the House of Lords make it essential for this to be reinstated on the Lord Chancellor's reform agenda. The third requirement is for the Lord Chancellor to relinquish both his position as head of the judiciary and his right to sit as a judge, and for the Law Lords to remove themselves from the legislature. These changes, which would enhance the authority and independence of the court, would help to promote public confidence in its ability to determine issues of *vires*. More widely, they would challenge Labour to move away from the tradition of pragmatic and incremental change towards an approach which is more aspirational and which recognizes that for constitutional reform to be successful and lasting, a degree of lateral thinking is required.

Roy Jenkins

Britain and Europe:
The problem with being
half pregnant

This short paper falls into three parts. First of all I will outline what I regard as the best strategy for Britain in relation to Europe in general and to the single currency in
particular. Secondly I will say why I regard the single currency
as beneficial. Thirdly, as a former President, I think I should
say a few words about the role of the Commission.

I

My central belief is that there are only two coherent British
attitudes to Europe. One is to participate fully in all the main
activities of the Union and to endeavour to exercise as much
influence and gain as much benefit as possible from inside.
The other is to recognize that Britain's history, national psychology and political culture may be such that we can never be
other than a foot-dragging and constantly complaining member. If so, it would be better, and certainly would produce less
friction, to accept this and move towards an orderly and, if
possible, reasonably amicable withdrawal.

This latter course would be a high-risk strategy, and it
would be impossible without getting the support of a majority
in a referendum to reverse the overwhelming result of the
1975 poll. Taking that course without another referendum
would be an affront to democracy, compared to which any

peccadilloes in the working of European democracy would fade into insignificance.

It is no use pointing to highly uncertain opinion polls. Six months before the 1975 referendum, with its two–to–one pro-European majority, the polls looked even more hostile than they do today. But I detect no great enthusiasm for an early referendum, certainly not on a straight in or out basis, amongst the Eurosceptics — not most of them, at any rate. As regards those who have recently pronounced themselves as basically Euro-enthusiasts, but who are nonetheless against the main and dominating activity of Europe today — that of the single currency — their prime objective seems to be to get the Government to postpone the European referendum as long as possible. That trumpet, therefore, is sounding a very uncertain note.

Indeed the whole position, which is that of being half in and half out, of believing that if we have to join anything we should make it as late as possible, is something which every episode of post-war history should have convinced us is ineffective. We should remember that almost every Prime Minister of the past half century has had his or her reputation damaged, and several have had their careers destroyed, by equivocation on the European issue.

Mr Attlee (or his Government) kept us out of the Iron and Steel Community. Sir Anthony Eden is widely regarded by pro-Europeans as the evil genius who made the generosity of Churchill's fine words and late-1940s sentiments about a united Europe run into the dismal sands — with Britain standing aside from the Messina Conference. This led to the Treaty of Rome and to the European Economic Community — in particular the common agricultural policy — being established and almost frozen until recently in a mould that suited other countries but did not suit us.

Harold Wilson boxed several compasses on the issue, and eventually walked backwards into a successful pro-European referendum, but nonetheless damaged both his reputation and his self-confidence by a zigzag of equivocation on the issue. James Callaghan maintained Britain's offshore record by being the only one of the then Community of nine to refuse fully to join the European monetary system.

Margaret Thatcher signed the Single European Act, thereby surrendering more sovereignty than was involved in the Treaties of either Maastricht or Amsterdam, but then swung her handbag so ferociously—not only at the Summits of Madrid and Milan, but also against Sir Geoffrey Howe and Nigel Lawson—that she ensured her own downfall.

Mr Major was simply poleaxed by the European issue. It ruined his Government and made him a figure without influence on the Continent and a cork bobbing on the top of competing Tory waves at home.

So there is plenty of warning from the past, and it is in my view firmly both in the national interest and in the interests of the reputations of individual politicians—Mr Blair included—that we take a firm, clear, unequivocal approach in favour of being fully in or out. It is always unwise to hang about in the middle of the road, where you are merely asking to be run down.

II

I would nonetheless be uneasy about advocating participation in the single currency solely on the ground that it is necessary to avoid the mistakes which we have made at least three times before. It needs positive reasons as well, and these I have no difficulty in finding.

First, the single market, Mrs Thatcher's proudest creation in Europe, is half hobbled without a single currency—or for the countries which are outside a single currency.

Secondly, I discount heavily the view that because different parts of the European Union are at different levels of economic prosperity this makes a single currency undesirable. A single currency in practice came into being in America only after the Civil War, when the disparities between, say, Pennsylvania and Alabama were far greater, I think, than those between Germany and Portugal today. Yet I firmly believe that both rich and poor America, over the past century and a third, have been better off with a single currency than they would have been with a New York dollar fluctuating against a Chicago dollar, and an Atlanta dollar fluctuating against a San Francisco dollar.

There are, of course, certain differences, which I shall come to shortly, between America and what I think will happen in Europe. But I greatly fear for the future of sterling caught off-shore from the euro, between the euro and the dollar. We should not forget how you can be battered about by fluctuating exchange rates. Remember how in the mid-1980s the sterling–dollar exchange rate varied within a few years from $2.40 to $1.08 – I think that was the lowest point. There was no rational basis for that; there was nothing in compara-tive costs, in comparative trading performance, in relative inflation rates, which remotely justified it. It was just an irra-tional fluctuation of sentiment, but one which was devastat-ingly unstable for trading companies.

Nor should the popular, if you like, the demotic, argument be entirely disregarded. Having a lot of different currencies is extremely inconvenient and expensive. I have twice made the mistake – I did not intend to make it the second time, but I for-got – of paying in a small cheque drawn on a French bank. I sent the cheque to my bank, a leading bank, and what do you think the charge was? On £150 it was £17.50; only £132.50 was credited to my account. This is not a major argument, but nei-ther is it a negligible one.

It is of course the case, as has often been pointed out, that in America the single currency has been contained within a sin-gle, although fairly devolved, federal Government. But I agree with those like Mr Clarke, Mr Heseltine – and probably Mr Blair too – who believe that a single currency can operate without implying any great advance towards political union. We may or may not go further in the direction of a single Euro-pean state. I think the whole argument on this is largely a form of shadow boxing involving those who look back in nostalgia to a Britain which never was and who look forward with fear to a Europe which never will be.

There is no good reason to think that there is any question of France and Germany becoming the equivalent of North Dakota and South Dakota, nor even of Massachusetts and Texas. I agree with Helmut Schmidt's remarks at the ICR *Britian and Europe* conference that the differences – of lan-guage, culture and history – are such that individual states will always maintain a great deal of their individuality. That does not mean that they cannot work closely and effectively together.

There is one forgotten thing that is, curiously, hardly ever mentioned: the European Currency Union, which persisted from 1860 to 1914. It had a rather unlikely list of participants: France, Italy, Belgium, Switzerland and Greece. Greece in particular is surprising. Over this period of 54 years — certainly not of common government — the position was maintained with total interchangeability, and no fluctuations in exchange rates, until it was all blown up in 1914.

III

Now I come briefly to my third part, which is about the Commission. The first thing I want to say is that a Commission is essential to Europe. There is quite a lot wrong with the Commission, and I shall say something about that, but it is essential to Europe. If you just got rid of it, and replaced it with a simple secretariat, a subordinate secretariat, you would destroy a great part of the idea of Europe. Some people would like to do that, but it is no good saying that there just ought to be a bureaucratic secretariat, with no views of its own, doing nothing worthwhile.

First, the small countries — there are now ten small countries in Europe, and there may well be quite a few more — regard the Commission as a very important defence of their interests against being pushed around by the big five, or as they sometimes see it, the big two that have been in the lead recently.

Secondly, there are ambassadors in Brussels, permanent representatives, who haggle over the interests of the Member States. But it is desirable to have some body that tries, sometimes imperfectly, to take a wider view of the interests of Europe as a whole, which is what the Commission is supposed to do.

Nonetheless I welcome, or at least half welcome, the catharsis of 1999, which led to the resignation of the entire Commission. The Commission has functioned within a brilliantly successful Europe in the past 40 years. It has been an area of great prosperity. We should remember in this country that while we have had relatively good years recently compared with our European neighbours, it is still the hard fact that national income per head in France and Germany is substantially higher than in Britain, as is productivity per head.[1]

At any rate, Europe has been a success story and it has also been an area of peace. Look at the history of Europe and the fact that there has been peace, that war has been inconceivable within the European Union. Then look at the effect on the world, and not only on Europe. Historically Europe has been a plague spot for wars — wars which have devastated Europe twice if not three times — and which have spread into the rest of the world.

I would agree that the European Union has not been very good at dealing with trouble spots outside its borders, whether in Kosovo or Bosnia. But the history of the great Powers does not on the whole show that they are very good at that. Certainly in the nineteenth century and the early twentieth century, when Britain was indisputably a great Power, we were not very good at dealing with Ireland. I do not think America, indisputably a great Power, has been very good at dealing with the Central American republics. So although no one can claim that our handling of the Balkans has been brilliant, I do not think that for a moment settles the issue.

Now, what happened in 1999 was that the European Parliament, which was mocked previously for being a paper tiger and running away, asserted itself. It has come of age and shown that it has teeth, and it has given the Commission, I think, a salutary shock.

What does the Commission need in the future? Above all, we need a smaller Commission. Even in my day — I had twelve Commissioners apart from myself, with nine member countries — it was at least two too big; you had to make up jobs for two of the Commissioners. There are now twenty. What will the figure be in the future, when we get enlargement?

---

[1] Just for a moment I am going to switch back to the single currency. If I were going to choose a national virility symbol for a Britain unwilling to merge any part of its sovereignty, I am bound to say I would not choose the pound sterling. I would not choose a currency which in the early 1960s bought 12 deutschmarks and now buys barely a sixth of that. Even in the 1970s it bought eight deutschmarks. If you are to have a go-it-alone policy, you need something a little more inspiring than that.

Another fact that is worthy of note with regard to the effective working of Europe is that nobody has wanted to leave the European Union. If the Eurosceptics have their way they will blaze a trail. If anything only too many countries have urgently and pressingly wanted to join. It is not exactly a record of failure.

I am in favour of enlargement; I am in favour of the enlargement of Europe, but I am certainly not in favour of the enlargement of the Commission to nearly thirty members. That would assist neither the quality of the membership nor collegiality.

What do you do about choosing the members? Of course, the bold step would be to have a directly elected President of the Commission, directly elected throughout Europe. I think that would be a bridge too far, at the present stage — maybe for ever. It would certainly be resisted by the member governments, because the President would then have a towering authority greater than that which they have themselves. I do not think Europe is ready for that. But I would certainly be in favour of the President being endorsed, proposed even, by the European Parliament. Somebody has to nominate the President, but the Parliament should have the right to turn people down and say 'We want someone else'. It should not just be rather weakly rubber-stamped, as at present.

Institutions often need a shake-up after about 40 years. I think the events of 1999 have given the Commission a good shake-up. But one should not assume from it that one does not want a Commission or that these things cannot be considerably improved.

Acknowledgements

An earlier version of this paper was presented at the conference *Britain and Europe*, 22 March 1999, sponsored by the Institute for Constitutional Research and *The Daily Telegraph*.

Jeremy Black

Foreign and Defence Policies: The challenge of Europe

Addressing current developments is always hazardous for the historian. The archival sources are not accessible and one knows that when they are they may show one up to be totally wrong. It may be the case that the records of the late 1990s will reveal that Tony Blair and his Government had a sound grasp of national interests and made a robust, intelligent and successful defence of them. It may be so, but I doubt it.

Yet, before suggesting why, it is necessary to consider an important lesson that does come from the historian's training, namely the extent to which concepts are open to different interpretations. Take the notion of national interests. That has been subject to different interpretations and at moments of tension there has frequently been no agreement as to the definition of these interests or as to how best to advance them. Furthermore it is possible to show that particular perceptions of national interest have been deliberately advanced at particular junctures.

All this appears to contribute to the idea of the 'invention of tradition', a notion that has been employed by historians close to the government, or judged sympathetic to its attitudes, such as David Cannadine, Linda Colley and Norman Davies. If, after all, the earlier policies and values can be displayed as contingent and 'manufactured', then they appear to have no inherent value and it is reasonable to replace them by modern counterparts.

Such an approach has many weaknesses, not least being its inability to consider adequately the consensual aspect of 'manufactured' traditions—more specifically the extent to which they reflect a measure of popular will. Furthermore, to prove that there is no one conception of national interest, or single constitution, that has lasted without change or criticism for hundreds of years is not the same as arguing that all conceptions or constitutions are of equal value, or that it is a good idea to reject existing systems in favour of an untried future.

Concern about the philosophical or methodological assumptions of the government are, in this case, accentuated by the degree to which its members do not appear to have a clear understanding of what they mean by the nation. No nation, no national interests? That is too simple, but the extent to which constitutional experimentation at present seems likely to lead to a replacement of the United Kingdom by at best a coalition necessarily has implications for foreign and defence policies. These will need to be 'negotiated' within the British Isles—especially if rival political groupings are in power in Belfast, Cardiff, Edinburgh and London. This process of negotiation, never easy, will be even less so because the pretensions and prerogatives of the European Union extend far into what has until recently been regarded as domestic policy. It is naive to imagine that it will be possible to keep this process politically separate from that of the settlement of differences between parts of the British Isles.

Thus, aside from the policy of the EU, it is likely that the constitutional policies of the current UK Government will have a major impact on British foreign and military power. In particular, the desire to keep the Scottish Nationalist Party from power in Scotland is likely to drive UK government policy to an extent greater than the latter intends. This will not be presented as an expedient, but that element will be powerfully present.

Aside from the 'British' dimension to the question, there is also the problem of optimism. A government that came to power on the basis of welcoming change and rejecting the past is necessarily one that is optimistic about the prospect for improvement and a better future. This also has a partisan aspect with the specific denial of both Conservative and 'Old Labour' policies. Indeed the very notion of 'Old Labour' helps 'New Labour' to reject the traditional assumptions of State interest and foreign policy because they can be associated with 'Old Labour'. However, an assessment of positions in terms of 'New Labour' confuses what might at present be thus identified and the more long-term plasticity of the concept. There is a danger in particular that Mr Blair's views will be seen as co-terminous with, indeed the definition of, New Labour, when in practice the rejection of what is presented as Old Labour draws on a wider range of attitudes and developements. Furthermore Blair will eventually go and then his identification of New Labour with his views may be a major problem. The long term is a sequence and sum of short terms, but commentators should try to look beyond the particular moment in order to consider how attitudes to foreign policy held among the major political groupings may change. Certainly, recent history suggests the need to be adaptable to rapid shifts in international circumstances.

The rejection of the past currently associated with New Labour is assisted by the sense that the end of the Cold War has created an opportunity and need for new assumptions. The end of the Cold War had certainly led to a downplaying of NATO and of the Anglo–American alignment. This has been mitigated by the close relations between Blair and Clinton, but that itself is troubling because there is every likelihood that such relations will not survive a change in government. This can be seen as a reason to encourage a stronger EU foreign policy and defence identity for the UK, and it is possible that future strains in transatlantic relations will lead in that very direction.

However, it is by no means clear that the EU is capable of fulfilling the hopes placed upon it in this sphere. This specific problem of the moment can be related to a wider shift. For long it has been apparent that Britain's role in the world has diminished, but that many politicians, commentators and much of the public were reluctant to accept this and to think through the possible implications. For many decades, the situation was partially disguised by the generally pliable attitude of Dominion governments and colonial populations, and because Britain was fortunate that her major ally was America. When, however, the latter alliance was absent or weak, as in the 1930s, the situation was far more difficult. Furthermore within the EEC and then EU Britain lacked any such ally to shield her or protect her interests. This became increasingly

apparent from the 1980s. The linkage of rival states may have
worked in the case of France and Germany, but has not done
so for Britain and France or, arguably, Britain and Germany.
Furthermore the EU has failed not only to meet Britain's needs
for an effectively-managed free trading area, but also proved
inadequate as a body through which to advance wider interests elsewhere in Europe. Thus Britain has found its freedom
in international trade negotiations, a key aspect of foreign
relations, circumscribed and its interests slighted. The EU
itself suffers from disunity, a lack of military resources, and an
ambitious extension of interests and commitments that have
taken it into the Balkans and threatens to take it to the borders
of Syria, Iraq and Iran.

This is the dangerous policy of recent years, and it is shot
through with an optimism and universalism that is troubling.
The latter rests in large part on the attempt to make human
rights a central feature in policy, at once replacing the moral
imperative of resisting Soviet imperialism and explaining and
justifying power projection. Yet, as there are areas where such
projection is well beyond EU capability, there is reliance instead
on the idea of regional security systems supportive of an international order. That *might* work in East Timor or, less plausibly, Sierra Leone and Liberia, but it will have scant impact on
China or Russia.

Furthermore the region in question for the UK – Europe – is
one that bears little relationship to long-established national
interests. Instead these are being reconfigured or European-
ized in a policy that at once testifies to the Government's view
that Europe is the crucial international unit for Britain and the
optimistic hope that it can be made to work. The logic, however, is somewhat limited. Apparently, as we are in Europe,
Europe should be our unit of concern – an approach that
could as easily justify globalism or the hemispheralism of
Haushofer and the geopoliticians of the 1930s. There is an
old-fashioned emphasis on propinquity which very much
dates from mid-century assessments of security and economic
relations. This means far less in terms of the global economics
and geopolitics of the present day.

In addition, the emphasis on Europe is a flawed assessment
of the multiple links of the UK. For centuries the UK has been
closer to Boston, Kingston or New York than to Bari, Cracow

or Zagreb, and this situation has not changed. Indeed, cultural and demographic developments over the last half century, ranging from the impact of American television to New Commonwealth immigration have accentuated these links and indicated the unhelpfulness of a definition of Britain in terms of Europe.

As with some earlier governments, there is a misleading tendency to argue that Britain's relations with Europe entail specific commitments. In practice, an argument about interdependability did, and does, not dictate the contours and consequences of such relationships. Choices existed, and exist, but that has long been denied by politicians and polemicists keen to advocate a particular point of view.

The optimistic Mr Blair—the youthful Mr Toad of British politics, with his faddish enthusiam for novelty and his determination to ignore an ancestral heritage—clearly feels that he can square the circle, or rather circles. He intends to reconcile traditional assumptions with new identities and to keep different alignments and commitments in concert and, indeed, mutually supportive. Maybe they can be made so, but the basis is unclear. Certainly, EU policy in the Balkans was not an encouraging precedent. Instead, Britain and France found themselves bearing most of the burden. Furthermore, the reduction in the military expenditure by other states, such as Germany and Belgium, suggests that future crises will find Britain bearing a disproportionate share. In addition, the history of Britain's relations within the EU in the late 1990s does not suggest that bearing a heavy burden will yield benefits in other fields. This failure can ironically be seen as part of a postwar trend in which successive governments have exaggerated the likely benefit that would flow from high military expenditure. In the case of New Labour, seeing the benefit in European terms does not lessen the error.

There is little room in my allocated space to turn to other specifics, but two points must be underlined. First, the resort to force in the Kosovo crisis neither prevented the Serbian brutalization of the local population nor ensured subsequent peace and order, let alone reconciliation.

Second, the use of universalist language by the British government (and to a more cautious extent by that of the USA) has helped to drive China and Russia together. In geopolitical terms this is disturbing. The Cold War became less threatening when the two powers split and even more so when they became rivals. To encourage them to look on each other as allies facing the West is thus foolish and will probably register in greater difficulties in dealing with crises in the Balkans, the Middle East and other parts of the World.

Lastly, as other writers have indicated, the government's support for greater European integration and for a European identity for the UK has lessened our ability to retain practices and politics of self-reliance, of national accountability, and of reacting to developments on their merits and with reference to the contingencies of the moment. In short, it will be harder to keep a distance from much that is difficult and intractable. Two philosophies are at issue. Mr Blair falls squarely into the Whiggish tradition of interventionism and the creation of systems to solve problems and prevent their recurrence. This is not one that has served the UK well this century, but at least under his predecessors there was a national not a European basis to this interventionism.

Alongside the Whiggish tradition there is also that which would emphasize the mutability and uncertainty of human affairs and the risks of a system-based approach. The pragmatic and prudential approach to foreign commitments needs to be recovered. As Samuel Johnson pointed out, in his *Thoughts on the Late Transactions Respecting Falkland's Islands* (1771):

> It seems to be almost the universal error of historians to suppose it politically, as it is physical true, that every effort has a proportionate cause. In the inanimate action of matter upon matter, the motion produced can be but equal to the force of the moving power; but the operations of life, whether private or publick admit no such laws. The caprices of voluntary agents laugh at calculation.

Norman Tebbit

Britain and Europe:
The issue of sovereignty

By 'Britain' I presume we mean not the British Isles which, to the chagrin of some, includes the whole of Ireland, nor Great Britain which, curiously, excludes both Northern and Southern Ireland, but the United Kingdom of Great Britain and Northern Ireland. By 'Europe' I suspect that most people mean not the geographers' Europe, which includes both Norway and Switzerland, the Baltic states, the Balkans, the central European states and the lands and states eastwards to the Urals, but our fellow members of the European Union.

I hope you will not think it pedantic of me to make these distinctions. The use of the same words to mean different things to different people, or different things at different times, is a useful means of obscuring issues and fudging conclusions but is seldom a help in analysis or debate intended to clarify rather than to confuse.

I will take Britain to mean the United Kingdom, a formerly self-governing state, and Europe to mean the European Union, both as it was and is, and as it is developing to be.

Until the United Kingdom acceded to the Treaty of Rome in 1972 it was not just a self-governing state. It was a democracy, it was independent and it possessed sovereignty.

The then Prime Minister said on 24 May 1971:

> Joining the Community does not entail a loss of national identity or an erosion of national sovereignty.

Others took a different view.

The problem besetting the relationship between Britain and Europe is that since its very inception it has been shot through with muddle, misconception, misunderstanding, deception and self-deception. The same words have meant different things to different people.

Entry to the European Economic Community was sold in Britain as entry into a trading system, not as a ticket on a train to economic, monetary and political union. In Brussels it was seen as a commitment — an irreversible commitment — to an ever closer union, which was taken there to mean a political union.

The Prime Minister's broadcast on 8 July 1971 was all about economic opportunity. I offer you some quotes:

> Traditional markets are being taken from us and new ones are not automatically opening up in front of us.

> The European Community provides us with our chance. It opens up one of the biggest markets to us.

> An agreement which will give our farmers opportunities of expansion they have never had before.

> We have got the Community to agree that their rules for fishing must be changed to safeguard our fishermen.

In the whole of that broadcast there was just this:

> Nor shall we be any less British. They have their parliaments. So shall we. They have their own laws and courts. So shall we.

Jim Callaghan, of course, saw it differently:

> Most people in Brussels, especially the economists, will tell you that if the EEC is to overcome its problems and have a common policy in agriculture and trade and economic matters it will have to be transformed into a federal state.

Jim Callaghan saw that in 1971. Not for the first time, his first reaction was profoundly sensible. I will not go on about his second. He was frustrated that the arguments at that time concentrated on economic issues and ignored the political and constitutional implications. 'Trying to get a pro-marketeer to state the political case for entry is like trying to nail custard to the wall', he complained.

All this was nearly 30 years ago. Yet the issue of the Euro — let me define that, too, a little more sharply — the issue of economic and monetary union, is being debated in precisely the same way.

There is even a danger of a consensus that the campaigners on either side of the question should best be businessmen, not politicians. A fusillade from Lord Marshall of British Airways is met by a barrage from Sir Stanley Kalms of Dixons. The cost of converting slot machines and tills is set against the joys of using the same notes and coins in a McDonalds in Manchester and a taverna in Tuscany.

But economic decisions have political repercussions. A single market in sheepmeat — a vile word — requires competence to set standards for the welfare of animals in transit, and it requires that power to migrate from national parliaments to Brussels, which I use as a portmanteau word for the Council of Ministers, the Commission and the Parliament. The political consequence is that our Westminster Government has responsibility but no authority over these matters. Animal rights activists have to be told that we cannot refuse to export live animals to countries which allow the abuse of animals, despite the Euro-laws which should protect them.

Power without responsibility, said Stanley Baldwin, is the prerogative of the harlot. Responsibility without power is the prerogative of the satrapy, not the sovereign self-governing nation.

Set against the economic advantages believed to flow from membership of the European Union, or those forecast by some from European monetary union, does it matter if a few sheep get a rough time in the last days of their lives? There is a moral argument here about animal rights or, as I would term it, human obligations towards animals, which, important as it is, is not relevant to the topic under discussion.

It is a constitutional issue, however, of where power and responsibility lie, an issue of government and of democracy.

Let me take the discussion away from such grassroots detail — and there are plenty of other examples — to a more rarefied level. This — the United Kingdom — what is it? To constitute a State the entity must have certain attributes. It must have people to constitute a nation. It must have territory too and a government with power to protect both territory and people and govern their conduct one with another and to govern conduct with other states.

To maintain statehood our government must fulfil five key functions.

1. It must be able to defend the territory of the state, the Queen's realm, in our case, against outsiders, and protect her subjects overseas.

2. It must maintain order — preserve the Queen's peace within her kingdom and allow her subjects to go about their lawful business in peace.

3. It must provide a currency to act as a medium of exchange and a store of value to allow commerce to be done and savings to be secure.

4. It must provide a system of law and justice to uphold the Queen's peace and to arbitrate between citizen and citizen and between citizen and the state.

5. To exercise these functions, it must have a monopoly power to tax the Queen's subjects.

In these days of peace and prosperity, there is a temptation to think more about the other desirable but optional services which we expect the state to provide, and to forget those key essentials. Desirable some of those things may be, but they can be provided by the state or by the private sector, nor does their absence constitute the absence of the state. Were it to do so, we would have to assume that the England of Queen Elizabeth did not constitute a state.

At the turn of the last millennium the Anglo-Saxon state formed by the merger of Wessex and Mercia was falling apart since Ethelred was unable to fulfil the five key functions of the state. We recollect what happened fairly soon after that. At the turn of the last century, in contrast, there could be no doubt of the capacity of the state which was the United Kingdom.

How do things look now?

Function five — the monopoly power to tax — has already been eroded. The principle that only the state by virtue of the powers endowed in parliament may choose to tax or not to tax has been fatally breached. In the words of a recent parliamentary answer, extracted, I have to say, with no less effort than must be devoted to the extraction of dragons' teeth:

> The European Community's sixth VAT directive provides a framework for the coverage of VAT and the rates which may be applied by Member States. Within that framework [notice that expression] the United Kingdom is able to decide a number of important issues [but not, of course, to abolish VAT, nor to reduce the standard rate to 10 per cent, nor to extend or reduce its coverage].

This may not yet be a huge intrusion upon parliament's right to tax — but nor would an uninvited garrison of foreign troops occupying, say, the Isle of Wight be a huge intrusion upon our territory, but it marks the beginning of the end of parliament's monopoly over tax.

I sometimes think I can hear the words of Gladstone drifting away on a wind blowing from the Continent. He said on 17 March 1891 at Hastings:

> The finance of this country is intimately associated with the liberties of the country. It is a powerful leverage by which English liberty has been gradually acquired. If these powers of the House of Commons come to be encroached upon, it will be by tacit and insidious measures, and therefore I say public attention should be called to this.

How well the Sixth Directive fits the bill! It is exactly fitting to the warning which Gladstone gave.

What of function four of the state? Is parliament still free to make the laws which uphold the Queen's peace or arbitrate between citizens, or between citizens and the state? Clearly not so. The European Court of Justice is the supreme court of this land, set above those of England and Wales and of Scotland and Northern Ireland. Across steadily widening swathes of our law, European law is now supreme. Should parliament legislate in contravention of Euro-law, parliament's law would have no validity. That is not to mention that other self-inflicted wound — our accession to the European Convention on Human Rights — which has led to the lunatic, *Catch 22* situation in which the European Court of Human Rights has ruled that the European Communities (Amendment) Act of 1986 is in breach of the Convention on Human Rights, because it denies Gibraltar the right to vote in Euro elections, but parliament has no power to amend that Act without the consent of every other Member State — including Spain. Whose jurisdiction are we in?

To be subject to two overlapping but separate foreign jurisdictions cannot, surely, be the mark of an independent, self-governing state. Nor can it be the mark of a democracy that the people cannot secure through the ballot box the enactment, amendment or repeal of the laws by which they are governed.

What of the third function of the state, the provision of the currency? Can that be contracted out by an irreversible Act and parliament remain sovereign? Again listen to the echoes of Gladstone's words. A state can lose its gold and currency reserves and remain sovereign even if not solvent. But when it yields to a higher authority power not only over taxation, but over borrowing and total expenditure, we can hardly delude ourselves that it remains sovereign.

In a Selsdon Group paper, Professor Tim Congdon sets out most cogently the reasons why the Euro requires a single central political authority for its success. Nearly 30 years ago Jim Callaghan made the same argument:

> If there is to be a successful economic and monetary union, then Member States will have to subordinate their own fiscal, taxation, and monetary policies to a central governing body and surrender their powers over these matters. Such a possibility is, in my view, a long way ahead, perhaps 10 years from now, but I am quite clear that it cannot be achieved through a confederation of European States.

Or, as I have put it, in rather less cerebral terms, no currency can have two Chancellors of the Exchequer, no independent government can be without their own Chancellor, and no Chancellor can be without a currency of his own to his name.

As to function two — the preservation of law and order — there has been more erosion by the European Court of

Human Rights than by Brussels, but the threat of *corpus juris*, with, amongst other things, its impact on *habeas corpus*, is already to be seen.

Function one—defence and foreign policy—began to be eroded by the Maastricht Treaty, and a single foreign and defence policy with a single defence force remains an ambition of some of our partners. The United Kingdom no longer resists the steps towards the creation of a European defence force. As usual, we are told that the proposed European Rapid Reaction Force will remain under sovereign national control and that it will operate (usually) within NATO. Yet the history of all such European empire building should warn us that the shortcomings of the ERRF will soon be used as a reason to centralize control. The force may not unduly frighten our external enemies, although it is already making our American allies nervous. Even worse there are no restraints, in being or proposed, against its use within the European Union. So the noose is tightened.

In short, much authority over the key functions of government, without which a state ceases to be a state, has already been lost, and more is being lost.

Entry into the European monetary union would accelerate the process and make it near irreversible. Is that inevitable? No. We are a developed nation, well able to govern ourselves. We are the fifth largest economy in the world—and who would seriously claim that there are only four nations in the world capable of self-government?

Is it desirable? There is—and one must recognize it—a case for selling one's birthright for a mess of pottage, but it has its downside.

All experience across the world suggests that no nation, no people, is willing to be governed by those who do not share its language, its religion and its history. Those states comprising separate nations are subject to increasingly fissiparous forces. There is little popular demand in the world today for an end to independence or self-government.

I believe the European monetary union will inevitably compel the creation of a state called Europe. That is a view that is shared by Chancellor Schröder and his predecessor, Helmut Kohl. Already 'Europe' has its citizens, its flag, its national anthem, its supreme court, its own external borders (it is extinguishing its internal borders), its parliament, overseas diplomatic representation, a currency, a central bank, a civil service, and a capacity to create foreign policy. As my American friends say, if it looks like a duck, walks like a duck and quacks like a duck, then it probably is a duck.

In the meantime, this United Kingdom looks less like a state as Europe looks more like a state.

The question for those who do not wish this Kingdom to become a province or a satrapy is 'What should be our relationship to Euroland?' Is there a possible relationship within a modified, new Treaty of Rome, or must we either integrate totally or withdraw? There may be. As the events of 1999 have shown, the state of Euro institutions is rotten, and they are over-ripe for radical reform.

I say, let those who wish to accept economic, monetary and political union get on with it without hindrance from us. Let the Commission become their elected Government, responsible to their parliament. But let the jurisdiction of the Council be limited to trade relations, and create a new, minimalist secretariat to serve that Council. In short, why not create a European version of NAFTA, with one big state and several smaller ones amongst its members, and let the British dog cease to occupy the federalist manger and try to deny it to those who wish to live there?

The United Kingdom cannot exist in the sovereign state of Europe. There cannot be two sovereign states in one territory. We can co-exist with it, and so can many other European states, and that can open the way to the admission of all the other Europeans, right the way through to the Urals, into the European Common Market.

What is certain is that Britain should not become part of a would-be super-Power which has at its heart the ambition to challenge the United States on the world stage.

Acknowledgements

An earlier version of this paper was presented at the conference *Britain and Europe*, 22 March 1999, sponsored by the Institute for Constitutional Research and *The Daily Telegraph*.

Peter Shore

European Union Takeover of UK

We are ceasing to be an independent sovereign state and we are ceasing to be a Parliamentary democracy.

I made that judgment long before the 1997 General Election and so it has no direct connection with Prime Minister Tony Blair's programme for the so-called 'modernization' of the British Constitution. Nevertheless, those measures, in particular the devolution of powers to the Scottish Parliament and the Welsh Assembly, the new methods of electing Members to the European Parliament, the reform of the House of Lords and the threatened change to our system of electing MPs to the Westminster Parliament will undoubtedly contribute to either strengthening or, more probably, weakening British democracy.

At this stage, only a provisional balance sheet is possible. But clearly Scottish and Welsh devolution, desirable in many ways as it is, is a much more risky enterprise in the late 1990s than it was when first conceived some 25 years ago: more risky because they are, as devolved assemblies, clear targets for the power brokers in the European Commission who foster separatist, regional and ethnic identities within the European nation states as part of their continuing drive to dismantle the nation state and to put in its place a 'Europe of Regions'. To turn substantial areas of the European Union into client states and regions, heavily dependent upon grants from Brussels and directly linked to the Brussels Commission is of course one of the strategies of 'ever closer union'. Moreover the introduction of continental voting systems, proportional representation and regional lists, into the elections for our new Scottish Parliament and Welsh Assembly, for the June 1999 election of Members of the European Parliament and the campaign to introduce a similar system for the future election of MPs to the House of Commons itself would undoubtedly further weaken British democracy — not least by making coalition government the norm in British politics. Against this however a decisive rejection in the promised — but now postponed — referendum on proportional representation for the Westminster Parliament and a particular enhancement of powers in the reformed second chamber, as discussed later, would have the opposite effect of strengthening our democracy and presenting an obstacle to any further erosion of our sovereign powers.

But let us turn now to the real issue: Europe. Long before the new Labour Government of 1997, when our present Prime Minister was still a schoolboy, the first crucial step in what has turned out to be a prolonged downhill journey was taken when Edward Heath as Prime Minister signed and negotiated the Treaty of Accession that brought the United Kingdom into membership of the Common Market on 1 January 1973. From the start, the Government accepted that, in a large area of our affairs, the British electorate and their elected Westminster Parliament were no longer sovereign; that we were henceforth to be subject to the provisions of the Treaty of Rome and to all the laws and treaties that had been subsequently made under its authority in the 16 years before we joined. Along with this surrender of a large chunk of our Parliamentary sovereignty went the supremacy of our courts of law. Henceforth, on all matters relating to the Treaty of Rome, the European Court of Justice was to be the final arbiter.

Of course, the Treaty of Rome covered a substantial part but by no means the whole of our national affairs. Nevertheless we surrendered the crucial power not just of regulating trade within the Common Market but also with the world outside. Henceforth, our external relations with other countries, which in peacetime largely consist of trade agreements and preferential and free trade arrangements, would be governed not by the Secretary of State for Trade in London and his Cabinet colleagues but by the European Commission in Brussels. As part of the internal market, a vast area of policy — all related to the free movement of goods, services, establishments and people, and to the achievement of 'a level playing field' — was transferred to the regulatory and law-making agencies of the Brussels Commission. In the years since 1973, as the Brussels Commission and the Council of Ministers have activated different dormant clauses of the Rome Treaty and added to that Treaty the Single European Act, the Maastricht Treaty and the Treaty of Amsterdam, there is left now hardly an aspect of our affairs, however trivial, over which the European Institutions, the Commission and the European Court of Justice, does not claim and indeed possess exclusive or shared 'competence' or control.

The process is far, far from over. There is a grinding, relentless logic built in to the European treaties, a logic that leads unmistakably to a single European state. The Common Market led to the Single Market; the Single Market to the Single Currency and Economic and Monetary Union. The Economic and Monetary Union leads on to the next target, a Fiscal Union. Within weeks of the May 1998 agreement to launch the Single Currency, the Euro, a strong new offensive was launched to bring the realm of indirect taxation within the scope of Community competence and control. Just as the possession of a national currency and a national central bank and the power to tax are the indispensable tools of a sovereign state, so their transfer to European institutions is both an abandonment of our own powers of self-government and the equipment of the European institutions with these crucial powers of statehood. Of course, we have an opt-out protocol, giving us the right to retain the pound sterling but not exempting us from many other obligations of Economic and Monetary Union. The pressures are now strongly upon the Government (which is a willing accomplice in the enterprise, but scared that the electorate would vote it down), to cancel our opt-out, to abandon sterling, to immerse ourselves into the Single Currency and the European Central Bank and to accept ever-increasing measures of tax harmonization.

The process of 'ever closer union' extends even far beyond the economy and everything related to it: it embraces increasingly our social policy, and a growing area of domestic law. Whether the British people are aware of it or not, the Treaty of Maastricht signed in 1991 has made us all, from the Queen to her humblest subject, citizens of the European Union, and citizenship carries with it not only rights but obligations and duties, although these have yet to be spelt out. The Treaty of Amsterdam, signed only in the Summer of 1997, seeks to embrace the whole of asylum law, immigration policy and to bring us within what the Treaty pleases to call an area of 'freedom, security and justice'.

The implication of all these measures on our previously sovereign parliament can easily be demonstrated. We can no longer decide our food and agriculture policy; that has been transferred *en bloc* to the European Commission; our fisheries are now governed by the so-called Common Fisheries Policy and all the waters and seas around our coasts — apart from a six mile coastal strip, and a further six to twelve mile strip shared with other European coastal states — have become the common property of the European Union. An Act of Parliament designed, in 1988, to give some protection to British fishing vessels, was taken before the European Court of Justice and struck down. What Parliament had decreed, the European Court simply overruled. Not only has new legislation, designed to meet particular British needs, to obtain the prior approval of the authorities in Brussels but parliament has lost the power, however strongly the British people wish it were otherwise, to repeal any of the laws and directives which, over the past 26 years of our membership, have been imposed upon the British people by the European Authorities.

Even that does not end the story. In the months since June 1999, a range of issues have come before parliament and people. We have been instructed and obliged to abandon duty-free sales of strictly limited quantities of tobacco and alcohol on British airlines to British passengers flying to and from European Union destinations. What looked like a very welcome outcome to the long negotiations between the Secretary of State for Trade and the German motor car giant, BMW, to invest heavily in Britain's obsolescent Rover car plants in Birmingham and Oxford, is now at risk. The European Commission intervened and told the British and German Governments that it is not satisfied with the arrangements and that they therefore cannot go ahead unless and until they received Commission approval. Again, in the middle of June 1999, the art market in London was obliged to accept a doubling of tax on the sale of works of art from the previous VAT at 2.5% to VAT at 5%. It will of course lead to a weakening of the London art market against the competition of its untaxed rivals in New York and elsewhere. None of these measures have the support — on the contrary, they have the stated opposition — of the British Government. But Her Majesty's Government no longer governs in these as in so many other and much more important areas of our national life.

But there is still one other area of decision making that has to be transferred before the United Kingdom is reduced to the status of a province of the European Union. Foreign policy, security policy and defence policy are still outside the control of the European institutions — but for how long this will be so and what bridgeheads the European Union has already established in all three areas are developments to which we must now turn. In this vital area developments began with the aim of 'co-operation' in foreign and security matters. Fine. But then we moved on to the declared aim of a common European foreign and security policy which, when agreed unanimously by the Heads of Government meeting in the European Council, can thereafter be developed by qualified majority voting to implement the policy goals. How all this will develop has yet to be clearly established. But the Treaty of Amsterdam, in force since May 1999, has now established a joint high policy- making secretariat in Brussels, headed by a senior European politician who is to become 'Mr Europe'. He will be responsible, as the decisions taken at the Cologne and Helsinki summit meetings make clear, for the implementation of ongoing agreed policies and no doubt he will meet the foreign and defence ministers of other independent sovereign nations such as the United States, Russia, Japan and the rest. Already Mr Europe has been appointed: Snr Solana, the former Secretary General of NATO.

Conventions have been signed between the Governments of Germany, France, Italy and the United Kingdom aimed at bringing together and rationalizing their defence industries. Finally, to crown it all, the European Council appointed in summer 1999 (with enthusiastic British support) as the new President of the European Commission, the most powerful single post in the European Union, Snr Prodi, a former Italian Prime Minister and an ardent enthusiast for creating a federal union, the United States of Europe. Within days of his appointment Snr Prodi has gone on the record to call for a single European army. We shall hear, again and again, in the months ahead how necessary it is for the European Union to have defence forces of its own, independent of the NATO alliance, to give substance and effect to the common foreign policy of the European Union. Already, at the December 1999 summit meeting the Heads of Government agreed a target of 60,000 for the planned 'rapid-reaction force'.

There is no doubt about what has happened and what is continuing to happen. The question is: how has it come about that so much of our most treasured possessions, our independence and our democratically-elected parliament and government — national possessions for which over the centuries and indeed as recently as the Second World War successive generations of British people have fought and died — have been surrendered with so little public and parliamentary protest by successive British governments since Prime Minister Heath made the first and fatal error of joining the Common Market and of signing up to the Rome Treaty.

The answer is not simple. Many factors contributed to this initial decision and to the subsequent treaties that we have accepted. But one factor is very clear: our unwritten Constitution, with all its other splendid strengths, does leave us peculiarly vulnerable to fundamental constitutional change. Other countries, with their written constitutions, usually provide that for a limited class of extremely important constitutional measures, simple majority voting in parliament is not enough. So, most written constitutions have provisions for the need to obtain a particularly large majority in parliament (up to two-thirds of members in favour is required) or — and sometimes and — that a referendum be held, before any substantial change can take effect.

Of course, until the arrival of Harold Macmillan and Edward Heath as Prime Ministers and Leaders of the Conservative Party in the 1960s, no one in our long history would have dreamt of the UK surrendering the powers of its government and parliament to foreign institutions. So, the Treaty of Accession signed in 1972 and the Act of Parliament to give effect to its obligations in 1973 required only a simple majority in the House of Commons. That Bill was fiercely con-

tested in the Chamber, and its Second Reading — and later the
guillotine motion that the Government imposed — were
passed by majorities as low as six.

Second, the whole strategy for achieving the European
state, which owed so much to the thinking and action of Jean
Monnet, was one of committed advance to the goals of 'ever
closer union' but to their achievement through an astonish-
ingly flexible tactic of 'gradualness', with long 'transition'
periods allowed to member states. All of this was well
designed to meet traditional British resistance to sudden
change, and the long-established British preference for gradual adaptation and incremental change.

Impressive though the tactics of the Euro-integrationists
have been, their success in disarming the resistance and gaining acquiescence of the British people could never have been
achieved without the connivance of successive British Governments, without the front bench collusion of the main political parties and without the continuing deception of the British
people about the real purposes and objectives of at least the
core members of the Common Market. The deceptions ranged
from Heath's original assurance that no significant loss of British Sovereignty was involved in membership, through Harold
Wilson's belief that the Single Currency project had been per-
manently abandoned and that the UK retained a veto over the
whole range of matters covered by the Rome Treaty, through
Mrs Thatcher's failure to recognize that the 1986 Single European Act involved not just more open-market competition
between the European economies, but the abandonment of
the UK veto over an immense area of the Treaties, through
John Major's self-deluding claim, on signing the Maastricht
Treaty, that it was 'game, set and match' for the UK, to Tony
Blair's blurred picture of Europe as 'an alliance of independent nations choosing to co-operate to achieve the goals they
cannot achieve alone'. Throughout these past 28 years successive Prime Ministers and most Leaders of the Opposition,
have either deceived themselves or been deceived and most
certainly have deceived the British people as to the central aim
of the founding members to achieve 'an ever closer union' of
peoples and institutions in Europe, culminating in a single
European state, a United States of Europe. So, by a process of
deception and stealth, much of the birthright of the British

people has been surrendered and what is still left is danger-
ously at risk.

How best to describe or label what has taken place? A rape
of our Constitution? Or a seduction accomplished by a mix of
false promises of future rewards and dire threats on refusal to
surrender? Or should we say that the British Government of
1973—and a number of its successors—simply played the
whore? Take your pick: but the fact is that our Constitution,
our democracy, our independence and our rights as British citizens and electors have been violated and diminished in a
truly disgraceful way.

That brings me to the third and last of the main questions
that have to be addressed: namely, what can be done to ensure
that the transfer of sovereign powers has now come to an end;
that there will be no further extensions of EU competence and
control and that we can set about the task of repatriating to
Westminster as many powers as a self-governing nation genuinely needs. Certainly the second part of this operation will
take time and effort; it can best be compared to a salvage operation to rescue as much of the cargo as still survives from the
sunken ship of British sovereignty.

Clearly we need both to signal and to define the new course
that Britain should take. In terms of immediate impact, nothing would signal more clearly the UK's new course than to
bring the question of the Euro to an early resolution. The Government and the Opposition are committed to the holding of a
referendum. The rules of that referendum have yet to be
agreed but, with the advice of the Neill Committee and the
experience of previous referendums to draw upon, rules for
their conduct could be swiftly established. The referendum,
with the decisive NO that the British people will register, will
have a tonic effect on the whole nation. If the Government
tries to delay the referendum beyond the first year of the next
Parliament, a national campaign should be mounted with the
purpose of forcing either a referendum or a clear statement
from the Government that they have abandoned the Single
Currency project.

Looking to the future, we urgently need to erect some constitutional barriers that will prevent any future government
from surrendering the rights of the British people and their

elected parliament without some procedures that include an explicit vote of consent by the electorate.

Proposals to achieve this end could indeed become part of the functions and powers of the reformed second chamber, following the removal of the Hereditary Peers and the fulfilment of the Government's pledge that the reformed chamber's composition would, by Act of Parliament, ensure that no one party could ever be allowed an overall majority in the chamber and that a substantial minority should consist of non-party, cross-bench Members who would be independent of party loyalties and disciplines.

This new and more authoritative second chamber should be granted one additional power. In a limited but supremely important category of legislation, constitutional legislation (defined as such by the Speaker of the House of Commons), which would certainly embrace any further transfer of electoral or Parliamentary powers from Britain to Europe, the new second chamber should be empowered, where it sees fit, to declare that the measure requires the specific approval of the British people, and then to require the Government of the day, should it wish to persist, to hold a referendum on the issue. Regrettably such a proposal is not in the Wakeham Commission report. But in the long process of debate and legislation that lies ahead, there is ample time to rectify that defect.

This clear expression of our determination to loosen the embrace of the 'ever closer union' and the establishment of constitutional checks to prevent any further erosion of parliamentary powers, would in themselves enormously raise the diminished status of our Westminster Parliament — as well as improve the morale and self respect of the 651 MPs whom we send to the House of Commons. Instead of tacitly accepting, as so many do, that the Westminster Parliament, the Mother of Parliaments, is doomed to become a parliamentary museum, they will know that among their many tasks they must now give first place to the defence, maintenance and restoration of the powers of the House of Commons and of the British electorate whom they are elected to serve.

There is much that they as Members of Parliament and their colleagues as Ministers of the Crown can do to encourage this process and to help restore the prestige and dignity of their House. At the very least, the House collectively should insist that Ministers no longer make policy statements outside the House but that statements of policy should *always* be made first from the Despatch Box in the House of Commons. Of course, Ministers and MPs must appear on TV and must be heard on radio. But, Ministers should be precluded from making statements on the *Today* programme and on other channels *before* they have addressed the House of Commons. On matters of great importance and strong public interest, parliament should insist that when in session, Ministers, including the Prime Minister, should be interrogated by either the House itself or by ad hoc Select Committees rather than be held to account in a BBC studio by such unelected tribunes as John Humphries, Jeremy Paxman or James Naughtie. Ministers who are derelict in this duty should be subjected, not only to stern and immediate rebuke from the Speaker, but to formal complaints to either or both the Select Committee on Procedure or the Select Committee on Standards and Privileges.

Lastly, MPs can make a direct and immediate contribution to restoring some of their own lost prestige. They should be there, in the Chamber of the House of Commons, when statements are made, when debates are opened and when they are wound up between 9pm and 10pm. In this Parliament in particular the prolonged absence of MPs from the Chamber, the vast expanse of green leather that is to be seen in every television snippet — apart from Prime Minister's Question Time on Wednesday at 3pm — at all hours on virtually every sitting day, is little short of a national scandal.

Peter Oborne

The Rise of the Media Class

The rise in the status of journalism in all its manifestations has been one of the most striking developments of our time. Little more than a generation ago, journalism was a dishonourable and poorly esteemed profession. Now talented journalists have become fêted celebrities. They wield immense social, economic and political power which the Media Class has gathered unto itself at the expense of the great institutions of the state, the monarchy and the church.

Nowhere is the elevation of the humble jobbing journalist more apparent than in political reporting. In the immediate post-war epoch, right up to the election of Harold Wilson as Prime Minister in 1964, the attitude of political reporters to the House of Commons and to politicians was profoundly deferential. It was practically unheard of for parliamentary correspondents—the title Political Editor and the grandeur that implies did not develop until the late 1960s—to have lunch with a Cabinet minister. Indeed, one of the primary requirements of the lobby man was to arrange, though not to attend, lunches on behalf of his proprietor. Gerald Herlihy, the political correspondent of the *Graphic*, was for a number of years in effect the social secretary to his proprietor's wife, Lady Kemsley.

Political reporters were divided between 'parliamentary' correspondents and 'political' correspondents. It was the function of the former to report, partly in the flamboyant manner of a theatre critic, the events of the previous day in the Commons chamber. These articles were given abundant space. Parliamentary correspondents were considered very much more important than political correspondents, whose membership of the lobby enabled them to share some of the privileges of Members of Parliament. These lobby men would add a few lines to the account of the previous day's parliamentary drama, modestly drawing attention to items of particular significance. This division of power within the profession indicates how political reporters accepted Parliament on its own terms. Politicians were judged very much in the way they wanted to be judged.

Prime Ministers in the post-war period did not deal with political reporters at all, and very rarely even with newspaper editors. They maintained a warm relationship with the great press proprietors, whom they met at society functions and country houses. When Churchill suffered a stroke in June 1953 the illness was never reported. This serious disruption in the life of a serving Prime Minister was one of the biggest stories the press had had to cope with since the war. Yet it was covered up with ease. Downing Street merely indicated to the great proprietors — Beaverbrook, Bracken and Camrose — that it would be inconvenient if this distressing illness got out, and it never did. Eventually it was Churchill himself, restored and at the despatch box of the Commons, who chose to reveal that he had had a stroke: a tribute to the then inviolate power of Parliament.

Churchill, during his second term as Prime Minister, held reporters in such low esteem that he refused to let them in through the front door of Downing Street when they turned up for their diet of daily official announcements. He banned them from the building and insisted that they use a room in the Cabinet Office further up Whitehall instead. When he reluctantly handed over power in April 1955, his successor Anthony Eden attempted to ingratiate himself with the press by rescinding the ban. But the feudal spirit remained. Harold Evans, who served as Press Secretary to both Harold Macmillan and Sir Alec Douglas-Home, adopted the demeanour and approach of a superior gentleman's gentleman. Downing Street briefings were conducted in the spirit of the butler at a great country estate addressing the domestic staff. Nobody thought this was odd or offensive. Lord Poole, chairman of the Tory Party under Macmillan, once pronounced on the subject of lobby correspondents at a Chatham House discussion. They were very decent fellows, he opined, but not quite the sort of people one would invite into one's own home.

The parliamentary reporter needed two qualities: an outstanding shorthand note and the ability to keep his head down. Very few of them had been to university: they had come up the hard way, starting with local papers in the provinces. Anthony Howard, who later became editor of the *New Statesman*, entered the lobby as a reporter for *Reynolds News* in 1958. He recollects that there were two other graduates in the Press Gallery: Bernard Levin of the *Spectator* and T.F. Lindsay, the sketchwriter for the *Daily Telegraph*. 'Lindsay practically fell round my neck. He greeted me like a long lost soul', records Howard. When Harold Wilson entered No. 12 Downing Street (the house which serves as the Whips' Hall, the large back room of which is sometimes used for Prime Ministerial press conferences) to give his first lobby briefing the day he became Prime Minister in 1964, the room stood to attention as he walked in. That sort of behaviour is inconceivable today. Perhaps the change reflects no more than the impoverishment of modern manners and the collapse of deference. But the collapse of deference is synonymous with and part of the story of the rise of the Media Class.

It was Wilson who first gave parliamentary reporters some kind of self-respect. He regarded them as important people. He called them by their Christian names. He read their work and was able to contrast their individual styles and modes of operation. He was at ease with them socially and they with him. He would invite the more important members of the lobby fraternity down to Chequers. He awarded knighthoods to two working political journalists, Francis Boyd of the *Guardian* and Harry Boyne of the *Telegraph*. He took them with him on overseas trips, and frequently made himself available to brief the lobby in person. On such occasions the sign would go up on the lobby notice-board: 'Sunrise Red at 4 p.m.' This obliged the Tories to respond in kind. Their leader Edward Heath, in the curious Masonic terminology then favoured by lobby men, was known as 'Celestial Blue'.

Wilson was the first Prime Minister to grasp the rising importance of the press. Alan Watkins, the political columnist of the *Independent on Sunday*, is today an elder statesman of the Press Gallery. In the early 1960s he wrote the Crossbencher column for the *Sunday Express*. Throughout the two years before the 1964 General Election he would see Wilson once a week, on Fridays. The Leader of the Opposition would take endless trouble to furnish him with political gossip for his column. 'Like Senator Joe McCarthy, he knew the deadlines', recalls Watkins. On one occasion, Watkins recalls ringing the Labour Party to check some minor detail about defence policy. He was surprised to receive a call back from the Leader of the Opposition himself. 'Even I was surprised', states Watkins, 'that Harold Wilson was taking an interest in what I might be writing.'

But it all went horribly wrong with Wilson. After a short space of time political reporters started to conclude that they had been taken for a ride. Devaluation of the pound in the autumn of 1967 perhaps sealed things. Thereafter the easy friendliness of the early days was replaced by bitter enmity and mutual contempt. But Wilson's fascination with the press continued, only this time it was malevolent. He would plot and intrigue against individual reporters. David Wood, political correspondent of *The Times*, was an early case. The Prime Minister went to extreme and demeaning lengths to prevail upon the editor and proprietors of *The Times* to dismiss Wood. William Rees-Mogg, then *Times* editor, responded to these endeavours in the only way possible: by promoting David Wood to the rank of political editor. Another subject of Wilson's obsession was Nora Beloff, the *Observer* journalist who was first to draw attention to the powerful and to this day highly mysterious influence exercised by Marcia Williams on the Prime Minister. Wilson summoned David Astor, the owner and editor of the *Observer*, to see him in his office at the Commons. When Astor arrived, Wilson produced bulky files of Beloff's newspaper cuttings, heavily annotated and underlined. After rambling on like a man obsessed on the subject of the sinister influences at work upon Beloff, the Prime Minister then announced: 'Of course, I know all about the people she sees. In fact our people keep an eye on her to see just what she is up to.' Names, offices and meetings were provided for Astor's inspection. When checked back with Beloff later they proved accurate in all respects. Astor presumed that Labour Party trusties rather than MI5 officers were behind the surveillance, though the matter has never been satisfactorily explained.

Late at night Harold Wilson would sit up with his tiny coterie of advisers, among them Gerald Kaufman and Marcia Williams, sifting through the first editions. They would assess likely sources for stories, always alert for signs of conspiracies being hatched against the Prime Minister. Any item that proved particularly difficult would result in a call from George Wigg, the Paymaster General, to the editor or the correspondent concerned. A generation later, Tony Blair's New Labour would take an even greater interest in the press. For the most part, however, the assessment and analysis were devolved to party officials rather than carried out by the Party Leader himself.

Harold Wilson was the first Prime Minister to understand the importance of 'spin-doctoring'. The expression was not current in his day; 'Public Relations Officer' was the expression used then. The word 'spin-doctor', which conveys the greater degree of menace, subterfuge and mystique in the modern PRO's job, came later. It originated in the United States and is said to have derived from baseball. According to Dr Emma Lenz of the *Oxford English Dictionary*, the first recorded use of the term was by Saul Bellow in his 1977 Jefferson Lectures. The *Collins English Dictionary* (1999 edition) defines 'spin-doctor' as 'a person who provides a favourable slant to an item of news, potentially unpopular policy etcetera, especially on behalf of a political personality or party'. The word was not taken up in Britain until the early 1990s, when it was indelibly associated with the rise to public prominence of Peter Mandelson and his school of New Labour media experts.

Wilson's catastrophic error was to try and carry out the task of spin-doctoring himself rather than delegate it to others. His first Press Secretary, Sir Trevor Lloyd-Hughes, was too scrupulous to fulfil the demands of the job. By the time that Joe Haines, an experienced press gallery hand with a fine political brain, was brought to bear in 1969, the problem had got out of control. Haines was condemned to fight a defensive war. It was often conducted with marvellous tactical astuteness but the chance to seize and then control the agenda, which was to be grasped with such brutal skill and strategic finesse by his successor Alastair Campbell twenty-five years later, had been well and truly cast away by the time Haines arrived on the scene.

The Media Class began to sense an intimation of its own future power during the Wilson premiership, but it did not emerge as a fully-fledged force on the national stage until the 1980s. Margaret Thatcher was a vital part of the story. The Media Class was her closest ally as she smashed down national institutions and challenged traditional sources of authority. She was often embattled and isolated within Parliament and even her own Tory Party, and the close alliances she formed with press proprietors, and through them with the political editors, became a key source of her power. The political press was no longer content, as it had been in the 1950s and the first half of the 1960s, to be a passive and neutral player in national debate. In the 1980s it developed with staggering speed into a brilliant, potent and deeply destructive force in its own right. For a long time that force was harnessed to Margaret Thatcher and the Tory Party. Some observers lazily considered that the alliance would last for ever.

There was much that was new about the press of the 1980s. Though nobody was yet fully aware of it, the balance of power between reporter and reported had switched. The reporter now met his subject on equal terms. In some areas — financial reporting is an example — the old deference held. But in politics it first collapsed, then went into reverse. The Media Class became an elite at Westminster. It suddenly became the case that journalists, now for the most part graduates, were cleverer, more self-assured, far better paid and very much more influential than most of the people they were writing about. The brightest and the best were going into the media, by contrast it seemed the dunderheads who went into politics. The cold cult of exposure made the problem worse. Brilliant men and women who felt drawn to public life steered clear for fear that some private vice or past misdemeanour would come to light: some of them became journalists and joined the Media Class instead.

Parliamentary correspondents — the old breed of gallery reporters who ruled the roost up to the 1960s — went into rapid, terminal decline. Their shortcoming was that they reported politics straight. Political correspondents — whose training was to put a slant on the news rather than merely report — had become the dominant force. Newsdesks and editors made it plain that they wanted stories with a sharp, polemical edge. Lobby men used their privileges to trawl the corridors of the Commons in search of rifts and scandal. Neither was in short supply.

Television was the decisive force behind the rise of the Media Class. All democratic politicians can have only one overwhelming preoccupation: the voter. There are 30 million of them out there but no one really knows what these mysterious creatures want or why they behave the way they do. Numerous experts claim special insights of one sort or another. There is no final way of telling whether they are right or whether they are talking gibberish. A previous generation of statesmen at least had the advantage of dealing with the voter direct. Open-air meetings, the verbatim publication of political speeches in newspapers, door-to-door canvassing: all gave that opportunity. Television took most of that away. The last generation of great political orators went out with Aneurin Bevan in the 1950s — Neil Kinnock, a natural orator of genius, was born a generation too late. Newspapers abandoned the practice of handing over precious space to unprocessed political discourse not much later. With the rise of television politicians were handed over, trussed and bound, into the hands of the Media Class.

From then on politicians could set their own agenda only with the greatest difficulty, and only on the terms set by the Media Class. Media Class values had to apply. The media have no morality in the sense that the word is traditionally understood. But they prefer the short-term to the long-term, sentimentality to compassion, simplicity to complexity, the dramatic to the mundane, confrontation to the sensible compromise. They can destroy with a pitiless and awesome brutality, but they can rarely create anything new, original and good. They yearn for the stark contrast between hero and villain. It is hard to imagine any environment for political decision-making that could be more damaging and unhelpful. By the 1980s, however, the Media Class had established itself as the most powerful force in British national life, comparable in a number of ways to the over-mighty trade unions in the 1970s.

For nearly a decade Margaret Thatcher rode the monster. The Media Class was not her natural ally, though it appeared to be so at the time. Large sections of the Media Class, above all the liberal elites which congregated in the broadsheets and the BBC, were always ranged against her. But they were unable to challenge the dominance she achieved through her alliance with the proprietors of United Newspapers, Associated Newspapers and above all News International. They gave an agenda to their editors, which was put into brilliant effect by two newspaper geniuses in particular: Kelvin MacKenzie of the *Sun* and David English at the *Daily Mail*. Their journalism was so well-focused and brilliant that its influence was impossible to resist, even by those who detested it most. And Margaret Thatcher's extraordinary personality fitted like a glove with the screaming Media Class demand for heroics, for confrontation and for drama. The eventual downfall of Thatcher, however, created an entirely new state of affairs and in due course unleashed the Media Class in a new direction. Under the bland and weak new Conservative Prime Minister John Major, the Media Class finally came of age. It threw off the Tory agenda and set about creating one of its own. It turned on the Conservative Party with an unspeakable ferocity and tore it apart.

It is impossible to understand Alastair Campbell, Tony Blair or New Labour without grasping all of the above. Campbell's earliest and most formative political experience was as a member of the tiny team of Neil Kinnock loyalists. He suffered at first hand as the Tory political editors ripped the man he loved to sheds and destroyed his chance of ever becoming Prime Minister. Nowadays Neil Kinnock, a warm and decent human being, blames his own personality defects for his failure to win in 1992. He need not be so hard on himself. The tabloid campaign to destroy Kinnock was the Media Class at its most brilliant, effective and repellent. Certainly Kinnock had weaknesses: they were magnified out of all proportion. Today William Hague, the Conservative Party leader, is a victim of the identical process of slaughter, carried out in many cases by the very same reporters. Campbell was a senior member of the Kinnock court in both the 1987 and 1992 General Elections. The experience scarred him for life, and this goes far to explain the strange bunkered isolation that persists inside Downing

Street today: former members of Neil Kinnock's court are like dogs which have been brutalized by a cruel owner as puppies. They are never happy with outsiders, only at ease within a tiny circle of trusted intimates.

But Campbell, with his cool, urbane and powerful intelligence, made certain that he learnt all the lessons going from the obliteration of Kinnock, and when the Tories fell into difficulties in the first half of the 1990s he was ready to apply them. First of all he did so, to vicious effect, as a journalist. No-one else spotted Major's weaknesses so quickly or exploited them so clinically. This painfully-acquired knowledge is what made him such a perfect choice to become press spokesman for Tony Blair.

It was immediately apparent to Campbell, just as it was to Tony Blair, that there was an extraordinary opportunity opening up for the Labour Party in 1994. The two men discussed it in great depth that summer as they talked about the task ahead at the Campbell villa in the hills above Avignon. The chance was there to claim the Media Class — for more than a decade the insuperable obstacle that lay between the Labour Party and government — for themselves. It was a chance that the vilified and despised Neil Kinnock would never have been able to seize. It was a chance that John Smith, with his old-fashioned attitudes and rather admirable imperviousness to the North London media establishment, would never have wanted to grasp. But it was a chance that was tailor-made for Tony Blair, the new media-friendly leader of the Labour Opposition.

The best that Neil Kinnock had ever been able to look for was to neutralize the awesome hostility of the British media — and that in itself was a forlorn enough hope. With Alastair Campbell to help him, Blair would pursue a far more audacious objective and seek to turn the domestic media into allies and friends. Campbell's view, which he expressed again and again with considerable force, was that the tabloid press, in the past such an enemy of Labour, held the key. Campbell made it a condition of his job that every possible means should be exerted to bring the *Sun* aboard. Not that the Labour leader, whose own views already lay in that direction, needed any convincing.

New Labour and the Civil Service

After the General Election of 1997 New Labour made no secret of its belief that the Government Information and Communication Service (GICS) should be transformed. In opposition Peter Mandelson and others had pioneered the most sophisticated media machine in history. Once New Labour had secured power it was only natural to compare the expertise, ruthlessness and sheer commitment of the pre-election Millbank office with the somewhat cumbersome and lacklustre government equivalent. In almost every way the GICS was found wanting.

Soon after the General Election Peter Mandelson, then Minister Without Portfolio in the Cabinet Office, and Alastair Campbell called a meeting of heads of government information departments in 10 Downing Street. Drinks were served, though neither Mandelson nor Campbell drank. Campbell spoke first. He was, in the words of one present, 'very kindly and friendly'. He explained that New Labour intended to place government communications right at the heart of policy-making. He insisted that New Labour would want to maintain control of the media agenda in the same way as it had done in opposition. He insisted that he wanted a 24-hour service and that he needed to know 'tomorrow's news' rather than what had already appeared in the papers. He said that if first editions got the story wrong, he wanted the failure corrected at once. He called on government information departments to be more interventionist and proactive. He spoke of the importance of reiterating the central government messages. 'When you and I are heartily sick of repetition, that is when we are getting through to the outside world', he insisted. Campbell made reassuring noises that New Labour had no intention of using the government information service for party political advantage and he gave assurances that no great purge of Civil Service jobs was planned.

There is no reason whatever to believe that Campbell's last assurance was not honestly meant, but that is not how things worked out. Between 1 May 1997 and 1 June 1998, no less than 25 heads of information or deputy heads were replaced, a turnover of more than 50%. That attrition continued. By August 1999, all but two of Whitehall's 17 directors of communications had been replaced since May 1997, a staggeringly high and completely unprecedented turnover. Some of the changes were entirely routine career moves, but others were forced moves and effective sackings which gave cause for unease.

The one head of information to speak out at the Downing Street meeting was Steve Reardon at the Department of Social Security. When Mandelson and Campbell had stopped talking there was what one witness refers to as 'an uneasy silence'. Then Reardon began a passionate defence of his profession: 'You see in front of you in this room a set of people generally reckoned by the outside world to be the *crème de la crème.'* Reardon was one of the earliest casualties of the new regime. Some of those present believe that Reardon did himself no good with this stance; within six months he was gone, so were Andy Wood from the Northern Ireland Office, Liz Drummond of the Scottish Office, Gill Samuel from the Ministry of Defence, Jonathan Haslam from Agriculture, Jill Rutter from the Treasury, as well as a number of others.

Two charges could never be made against these people. First: incompetence. They were all highly respected within the Civil Service. One or two of them were high-flyers recognized for their outstanding qualities, and most of them were snapped up by the private sector. Second: political bias. As a group they were simply not open to the charge of being anti-Labour. If anything the reverse was the case, much of the Civil Service had looked forward keenly to a Labour victory. Wood, for instance, had been a party member before entering government service.

Wood was informed by the Permanent Secretary at the Northern Ireland Office that 'personal chemistry' in his relationship with the Ulster Secretary Mo Mowlam meant that he had to be moved from his post. Reardon clashed with Harriet Harman and her two Special Advisers, accusing them of improper interference in the work of his department. In an important piece of evidence to the Select Committee on Public Administration, Reardon claimed that:

> In particular the drafting of departmental press releases was closely scrutinised to the point of obsession by the Special Advisers who frequently

issued instructions about drafting and re-drafting directly to junior press office staff without my knowledge. There were frequent arguments about the proper language to be employed in a departmental draft and Special Advisers sought to reproduce the tone of the Labour manifesto and repeat its election commitments as emerging news.

The most disturbing case of all was that of Jill Rutter, whom Gordon Brown inherited as his Treasury Press Secretary from Kenneth Clarke. Rutter was an outstanding civil servant who had made her career at the Treasury. The arrival of Charlie Whelan and Ed Balls as the new Chancellor's Special Advisers cut the ground from under her. They took a vigorous interest in press handling and it was often all too obvious that they were better briefed than she was. Rutter asked her Permanent Secretary Sir Terence Burns for a transfer. She complained that three-quarters of her job had been taken away. He told her to carry on with the other quarter 'for the sake of the service'. Eventually life became impossible and she left the Treasury altogether.

New Labour set about not merely changing the personnel within the GICS; it also set about changing its structure. Campbell wisely decided not to follow the example of his predecessor Sir Bernard Ingham and head up the GICS himself. He left that role to Mike Granatt, all the while retaining and strengthening the mechanisms of central control of the GICS as a whole. Within weeks of the election victory the Cabinet Secretary, Sir Robin Butler, was prevailed upon to commission a report into the GICS. Sir Robin commissioned the Permanent Secretary at the Office of Public Service, Sir Robin Mountfield, to undertake the task. His report was received in November 1997.

Press attention at the time of publication of the Mountfield Report focused upon its least interesting and most conservative recommendations: these concerned the attribution of statements by Alastair Campbell. In the past there had been a fiction that Downing Street spokesmen, like the Secret Service, did not exist. This convention had already been breaking down: Mountfield did away with it altogether. After the publication of his report a new entity emerged: the Prime Minister's

Official Spokesman—or PMOS as Campbell has come to be known around Whitehall. The Mountfield Report stopped short, however, of permitting Campbell to be identified by name or broadcasting lobby briefings. This was the key decision: the secretive lobby system has been too useful to the government for it to be done away with altogether. Furthermore, the Prime Minister's Press Secretary was well aware of the dangers of allowing himself to become a public figure in his own right.

More important were Mountfield's other recommendations. They brought many of the innovations of the Millbank system into the heart of Whitehall. His report recommended a new body to coordinate departmental announcements and government initiatives. Thus the Strategic Communications Unit was born. This small cadre, made up of a mixture of Labour appointees and civil servants, was given an office in 10 Downing Street formerly used for the appointment of bishops.

Mountfield announced the creation of a central media monitoring unit 'to provide 24-hour monitoring of emergency stories, and immediate warning to Departmental Press Offices and the centre'. This was a direct lift from Millbank and, according to those who saw its product, not as accomplished as the original version. Mountfield also referred to plans for a new computer to replace the Cab-E-Net electronic information system which had served the Tories. Cab-E-Net had been constantly dogged with technical difficulties; not so its replacement. Given the name Agenda, it listed forthcoming events, lines to take and ministerial speeches. It became a vital tool of government.

Most of these changes were pure common sense, designed to lift the government out of the media stone age. New Labour was not content merely with these improvements, however. A hugely enhanced role was also given to Special Advisers in government. Special Advisers have a unique, and in some way contradictory, status in Whitehall. They do not have to abide by Civil Service rules of neutrality. On the other hand, they are paid for by the taxpayer. New Labour in government has seized on the freedom offered by Special Advisers, increasing the numbers from 35 at the end of the last government to over 70 at the last count. Many of these Special

Advisers are given a purely media-relations role. The most notable example of this was Charlie Whelan at the Treasury, who to a large but informal extent took on the role of Press Secretary. But he was merely the best-known and noisiest example. More unobtrusive and typical was Joe McCrea, Frank Dobson's Special Adviser at the Department of Health.

In 1998, McCrea wrote an account of his first year in government for *Progress*, a magazine for Labour Party members. It was clear from McCrea's article that his work was overwhelmingly concerned with the media. 'My overriding impression of the first seven months is one of having to battle to bring the government standards of briefing up to those which we developed in the run-up to May 1997.' McCrea went on to explain how he had told civil servants: 'you can't win 21st century political battles with techniques and technology from 30 years ago'. McCrea appears not to ask himself whether it is the role of government departments to fight and win political battles. He cheerfully accepts the equivalence between the Millbank fighting machine and the domestic Civil Service. His article shows little awareness of the distinction between a neutral Civil Service and an election-fighting political machine. It highlights a distinctive feature of Tony Blair's New Labour Government, which is its apparent lack of respect for the traditional detachment of the British Civil Service.

McCrea lost his job when Frank Dobson left the Cabinet to stand in the London mayorality elections in autumn 1999. He soon re-emerged in another shadowy Whitehall role, given the job of setting up a government rebuttal system operating out of the Cabinet Office. Named the 'Knowledge Network Project', McCrea's new unit bore a striking similiarity to the Millbank 'Excalibur' rebuttal machine designed to provide Labour politicians with a line to take ahead of the last election. Claims that the Knowledge Network Project marked a further stage in the politicization of the British civil service were duly rebutted. Nevertheless it was striking that a Labour Party operative rather than an impartial civil servant should have been involved in the creation of such a sensitive and novel part of the government machine.

The claim of 'politicization' has been made against all recent governments. It was made against the Wilson administration, against Margaret Thatcher's Government and against John

Major. In the final years of the previous Government the New Labour opposition was reckless with charges of politicization against the Tories. Yet the transgressions which Tory ministers were accused of were minor compared to New Labour's cull of government information officers or its doubling of the number of Special Advisers.

Campbell's own appointment, as a party political man placed in a key government role, raised huge questions about the neutrality of the Civil Service. Previous occupants of his post have been civil servants. Tony Blair's decision to lift the restrictions on civil servants in Campbell's case created problems. The Civil Service Order in Council 1995 created an obligation that all Home Civil Service appointments should be made 'on the basis of fair and open competition'. One exemption was allowed, for Special Advisers. But they were forbidden to exercise executive authority over civil servants, and so the exemption was useless for either Campbell or the Downing Street Chief of Staff Jonathan Powell. That was why, acting on the advice of officials, the incoming government changed the Order in Council to allow up to three posts at No. 10 to be both party political and to carry executive responsibilities.

Senior officials say that they welcome the new formula. Sir Richard Wilson, the Cabinet Secretary, made a virtue of it when questioned by the 1998 Select Committee on Public Administration, saying that 'everybody knows where he [Alastair Campbell] is coming from'. Senior Tories (and ex-Tories) are also supportive. Tim Collins, now a Tory MP and formerly the party Director of Communications, says that the politicization of the Press Secretary role is a 'welcome, sensible and entirely legitimate change'. Another former Tory Director of Communications, Shaun Woodward, goes further still. He says that 'criticising the Blair machine is a bit like attacking Sainsbury's for having a PR Department. What Campbell and others have done is to professionalize a department which until then was run by amateurs.'

Critics, however, note the dangers of an erosion of the distinction between the political party and the Civil Service. The government machine in Britain has not been the servant of a single political party since the reforms of the mid-nineteenth century aimed at rooting out nepotism and corruption. Under

New Labour the Civil Service is coming to bear a closer resemblance to the American system, where Civil Service jobs routinely change hands with an incoming administration.

Acknowledgements

This essay was abridged and updated from the author's book, *Alastair Campbell. New Labour and the Rise of the Media Class* (Aurum Press, 1999).

Mick Hume

What if They Gave an Election and Nobody Came?

Criminals, lunatics and members of the House of Lords are three groups traditionally denied the right to vote in Britain. However, now that most of them are being released back into the care of the community, Hereditary Peers are to be allowed to vote in the polling booth, if not in Parliament. What's more, under the provisions of the new Representation of the People Bill announced in the Queen's Speech in November 1999, Home Secretary Jack Straw proposes to grant the vote to 'those in mental institutions'.

While several of the Home Secretary's other proposed legislative changes, such as restricting the right to trial by jury, met with fierce public criticism, the Government's plans to extend the franchise to the mentally ill attracted little attention. Yet this extraordinary proposal reveals a lot about the New Labour Government's attitude to democratic politics.

Granting the vote to people who are, in common parlance, mad, calls into question the moral foundations of representative democracy. That system, whatever its imperfections might be, is at least based upon the idea that adults are rational individuals capable of making conscious choices about what they deem to be right and wrong. By suggesting instead that mental patients are as well qualified as those of sound mind to participate in the political process, Jack Straw's proposal threatens to degrade the entire electorate and democracy itself. It implies that we should all be deemed to be as irrational and incompetent as the insane. Perhaps that helps to explain why, while the therapeutic state wants to grant the vote to the mentally ill, it no longer trusts the rest of its supposedly sane citizens to sit on juries and find their peers guilty in sufficiently large numbers.

The proposals to extend the franchise to mental patients, the homeless and those held on remand will no doubt be nodded through, as a worthy part of what the 1999 Queen's Speech described as New Labour's plan to 'modernize the country'. The Government is always banging on about the importance of combating the social exclusion of marginalized groups such as the lunatic community. Yet the true motive behind the extension of the franchise seems to have little to do with any Government commitment to the 'rights' of the mentally ill. After all, at the same time as Jack Straw was promising them the vote, he was also planning to impose compulsory treatment orders, and to allow the courts to lock up people with psychological disorders who have been convicted of no offence.[1]

The primary motive behind the Government's package of voting reforms is simply to get more people, any people, into the polling stations. It is a rather pathetic attempt to bump up the vote and combat the increasing alienation of the electorate from the political system, to bridge the widening gap between *demos* — the people — and parliamentary democracy. The effect of the Government's approach, however, can only be further to degrade and depoliticize the democratic process, by reducing it to a bean-counting exercise.

These reforms reveal the Government flailing around for a technical solution to the political malaise that is now being experienced by every Western society. From America to Austria and from Belgium to Britain, it appears that a disenchanted public has little time for the old political parties, policies or identities. The mood of mistrust is most obviously reflected in the growing alienation of people from the electoral system. The kind of voter apathy that has long been the norm in the USA is creeping across Europe, as more people draw the conclusion that voting is a waste of time.

In the USA, there has been a steady decline in turnout for presidential elections over the past 40 years. In 1960 62.5% of

---

[1] Bizarrely, under the new franchise proposals these non-criminal psychopaths would still be entitled to vote.

those entitled to vote turned out for the election that gave John F. Kennedy a narrow victory over Richard Nixon. By 1988 only 50.1% bothered to vote in the election that put George Bush in the White House. In 1996 Bill Clinton won his second term in a poll where just 49% participated—the lowest turnout since the '20s. Elections for the House of Representatives fare far worse, with turnouts averaging around 35% through the '90s.

Voter disenchantment is at least one area in which Britain is fast catching up with the USA. With overall turnout the lowest at any general election since the Second World War, the New Labour landslide of 1997, widely hailed as a sea change in British political life, was achieved with the support of only 31% of those entitled to vote. Nor did the major public elections of 1999 succeed in capturing the public imagination. The votes for the new Scottish and Welsh assemblies, for example, hardly lived up to the hype about 'historic' elections. In Wales the majority did not bother to vote at all. In Scotland it took the PR efforts of the entire political class to achieve a 59% vote. On the same day in May 1999, local elections in England attracted a 29% turnout. The June 1999 UK elections to the European Parliament marked an all time low for national polls in Britain, as only 23% turned out to vote. Turnout figures for some parliamentary by-elections even dipped below that desperate mark.

In the face of this trend, the plans to extend the franchise to the mentally ill, homeless and prisoners held on remand formed part of a package of measures in the Representation of the People Bill that is supposed to counter public disengagement from politics.[2] Other proposals in the Bill include plans for weekend elections and to allow voting at more convenient venues such as supermarkets, while considering the possibility of internet voting in the future.

As a response to the serious decline of public participation in electoral politics these measures look like a cross between naivety and arrogance. They appear to be based on the

---

[2] Remand prisoners could turn out to be a particularly sizeable constituency, if the Government keeps inventing so many new offences with prison sentences attached, the latest of which includes the crime of recklessly damaging a bird's nest.

assumption that the main reason why more people don't vote is that the masses are too lazy or too short-sighted to appreciate the great candidates and policies that are being set before them. The solution, then, is simply to make it easier for people to cast their votes. Somebody up there seems to believe that only 20–30% of people voted in some major elections last year because the rest had to get the shopping in or watch *Who Wants to Be a Millionaire?* on a Thursday. It seems not to have occurred to them that millions might have abstained because they did not fancy any of the shoddy political goods on offer.

Supermarket polling stations and votes for the mentally ill can do nothing to breathe life into democracy. They are simply intended to improve appearances by getting more bums on seats — or in this case, more crosses in boxes. Most people already know how and where to cast their vote. If they do not bother to do so it is likely to be because they see no party offering the kind of positive vision that might inspire their support. Voter alienation reflects the widespread conviction that politics does not matter, that politicians are all the same, and that election results make little difference to voters' lives.

To gauge the depth of public distrust of the political system, look at the way that the media-backed crusade against 'sleaze' has come to dominate so much of political debate in recent times. It is an issue that draws its strength from the general view that politics and government is another way of saying graft and corruption. Politicians always come bottom in surveys of which professions the public trusts. A June 1999 poll found that only 10% of respondents trusted politicians a lot, 65% a little, and 25% not at all. This mood does not recognize party lines. New Labour successfully portrayed the Conservatives as the party of sleaze in the 1997 general election. Yet within months of taking office the new government itself was embroiled in a series of minor scandals involving Labour MPs and ministers.

The obsession with sleaze is a symptom of the low standing of the political system, but it is not the cause. In recent times we have witnessed nothing less than the end of politics as we know it. A century ago political life was about a contest between radically different views of the future. Competing political philosophies offered contrasting visions of the good society. Conflict between Left and Right was an often fierce and sometimes violent clash of views about the good society. Over the past two decades, however, politics has been drained of the passions and conflicts that shaped the past century. The traditional politics of both Right and Left are now exhausted. As both of the major British parties self-consciously distance themselves from their past principles, parliamentary politics collapses into a blancmange of the centre ground. Little wonder, then, that voters should appear less loyal to any party, and less enthusiastic about voting for anybody. Who could get very excited about the mighty clash of minds between Tony Blair and William Hague?

If the anti-politics mood simply reflected a loss of support for the tired traditions of the established parties it might be no bad thing. But the problem goes much further. At root, it betrays a loss of faith in the human potential to shape our common destiny. Mrs Thatcher may be long gone, but her friend Tina—There Is No Alternative—still bestrides public life, keeping any notion of purposeful social change off the agenda. Instead, people experience change as an external force, something frightening that is beyond the control of us poor little humans, like a permanent strain of the mythical Millennium Bug. The fashionable 'ism' of the age is not socialism or even capitalism, but fatalism. It is summed up by the popular theories of 'globalization' which, with their vision of a world spinning out of anybody's control, sound like a new language for blaming our problems on Acts of God.

Once it becomes accepted that there is no alternative, then politics can have little meaning. Without alternatives, political life is reduced to empty posturing and PR stunts. Today, the failure of the political imagination means that there are no ideologies or political principles worthy of the name. Instead it seems that every party operates according to the simple slogan, 'Something Must Be Done'. Politicians sense that something must be done to make a new connection with the alienated electorate; that something must be done to give drifting governments an air of authority and sense of mission; that something must be done to re-create a moral consensus in societies that have lost touch with traditional notions of right and wrong. Since few of these politicians actually believe in anything much, the detail of what 'thing' they do is pretty unimportant. All that matters is that they do, and are seen to be doing, *something* to fill the moral/political vacuum.

That is why a government like Tony Blair's New Labour is constantly churning out parliamentary Bills, initiating policy reviews, setting up inquiries and appointing new officials. It also explains why the process of government in Britain has been turned into something resembling a permanent press conference (a technique, like many others, imported from the USA). The concern of all this furious activity is both to stake out the moral high ground for the government, and to bridge the legitimacy gap now separating politics from the people (whilst at the same time insulating the authorities from any genuine democratic pressure).

The trouble is, many initiatives from the 'Something Must Be Done' school of politics are too obviously trivial and stage-managed to have much effect. In an age when politics passes most people by, even a moral crusade like the war over Kosovo can have a limited effect in galvanizing the public. A government like Mr Blair's is left with no option but to launch further interventions at home and abroad, against everything from fox-hunting to child-smacking, in order to keep up the appearance of a crusading, purposeful party leading the people. But in the absence of any debate about fundamentals, such artificial exercises can inspire little depth of support. As the process of government becomes more technical and managerial, parliamentary politics is being transformed into a tedious irrelevance. The number of people who passionately identify with any political party has shrunk accordingly. For many, the unattractive state of public life at the start of a new century has been summed up by the politics of the madhouse surrounding the election for London mayor.

Despite all of this, however, New Labour's technocrats insist that it is our democratic duty to vote, apparently without considering that it might be their responsibility to offer us something worth voting for. The new citizenship classes now being enshrined in the national school curriculum partly rest on the assumption that people don't vote because of ignorance about the system, in which case boring children with lectures about parliamentary institutions and processes will eventually solve the problem. We might call it teaching them to vote by rote. These same citizenship classes even want to teach chil-

dren to chivvy their apathetic parents along to the polling station. It is unclear whether or not, in order to acquire their
certificate, they will be required to report those who fail to
comply.

As the search for technical solutions to the political problem
of disengagement intensifies there is now a growing New
Labour lobby to make voting compulsory in the UK. Supporters of such a measure often cite the successful example of
Australia, where citizens have to vote and election turnouts
regularly touch 95%. In fact, the Australian example demonstrates the shortcomings of such bureaucratic measures.
While almost all Australians might vote, most are just as alienated from their discredited political system as the stay-at-
homes in the UK or USA. In the 1999 referendum on the future
of the monarchy in Australia, for example, the majority voted
against a republic even though only a tiny number actually
want the Queen to remain as their head of state. Many Australian republicans simply could not stomach the proposed alternative of allowing the prime minister and his cronies in
parliament, rather than the people, to elect a president—a system contemptuously dismissed as 'the politicians' republic'. If
one is concerned about democracy as a clash of political ideas
in which people are offered some genuine choice, then making
them vote for candidates they don't support clearly offers no
solution. But if one simply wants to improve appearances by
inflating the turnout figures, perhaps it really does not matter
if voters trudge unwillingly to the polling booth.

In response to a crisis of faith in the political system, the
Government's dream seems to be to make us all into unthink-
ing lobby fodder—a kind of nation of New Labour MPs in fact.
You don't have to be mad to vote here, but it helps.

Moshe Berent & Keith Sutherland

Consensus Politics and the Modern State

Since Hobbes, the first philosopher of modernity, the very notion of politics has involved the idea of conflict or the advancement of political standing and private interest. However, the Hobbesian model has been explicitly disowned by Tony Blair, who claims that he wishes to adopt the classical Greek model and govern by consensus, in contrast to the 'factional' approach of his predecessors. The Greeks had an abhorrence of *stasis*, or factions — the democratic institutions of the *polis* were a direct attempt to overcome conflict and sectional interest.

James Madison and the other architects of the American Second Constitution retained the Greek disdain of factionalism. But Madison realized that the sort of consensus that was a prerequisite for the stability of the *polis* was both impossible to achieve and undesirable on a larger political stage. The *Federalist Papers* and the resulting Second Constitution depended more on a robust Hobbesian analysis of power and the need to hobble and constrain it by creating a constitutional balance between factions. Madison accepted that 'the causes of faction cannot be removed and the relief is only to be sought in the means of controlling its effects'. He also agreed, with Hobbes, that moral or religious motives cannot be relied on as an adequate control.

James Madison was working within the framework of eighteenth-century liberalism, whose main tenet was that private vices could be turned into public virtues. In the realm of society this was attributed to the 'invisible hand', while in the realm of politics it was the design of the constitution which was meant to achieve this goal. A recent protagonist of this approach, at least in the economic sphere, was Margaret Thatcher. Thatcherism is, at heart, nothing more than the simple recognition that people look after what they own and don't give a damn about what they don't. The extensive privatization process was partly fuelled by the recognition that open market competition leads to efficiency, but her main concern was to spread share ownership as widely as possible amongst the voters.

The Greek fear of 'faction' is mirrored by the Blairite call to overcome the 'divisiveness' of the previous government and to return to what is, in essence, a marriage of social democracy and one-nation toryism. Whereas to Thatcher, consensus meant weakness, fudge and compromise, to Blair consensus is the key to a stable society and harmonious change. Consensus is a question of shared values, so the Greek emphasis on moral inhibitions, strong public sentiment and education is back in fashion. The casting of Mr Blair as the Vicar of St Albion by Ian Hislop and Harry Enfield is not just a sign of the Prime Minister's oratorical style. The New Labour project and the 'People's Government' depend on a consensus of widely- shared values. But how applicable is the Greek notion of politics to modernity? Can any parallel be drawn between the *polis* and the modern nation state?

Analyses with an overt Marxist allegiance have taken a bit of a hammering in the last decade. But the key insight — that ideas follow practice, rather than the other way round — has lived on. This has revolutionized the study of history — the new understanding is that texts can only be understood in the context of their time. The chief anxiety of students of the history of political thought is to avoid judging the past in terms of the present. Thus those who would portray Locke as a bourgeois apologist, on account of his views on the reform of the Poor Law, are not really allowing for the harsh view of punishment that was characteristic of the time.

As another example of the old (discredited) approach to history, in his seminal study, *The Open Society and its Enemies* (1945), Karl Popper attributed the invention of democracy, politics and political philosophy to 'Greek rationality'. Moses

Finley contrasts the Western (Greek) response with the approach of the Eastern kingdoms, and implies that the 'Greeks took a radical step' towards democracy and politics. Both Popper and Finley assumed that the choice was equally open to the kingdoms of the East, and their failure to do so was because the Orientals did not possess the necessary rationality or courage.

The trouble with this idealist interpretation is that it fails to recognize that the Greeks didn't so much *choose* democracy, but rather they were *pushed* towards politics by the decentralized, unstratified nature of their society. The ancient Greek *polis* was quite unlike any other form of agrarian state — there was no monopoly of power and it was comparatively unstratified. Max Weber famously defined the state as the agency within society which has the monopoly of the application of violence. If so, then the *polis* was not a state, as private armies were recruited by factions on an *ad hoc* basis to deal with struggles as they occurred. With the partial exceptions of Sparta, the Athenian navy and the tyrannies, the *polis* had no standing army, and never developed a proper police force. Policing was largely done by self-help and self-defence (that is with the help of friends, neighbours and family). So, due to the *lack of alternative political institutions*, the Greeks had to resort to open debate, voting and consensus to resolve any potential conflicts. As there were no organs of state power, the system could only work if there was overall consensus — the goal was to establish a community of *homonoia* (same-mindedness). Thus politics became a branch of moral philosophy, for the external checks of the coercive state were simply not available. In the words of Ernest Barker, 'political science...became in the hands of the Greeks particularly and predominantly ethical'.

The distinction drawn by Robert Dahl in his *Preface to Democratic Theory* between external and internal checks could help us to understand further the difference between the Greek and the Hobbesian solution to the problem of faction. The modern solution which was proposed by Hobbes and by the fathers of the American Constitution, who were greatly influenced by Hobbes, was based upon 'external checks', that is the application of what Hobbes calls 'rewards and punishments' to the individual (or, in the Madisonian case, also to the group) from a source which is external to the individual or the group. Consequently it is based upon the idea of force and conflict. By contrast, the Greek solution was based upon 'internal checks' which means those moral inhibitions which are instilled in each member of the community by a strong public sentiment, morality and education. The purpose of all this is the development of self-restraint.

How does one adjudicate in this dispute between Greek politics-as-morality and Hobbesian and Madisonian *realpolitik*? Given the fragmented, pluralistic society of postmodernity, what does all this mean nowadays? How can consensus be achieved and what is the role of Greek-style politics-as-morality? Is political stability the result of the Greek 'internal policeman', Hobbes's *Leviathan* or Madison's constitutional balances?

One of the ways in which modern Anglo-American democracy differs fundamentally from its Greek counterpart is in the idea of *representation*. Although this is also largely a consequence of scale — the size of the *polis* meant that all citizens could participate directly in the decision-making process — the very idea of representation implies conflict, 'factions' and the impossibility of politics by general consent. When you tick the box on the election slip, you expect your chosen candidate to fight for the sort of views you believe in, whether in government or opposition. Nevertheless, as Madison observed, representation was supposed also to 'refine and enlarge the public views, by passing them through the medium of a chosen body of citizens, whose wisdom may best discern the true interest of their country, and whose patriotism and love of justice will be least likely to sacrifice it to temporary or partial considerations'. Thus while society was factional and selfish, it was for the representatives to work towards consensus politics.

The traditional eighteenth-century emphasis on the Member of Parliament as representative *of* the people has, of course, been undermined by the party whips and the new emphasis on media spin doctoring, with the party representing itself *to* the people. Although this has already gone a long way to undermine the contract of the MP with his constituents, the recommendations of the Jenkins Committee would go a lot further. Mr Blair, who has been known to dismiss parliament as a 'bunfight', has the worst attendance and voting record of any Prime Minister this century. John Prescott was obliged to present the 1999 *Spectator* award for Parliamentarian of the Year to the leader of the Opposition and Inquisitor of the Year to Rhodri Morgan, a less than popular figure in the New Labour establishment. Although the case for the reform of the Lords is being presented as part of the overall programme for modernization and rationalization, Jack Straw let slip that the Lords' scrutinization role was introducing unacceptable delays into the government's legislative programme.

One recent conflict between the Lords and the Commons was over the issue of representation in the European elections — the closed or open list system. But if representation is essentially factional do we really want it? *Prospect* magazine has published a survey on the rise of direct 'opinion poll' democracy. As Peter Mandelson pointed out, in the golden days of representational democracy, society was clearly divided into different 'orders', each with its own elites who between them represented most of the voters, whether they were landowners, shopkeepers or trade unionists. Voting habits used to be passed on from one generation to the next more or less intact. However this is no longer the case — society is much more opaque, fragmented and individualized. Largely due to the increase in social and occupational mobility, there are no longer any homogenous blocks of opinion to be represented. MPs no longer represent local or factional opinion so much as act as glorified 'gofers' and social workers, catering to the private needs and grievances of their individual constituents. Thus MPs today increasingly reflect factions rather than represent them and consequently parliamentary democracy is losing its powers of mitigation. As it becomes more difficult for consensus politics to be created in parliament, Blair's call for its creation in society makes little sense.

The Greek view, that consensus would emerge from open debate in the council, only worked for direct democracy and required a high level of political education amongst all the citizens. It is hard to apply these qualities to Britain at the end of the twentieth century. But if consensus won't emerge naturally, it can always be *created*, hence the importance of the media to the Blair project. New Labour has been clear all along that it intends to rule by newspaper headline. The government is remarkably sanguine about its ability to change public opinion on EMU. But what this means in practice is that the spin *is* the policy, and its success is judged not by events but by the impact of the resulting headlines on the focus group. This is the new age of virtual reality politics.

Here indeed lies a major difference between Greek and modern consensus. For while modern consensus could be created, the Greek consensus could not. The Greek citizen received his (political) education just by growing up in a highly politicized community. The absence of means of coercion, state-education or any other public means through which such a consensus could have been created meant that any common action needed to be consensual, that is everybody had to be consulted. Thus stateless communities tend towards democracy or open government.

Yet, while the Greek outlook was democratic it was certainly not liberal. Indeed one lesson that can be learned from Greek politics is how the Greeks treated those who fell outside the populist consensus. If the stability of the *polis* depended neither on the monopoly of force, nor the balance of factional power, but on consensus, then this is an important, fragile thing that needs to be treasured. Like ourselves, the Greeks put much emphasis on the role of the outstanding individual in politics (they had no kings or political caste to depend on). But, as they had no means of coercion other than that of consensus, there was a great nervousness towards the eccentric. This led to a moral dilemma in terms of the balance of rights and duties, and the Greeks dealt with anyone who got the balance wrong with great harshness. The penalties were typically ostracism, banishment or death. The dialogue between Socrates and the Laws in *Crito* shows both the fear of the outstanding individual and the importance of his moral decisions. As the system relies on consensus—the Laws beg and persuade, rather than command—then any eccentricity will destroy the Laws and the entire *polis*. In the context of this consensual model, the death of Socrates at the hand of the state was the only available option.

While, even in the absence of public means of coercion, consensus politics is illiberal, the dangers of consensus politics are much higher under the modern state, as it involves the use of public means, like coercion (overt or otherwise), state-education and the media, in order to achieve such a consensus. Here, perhaps, the British have to be more careful than other nations about conducting consensus politics. For there are indeed certain similarities between the British society and the ancient Greek *polis* as far as the existence of a strong public sentiment is concerned. One of us (Berent), as a stranger living in Britain could not help wondering at the extent to which Britain is still a 'shame society', where people are constantly moralized and educated by their fellow citizens in everyday life. Many would say that the tyranny of public opinion in Britain is too much as it is. As in the case of the Greek *polis* the existence of such strong public sentiment is a product of a society which values tradition. Yet it is also a product of Britain as an increasingly centralized society, with a system of government which gives all powers to Westminster (in fact, to the Government and the Prime Minister). Furthermore the media is highly centralized as well, the national channels are dominant and most of the national newspapers are published in London. This is all by sharp contrast with, say, the United States.

Of course, there will always be those who choose not to go along with the consensus. Then the problem arises of how to reconcile populist consensus and minority rights. This is a particular dilemma for a government that attempts to be both populist and liberal at the same time. In the case of New Labour this dilemma has shown itself in the issues of hunting with hounds and parity in the age of consent for homosexuals. In the former case the populist argument for abolition ran against a passionate country sports minority, whereas in the case of the age of consent the blocking vote of the House of Lords seemed to be more in touch with the *vox populi*. So far neither of these issues has been resolved, alongside the broader issue of whether it is possible to have populism and pluralism at the same time.

The public outpouring over the death of the Princess of Wales is another sign of this conflict. Those of us who were alienated by the orchestrated wailings in 1998 were dreading the anniversary re-run. True to form, most of the TV coverage was tacky hagiography, the one exception being Christopher Hitchen's *Diana: The Mourning After*. Hitchens focused on the media censorship — dissenters like Simon Heffer were told by their proprietors to go on holiday. Hitchens pointed out that half the country didn't watch the funeral, but there was considerable intimidation to conform. This is easy to confirm, with stories of businesses having excrement pushed through their letterbox when they announced their intention to remain open for the funeral, and the producers of the play *Discussing Diana* receiving death threats. This may all be 'the people's will' but it has more to do with Robespierre than genuine democracy. The appropriation of the People's Princess by the leader of the People's Government is perhaps a little ominous.

The so-called Third Way makes a lot of the balance of rights and duties. How the new governments of the Third Way will choose to deal with those who would depart from the consensus remains to be seen.

Anthony O'Hear

The People's Party

The old Labour Party used to like to call itself the People's Party. In those days, though, it was the 'people', as opposed to the bosses, the toffs, the establishment, the ruling class. There was no suggestion that 'the people' included everyone. The people were those who were more people than the others, the sort of people whom the old Daily Mirror wished to project forward, the old working class in fact.

The old working class had its virtues, as did the old Labour Party, though it has to be said that the populist *ressentiment* on which both tended to thrive was not always an edifying spectacle. But, we are told, neither old Labour nor the old working class have much of a future in 2000.

As old Labour has transformed itself into New Labour so the notion of 'the people' has undergone a subtle and, to my mind, unsettling change. Far from New Labour being the political arm of the working class, it now proclaims itself the political arm of the British people. It talks about the big tent and about joined-up politics. The implication is that it can somehow represent everyone and that only the infantile would reject it. It talks about destroying the 'forces of conservatism', and about the enactment of the will of the majority, as if the minority does not count. Or, rather, there is no minority any more: 'and now, at last, party and nation joined in the same cause', as the Prime Minister rather ungrammatically had it at the Labour Party Conference in 1999.

Even regarded purely as rhetoric there is something unpleasant about all this, as had already become clear over the reaction to the death of Princess Diana. Having been dubbed by the Prime Minister as the People's Princess—itself a not very veiled comment on the rest of the House of Windsor—it became necessary for the Prime Minister and his spokesman, no less, to accuse those who did not subscribe to Diana's canonization of being 'snobs' and 'out of touch'. In other words, scratch the surface of New Labour's all-inclusive populism and you get rather old-Labourish reactions and inverted snobbery.

But, despite similarities, there is a significant difference between old Labour's view of the people and New Labour's. It is this. New Labour actually does have a good claim to include in its ranks a far wider cross-section of the nation than old Labour ever did. Nowhere is this more clear than in that it has wooed and, on occasion, promoted and brought into the government rich and powerful figures from industry, architecture and the media—some of whom are, in turn, contributors to Labour funds.

As an example of New Labour's great and good, consider Greg Dyke, newly appointed Director-General of the BBC and Labour party donor; (Lord) David Puttnam (film director and government advisor on education); (Lord) Melvin Bragg (media mogul); (Lord) Waheed Alli (television executive and promoter of youth culture); (Lord) Richard Rogers (a high-flying architect whose 'credits' include the Millennium Dome and the Pompidou Centre in Paris); (Lord) David Sainsbury (of J. Sainsbury and government minister); (Lord) David Simon (of BP, one-time government minister and advisor on the structure of government); (Lord) Chris Haskins (of Northern Foods and head of the government task force on regulation); (Lord) Gus Macdonald (media executive and government minister); (Lord) Robert Gavron (former chairman of the group which owns the *Guardian* newspaper); and (Lord) Michael Levy (music promoter).

It will be said that there is nothing new in a government rewarding its supporters and benefactors with peerages and influence, though one does have to wonder whether any previous government has given ministerial or quasi-ministerial posts to quite so many of those it has raised to the peerage.

But what *is* new is the way a *Labour* government has co-opted so many from industry. While it can still (more or less) count on support from the trade unions it is bringing in what has traditionally been seen as the other side—and not just

industrialists and big money; at the same time there has been a
concerted, and not unsuccessful effort on the Government's
part to enlist various Tory and ex-Tory bigwigs on various
projects. There has been analogous emasculation of the Liberal Democrats at the parliamentary level through joint cabinet committees and discussions.

In short: the inclusiveness of 'joined-up' politics is that of
the corporate state. That is, a state in which government, corporations, media and trade unions are all in the same political
party, with any opposition made to look irrelevant, petulant
and out of touch.

At the same time as establishing a parliamentary-cum-
business-cum-trade-union corporate consensus, many other
aspects of our lives are being run from the centre. Despite
criticizing the Tories for undermining local autonomy, New
Labour, once in power, is no more enamoured of local initiative or the small platoons. It has not, for example, relaxed any
of the centralized control of education instituted under the
Tories. In fact, it has further circumscribed the powers of both
individual schools and local education authorities. Schools
are subject even more to central direction, even in the way
they teach reading and arithmetic, something the Tories
would never have dared to prescribe. At the same time Local
Education Authorities are subject to all kinds of constraints
and centrally-dictated targets and then criticized by the same
government for being too prescriptive. One imagines that the
Government would actually love to privatize educational provision in some localities; but they would undoubtedly be subject to stringent regulation from its own Department for
Education and Employment. Such a move would suit both its
modernizing and its controlling tendencies, and give 'consumers', as they would be called, the worst of both worlds:
centralized control and privatized gloss and flimflam.

Meanwhile in all kinds of other areas liberty and autonomy
are being eroded by central control. Businesses and employers
are being subjected to barrages of new legislation and regulations, costing an estimated £10 billion since the 1997 election.
These impositions, such as the working-time directive and the
minimum wage unfairly favour the big corporations who
have the resources to deal with such requirements far easier
than small businesses.

Under New Labour the state is intervening in such matters as preparation for marriage and the way adults are allowed to coach young people in sport. The Government is proposing to incarcerate indefinitely those deemed to be 'a serious risk' to the public. This is people not clinically insane nor actually guilty of a crime—so goes our ancient right to be deemed innocent until proved guilty. At the same time the Home Secretary is proposing to scrap defendants' right to trial by jury in some cases. We are also promised a national DNA data bank to include samples taken from everyone arrested for a criminal offence—however minor—and, in an increasing centralization of the law, an increase in the proportion of stipendiary as opposed to lay magistrates. It will of course be said that no law-abiding citizens have anything to fear from any of this. Much appeal is made by government spokesmen to the populist dislike of criminals and layabouts of various sorts; but those with a care for traditional liberties have a right to be worried when they see any government so careless with our basic freedoms.

Alongside this significant erosion of civil liberties goes radical revision of the Constitution. The two-staged removal of the Hereditary Peers from the House of Lords and their replacement by appointees had been widely and correctly earmarked as a device to get rid of a potentially awkward independent section of Parliament. But less widely noticed, and important at least for its symbolism, was the emasculation in November 1999 of the Quinquennial Act, the power by which the Lords could prorogue the Commons were it to try to exceed a five-year term by voting itself an extension of office. Of course, it is said, this is no threat to democracy. The Commons would never seek to extend its life undemocratically. Of course not, not in this country; we are all decent men and true, and all great upholders of British freedoms. But then why was the Government so keen to push the measure through? At the very least it is symptomatic of the widely-remarked disdain Blair and his associates have for parliamentary traditions and niceties, and for their preference for running things through extra-parliamentary channels.

Devolution in Scotland and Wales and elected mayors of big cities may seem to militate against the centralizing argument, and up to a point they could have consequences unpalatable to a centralizing government and party machine: but only if the party machine loses control of events. Certainly devolution is a way of weakening Parliament, and is thus consistent with the Government attempt to marginalize parliamentary opposition. Clearly, to judge by the shenanigans over the Welsh Assembly and the Mayor of London, the New Labour machine has no intention of losing its grip over events. Even if, as some think likely, Scottish devolution is the start of an inexorable drift towards full Scottish independence, from the Blairite point of view devolution combines 'modernization' with an extra-parliamentary concentration of power in the party, over which the party machine is able to exercise almost total authority, even in the devolved regions.

I have drawn attention to the *Volkisch* and corporatist aspects of New Labour, to its attempt systematically to marginalize opposition, to its involvement of business and managers in government, to its erosion of traditional liberties, and to its extra-parliamentary instincts and impulses. Some with a longer historical sense than that of our Prime Minister may be reminded in all this of Sir Oswald Mosley's 'Third Way' of the 1930s which combined many of the same elements as Blair's 'Third Way'.[1] We might also recall that in Italy at least fascism was supposed to be a centrist movement transcending class conflict and the polarities of traditional left and right. The fascists were also masters in the rhetoric and persuasion of 'the people' and, like Blair's publicity machine, rather good at rendering 'non-people' invisible, even while going on about social inclusion. The fascists also encouraged a kind of national amnesia, trying to persuade people that nothing good had ever happened before they came to power.

But it may be a hostage to fortune to raise the spectre of fascism at this point. There are many dissimilarities between New Labour and traditional fascism. For one thing New Labour is not nearly as *dirigiste* in economics. Nor is there any attempt formally to incorporate particular sectors of society into their own organizations which are then supposed to feed directly into the national policy-making. Nor, just to make the point I am making quite clear, is there any suggestion that New Labour has any truck with violence or the threat of vio-

---

[1] On this, see Mike Diboll's interesting chaper in the current volume.

lence or, of course, that its attitude to 'non-people' is at any level other than the rhetorical. But fascism and New Labour do share one fundamental belief, a belief they also share with communists of all types and nations. To my mind this belief is highly suspect, and not just on a theoretical level. It is the belief that in a modern democracy there can or could be just one party, able to express and promote the interests of everyone. For a society whose official ideology is that of 'pluralism', the notions of a single political party representing everyone is a nonsense. Pluralism means that there is no single vision of the good life, or even of the good political system. It means that competing visions survive, express themselves and are allowed to develop. Insofar as politics is partly about competing visions of the good life, pluralism entails thriving and competing political parties.

But even if we reject pluralism in that sense, and feel that we are in some sense all united by a single vision of the good life, single party politics would be by no means a good idea. For, practical politics being what it is, there will inevitably be competing ways of realizing that vision. Is, for example, the best way to eliminate deprivation to increase the welfare state or to try to get people out of it altogether? Can you improve education by central direction and control or do improvements require more autonomy at all levels? Do restrictions and regulations on business help workers and the economy or hinder these things? Should transport and basic utilities be in public or private hands? Can governments create real jobs or is the whole idea a sorry illusion, attractive in the short term but disastrous in the medium-to-long term?

These might all be regarded as questions of means to agreed ends, though I suspect that differences on some of these means actually reflect more fundamental differences in one's conception of human nature and society. Whether this is so or not, what is clear is that they are differences that cannot be fudged by 'Third Way' centralism. They are real differences. They reflect and imply differences in policy. The arguments need to be put and brought into the open. There should be alternative political parties representing these differences.

Apart from anything else, openness requires no less. A single party political system is inevitably one in which criticism and opposition decline by default. The difficulties with policies are just not raised and a hubristic executive, surrounded by flatterers and placemen, simply ignores complaints, if indeed it even hears them.

New Labour is accused of being arrogant, bullying and power mad. To a greater or lesser degree this is true of all governments and particularly true of governments who, like New Labour, see their position as unassailable. There is nothing new there — unpleasant, arrogant and dismissive as it is. But what is new and needs careful monitoring are New Labour's pretensions to represent all sections of opinion. It just cannot be done, for the reasons already given. But even the attempt is worrying. This is not just because of its implicit exclusion of those unwilling to enter the big tent (dismissed as 'conservatives', 'extremists' or purveyors of 'libertarian nonsense'.) More fundamentally it shows what those driving the project really think of individual liberty and of democratic right.

Mike Diboll

Democracy Direct

New Labour's first term in office has brought about extensive constitutional change: devolution in Northern Ireland, Scotland and Wales; the abolition of Hereditary Peers; and the introduction of executive mayors in British cities, beginning with London. What constitutional changes would be enacted in a second term in office? Reform of the monarchy? No chance. The introduction of some sort of proportional representation in general elections? Maybe, but this is looking increasingly less likely as Tony Blair grows accustomed to the powers and privileges of an 'elected dictator' which the first past the post system bestows on a Prime Minister with a huge majority. Restrictions on party donations and the funding of election campaigns? Quite possibly, provided this can be done in a way which favours New Labour.

However, one aspect of constitutional change which may well occur is the introduction of some sort of 'direct democracy'. New Labour has been careful not to run ahead of the game in its promotion of direct democracy. However, direct democracy's apparent chief advocate, Peter Mandelson, has mooted the idea over the last couple of years, often tucked away amid 'big picture' policy announcements. For example, in a piece in the *Independent* during the 1999 Party Conference, Mandelson asserts that 'to gain a second term...our organisation needs to be more than a smooth electoral machine and an efficient call centre'.

Of course, just how well New Labour oils its 'machine' should be the Party's own business, were it not for the now all to familiar elision of Party into State that is becoming one of New Labour's most disturbing traits. For Mandelson contin-

ues that having 'reinvented the political platform our party
stands on New Labour must now build a grass-roots political
movement fit for the twenty-first century'. No longer merely a
party but now a 'movement', changes in 'the ways we vote'
would take place in parallel to changes within New Labour's
'machine'. Thus, 'Elections will take place over two or three
days. People will be able to vote in libraries and supermarkets.
They will be able to live in one part of a town and vote in
another — or in another town altogether, with the assistance of
modern communications technology.'

All this may seem pretty harmless. Yet consider the implications of an earlier outing of Mandelsonian 'virtual Labour'. At
a keynote speech at a seminar held at the British Embassy in
Bonn in March 1998, Mandelson shocked his audience of German politicians by declaring that 'it may be that the era of pure
representative democracy is slowly coming to an end'. As
John Lloyd noted in *The Times*, Mandelson's speech was full of
weasel words and get-out clauses: 'may be', 'pure' and
'slowly'. Nevertheless, Mandelson went on to say unambiguously that:

> We entered the twentieth century with a society of
> elites, with a very different class structure. In those
> days, it seemed natural to delegate important deci-
> sions to members of the land-owning elite. When in
> Britain, Labour emerged as the party which repre-
> sented the industrial working class, it quickly devel-
> oped its own elite of trade union bureaucrats, city
> bosses and socialist intellectuals. But that age has
> passed away. People today want to be more
> involved. (*Guardian*, 16 March 1998)

For Mandelson, the twenty-first century would see a choice
between 'direct democracy or dying democracy', because
'people have no time for a style of government that talks down
to them and takes them for granted'. Mandelson's vision of
'direct democracy' included the use of focus groups, citizen's
movements, plebiscites and the internet. What so shocked
members of his German audience was that Mandelson's version of direct democracy amounted to the abrogation of political responsibility. The ex-leader of the Christian Democrat
Party, Wolfgang Schäuble, commented:

> I think that we politicians have to take the decisions.
> In short, Mr Mandelson's verdict is: 'representative
> democracy is over'. Translated that means, 'things
> must be brought closer to the people'. That means
> politicians are too cowardly to take decisions.
> Mandelson also argued that if Europe is to function
> at all, then it can only be through inter-governmental
> co-operation. That's the end of European integra-
> tion if you don't want to lead politically and take
> decisions. (*Ibid.*)

Mandelson was in the broadsheets within a few days, pointing out that he had not said that 'representative democracy
was over', only that it should be 'enhanced' or 'comple-
mented' by direct democracy. However, Mandelson did not
adequately address the Germans' historical objection to his
ideas. Modern Germany places a high value on representative
politics because the Nazis employed precisely such devices as
citizens' movements and plebiscites to undermine Weimar
democracy and pave the way for one-party rule. For the Nazis
as well, traditional politicians (who Oswald Mosley called
'the old gang') were an out-of-touch elite who could no longer
retain the respect of the 'people'; the Nazi movement was able
to subvert and eventually abolish democracy — all democracy,
representative and direct — by exploiting popular dissatisfaction with the established political class and using 'direct'
means of consulting the masses which seemed to bypass the
conventional political system and reach the people without
mediation. Consequently, in post-war West Germany, the
establishment of a political class of integrity informed with an
ethos of public duty was a cornerstone of de-Nazification.
Mandelson's speech had evoked in the mind of his German
audience terrifying spectres from the past.

In Britain at the beginning of the twenty-first century, would
the introduction of Mandelsonian 'direct democracy' (in contrast to the Madesonian representative variety) enhance or
diminish democratic government? Would it really bring people and government closer together, or would it merely provide a 'democratic' rubber stamp which would enable a
government that has already displayed disturbingly authoritarian tendencies to claim some sort of popular legitimacy for

its policies? These questions are quite distinct from wider-ranging issues, such as 'is direct democracy a better system than representative democracy?' or 'is direct democracy workable in practice?'. The democratic deficit in British politics is very real: the British political settlement expects a seventeenth-century parliament to deal with the complexities of political life in the twenty-first century. Clearly, there is a real case for constitutional and democratic reform in the UK. However, this essay is not concerned with such questions; the issues being dealt with here relate to New Labour and the uses that it might make of its version of 'direct democracy'.

Nevertheless it is helpful to review just what is meant by 'direct democracy'. Traditionally, direct democracy has posed a radical challenge to established political systems, raising as it does the question 'why should responsible adults be debarred from deciding political issues by themselves?' Certainly, the election of governments at intervals of five years or so does not offer the voting public much say in the decisions which politicians regularly make on their behalf.

Direct democracy can mean the unmediated rule of the people; this form of direct democracy would involve open voting in public forums unmediated by political parties or professional politicians. The Athenian *polis* is often offered as an example of this kind of direct democracy. However, this is something of an idealization, since (apart from the fact that the Athenian economy depended heavily on the labour of slaves, who had no democratic rights) even in a society as small as Athens and even with Athens' highly literate and educated citizenry, direct democracy was only able to function effectively by the establishment of a community of *homonoia*, or 'same-mindedness'. On the one hand, the desire to achieve *homonoia* led the Athenians to inculcate within themselves a highly-developed sense of ethics; this aspect of Athenian culture has long been celebrated in the philosophical tradition of the modern West. On the other hand, however, the need of the Athenian *polis* for 'sameness' had a darker side — the suppression of alien, original or eccentric thought, for such thought would undermine the consensus upon which the Athenian system was predicated. The execution of Socrates is the prime example of this aspect of Athenian democracy.

It is unlikely that Mandelson had this version of direct democracy in mind when he spoke in Germany, since, apart from its patent unworkability in a country of 60 million souls (the internet notwithstanding), the application of Athenian-style unmediated direct democracy would necessitate the abolition of political parties and professional politicians. Nevertheless, an overview of Athenian direct democracy does illustrate ways in which some of the consequences of direct democracy might coincide with the New Labour programme. Blair promotes his own version of *homonoia*, despite his paying lip-service to the benefits of cultural and other diversity: Blair's vision of politics is fundamentally ethical and the Blairite concept of moral consensus seems to require a shocking degree of conformity.[1]

A more sophisticated concept of direct democracy involves a synthesis of direct and representative government. A party-based government would be chosen by electors, but this government would then put important bills to the popular vote, just as it currently does with legislative votes in Parliament. Such a model of direct democracy could be seen as being a pragmatic way of adapting Britain's seventeenth-century parliamentary system to the vast social and political changes which have taken place in British society during the last three centuries. Such an approach would also be technically feasible, since advances in information technology have the potential to make this a reality for everyone in the country within the next decade or so.

Even without such technological advances, some countries already offer systems of voting which come close to this synthesis of direct and representative democracy. Currently over half the popular consultations held at national level in the world are held in Switzerland, and this does not include the consultations which take place in the country's twenty-six cantons (indeed, some of the very small German-speaking cantons at the heart of the Swiss federation run something approaching the Athenian model of direct democracy, with popular assemblies in place of parliaments). However, Switzerland is a small country with a high level of general educa-

---

[1] As Glenn Hoddle, the England football manager found out to his cost— transubstantiation: one, reincarnation: nil.

tion and a very high per capita income and lacks the dynamic
heterogeneity of Britain. As a result it is unlikely that the Swiss
experiment in direct democracy has much to offer the UK.
Similarly, Italy, which has a long tradition of referenda, currently runs more plebiscites than any other major Western
democracy and in recent years has used referenda to decide
important social issues such as the legality of abortion and
rights to divorce. Unfortunately, Mussolini's abuse of referenda to consolidate Fascist rule over Italy via 'consultation'
with the people still casts a long shadow over Italian politics.

The American experience of direct democracy might be
more relevant to Britain. The system of checks and balances
restricting the power of the federal government in Washington is a distinct improvement on the Westminster 'elected dictatorship'; nevertheless, the remoteness of the federal
government to most Americans' daily lives, and subsequent
voter apathy, means that a 'democratic deficit' also applies in
the US at Federal government level. However, the situation in
many US states is quite different. There, instead of referenda,
citizens have recourse to the 'policy initiative'. This initiative
can be called on by any section of the population to oppose,
modify or suspend any state legislation or to propose new legislation provided that group can collect a sufficient number of
signatures to invoke the initiative.

Why then, when workable forms of 'enhanced' democracy
exist elsewhere in the Western world, should a future New
Labour initiative to enact some form of direct–representative
democratic synthesis be opposed? There are two arguments
for opposing the Mandelsonian version of direct democracy.
One is historical and structural, the other has to do with New
Labour's uses of constitutional reform and is ultimately (and
ironically) an ethical argument.

Imagine a continuum where at one end is absolute direct
democracy, which is completely unchecked and unmediated.
At the other end is absolute representative democracy, where
popular choice consists entirely of electing representatives to
the legislature. Near the absolutely direct pole on this continuum stands the idealized representation of Athenian democracy, a little further along towards the representative pole is
actual Athenian democracy (even Athens had Pericles). About
a quarter of the way along the continuum are the smaller

Swiss cantons, and about a third of the way on is the Swiss federal government. Just before the half-way mark on this continuum are various US states, and just over the mark is Italy. Three-quarters of the way towards the representative pole we find the US federal government, and four-fifths of the way there is the government of France. Nine-tenths of the way towards the absolutely representative pole stands Westminster.

In Switzerland and the United States direct democracy was not imposed as a gimmick by a populist politician desperate to give substance to the vacuous 'ism' that bears his name. Rather, it developed as an intrinsic part of those countries' political systems as a result of historical and cultural factors. Since the Middle Ages the German-speaking cantons at the heart of the Swiss federation fought hard to retain their guild-democracy independence from the larger Germanic kingdoms to the north and east. Later, French- and Italian-speaking cantons joined the federation to escape other forms of absolutism. The United States was born out of a struggle to tame the wilderness and a struggle against British absolutism. Both of these required a highly developed ethos of individual and community independence. Moreover, the Founding Fathers took great pains to establish a federal constitution which structurally inhibited the centralized accumulation of power enjoyed by British governments. Even the choice of the site for the capital, well away from America's financial and commercial centres on what was originally mosquito-infested marsh which froze in winter and sweltered in summer, neither north nor south slap in the middle of the original thirteen colonies was determined to *discourage* the inappropriately ambitious from pursuing a political career. Even Italy's love of the referendum (a Latin word) is rooted in its history and dates back (via Mussolini) to Imperial Rome—with the mob in the Coliseum entreating Caesar to give some hapless gladiator the thumbs-down—and to the Republic before.

Britain has no equivalent tradition of direct democracy. On the contrary, the last three-hundred years of British political history have been largely defined by statism and the concentration of power; even Mrs Thatcher could not bring herself to liberalize the secretive British state. None of this means that an ethos of direct democracy cannot be inculcated within British society. However, to do so would require a raft of far-reaching constitutional reforms for which New Labour shows no stomach; something along the lines of Jonathan Freedland's 'Ten Steps to the Revolution', which encompasses a republic, the separation of rights and a written constitution.

What Mandelson is proposing is to take a political *modus operandi* from the direct end of the democratic continuum, and superimpose it on an otherwise unreformed governmental system which is positioned at the extreme end of the representative pole of the continuum. The result is neither direct nor representative democracy, but a chimera, a hybrid that manages only to combine the incompatible aspects of both systems.

This leads on to the issue of New Labour's use of constitutional reform to date. Consider (since we have just mentioned Freedland) Blairism's selective borrowings from America; these do not make Britain 'more like America', for to do so in any meaningful way would mean engaging in a wide-ranging series of structural changes to the British body politic which would go against the centralizing thrust of the Project. Rather, such borrowings merely enable New Labour to cherry-pick repressive measures from the USA—a private prison here, a 'three strikes and you're out' policy there—and call this 'modernization'.[2] Likewise, arguably much-needed constitutional reforms have been taken up selectively so as to further entrench New Labour hegemony; there is no reason to believe that the Mandelsonian 'take' on 'direct democracy' would be an exception to this trend.

New Labour makes much of the claim that it is 'giving power back to the people', yet much of this 'handover' of power is mere window dressing to disguise an unprecedented centralization of power. The power to vary exchange rates was taken away from 'the people's' elected representitives and given to technocrats from the Bank of England, in keeping with New Labour's neo-corporatism. The Welsh Assembly was an attempt to stymie the establishment of a full-blooded Welsh Parliament. The Welsh people's lukewarm reception of

---

[2] New Labour are fond of such cherry-picking—according to Jack Straw deficiencies in the Scottish system mean it is admissible to restrict the right to trial by jury in the rest of the United Kingdom.

the Assembly reflects their disgust at Blair's abortive para-chuting in of his gauliter, Alun Michael, as the Assembly's first First Secretary. For Downing Street the Severn proved a bridge too far.[3] Executive mayors and assemblies for the regions are showcased as an example of New Labour's sup-posed commitment to extending democracy; however, a less well discussed aspect of 'the modernization of local govern-ment' involves the creeping abolition of 'old-fashioned' local council democracy and replacing it with an 'executive cabinet' of a few individuals who decide policy from behind closed doors. This is the political culture onto which Mandelsonian 'direct democracy' would be superimposed to add the fig-leaf of popular consent to the activities of one of the most centralist peace-time British governments since Cromwell.

It could be objected that to view automatically a New Labour 'reform' in such a negative light is to be guilty of one of the most heinous thought crimes of Blair's Britain — cynicism. Yet greater cynicism accrues to Blair and followers than to those who have the temerity to criticize. Following the Anthony Giddens school of political nomenclature, Blairism likes to take vague and abstract ethical categories such as 'risk' and make of them policy. So let us look at that most Blairite policy ethos 'trust'. Blair first asked us to 'trust him' when it appeared that donations from an entrepreneur who was heavily dependent on the tobacco industry had influenced New Labour health policy. Yet the currency of Blairite trust has become devalued through supply-side imprudence. After the death of ohn Smith, Blair asked Mo Molam to 'trust him' that Mandelson was not pulling the strings of the Blair leader-ship campaign; later it transpired that Mandelson had been doing just that. Five times on the broadcast media in the run-

---

[3] The obvious exception to this trend is the Scottish Parliament. However, Blair inherited from his predecessors a cast-iron commitment to a Scottish parlia-ment on which, in the context of Scottish politics and society, it would have been foolhardy to try to renege. Moreover, if Blairism is to establish a hege-mony in middle England, why not let heavily-subsidized Scotland, with its awkward traditions of 'Old Labour' socialism and Scottish nationalism, go its own way, much as the Czech Republic did with Slovakia? Italy's Northern League has recognized that the politics of the *mittlestand* in a 'Europe of nations' might require the shedding of incovenient bits of the nineteenth-century nation-state.

up to the exclusion of most of the Hereditary Peers from the House of Lords) Blair claimed that a Private Member's Bill to outlaw foxhunting was blocked in the Lords when in fact it was the Government that refused to allow the bill sufficient Commons time — once a mistake, but five times a lie. The public were served up a similar diet of Melton Mowbrays when Blair claimed that he had been elected leader of the Labour Party by 'the same' electoral college that had been cobbled together to block Ken Livingstone's candidature for the London mayoralty. Even Blair's promises to the Liberals regarding PR look set to amount to nothing. Are these really the sort of people that we should 'trust' with the reform of British democracy?

Away from the risky abstractions of 'trust', consider something more 'hands on'. Since Mandelson is so enthusiastic that 'new technology' should be used as a means by which 'direct democracy' should 'supplement' creaky, elitist representative democracy, consider New Labour's new toy: the 'Knowledge Network Project' (its new electronic information and rebuttal system). This system sets out to 'explain the Government's core message' so that 'citizens can get the full facts without going through the distorting prism of the press'. It also seeks to tell politicians from the Cabinet down to the humblest councillor the No 10-approved 'line to take' on any given issue. Unlike Excalibur, New Labour's general election 'rebuttal machine', all this is to be paid for by the public purse. Yet the 'knowledge' that can be accessed from this network has several grades. Only the clique around the Prime Minister will have access to 'quality' (*i.e.* unfiltered) information. Cabinet ministers get less. MPs less still, the 'three best arguments' and 'five best quotes' with which to support any given policy. Party members will get platitudes. The general public just gets propaganda — carefully filtered and doctored feel-good blanditudes with zero verifiable content. No wonder Blair had Jack Straw throttle the Freedom of Information Bill with its own legislative umbilical cord. Even the *Guardian*'s editorial came out and said plainly that no government should have such power, and feared what any government 'even a Labour government' might do with such a powerful propaganda tool. Leaving aside New Labour's selective abuses of its constitutional 'reforms', the Upper House of placemen and the knobbling of Livingstone and Morgan, the Knowledge Network makes the most eloquent case against Mandelsonian 'direct democracy' since it provides a real example of the quality of the information with which Mandelson's 'direct' voters would be expected to make their decisions.

If, in a country where one is more likely to die of cancer or heart disease than in any comparable Western nation, 'NHS Direct' is a sick joke, then 'Democracy Direct' is an insult. Mandelson's audience, aware that in Germany the Nazi corruption and subversion of democracy lives on still in the memories of older people, were right in their scepticism.

* * *

Some readers may be surprised at the comparison between Peter Mandelson's argument for direct democracy with the history of Nazi Germany. It is often argued that fascism is a movement of the 'far-right', but this is not the case. Far-right extremists — authoritarian conservatives such as Franco in Spain or Pinochet in Chile, may have adopted some of the trappings of inter-war European fascism, but to conflate the authoritarian far-right with fascism is to misunderstand the nature of the beast. Fascism can be more usefully theorized not as right-wing extremism but as an extremism of the *authoritarian centre*, a kind of modernizing dictatorship. The idea of a 'Third Way' between or transcending left and right has been definitive of fascist thinking from the movement's earliest years right through to the present, clearly illustrating fascism's essential centrism. Moreover, the congruence between the Blairite and the fascist takes on the Third Way goes far deeper than a shared rhetoric. Despite its radical rhetoric, fascism sought to maintain capitalism, retaining its essential core — the private accumulation of capital — intact. However rather than simply aiming to conserve the status quo, fascism seeks to manage capitalism more effectively by bringing about a new society peopled by citizens with new moral values and a renewed sense of purpose. Much the same can be said of Blairism, with its 'New Britain' built on a 'new moral purpose for the new millennium'.

Thus, from the mainstream, Blair — a Prime Minister of the 'radical centre' — is leading a European crusade advocating the 'Third Way' for parties of the left and centre. Consequently, European politics are being trapped in a pincer movement. On the one hand, Europe's more media-savvy neo- fascists have become consumer-friendly 'post-fascists'. These 'post-fascists' eschew the mimetic fascism of the boot-boys, rabid anti-Semites, white supremacists and Nazi-fetishists who have dominated post-war neo-fascism in Europe; on the contrary, these groups model themselves as the 'Third Position' transcending left and right, a chilling reminder of the fact that the idea of the 'Third Way' adopted by New Labour as its defining creed originated with Mussolini. On the other hand, Blair is offering the European centre a means with which they can re-invent themselves from *within* the political mainstream. No doubt Blair and his fellow travellers of the Third Way would be horrified to be compared to the Third Positionists of Italy's *Alleanza Nationale* or Austria's Freedom Party. Yet however much New Labour may 'deplore' Jorg Haider entering the Austrian government, the parallels between Haider's overt and Blairism's covert third positionism cannot be avioded, as a pro-Haider correspondent put it in the *Guardian*:

> All the allegations [about Haider] are smears, slander and deliberate distortions...he is a postmodern politician who wishes to move his country beyond the tyranny of tradition. Just as Mr Blair is looking for a 'Third Way'...Mr Haider believes, like Great Britain, that unlimited immigration is not possible without serious social consequences. He is no more racist than Mr Straw...' (*Guardian*, 5 February 2000).

Or in Mr Haider's own words (swiftly denied by Downing Street), 'I think there are a lot of similarites between our programmes'. Karl-Heinz Grasser, the Austrian finance minister, described his new leader as 'very New Labour', advancing socially responsible policies alongside the interests of business.

As post-Schengen Europe moves away from models of citizenship based on *jus soli* (the republican concept of citizenship), towards one based on *jus sanguinus* (citizenship based on ethnic or racial origins), an emerging authoritarian centrism would ensure that the two streams of the Third Way and the Third Position could converge to form something akin to *Europa*, the united Europe of fascist nations of which Hitler, Mosley and Mussolini dreamt.

To many it may seem far-fetched or even paranoid to equate Blairism with fascism, but consider the following scenario. A dynamic Labour outsider swims against the tide of the Party's traditions to depose the 'Old Gang' who have held back both Party and country. Abandoning Labour's socialism, he proposes a 'Third Way' transcending left and right: class conflict and *laissez-faire* competition would both be made subordinate to a new national consensus. At the head of this renewed Britain stands a leader figure with Caesarian pretensions, on a mission to rescue Britain from decadence. The radical surgery that Britain needed required 'a revolution in the machinery of government'. Hence, the roles of Cabinet and Parliament would be marginalized and key decisions taken by a handful of ministers around the leader. Technocrats would be brought in to run the economy, with MPs left with presentational roles and the public 'consulted' on the government's performance via referenda.

The labour modernizer described above is Sir Oswald Mosley. Frustrated with the Labour Party's reluctance to adopt his radical 'modernizing' agenda, Mosley eventually formed his New Party, which then evolved into the British Union of Fascists, to finally become the British Union of Fascists and National Socialists. As modernizing parties of the authoritarian centre, the symmetry between the New Party and New Labour is almost perfect. However, Mosley left a mainstream party, the Labour Party, to form a party of his own; Blair, on the other hand, has transformed the Labour Party from within, converting it from a party of the social-democratic left to a party of the authoritarian centre. The effectiveness of the Blair clique's entryism into Labour should leave the Trotskyists of *Militant* green with envy.[4]

---

[4] Ex-New Labour minister Peter Kilfoyle attributed his resignation from the government in part to his experiences fighting *Militant* in the 1980's: 'The increasing control exerted by Labour's headquarters is not unlike the democratic centralism of the Trotskyites [says Kilfoyle]. It can work for a short time then the bottom starts to erode and crumble because people want an input.' (Rachel Sylvester, *Daily Telegraph*, 5 February 2000.)

Blair has succeeded in achieving the third positionist re-alignment of British politics which Mosley, with his black-shirted aping of '30s fascism failed to do. By the early '60s Mosley was struggling to preserve his dying Union Movement, the withered stump of the BUF, from the 'crackpot-fascism' of the likes of the Hitler-worshipping BNP and National Socialist Movement.

The true inheritor of the Union Movement's vision — 'class harmony, economic dynamism and European unity through a consensus of the nation achieved by a government of national union drawn from all that is best and most vital in the nation' — is New Labour. The thoroughness of the Blairite transformation of British politics is evidenced by the fact that at the next general election the electorate will be faced with a Hobson's choice between New Labour, an ever-more extremist party of the authoritarian centre, and the Conservatives who are on a vain mission to try to out-flank Blairism from the right, thereby condemning themselves to becoming merely a party of right-wing reaction to Blair's incremental totalitarianism of the centre.

Fascism required, and Blairism requires, a strong government as unimpeded by parliamentary niceties as possible with which to impose a synthesis of the conflicting elements that make up society: such a dangerous subversive as Speaker of the House Betty Boothroyd, a staunch defender of the rights of Parliament over the executive, finds herself on the receiving end of smears and whispering campaigns. Where liberalism seeks to contain conflict and competition within reasonable bounds, third positionism sees liberal freedom as encouraging harmful social division and indiscipline that must be surpressed. Thus, New Labour proposes compulsory DNA testing for anyone convicted of a criminal offence, no matter how minor; curfews on children; increased video surveillance of daily life; and the policing of electronic communication. It proposes 'anti- terrorist' legislation that would make 'terrorists' out of the likes of Greenpeace and would lead, as one commentator put it, 'to a situation where there is a real danger that some government, at some stage, and some police forces will use the new forces to catch individuals or groups who should never be detained or caught in the criminal net of a liberal democracy'. Nevertheless, enough of the centrist programme remains for many liberals to be brought into the corporatist 'big tent' with the vain hope that they can curb the authoritarianism of Blair's third positionism. Thus liberals can still co-operate with New Labour as fellow travellers of the centre even as New Labour sets out to curb such historic guarantees of individual liberty as the right to trial by a jury of one's peers.

Similarly, in the name of national unity, Blairism is able to co-opt support from a desperate left by enacting measures such as the minimum wage and the banishing of the bulk of the Herditary Peers from the House of Lords, even as it pursues a policy of crypto-privatization in areas where even the Tories feared to tread — in education, for example. Likewise it also draws support from the unthinking right — the *mittlestand* of Middle England so beloved by Blair and New Labour — by milking reactionary populism for all it is worth. Claiming to be 'tough' on law and order (when in fact it is 'tough' on civil liberties), and knocking down patsies such as asylum seekers and lefty teachers, Blairism appeases saloon-bar bigotry, but nevertheless ruins the things dearest to the right: mauling traditional institutions for its own ends and declaring war on individual liberty.

Genuine liberals, social democrats, socialists, traditionalist conservatives, and right-wing libertarians differ on many things, but at least have one thing in common: they live in the real world and realize that conflict and competition are inevitable and even desirable in a mature and healthy society. Third positionists, on the other hand, live in a never-never land where they dream that all conflict has been abolished by a strong and popular government: the triumph of the authoritarian centre.

Chillingly for a party which is still ostensibly socialist, New Labour is developing a nationalist strand to complement its 'socialism'; nationalism has become the touchstone of the New Labour 'project'. Moreover, New Labour's nationalism is not merely patriotism, a generalized liking for one's country and a desire to see it flourish. Rather, Blairite nationalism recalls the fascist idea of the 'organic' nation, wherein a strong government of the authoritarian centre has transcended left and right, imposed a new national consensus upon society and resolved class and other conflict. Enemies of the 'nation' or 'the people' have been neutralized or marginalized, and the collective will of the nation flows through the party and ultimately the leader. Competition becomes nationalized – under third positionism the individualized competition of liberalism and Marxian ideas about competing social classes are replaced with the idea of the competitive nation. Under Blairism, it is 'Britain' or 'the nation' that must be competitive, not individuals within it. European nations are not to compete with each other, but for control of world markets. The thousands of protestors who gathered in Seattle in November 1999 to demonstrate against the WTO attempt to control the world economy on behalf of the West would recognize Mosley's formula for, 'a system of international order based on corporate empires, or geographical blocs, which would enable nations to discuss rationally and peacefully the allocations of raw materials markets'. Countries that can't, or won't be brought into line by economic means, such as Iraq or Serbia, go the way of Albania or Libya under Mussolini and are bombed into submission and, to add insult to injury, banded 'fascist' into the bargain.

The spectre of the fascist idea of the 'organic nation' haunted New Labour's 1999 Party Conference; as at previous New Labour conferences, the words 'Britain', British' and 'nation' rang out hundreds of times. According to Blair's keynote speech, Britain was 'on the frontier of the new millennium', where 'One Prime Minister, One Party', our 'guide' sets out on his 'mission' to 'renew British strength', laying down the 'foundations for a New Britain', a 'nation' which 'will master its future', with New Labour as 'the nation's only hope for salvation', where 'there is no greater privilege than serving your country' on its 'moral purpose' and promoting 'a strong community'. Predictably, the twenty-first century will be a 'battleground'. True to Blairism's authoritarian centrist form, the 'battle' will not be 'between capitalism and socialism', since Blair's nationalist post-socialism likes to imagine that it has resolved that particular conflict. Rather it is between 'the forces of progress and the forces of conservatism'. The forces of progress are 'the national creative forces of the British people', a phrase which could have come straight from Mosley. The forces of conservatism are 'not just the Conservative party' who are 'weird, weird, weird' and 'far right, far out' (thus Blair diverts attention from New Labour's own centrist brand of extremism), but 'the forces of conservatism of the right and the left' who 'are within us, within our nation', as if these 'forces' were some sort of disease to be expunged from the nation's coporate organism. Blair says (offering a massive hostage to fortune) that these dissidents 'do not understand that creating a New Britain of true equality is no more a betrayal of Britain's history than New Labour is of Labour's values'. The speech ends sounding like a poor Blairite 'take' on *vers libre*:

> The battleground, the new millennium
> Our values are our guide
> Our job is to serve
> Our workplace, the future
> Let us step up the pace. Be confident. Be radical.
> To every nation a purpose.
> To every party a cause.
> And now, at last, Party and nation joined in the same
> cause for the same purpose: to set our people free.

Hitler's speeches were often full of sentiments remarkably similar to those in Blair's keynote conference speech, as a random sample shows:

> The splitting up of the nation into groups with irrec-
> oncilable views systematically brought about by
> false doctrines means the destruction of the basis of
> a possible communal life. It is only the creation of a
> real national community rising above the interests
> of rank and class that can permanently remove the
> source of these aberrations of the human mind.
> Simultaneously with this political purification of
> our public life the government of the Reich under-
> take a moral purging of the body corporate of the
> nation. (Berlin, Reichstag, 23 March 1933)

Blair's interest in the idea of the organic national community pre-dates the 1997 general election. In his 1995 Party Conference speech he had similar things to say about 'one nation' and a 'young country':

> Let us build a new and young country that can lay
> aside the old prejudices that have dominated our

land for generations. A nation for all the people
where old divisions are cast out. A new spirit in the
nation based on working together, unity, solidarity,
partnership. One Britain. That is the patriotism of
the future. Where never again do we fight our politics by appealing to one section of the nation at the
expense of another. Where your child in distress is
my child, your parent ill or in pain is my parent,
your friend unemployed or homeless is my friend,
your neighbour, my neighbour. That is the patriotism of a nation.

How on earth must Blair's rhetoric read when translated into
German or Italian? No wonder France, that still remembers
the collaborationist Vichy regime was lukewarm about *La
Troisieme Voie.*

The road to fascist hell is paved with good intentions. As
Gita Serany pointed out in her book *Into That Darkness*, the
Holocaust had its roots in Nazi Germany's pre-war programme of 'merciful' involuntary euthanasia for imbeciles
and other 'unproductives'; in New Britain's crumbling health
service, where a human life has long had a price-tag, doctors
are beginning to blow the whistle on a policy of *de facto* involuntary euthanasia on such unproductives as the senile, the ter-
minally ill and the long-term comatose. Both Hitler and
Mussolini came to power as elected politicians, neither cam-
paigned on a manifesto that promised a totalitarian state,
genocide, total war and eventual defeat and occupation.
Rather totalitarianism and the moral and political darkness
that accompanies it advances by increments; it was the naive
unworkability of fascism's national consensus that planted
the seeds of the catastrophe that was the Second World War:
fascist governments had to become ever more dictatorial,
authoritarian and belligerent in order to stay in power. It is
not, as some might claim, a 'defamation of the dead' to investi-
gate parallels between fascist totalitarianism and the creeping
totalitarianism that is Blairism; rather, we defame the dead of
the Second World War and the Holocaust if we glibly buy into
the cosy Liberal assumption that the fascism of the Axis powers was some kind of extraordinary and unique aberration in
Western politics that will never again be repeated: Liberty

depends on the vigilance of her Minutemen. If our children must have classes in citizenship, then the inculcation of such vigilance must take preference over the partisan propaganda of a party which, its bogus Holocaust Memorial Day notwithstanding, seeks daily to entrench what is beginning to look frighteningly like one-party rule. As the *Observer*'s Nick Cohen put it, one needs to grow (if one does not already have one) a Jewish nose; one needs to be able to sniff out creeping totalitarianism from where ever it might arise. If in so doing one offends the sensibilities and comfortable assumptions of the odd liberal who is drawn into the Blairite Big Tent, then so be it. To be wrong about Blairism–Fascism is merely to be wrong; to have nipped in the bud incremental totalitarianism before it does real harm is to have acknowledged the real debt that the comfortable post-War generation owe their ancestors.

Blairism daily accomplishes incremental erosions of parliamentary sovereignty and cabinet accountability, while the Labour Party itself is ever more centralized and purged of dissent. Ever more authoritarian laws are proposed and enacted, whilst sleight-of-hand constitutional reform camouflages the consolidation of Blairite power by pretending it is really the extension of democracy. Already leader of one of the bloodiest and most belligerent of post-war British governments, Blair advocates for Europe a growing web of treaty obligations in support of precarious Eastern states. This has given NATO a common border with an unstable and nuclear-armed Russia: the cold war bunkers may yet have their uses.

Meanwhile, the better to stupefy 'the people', New Labour trivializes public life by emotionalizing politics. Fascist Italy had its 'Oceanic Rallies' and Nazi Germany had Nuremburg and the 1936 Olympic Games as spectacular means of making politics out of emotion and emotion out of politics. The farcical Blairite repetition of the fascist tragedy has its Millennium Dome — at least Leni Reifenstahl's *Triumph of the Will* had aesthetic integrity, even if its politics stank. A true child of the television-age, New Labour also seeks to emotionalize politics by reducing it to the level of a soap opera. Blair's politics-as-soap began with his (actually Alastair Campbell's) canonization of Diana as the (oxy)moronic 'people's princess' and the Shared National Experience (SNE) of her funeral. The latest episode of the soap is the immaculately-timed conception of

Mrs Blair's baby. This is to be no mere pregnancy, for it will take the SNE one step further; for according to Peter Mandelson 'the whole nation will be sharing it' (whither the *vomitorium*), as New Labour gears up for the next general election. Fascism promoted *Il Duce* as 'a hero of virility', and promoted among women a 'battle for births'. If Mr Blair's messianic monomania extends to the engineering of a new baby for a New Britain in the New Millennium, that is a matter on which psychologists may be best qualified to comment. However, the Blairs' labour may have been in vain; the refreshing indifference with which the British public has greeted the Dome, and the revived interest in substantive political issues such as health may indicate that New Labour hubris has gone too far.

Predictably, however, the public snubbing of Blair's 'beacon to the world' has not led to a reining in of Blairite hubris, but to recourse to a yet more sinister propaganda ploy. Not content with turning politics into soap opera, the latest Millbank wheeze is to turn soap opera into politics. Thus, carefully spun policy lines will be woven into plot-lines in popular national episodic dramas such as *The Archers*, *Eastenders* and *Coronation Street*, along with subliminal on-message messages on such topics as the minimum wage and the New Deal. It would be inaccurate to describe this measure as 'Orwellian', for New Labour's New British Gvernment of the New Millennium would regard Big Brother's mid-eighties propaganda techniques as hopelessly dated. Given New Labour's proven contempt for the public's ability to make informed decisions free of spin, hype, manipulation and propaganda, it is not unreasonable to fear the abuses to which Blair's government might subject an IT-based system of 'direct democracy'.

Clearly, Blairism's Third Way represents, in a Europe that is increasingly falling into the thrall of overt or covert third positionism, a threat to democratic liberty. A battle needs be fought for the conservation of meaningful democracy in British politics. The right and the left should, for the present, put aside their differences, just as the Western democracies once made common cause with the USSR against the Axis during the Second World War. The forces of radicalism on the right and on the left must be deployed against the incremental totalitarianism of the extremists of the authoritarian centre: tomorrow must not belong to the Blairites.

Dumbing Down: Culture, politics and the mass media
Edited by Ivo Mosley

Never before in human history has so much cleverness been used to such stupid ends. The cleverness is in the creation and manipulation of markets, media and power; the stupid ends are in the destruction of community, responsibility, morality, art, religion and the natural world.

Dumbocracy in Government

Tam Dalyell, *On the Decline of Intelligent Government*; **Ivo Mosley**, *Dumbing Down Democracy*; **Michael Oakeshott**, *The Masses in Representative Democracy*; **Redmond Mullin**, *States, Dissent & Constructive Disorder*; **Michael Johnson**, *The Consequences of Permanent Revolution in the Civil Service*; **Dominic Hobson**, *Government as Business*.

Dumbocracy and Culture

Ravi Shankar, *Interview*; **Philip Rieff**, *The Impossible Culture*; **Robert Brustein**, *When PC becomes Dumbocracy;***Anne Glyn-Jones**, *Sensationalism in Modern Entertainment*; **Roger Deakin**, *Stupidity*; **Mark Ryan**, *Turning on the Audience*.

Dumbocracy and the Media

Adam Boulton, *Not so Dumb – In Defence of Soundbites*; **Oliver O'Donovan**, *Publicity*

Dumbocracy in the Visual Arts

Laura Gascoigne, *Mumbo-Dumbo*; **David Lee**, *What Contemporary Art Means To Me*; **Peter Randall-Page**, *Form, Transformation and a Common Humanity*; **Bill Hare**, *Glasgow Belongs to Whom?*

Dumbocracy in Education

Michael Polanyi, *The Eclipse of Thought*; **Claire Fox**, *Education: Dumbing Down or Wising Up?*; **Andrew Williams**, *The Dumbing Down of the Young Consumer*.

Dumbocracy and Science

Joan Leach, Shaun Mosley and I. Mosley, *Science: The Stuff of Dreams or Nightmares?*; **John Ziman**, *Heeding Voices*; **Jaron Lanier**, *Agents of Alienation*; **Walter Freeman**, *Happiness Doesn't Come in Bottles*.

Dumbocracy and Religion

Helen Oppenheimer, *The Truth-Telling Animal*; **Nicholas Mosley**, *Dumbing Down/Dumbing Up in Religion*.

Dumbocracy and 'The Environment'

C.D. Darlington, *The Impact of Man on Nature*; **Demelza Spargo**, *The Cultivation of Society*

Imprint Academic, 336 pp., £12.95/$19.95, 0907845 657 (pbk.)
http://www.imprint.co.uk

HOLDING UP A MIRROR
How Civilizations Decline
Anne Glyn-Jones

According to Glyn-Jones, the central dilemma of history is this: the dynamic that promotes economic prosperity leads inexorably to the destruction of the very security and artistic achievement on which civilizations rest their claim to greatness. This book argues that the growth of prosperity is driven largely by the conviction that the material world alone constitutes true 'reality'. Yet that self-same dynamic — developing a critique of all belief in the supernatural as at best superfluous, and at worst a damaging superstition — undermines the authority of moral standards and so leads to social and cultural disintegration.

Focussing on dramatic entertainment as the barometer of social change, the author shows in vivid detail how the thesis worked itself out in four different civilizations: those of Greece, Rome, medieval Christendom, and now in our own contemporary society.

Critical acclaim for *Holding Up A Mirror*

This is a visionary book. Painful yet true in its portrait of the present, it is clearly driven by the anxieties of a sensitive and conscientious observer. **Bryan Appleyard**, The Sunday Times

Those who share Anne Glyn-Jones's belief in objective values will congratulate her on a thoroughly researched and illuminating reinterpretation of what Sorokin saw as 'The Crisis of Our Age'. **Angela Ellis-Jones**, TLS

It is a strength of this rich and engrossing book that it provokes on almost every page a willingness to argue with the author. Her thesis is challenging, and her examples abundantly interesting. **Alan Massie**, Daily Telegraph

Her focus on the theatre . . . gives her book an interest and a solid core that lend credibility to the main thesis. **John Habgood**, THES

Glyn-Jones's intriguing book puts an entirely new gloss on the stereotyped picture of fanatical Islamic theocracy. **Frank McLynn**, New Statesman

She excels in vivid, informative presentation of detail drawn together into a lucid, robust and fair-minded narrative. **Helen Oppenheimer**

Imprint Academic, 652 pp., £14.95/$24.95, 0907845 606 (pbk.)
http://www.imprint.co.uk